A Norse Farmstead in the Outer Hebrides

Excavations at Mound 3, Bornais, South Uist

A Norse Farmstead in the Outer Hebrides
Excavations at Mound 3, Bornais, South Uist

edited by

Niall Sharples

With contributions by

J Bond, J Cartledge, A Clarke, S Colledge, I Dennis, R Gale, M Hamilton, C Ingrem, A Lane, J Light, P Macdonald, P Marshall, K Milek, J Mulville, A Smith, H Smith and T Young

Cardiff Studies in Archaeology

Oxbow Books

Published by
Oxbow Books, Park End Place, Oxford OX1 1HN

ISBN 1 84217 169 0

This book is available direct from

Oxbow Books, Park End Place, Oxford OX1 1HN
(*Phone:* 01865-241249; *Fax:* 01865-794449)

and

The David Brown Book Company
PC Box 511, Oakville, CT 06779, USA
(*Phone:* 860-945-9329; *Fax:* 860-945-9468)

or from our website

www.oxbowbooks.com

Printed in Great Britain at
The Short Run Press
Exeter

Contents

Illustrations

Tables

List of Contributors

J Bond
Richmond Road
Roath, Cardiff
Wales

J Cartledge
15 Pengeston Road
Penistone
South Yorkshire, S36 6GW

A Clarke
Rockville Lodge, By Kingston
North Berwick, East Lothian
Scotland

S Colledge
Institute of Archaeology, University College London
31–34 Gordon Square
London, WC1H 0PY

I Dennis
HISAR, Cardiff University
Humanities Bulding, Colum Drive
Cardiff, CF10 3XU

R Gale
Bachefield House
Kimbolton
Leominster, HR6 0EP

M Hamilton
SCARAB, School of Humanities and Science
University of Wales Newport, Caerleon Campus
PO Box 101, Newport
Wales, NP18 3YH

C Ingrem
Faunal Remains Unit, Archaeology,
University of Southampton, Avenue Campus
Highfield
Southampton, SO17 1BF

A Lane
HISAR, Cardiff University
Humanities Bulding, Colum Drive
Cardiff, CF10 3XU

J Light
88 Peperharow Road
Godalming
Surrey, GU7 2PN

P Macdonald
Centre for Archaeological Fieldwork
School of Archaeology and Palaeoecology
The Queen's University of Belfast
Northern Ireland, BT7 1NN

P Marshall
English Heritage
23 Saville Row
London, WS1 2ET

K Milek
Dept. of Archaeology, University of Cambridge
Downing St
Cambridge, CB2 3DZ

J Mulville
HISAR, Cardiff University
Humanities Bulding, Colum Drive
Cardiff, CF10 3XU

N Sharples
HISAR, Cardiff University
Humanities Bulding, Colum Drive
Cardiff, CF10 3XU

A Smith
Society of Antiquaries of Scotland, Royal Museum
Chambers Street
Edinburgh, EH1 1JF

H Smith
School of Conservation Sciences
Bournemouth University, Talbot Campus
Poole
Dorset, BH12 5BB

T Young
GeoArch
54 Heol y Cadno, Thornhill
Cardiff, CF14 9DY

1 Introduction

The beginning

The excavation and survey reported here is part of a long-term project to investigate the archaeology of the island of South Uist in the Outer Hebrides of Scotland (Figure 1). The southern Hebrides project was instigated in 1988 by the University of Sheffield but as the years passed a variety of researchers from many universities have become involved (see Sharples, Parker Pearson and Symonds 2004 for a full list). The editor of the current volume became involved with the project in 1991 when he co-directed the excavation of the broch of Dun Vulan on the west coast of the island with Mike Parker Pearson. There was clear evidence that Dun Vulan was being eroded by the sea (identified by Alex Woolf) and consequently funding was obtained from Historic Scotland for rescue excavation. The Dun Vulan excavations provided a valuable introduction to the archaeology of South Uist and a base from which to develop other projects that would have a longer temporal and broader spatial scale.

Prior to excavation Dun Vulan was a recognisable monumental roundhouse. This was expected to date to the Middle Iron Age but it was hoped that it would prove to have been built on earlier deposits and have an occupation that continued into the Late Iron Age and Medieval periods. These predictions proved to be correct (Parker Pearson and Sharples 1999) but unfortunately, in the areas excavated, the later deposits were badly eroded and the complexity of the surviving Middle Iron Age deposits made it difficult to examine the earlier deposits. It consequently became clear from early in the excavation that to obtain information from other periods additional excavations would be necessary. Fortunately our daily journey to and from Dun Vulan identified an appropriate settlement for exploration.

South Uist

South Uist is a small island, approximately 36,467 ha (Angus 1997, tbl. 9.1), in the southern half of the Outer Hebrides or Western Isles (Figure 1). To the north the island is currently joined to the neighbouring island of Benbecula by an artificial causeway; however, access between the islands at low tide is possible and for much of prehistory South Uist, Benbecula and North Uist would have formed a single landmass (Ritchie 1985). The channel between South Uist and Barra is more substantial and would have separated the islands from relatively early in the postglacial period. The current island is rectangular, roughly 35 km long and up to 13.6 km wide with its long axis oriented to the north (Figure 2). The landscape can be divided into three very distinctive environments that divide the island into strips running from north to south.

- The east half of the island is an inhospitable region dominated by mountains and bogs. The highest mountain is Beinn Mhor, which reaches a height of 608 metres. Interspersed with these mountains are large expanses of peat moorland. The coastline varies from cliffs to small sheltered bays, but its most important features are the three deep sea lochs, Loch Baghasdail, Loch Aineort and Loch Sgiopoirt, which penetrate through the mountains to the low-lying land which lies at the centre of the island.
- As one moves west the land gradually descends, first through an area of moorland then to an area distinguished by extensive freshwater lochs separated by rocky outcrops.
- The west coast is characterised by the shell sand deposit known as the machair (Ritchie 1979), which on South Uist extends as a continuous plain, up to 2 km wide, from the south to the north coast, and indeed continues along the west coast of Benbecula and North Uist. Projecting from this coastline are two distinctive promontories; in the middle of the island is Rubha Ardvule, a low promontory and at the south end is Orosay, a steep-sided tidal islet.

The central and eastern part of the islands can be collectively referred to as the blacklands. Today, settlement is concentrated on the rocky outcrops between the freshwater lochs on the blacklands but adjacent to the machair plain of the west coast. The occupants of these settlements exploit the land in their immediate vicinity, but they also cultivate the machair plain and use the eastern uplands as a summer grazing resource. The sea lochs of the east coast provide sheltered anchorages and small settlements oriented on fishing, or fish farming, are found scattered around their shores. Access to the Scottish mainland is also channelled through these sea lochs and has resulted in the development of a port at Lochboisdale.

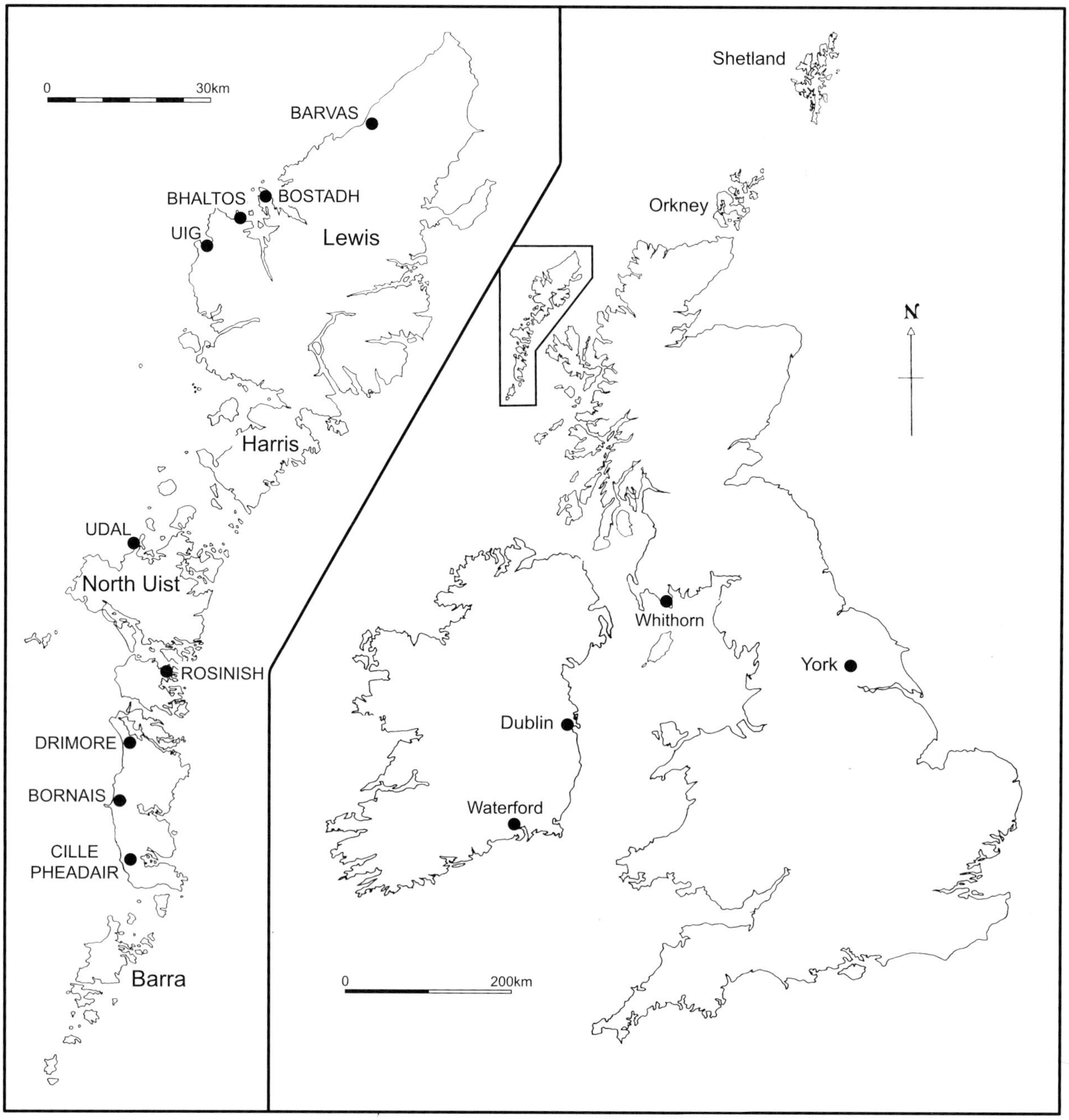

Figure 1. The Western Isles in relation to Britain and Ireland showing major Viking and Norse sites

The history of recent research on South Uist

Dun Vulan is located on the rocky promontory of Rubha Ardvule (Figure 3). The machair plain of the area adjacent to Dun Vulan lies in the township of Bornais and, partially as a result of recent erosion (Angus 1997, 167–169), this plain is particularly flat and low-lying. Settlements on this plain are highly visible mounds full of debris such as animal bones, seashells, pottery and other artefacts which can be recovered by a cursory examination of the spoil dumped in front of the many rabbit burrows that riddle the mounds. The machair plain of Bornais is dominated by three particularly prominent mounds, which are amongst the largest recorded on the island (Parker Pearson 1996). These mounds were clearly visible as we crossed the machair to Dun Vulan and, prior to our arrival on the island, they had been visited by Alex Woolf, who established their archaeological significance.

In 1993, during the period when Dun Vulan was under excavation, Mike Parker Pearson began an exhaustive survey of the machair plain. In the first year he concentrated on the five square kilometres nearest Dun Vulan but in later years this was expanded to cover the whole of the west coast of the island (Parker Pearson 1996). Approximately 40 archaeological settlements were initial-

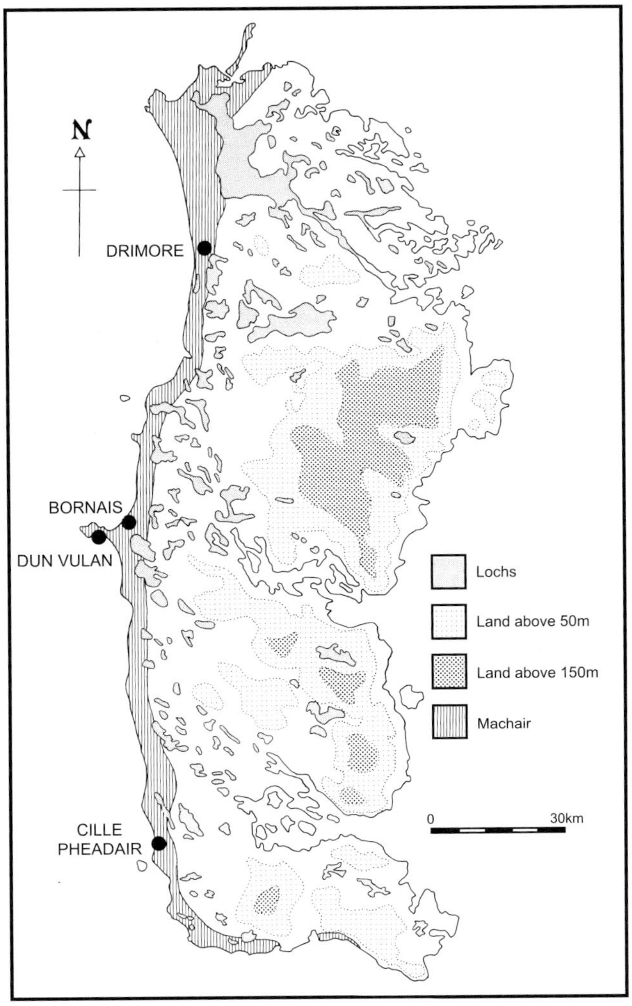

Figure 2. The island of South Uist showing topography and the principal Norse settlements

ly identified in this survey area (Figure 3) and some produced pottery or other finds that could be dated using comparanda from other areas of the Outer Hebrides (Lane 1990). This survey provides a chronological background to the settlement of the west coast of South Uist and highlighted the significance of the mounds at Bornais. One of these mounds (2) could be dated to the Norse period because of the presence of platter and other grass-marked pottery, which the excavations at The Udal suggested were restricted to the Viking and Norse period settlement of the island (Lane 1990). A small number of Iron Age sherds from mound 1 suggested that the settlement would include pre-Norse settlement and might include material from the period of the initial Viking settlement.

In 1994 the excavations at Dun Vulan had ceased (there was a final consolidation season in 1995) and Mike Parker Pearson began to test other settlement mounds to identify sites that would show the historical development of the settlements before and after the Middle Iron Age. The Middle Iron Age was a period that was now relatively well documented on South Uist by the excavations at Dun Vulan (Parker Pearson and Sharples 1999), and the wheelhouses of Cill Donnain, Cille Pheadair, A'Cheardach Mhor and A'Cheardach Bheag (Zvelebil 1991; Lethbridge 1952; Young and Richardson 1960; Fairhurst 1971) but no unambiguous Late Bronze Age/Early Iron Age settlements had been excavated, on any of the islands of the Outer Hebrides, and only one Norse settlement, Drimore (MacLaren 1974) had been excavated. The mounds at Bornais were an obvious place to begin, as they appeared to indicate a Norse settlement. Exploration of the mounds began with the excavation of mound 2. The excavation was initially undertaken by Mike Parker Pearson and Jane Webster and it was only in 1995 that Niall Sharples took over direction, initially with the help of Jane Webster. The history of the excavation of Bornais is fully described in chapter 3 but, before we deal with the site, it is necessary to outline the various other projects that were undertaken on the island at the same time as these excavations.

At the same time as the excavation of Bornais commenced another long-term project began with the examination of a prehistoric settlement at Cladh Hallan, some 8.5 km to the south of Bornais (Figure 4). This site, though outside the principal area of research, had been examined in 1989 (Parker Pearson and Roper 1994). However, following the initial work there had been considerable quarrying of the location and this had exposed a building that was clearly under threat. The early work at the site had revealed a midden, radiocarbon dated to the Late Bronze Age, and this was cut by the newly exposed building. It seemed likely that this site would provide the opportunity to explore a settlement earlier than Dun Vulan, as there were no obvious Middle Iron Age ceramics from the initial work. Excavation continued at Cladh Hallan every year from 1994 to 2002 and has revealed an extensive and extremely important settlement that does indeed span the period from the middle of the second millennium BC to the middle of the first millennium BC. This is the only settlement site known from this period to be examined in any detail on the Western Isles and it will provide an invaluable contribution to an understanding of the settlement history of the island.

Of more relevance to the excavation of Bornais was the discovery and excavation of a Norse settlement at Cille Pheadair (Parker Pearson, Brennand and Smith 1996; Parker Pearson and Smith forthcoming). This settlement was exposed by a heavy storm in the winter of 1993/4. The machair in this area is subject to severe coastal erosion and several archaeological sites are believed to have been completely destroyed in this area over the last century. However, there was no evidence for this settlement prior to 1993/4 and excavation subsequently demonstrated that the erosion of this settlement had only just begun. A layer of occupation soils and structural remains about 40 m long and 1.20 m thick

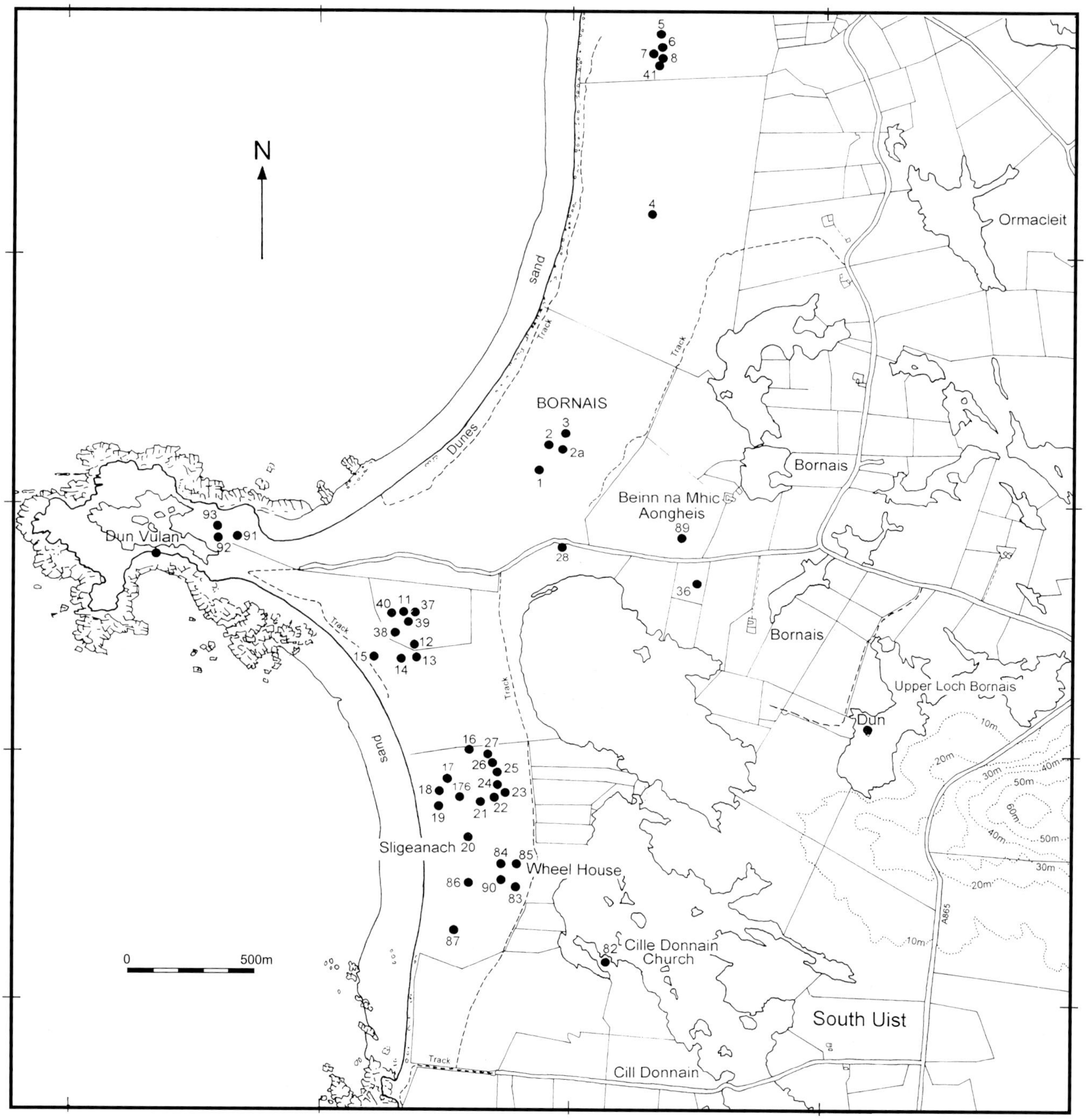

Figure 3. A detailed map of the area around Bornais showing sites located by the machair survey (Parker Pearson 1996)

defined the site. These deposits were sealed by 2–3 m of sterile wind-blown sand and the site was consequently not identified through surface field walking. It was built on sterile sand of unknown thickness and there was no evidence for an earlier Iron Age precursor.

The site was clearly threatened by coastal erosion and required immediate excavation. Mike Parker Pearson commenced work in 1996 and this was completed in 1998 by which time the centre of the settlement and all the principal buildings were completely excavated (Brennand, Parker Pearson and Smith 1998). The excavations revealed a Norse settlement occupied from approximately AD 1050–1350, with no Iron Age or Later Medieval contamination. A consecutive sequence of five buildings were present, some of which were accompanied by small subsidiary buildings. Large quantities of artefacts and ecofacts were recovered and the analysis of this material should provide a detailed picture of life in the Norse period. All of the material found was contemporary with the material recovered from Bornais and the two sites will eventually be compared and contrasted to provide a more complex and balanced view of Norse settlement in the Outer Hebrides. This comparison is particularly important, as there is no data set comparable to these settlements from any other excavation on the Western Isles and because it is already clear that there are significant differences in the settlements. Bornais is a much more substantial settlement and, in contrast to Cille Pheadair, the location was occupied prior to the Viking colonisation of the islands.

The excavations at Bornais, Cille Pheadair and Cladh Hallan were the main SEARCH projects under way in the second half of the 1990's but a variety of small-scale excavations (Figure 4) were also undertaken as part of the overall landscape project and some of these are directly relevant to the Bornais excavations.

- In 1995 trial trenching was undertaken on the church at Cille Donnain in the township immediately to the south of Bornais. This church had been identified in a field survey undertaken by Andrew Fleming (Fleming and Woolf 1992) and was thought to date to around AD 1100. The excavations did not recover any material contemporary with the primary phase of the church but they did recover sherds of Late Medieval date (Parker Pearson 1995).
- In the following year (1996) excavations were undertaken at Beinn na mhic Aongheis, Bornais (site 89, Marshall, Mulville and Parker Pearson 1996). This is a large grassy knoll lying in a marshy area just to the east of the machair plain, approximately 0.6 kms southeast of the Norse settlement. This site was identified as the location of the pre-clearance settlement marked on William Bald's map of 1805 (Bald 1805). No surface evidence for the settlement existed and it was only located by test trenching a number of suitable locations in the vicinity. Excavation was limited but successfully identified structural remains and recovered hand-made pottery, that indicated occupation from the fourteenth to fifteenth centuries onwards, and a clay pipe, dating to the late seventeenth century.
- In 1997 an island 'dun' in Upper Loch Bornais was examined (Marshall and Parker Pearson 1997). A number of test pits were dug and these produced evidence for a

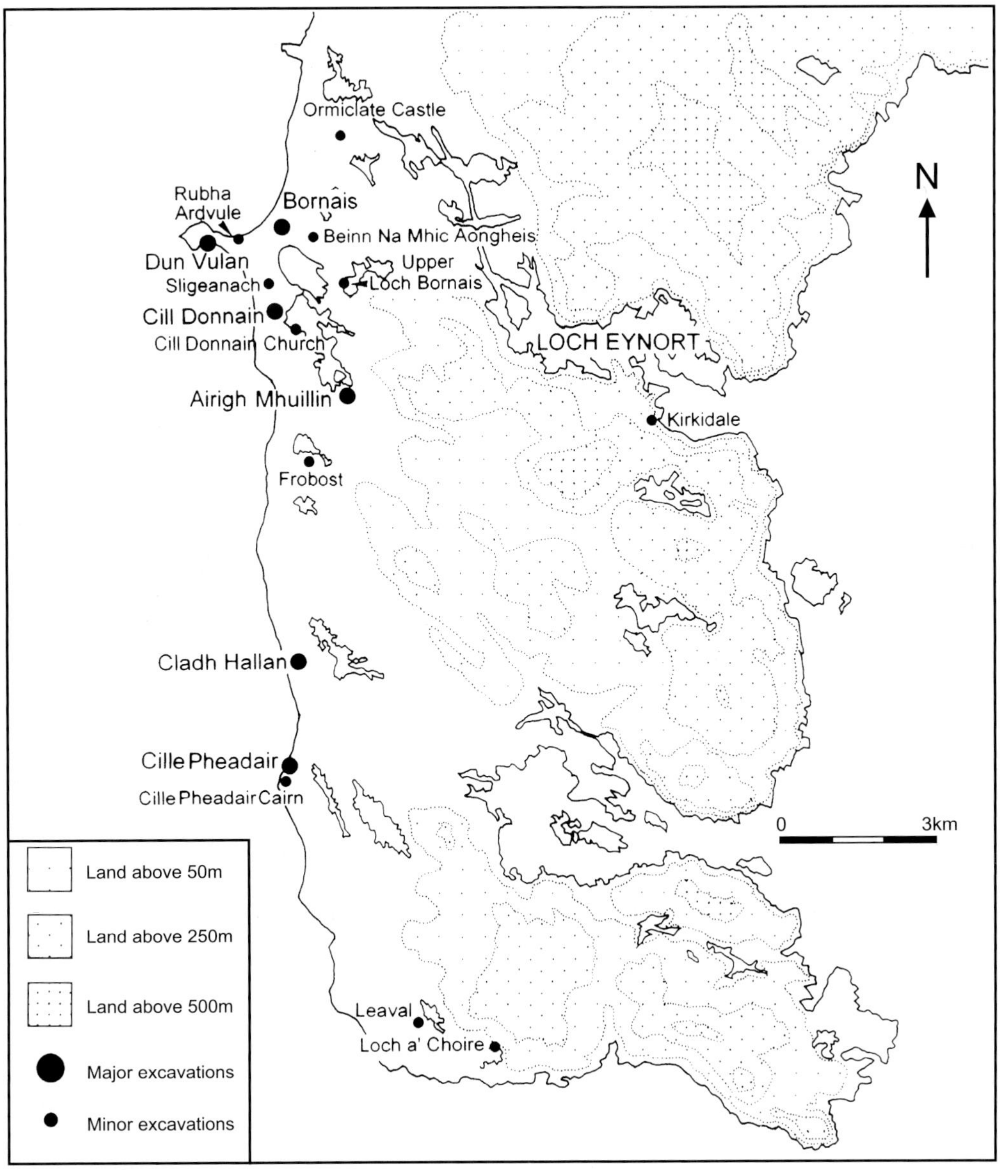

Figure 4. The south end of South Uist locating the excavations up to 2000

Late Bronze Age/Early Iron Age (c.600–300 BC) occupation of the island as well as limited evidence for occupation in the later Middle Iron Age (c. AD 100–300) and suggested that a large stone building existed at the centre of the island.

- In 1998 a number of mounds at Sligeanach, in the adjacent township of Cill Donnain, were test pitted. These excavations revealed the presence of an important Early Bronze Age settlement as well as an Early to Middle Iron Age settlement, which included a wheelhouse (Sharples 1998a).
- Contemporary with the SEARCH projects was the excavation of the post-Medieval township of Airigh Mhuillin, Milton (Symonds 1997; 1999c; 2000; Symonds and Badcock 2001) that lies only 3.73 km southeast of Bornais. Work here has provided an extensive and detailed examination of an eighteenth and nineteenth century township on the blacklands.

All of these excavations have been useful in providing a context for the more exhaustive excavations at Dun Vulan and Bornais and it is hoped to follow up the test-pitting programme by further work on the Early Bronze Age settlement at Sligeanach.

It was clear from the beginning of the South Uist project that a detailed understanding of the domestic architecture of the island was a worthwhile objective. The machair environment of the west coast of South Uist provides ideal conditions for the preservation of structures. There were few trees available on the island by the end of the Early Bronze Age and so stone and turf were the preferred media for the construction of house walls. In a relatively mobile environment such as the machair any structure built of stone will act as trap for the accumulation of wind-blown sand. Sand does not provide a surface that creates a compact and durable floor and so floors appear to have been created by the accumulation or deposition of organic material that provides a clear archaeological horizon associated with the occupation of the building. The accumulation of blown sand seals and preserves the floors and the walls. Finally the cultural tradition of the Western Isles apparently involves the repeated reconstruction of houses at the same location (Sharples forthcoming) and this forms a palimpsest of structures, which provides a detailed architectural history of a settlement.

Unfortunately the excavations at Dun Vulan were not sufficiently extensive to expose complete house floors and so we were not able to address this problem. However, researching house floors became a key research strategy for the second stage of the South Uist project (Smith, Marshall and Parker Pearson 2001). The excavations at Bornais, Cladh Hallan and Cille Pheadair specifically prioritised the excavation of complete buildings and a sampling strategy (detailed in chapter 3) was designed to maximise the examination of floors.

The Norse context for the excavations

In the last two decades archaeological exploration of the Norse settlements of the North Atlantic has been an area of increasing interest to scholars in a range of countries. Important new work is underway on settlements in Greenland, Iceland, the Faeroes and Norway. Much of this work has not yet been fully published but in recent years there have been several publications that place a considerable amount of information in the public domain (Morris and Rackham 1992; Batey, Jesch and Morris 1995). In Britain the principal focus of research (excluding the urban settlement at York) has been in the Northern Isles and Caithness. These areas have the benefit of a background of important research carried out in the first half of this century. Settlements such as Jarlshof, Shetland (Hamilton 1956), Birsay, Orkney (Curle 1982) and Freswick, Caithness (Curle 1939) provided invaluable evidence for the nature of Norse settlements throughout the North Atlantic. Recent work has involved either re-excavation or new work on these famous sites (e.g. Hunter 1986; Morris 1996) as well as the excavation of new sites, most importantly Tuquoy (Owen 1993) and Pool, Orkney (Hunter, Bond and Smith 1993) and The Biggings (Crawford and Ballin Smith 1999) and Sandwick, Shetland (Bigelow 1985).

In contrast to this activity, fieldwork on Norse sites in the Western Isles has been extremely limited (Figure 1). The only recent excavation on a scale comparable to the Northern Isles has been at The Udal on North Uist (Crawford 1986; Selkirk 1996). In the 1950's a 14 m longhouse was partly excavated at Drimore, South Uist (MacLaren 1974). Small-scale excavations have been undertaken on a settlement at Barvas on Lewis (Armit 1996, 192–193) and on the cemetery at Bhaltos on Lewis (Welander, Batey and Cowie 1987; Cowie, Bruce and Kerr 1994; Dunwell, Cowie, Bruce, Neighbour and Rees 1995) and Norse middens have been exposed and examined during the excavation of earlier structures at Rosinish (Shepherd and Tuckwell 1977) and Bostadh (Neighbour and Burgess 1996). Other unambiguous evidence of the Norse occupation of the islands is restricted to a handful of burials (Crawford 1987, figure 31; Graham-Campbell and Batey 1998, 74–76), three chance finds of silver money on Lewis and gold finger rings on North Uist (Graham-Campbell 1976; 1995; Graham-Campbell and Batey 1998, 75–76; Armit 1996, 194–195), a bronze pin from Bornais, and the famous chessmen from Uig sands on Lewis (Stratford 1997).

This relative imbalance in the extent of archaeological work between the Northern and Western Isles of Scotland could be related to the historical significance of the Northern Isles and the importance of the early work on sites such as Birsay and Jarlshof. However, this imbalance is visible in other periods and is more likely to be related to the uneven practice of archaeology in Scotland than to either the inherent attractions of the archaeological resource in the Northern Isles or the unimportance of the Western Isles in the context of the Viking settlement of the North Atlantic. The Western Isles sit astride the sea route from Norway to Dublin and it is clear that any movement down the western seaboard of Britain would inevitably have involved contact with, or provisioning from, the islands. Furthermore, work on the historical records suggests that the inhabitants played an important part in the colonisation of Iceland (Andersen 1991, 137).

A considerable impetus in the recent work on the settlements of the Northern Isles has been directed towards the recovery of environmental and economic data that enables a detailed recreation of subsistence activities of the inhabitants of the various excavated settlements (see in particular Morris and Rackham 1992). This was an important research objective as work on this aspect of the past had advanced immeasurably since the early excavations, where this type of information was barely recovered. Environmental sampling was also a priority for the excavations at Bornais. One of the long-term objectives of the South Uist project is to provide a detailed history of the changing environment and economy of the island from the earliest occupation through to the contemporary period and the project has included environmental and economic specialists from its inception (Gilbertson, Kent and Gratton 1996; Smith and Mulville 2004). The excavation methodology involves intensive sampling of the excavated contexts in all of the substantial field projects and as a result an extraordinarily large database of fish, bird, large and small mammal bones, carbonised plants, snail and eggshells and crustaceans has been recovered. This will provide a resource of considerable importance to future scholars and is directly comparable to the material available from excavations in the Northern Isles and in other comparable collections from excavations in Iceland and Norway.

In most of these excavations the emphasis has been on the exploration of middens where the concentrations of economic information have been at their most substantial and where relatively small-scale interventions have resulted in the recovery of large assemblages. However, as noted above, one of the main priorities of the South Uist project has been the examination of house floors. It was felt that a comparative analysis of the spatial organisation of activity in a house (and other buildings) would provide an invaluable aid to the interpretation of society and social change. In this respect the recent work in the North Atlantic is unfortunately less helpful. Most of the recent work in the Northern Isles has been unable to explore complete well-preserved house floors.

In the Western Isles the excavations at Drimore apparently exposed a complete Viking house (MacLaren 1974) and this was in the machair environment that should have preserved floors similar to those exposed at Bornais. However, the structural integrity of the Drimore house has recently been called into question (Graham-Campbell and Batey 1998, 175–177), the finds recovered were not published with locations and there was no intensive sampling of the floor. Several houses were excavated at The Udal on North Uist (Crawford 1974; 1981; 1986) and some of these are directly comparable to the structures excavated at Cille Pheadair and Bornais. However, none of this material has been published and it is impossible to assess the detailed characteristics of the buildings.

At Birsay a large number of Norse structures were excavated (Hunter 1986) but unfortunately most of these structures had been cleared in the early part of this century and the floors were largely removed. The excavation of previously untouched structures (such as Beachview Area 1, Morris 1996) has been restricted to very limited samples which whilst clearly identifying important floor deposits have not been large enough to gain a detailed understanding of the use of the house. Similar problems restrict the interpretation of many other sites. At Freswick (Morris, Batey and Rackham 1995) the new excavations of the houses exposed in the thirties were very restricted. Examination of the important Norse settlement at Tuquoy was restricted to cleaning the cliff section exposed on the beach (Owen 1993).

Only a limited number of Norse houses have seen anything like complete excavation in recent years. The principal examples are Skaill (Buteux 1997), Pool (Hunter, Bond and Smith 1993), Westness (Kaland 1993) on Orkney and Sandwick (Bigelow 1985) and The Biggings (Crawford and Ballin Smith 1999) on Shetland. Only two of these excavations have been fully published and in neither study was it possible to undertake a systematic analysis of the distribution of material inside the house, though they do provide very important information on the architecture of these structures. The most detailed analysis of a house floor was presented in an interim report on Sandwick (Bigelow 1985) where the author used the range of artefact types found in the two halves of the building to argue for the presence of a byre area. It was possible to compare the results with some of the houses at Jarlshof (Hamilton 1956) for which a considerable amount of distributional information was recorded and published.

Similar problems exist in other areas of the North Atlantic region. Rural excavations are rare and when houses have been excavated the emphasis tends to be on the architecture. Understanding the use of a house through a detailed analysis of the finds distribution is limited. A good example of the potential information that can be acquired from the analysis of finds distributions is Granastaðir in Iceland (Einarsson 1995, 128–135) and hopefully the analysis undertaken here will go someway towards surmounting the obstacle noted by Einarsson that 'we lack clear knowledge about plans of farms and the distribution of artefacts' (Einarsson 1995, 139).

Publication strategy

The excavation of the Bornais settlement is a long-term project, which has been underway since 1994 and was only completed in 2004. The timescale makes publication problematic. Ideally it would be best to publish when all the post-excavation has been undertaken. However, this ideal clashes with the desire to make the results of what is a very interesting project available to scholars and the general public in a reasonable period of time. It is very unlikely, given the vast quantities of data that have been collected, that the project can be completely published before the end of the decade (2010). This is a long time period and though it can, and will be, partially ameliorated by the publication of interim reports and detailed discursive papers, it still seems an unacceptable delay. The solution to the problem is to publish the excavations in several monographs. This is a reasonable response to the dilemma because the settlement at Bornais consists of several mounds and these mounds formed the focus for discrete excavations. Two of the mounds (1 and 3) were subject to only limited excavation and the fieldwork was completed in 1999. Post-excavation has prioritised the analysis of these completed excavations and as a result it is possible to publish these mounds as separate fascicules prior to the analysis of mounds 2 and 2A.

The first volume is primarily concerned with the excavation of mound 3 (Figure 5) but it includes a discussion of the topographic and geophysical survey of all the mounds (chapter 2). The geophysical survey provides an essential background to the understanding of the settlement at Bornais as it depicts the overall pattern of settlement activity across and around the different mounds. It is also possible to identify distinctive structures, which enables a provisional interpretation of the nature of the settlement of the different mounds. The topographic survey is less helpful as an interpretative tool but does provide a useful basis for monitoring the erosion of the mounds. It also provides some indication of how the settlement was used in its last century.

The excavation of mound 3 was superficial and the results are consequently relatively inconsequential compared to the more extensively excavated sequences of mounds 2 and 2A. The structures exposed (two houses and a kiln/barn) are simple and relatively low-status buildings, only a small number of finds were recovered and they are fragmented and lacking in prestige. Nevertheless these buildings have provided a considerable amount of new and exciting information about the Norse settlement of Scotland. The most important results have come from the analysis of the floors of the two completely excavated structures (the later house and kiln/barn). These produced substantial assemblages of carbonised plant remains and fish bones, which not only provide a detailed understanding of the occupation of the houses but also tell us a considerable amount about the agricultural practices and fishing strategies of the settlement's occupants.

The fish remains provide the first documented evidence for intensive herring fishery in Scotland. This was completely unexpected when we began the analysis as previous work in the Northern Isles (Barrett, Nicholson and Cerón-Carrasco 1999) had indicated that herring was not consumed, or actively hunted, in the North. Both the settlements and the specialised fishing sites of Orkney and Caithness produced large assemblages of codfish. Similarly the work at Dun Vulan yielded a fish assemblage dominated by codfish. The excavations of the Norse deposits at The Udal (Serjeantson pers. comm.) had produced a slightly larger collection of herring but this was not sufficiently large to be abnormal and with hindsight it appears likely that herring were seriously under-represented because of the sieving strategy. After the discovery of the herring at Bornais it became apparent that herring were present in other Norse settlements in the Western Isles. At Bostadh on the Isle of Lewis (Neighbour and Burgess 1996) the excavation of a Late Iron Age settlement also resulted in the discovery of a Norse midden and examination of this revealed a herring-dominated fish bone assemblage (Cerón-Carrasco pers. comm.). The Cille Pheadair fish bone assemblage is also dominated by herring (Ingrem in Parker Pearson and Smith forthcoming).

The carbonised plant remains have also provided important results and the significance of the results is enhanced by the excavation of a 'corn-drying kiln' in mound 3. The high density of carbonised plants found at this settlement indicates the increasing importance of cereals to the Norse economy in comparison to the Middle Iron Age economy. Analysis of the various floor layers, and associated contexts, has indicated significant differences in the assemblages present in the later house and the kiln/barn. These differences suggest a route for the processing of cereals, which entered the site via the kiln, and were initially processed in the adjacent 'barn' before final cleaning and presumably consumption in the house. The analysis of the species present, both cereals and weed seeds, indicates an expansion of arable agriculture into areas that were hitherto uncultivated. This evidence is of considerable importance for the understanding of the late Norse economy of Atlantic Scotland and the patterns observed are some of the best documented in Britain.

A detailed description and discussion of these two assemblages takes up much of this report but this publication also places on record the architectural features of a typical fourteenth to fifteenth century farm. This farm type originated in the Scandinavian milieu of the North Atlantic and its architectural evolution can be compared to similar settlements in the Norse regions of Orkney and Shetland and, further afield, in the Faeroes, Iceland and Norway. However, it is also possible to compare it with other Medieval settlements in mainland Britain that lie outside the Norse colonies, and although the Medieval evidence from the Scottish mainland is minimal, Highland domestic buildings provide a useful comparison. The Bornais buildings are similar to structures built in the Uists in the last century and these historically documented remains provide information essential to a detailed understanding of the excavated house.

The report begins with a detailed discussion of the survey evidence. This is followed by a chapter that presents

Figure 5. A plan of the Bornais mounds showing the trenches excavated up to 2003

the methodological approach to the excavation of the site and to the post-excavation analysis of the various material assemblages recovered by these excavations. There then follow three chapters that provide a detailed description of the evidence from the separate trenches excavated in mound 3. The organisation of these chapters follows the stratigraphy exposed during the excavations and involves the description of the contexts exposed and material recovered from these contexts. The following chapter provides a comparative analysis of the material from the different contexts in both trenches. Chapter 8 is a discussion of the radiocarbon dates. Three discussion chapters follow the descriptive chapters; these examine resource exploitation, management and production and place the site in the context of the archaeology of the North Atlantic in the Medieval or Norse period.

The structure is slightly unusual in fracturing the disciplinary boundaries of the find specialists and closely integrating the stratigraphic description with the artefact analysis. Both of these goals derive from my dissatisfaction with the shortcomings of traditional archaeological monographs (Sharples 1998b, 90) and I have made previous attempts to create a more readable archaeological report. The publication of the broch at Scalloway (Sharples 1998b) was my first attempt to integrate specialist reports and this was reasonably successful (though some specialists were not happy, Ballin Smith 2001). I was less happy with the way the finds reporting was integrated with the stratigraphy in the Scalloway report and this aspect was more successfully implemented in the Dun Vulan report (Parker Pearson and Sharples 1999). However, it was not possible to carry out the integrated analysis of the finds in the Dun Vulan report. It is hoped that this report will successfully amalgamate the positive features of the Dun Vulan and Scalloway reports and that this can be carried on into succeeding volumes.

The intention is to provide a companion volume on mound 1, and then, some time later, provide volumes on mounds 2A and 2. The quantity of finds from mound 2 may necessitate two volumes and a final discussion volume that integrates the various sites may be required but that is some time in the future and it is best not to plan too far ahead.

Acknowledgements

The fieldwork undertaken at Bornais would not have been possible without the support of many people. Permission to excavate was given by the Bornais Grazing Committee through Ewan Steele, South Uist Estates through Tim Atkinson, and Scottish Natural Heritage through Mary Harman. Throughout the project we have received much invaluable support from the members of Comann Eachdraidh Uibhist a Deas, Kathy Bruce, James and Calum MacDonald, Alasdair MacIntyre, the late Gill MacLean, Neil Macmillan, Effie MacMillan and Robert Tye.

Cardiff University, Historic Scotland and Sheffield University supplied financial support. P Ashmore, S Foster, N Fojut and R McCullagh of Historic Scotland have all provided considerable help and P Ashmore supported the extensive programme of radiocarbon dating.

K Frazer, M MacIsaac, A J MacKinnon, M K Morrison, and Col H Massey kindly provided accommodation. J J MacDonald Builders, Norman MacAskill, Laing Motors and Uist Builders Construction provided technical help.

The excavations still operate within the overarching structure of the now much modified SEARCH project and have benefited from the critical comment of the main surviving participants; Jacqui Mulville, Mike Parker Pearson and Helen Smith. Helen Smith organised and carried out the flotation programme and was responsible for the overall coordination of the analysis of the plant and soil samples. She enlisted Sue Colledge, Karen Milek and Pete Marshall who have provided important contributions to this volume. Jacqui Mulville has coordinated the analysis of the animal remains and, as well as undertaking the analysis of the large mammal bones, she enlisted Claire Ingrem, Judy Cartledge and Jan Light to undertake the specialist analysis of the fish bone, the bird bone and the crab remains. The finds specialists were organised by Niall Sharples and I am indebted to my colleague Alan Lane, for organising the report on the pottery, and undertaking the analysis with Jerry Bond; to Ann Clarke for the stone report, Phil Macdonald for the report on the iron, Andrea Smith for the report on the worked bone and Tim Young for the analysis of the slag. Publication drawings were produced by Ian Dennis.

The excavation of trench D was largely supervised by Mike Hamilton but with an important initial contribution by Jane Webster. Trench F was started by Dave Wyatt and finished by Rachel Jackson. We would like to thank all the students, from Cardiff and Sheffield Universities, who worked on these trenches for the skill and effort they put into the job. Mike Hamilton's initial involvement with the site began with the geophysical survey and this is an immensely important document for the future analysis and preservation of the settlement. Its final format has benefited from a re-analysis of the data by Tim Young.

The iron was x–rayed and cleaned by undergraduate students in the Conservation Department of the School of History and Archaeology, Cardiff University and Phil Parkes of Cardiff Conservation Services, School of History and Archaeology, Cardiff University. Soil thin sections were manufactured by Julie Miller at the McBurney Geoarchaeology Laboratory, University of Cambridge. Funding for travel to South Uist for the collection of reference samples of peat and dune sand, and for the continuation of the micromorphology sampling program at Bornais, was provided by the Kathleen Hughes Fund, for which K Milek gratefully thanks the Department of Anglo-Saxon, Norse and Celtic at the University of Cambridge. Lydia Zapata (University of the Basque Country, Spain) and Marco Madella (McDonald Institute for Archaeological Research, University of Cambridge) assisted with the identification of the botanical remains in the thin sections. Katinka Stentoft has provided a very useful translation of several important Scandinavian papers.

2 Surveying the Mounds

The original approach to the surveying of the site was to lay out a base line that ran from mound 3 across the low point between mounds 2 and 2A to mound 1. In 1995 this base line was used to undertake a contour survey of the mounds using a dumpy level and taking readings at every 5–10 m. This created a satisfactory visual impression of the mounds (Sharples 1997, figure 1), which could be used to document the relationship between the various trenches. In 1996 it was possible to undertake a geophysical survey (resistivity and gradiometer) of the mounds. The results of the geophysical survey made it clear that the settlement extended off the mounds and was considerably more complicated than had previously been thought. It was decided that a new contour survey was required that would record a larger area in more detail. This was undertaken in 1999 using an EDM with a datalogger (Figure 6). The digitised database made analysis and reproduction of the data easier and allowed for the integration of the contour and geophysical survey data.

The physical topography of the settlement – N Sharples

The settlement is located in a fairly flat machair landscape. There is a coastal dune system, characteristic of the machair (Ritchie 1979), and at Bornais this is very pronounced. The coastal dunes drop down to a flat, low-lying area which is flooded in the winter. The eastern edge of this seasonally flooded area is marked by a distinct scarp that rises from about 2.50 m OD to 3.25 m OD which defined the western edge of the surveyed area (Figure 6). The settlement mounds are located immediately to the east of this scarp (mound 1 lies just over 40 m from the scarp, mound 2 just over 30 m, and mound 3 approximately 80 m). Around the mounds there are localised, small dunes, particularly near mound 3 and to the north of the settlement, but to the east of the mounds the ground flattens off. The absence of high dunes makes the Bornais machair ideal for cultivation and most of the machair is cultivated, for barley or oats, on a two-year rotation. The cultivation area includes mounds 2A and 2B and the southern fringe of mound 3.

The settlement comprises three principal mounds:

- Mound 1 is a prominent isolated mound, which defines the southern edge of the site. It is 52 m by 59 m and rises 1.5 m, from a height of 3.5 m OD to just over 5 m OD.
- Mound 2 lies 60 m to the north of mound 1. It is an even more prominent mound, rising on the south side from 3.75 m OD to a height of just over 6 m OD. The mound is basically circular, 30 m by 33 m with a slight extension to the north.
- Mound 3 lies 43 m to the northeast of mound 2 and it is the most extensive mound but the least conspicuous. It is 58 m north to south by 28 m east to west. It has two separate summits, the principal one to the north and a subsidiary one to the south. On the north side the mound rises from 4 m OD to just above 5 m OD.

Two subsidiary mounds are visible on the contour survey, though they are difficult to define by surface features alone.

- Mound 2A lies 10 m to the east of mound 2 and it is 21 m in diameter.
- Mound 2B lies 6 m to the northeast of mound 2 and is 18 m in diameter.

Mounds 2, 2A, 2B and 3 all lie close to each other and form a fairly continuous complex. Mound 1, in contrast, is separated from the complex by a large, flat expanse apparently devoid of archaeological remains.

The geophysical survey – M A Hamilton, N Sharples and T Young

The geophysical survey was based on 20 x 20 m grids. Unfortunately, owing to problems rediscovering the survey pegs at the beginning of the 1996 season, the grid used for the geophysical survey was not identical to that used for surveying the site. The geophysical grid was 2.5 degrees askew from the original grid. It passed through peg 440/300 on the 1995 grid and was 6.4 m to the east of peg 440/120 (Figure 7). The geophysical baseline was surveyed by EDM, and then individual 20 x 20 m squares were created by triangulation using 50 m and 30 m tapes. 20 m strings, with measuring points indicated by coloured tape, were then laid out across the grids. Each gradiometer grid began with the first reading in the southwest corner and then proceeded north. The resistivity grids had their first reading in the northeast corner and then proceeded south. Each grid was given a number prefixed "R" or "M" depending on survey type. The numbers were sequential for each machine (M1 to M55 and R1 to R40). There was no attempt to retain the same numbers for

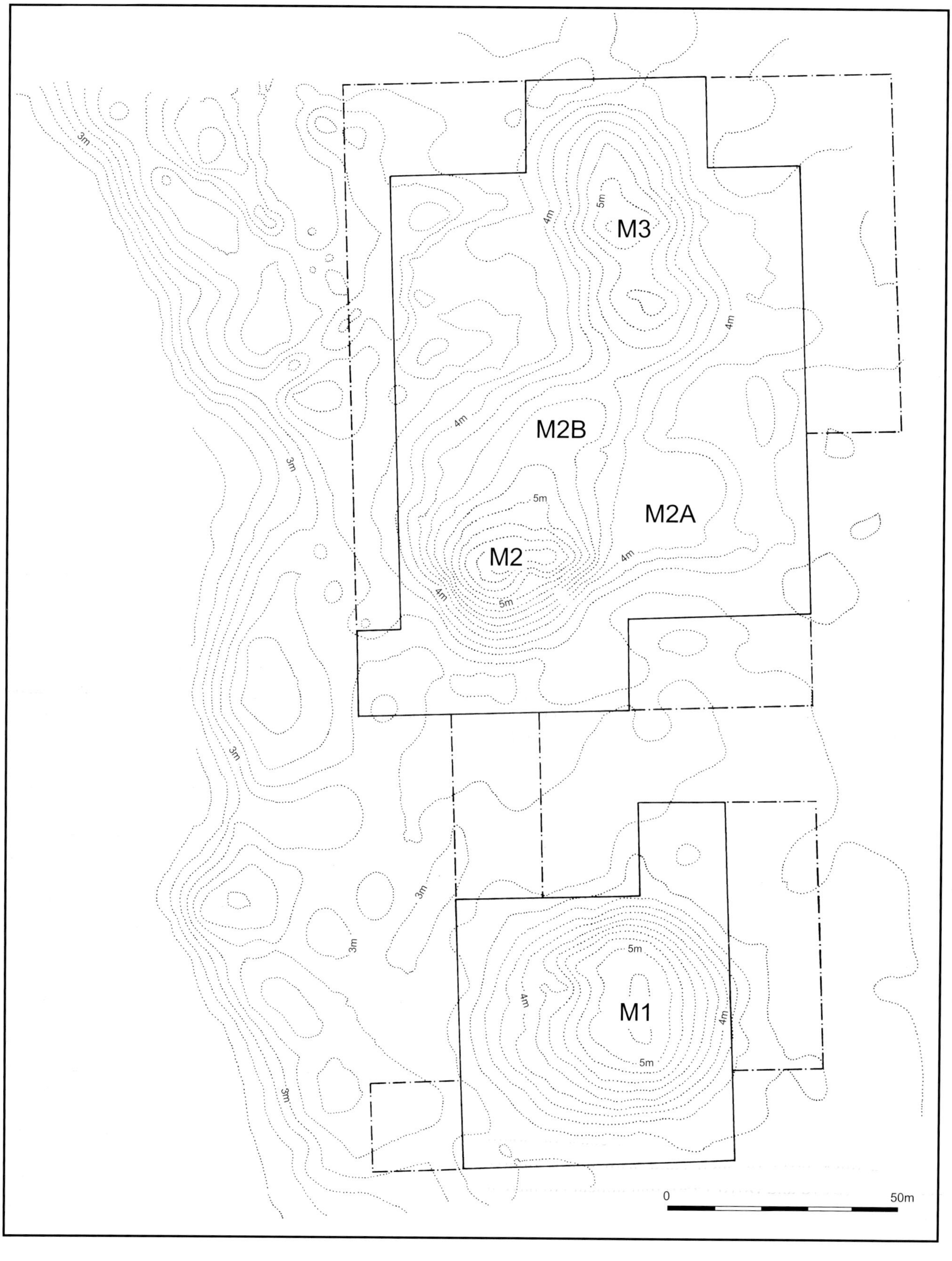

Figure 6. The contour survey of the mounds and the geophysical survey grids

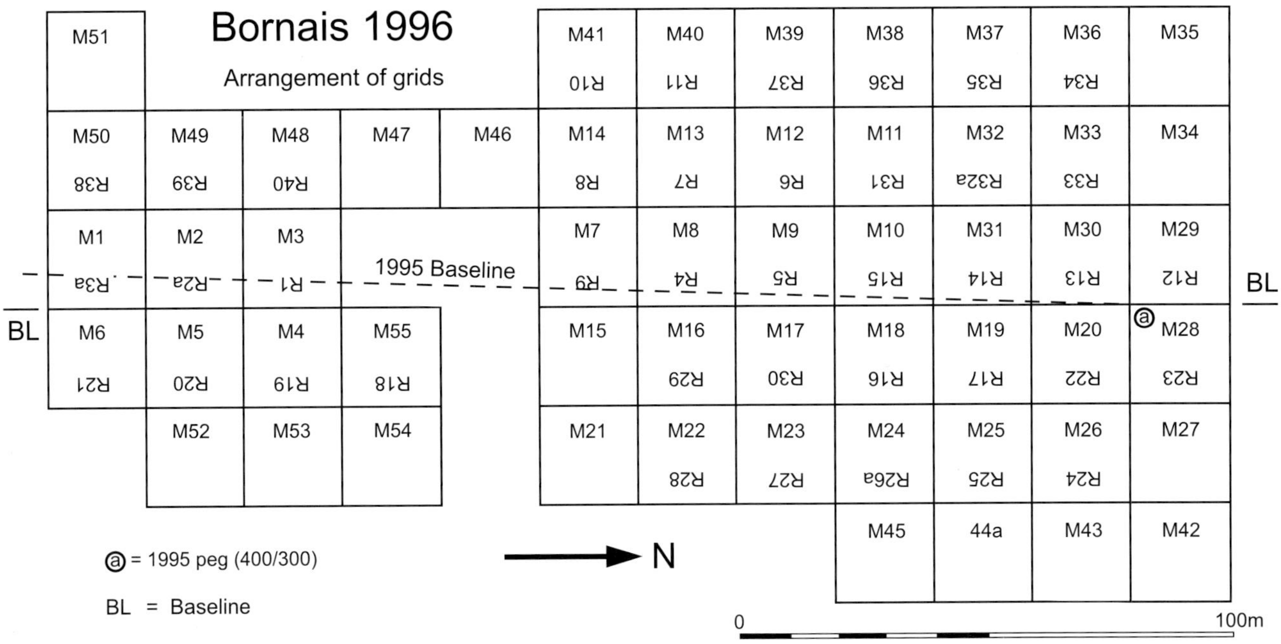

Figure 7. The geophysical survey grids

both techniques on the same grid (e.g. R16 is not the same grid as M16). Any grid number with an additional "a" refers to a grid which either was resurveyed or required additional processing.

A Geoscan FM36 fluxgate gradiometer was used with a sensitivity of 0.1nT. Readings were taken with a transverse interval of 1 m and a sampling interval of 0.5 m, making 800 readings for every grid. A Geoscan resistance meter (RM4) and datalogger (DL10) were also used. Each grid had transverse and sampling intervals of 1 m, resulting in 400 readings for every grid. The data was processed using a Triumph-Alder Walkstation 386SX running Geoscan Geoplot 1 and 2 programmes. The data were then exported from the completed composite and imported into Golden Software's Surfer software. The data were interpolated to a node spacing of 0.125 m in Surfer using kriging to produce a grid file for final imaging.

Gradiometer survey (Figures 8, 9)

The underlying geology of the Hebrides is largely metamorphic rock that is magnetic and therefore severely limits the effectiveness of the gradiometer (Clark 1990, 92). However, the machair of the west coast of South Uist is a thick layer of shell sand with a low quartz component (Boyd and Boyd 1990) that appears to have a neutral response from the gradiometer. If the sand is sufficiently deep then the effect of the geology is limited, but if the depth of the machair is less substantial then the effect of the geology completely obscures any archaeology. It is as yet unclear how thick the machair needs to be to mask the geology. The neutral areas to the west and east of the settlement at Bornais (Figure 8) demonstrate that the effect of the geology is insignificant at this location.

The principal features noted during the excavation of the site are buildings, sand layers with organic material and artefacts (which merge into heavily organic middens) and occupation surfaces. Ditches are not common features on machair sites owing to the free-draining nature of the sand and the problems caused by wind erosion if the unconsolidated sand is exposed. Furthermore any ditches that were created and naturally infilled with blown sand would not produce strongly magnetic anomalies.

The most obvious feature visible on the survey is an enclosure wall (Figures 8, 9) built in the 1870's. The visible and well-defined nature of this feature is due to the use of magnetic local stones. These stones are also used in facing the walls of buildings and it was expected that some of the geophysical anomalies should be walls. The gradiometer survey of mounds 1, 2 and 3 shows a number of high magnetic anomalies, none of which correspond to features visible on the surface. Many of these anomalies appear on the survey as roughly sub-rectangular shapes, defined by positive readings, and some of these have a hollow core, defined by negative readings. It was clear from our understanding of the enclosure that the high response is typical of the local stone, and this, together with the shape, suggested that these anomalies were rectangular buildings. To confirm this, a trial trench was excavated across feature S15 in 1996. This was a particularly clear rectangular anomaly, on the eastern edge of the settlement complex, visible on both the gradiometer and resistance surveys (Figures 8, 9, 11).

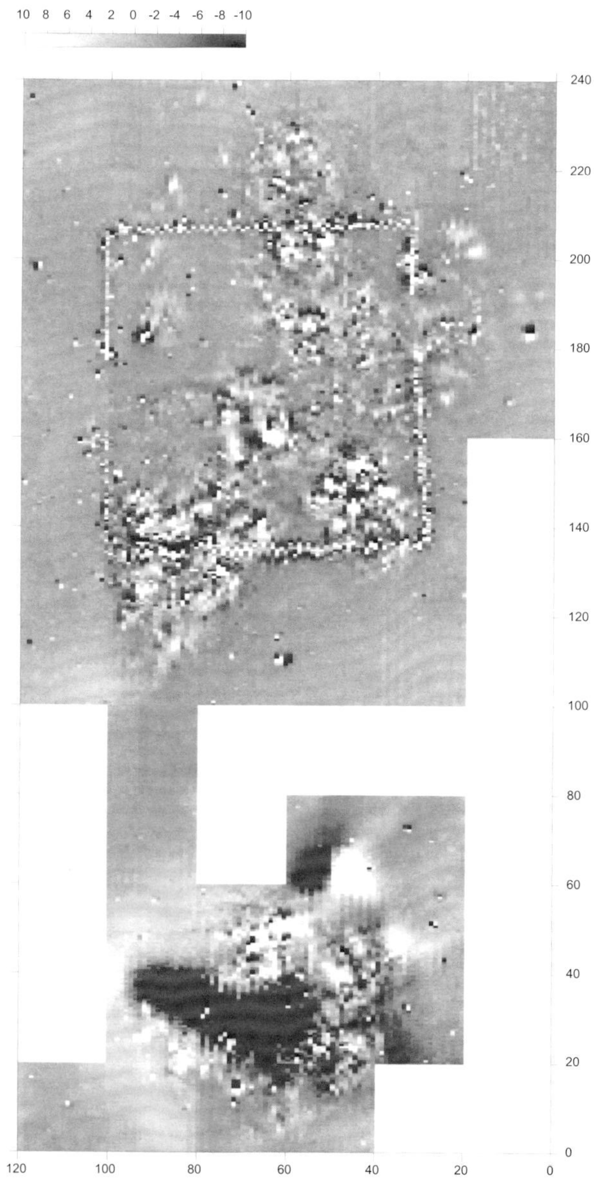

Figure 8. The gradiometer survey, raw data

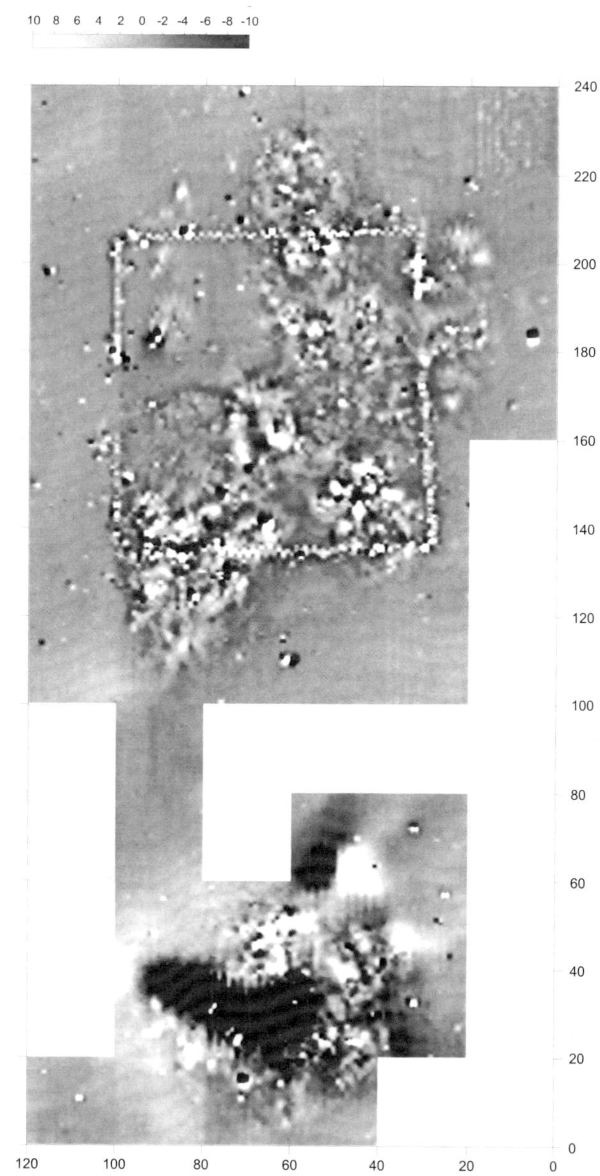

Figure 9. The gradiometer survey, kriged to 0.1 m nodes

Excavation exposed a wall and a floor (see chapter 6) that confirmed the interpretation that this was a house. It is notable that the magnetic response from the buildings generally produced a broader anomaly than that from the enclosure wall (Figure 12, A). This may be because they are buried deeper than the enclosure wall or because of collapsed rubble.

What is less clear is how successful the gradiometer is in detecting the organic-rich middens, occupation surfaces and hearths. Normally such features are detected because burning has enhanced the magnetism of the iron oxides found in soil and clays. The shell sand at Bornais, and elsewhere, does not contain significant iron oxides but these are present in peat, which is an important source of fuel and can be found in abundance to east of the settlement. Magnetic susceptibility studies at Bhaltos (Armit 1994, fiche 1:E6) demonstrated that middens and archaeological deposits on at least one machair site had significant susceptibility. The most likely source for this is the iron present in the peat that was used as fuel.

Resistivity survey (Figures 10, 11)

The main problem with this technique on the machair is that the sand is very well drained and this produces very high contact resistance. This was exacerbated by a prolonged period of dry weather in 1996 prior to the first day of surveying. When crossing the extensive rabbit warrens the machine occasionally refused to take any readings and those locations had to be dummied. Fortunately rain on the second day and all the subsequent days meant that, while contact resistance remained very high,

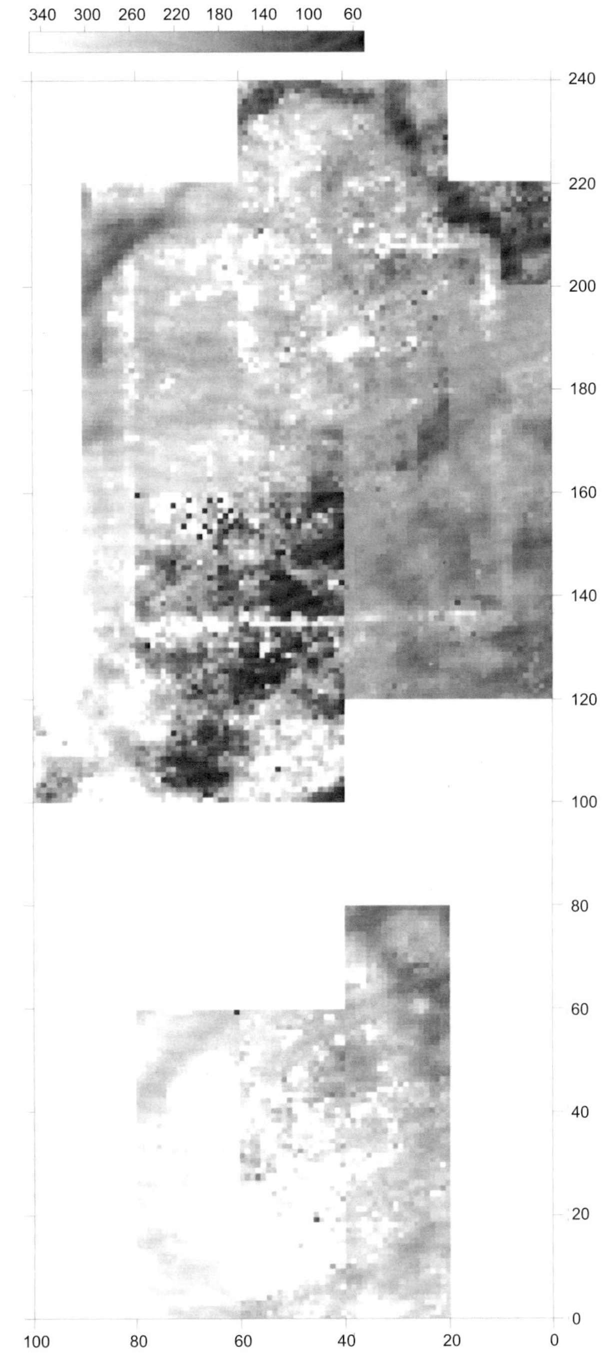

Figure 10. The resistivity survey, trace plot

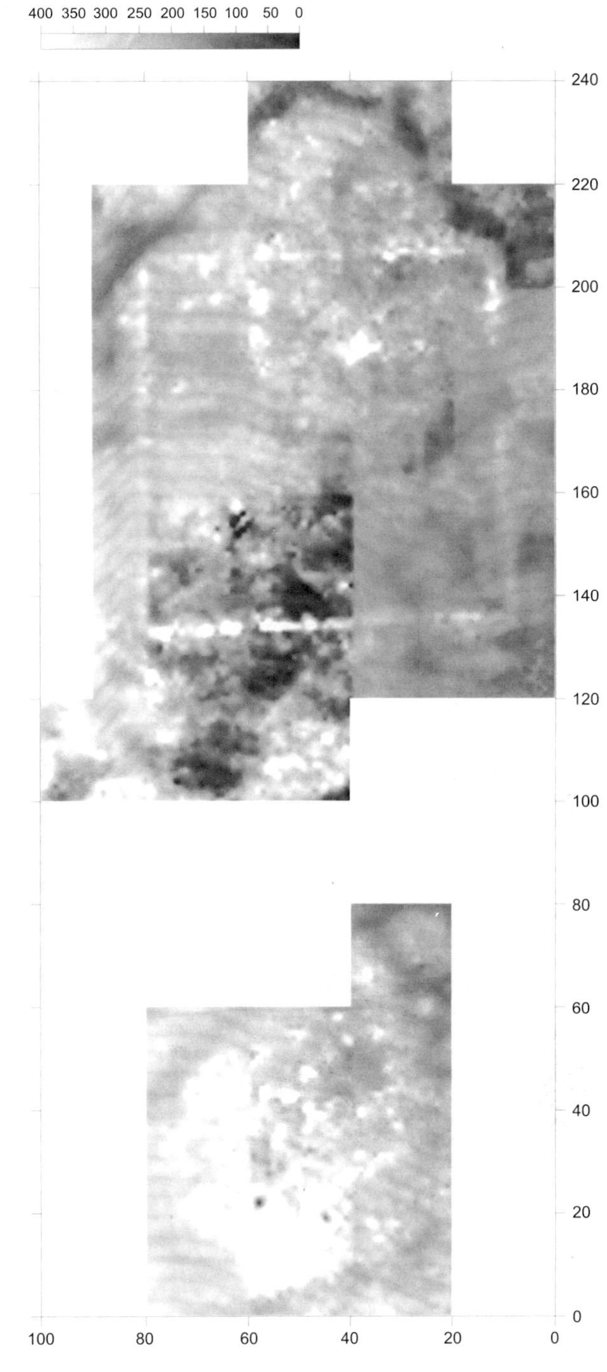

Figure 11. The resistivity survey, kriged to 0.1 m nodes

the problem was less significant. The Geoscan RM4 resistance meter has a warning for high contact resistance that remained permanently on for the whole of the survey and typical readings for the survey were 300 Ohms with the remote probes 1 m apart.

Atkinson used resistance to locate possible structures at Sollas, North Uist (Campbell 1991) but excavation showed that these anomalies were due to variation in sand depth. On other machair sites resistance surveying seems to do little more than confirm the topographical survey (Dockrill 1984; Armit 1994). However, Dockrill (1986) did locate structures in a mound on Sanday, Orkney that were represented by sub-circular bands of low resistance. At Bornais a building was identified by a very distinctive high resistance feature (Figure 12, S16). Excavations revealed a very well-preserved building infilled with a thick deposit of clean white sand. This sand does not retain moisture and this explains the high resistance.

The more general areas of higher resistance are difficult to interpret. They could reflect the depth of the wind-blown sand, but areas where there is known to be a

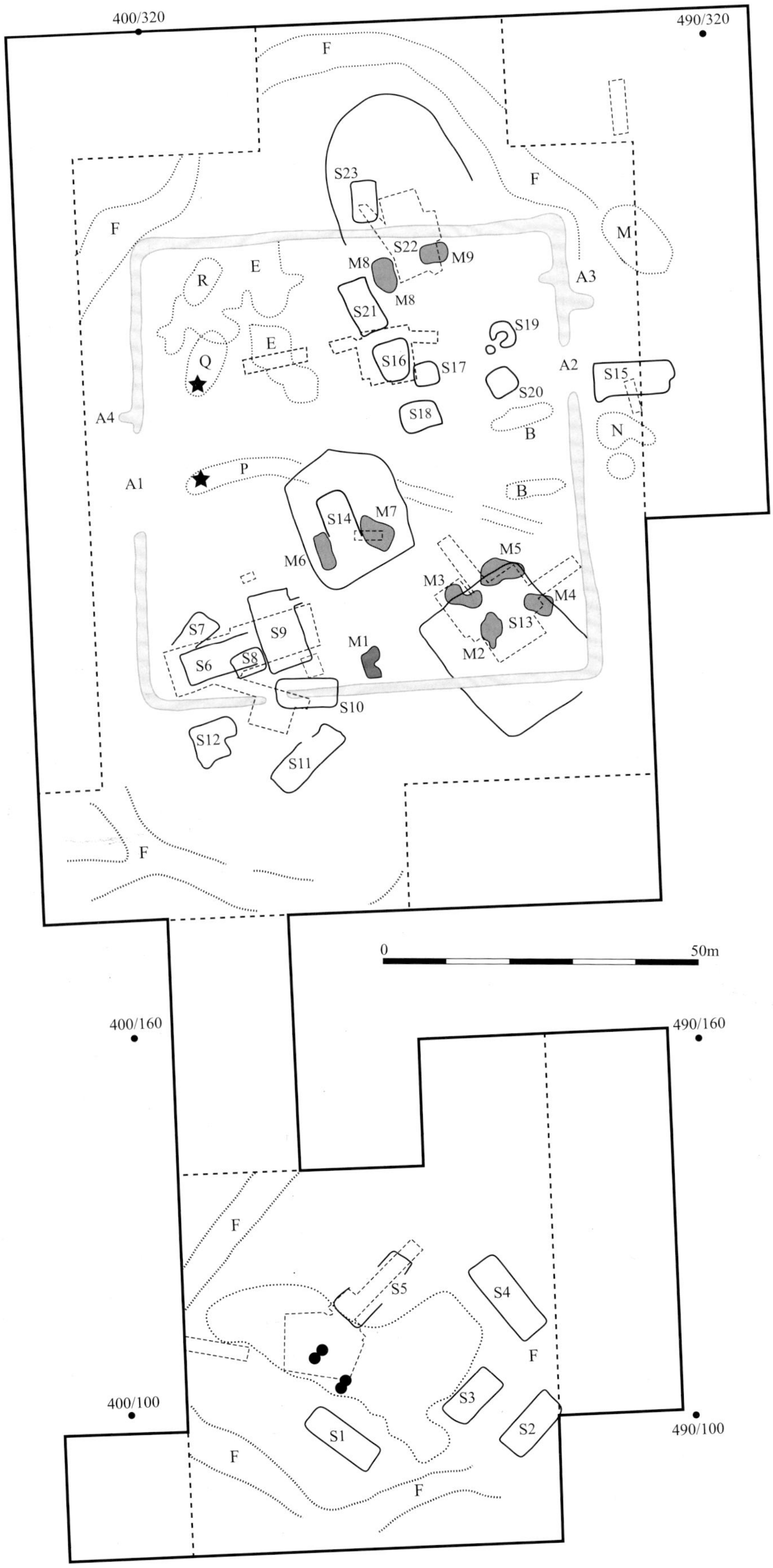

Figure 12. The interpretation plan

considerable depth of wind-blown sand (such as on top of mound 2) or where a depth would be expected to build up (such as along the enclosure wall) are not significant features. An alternative is that the areas which have generally higher readings (such as south and west of mound 2) reflect shell sand with a low organic content, perhaps because there has been little human activity in those areas. The low resistance areas to the east of the modern enclosure could be the result of higher water retention in this relatively low-lying area.

Mound 1 results (Figure 13)

The magnetic survey of mound 1 (Figure 13) is completely different from the survey of mounds 2 and 3. There is a massive negative anomaly which completely covers the southern half of the mound, spreading off the mound to the east and west, and a separate, similar anomaly which lies in the flat area to the north of the mound. The excavated trench cut across the northern edge of the principal negative anomaly and demonstrated that it coincided with an area of unaltered blown sand deposits that sealed and surrounded a stratified sequence of charcoal-rich Late Iron Age deposits and some Norse features. One of these Norse features was a rectangular stone-lined hearth and this shows up clearly as a distinctive double-peaked anomaly (Figure 13) in the centre of the excavated area. A very similar anomaly lay to the southeast just outside the trench and this presumably represents another hearth.

The northern boundary of the negative anomaly coincides with the edge of a rich Norse midden layer, which infilled a rectangular, stone-lined building. This building (Figure 13, S5) was oriented northeast – southwest which coincides with the orientation of several anomalies that lie around the edge of the mound. Most of these anomalies have a linearity that suggests they represent rectangular buildings arranged on a similar axis or perpendicular to the building excavated. In addition to the excavated structure, the presence of three or four further buildings could therefore be suggested:

- S1 lies on the south side of the mound and has a well-defined east end indicated by a high magnetic anomaly. Running perpendicular to this are two lesser anomalies, which appear to represent the side walls of the house. The west end of the house is more difficult to identify as the walls disappear into a general area of high magnetic readings but it is possible to suggest a building up to 12 m long and 4 m wide.
- S2 lies on the southeast side of the mound and is defined by two side walls and the northern gable; the south gable is more problematic. A possible partition wall divides the house in two. The building is estimated to be about 12 m long and up to 6 m wide.
- S3 runs parallel to this structure. It is not as well defined but again two discrete anomalies mark the gable walls and a strong anomaly in the centre of the building appears to indicate a partition wall. This house appears to be smaller, approximately 10 m long by 4 m wide. Lying between the north end of these two houses was an area of high magnetism that is more likely to indicate a midden than a structure.
- S4, the northern house, is well defined with a southern gable from which faint perpendicular side walls extend. These run into a large area of high magnetism which cannot simply be the northern gable but may indicate a midden infilling the northern half of the building. If the house ends at this point then it would be 10 m long and 5 m wide. However, there is some indication that the side walls continue to a less significant area of high magnetism, indicating the northern gable wall, which defines a house approximately 14 m long.

The most striking pattern of the resistivity survey is the alternate strip of high and low resistance running from southwest to northeast with a more generalised area of high resistance in the south and low resistance in the north. A band of low resistance surrounds the mound. It is very unclear what these patterns represent.

The enclosure

The most visible feature on both the gradiometer and resistivity survey (Figures 8 and 11) is an almost square enclosure (Figure 12, A), approximately 72 m by 70 m. Excavation on mounds 2 and 3 has revealed that the enclosure was defined by a stone wall approximately 2 m wide. The enclosure was designed to contain animals grazing on the machair in the evenings and has been dated to the 1870's by a local historian (G MacLean pers. comm.). It is notable that the wall is better defined on the surveys when it crosses the existing mounds. The construction of walls on the machair has the effect of altering the topography and it is probable that sand accumulation is more significant on the flat parts of the site and on the leeward sides of the mounds and this masks the line of the enclosure.

Excavations on mound 3 located a narrow entrance, with a gate post on the east side, and this is visible on both surveys. Two large gaps in the circuit have been identified by the survey (Figure 12): A1, clearly visible in the centre of the west side on the gradiometer survey but not so convincing on the resistivity survey, and A2, a large gap visible on both surveys two-thirds of the way along the east side. These may indicate where the wall is concealed by a thick build-up of sand but this is not a significant feature on the contour survey (Figure 6). It is possible the wall was never completed, robbed this century, or required large gaps. The gradiometer survey located short east-west walls at right angles to the enclosure wall at A3 and A4 (Figure 12). The resistivity survey suggests that the wall is wider at that point, with higher values than typical elsewhere on the east and west sides. The presence of two features very similar in response, shape and location, suggests these may be contemporary with the boundary wall and might have been small shelters for the individuals watching over the animals.

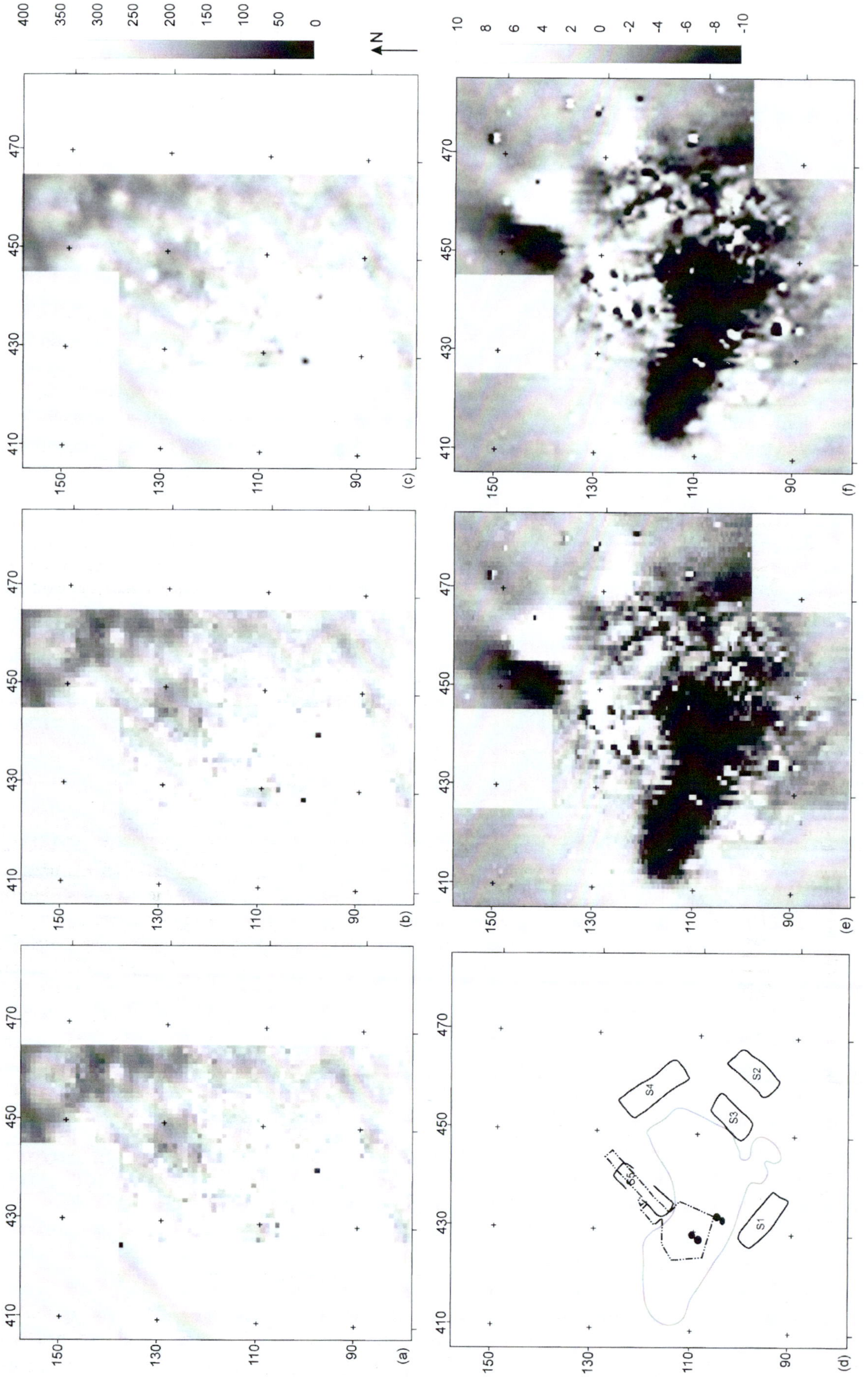

Figure 13. Mound 1: the geophysical data

Mounds 2 and 3 introduction

It is clear from the analysis of the contour survey that mounds 2 and 3 were the most prominent parts of a larger settlement represented by a more diffuse mound which encompassed the two mounds and spread to the east. This was dramatically confirmed by the geophysical survey with evidence for discrete settlement foci clearly visible to the east of mound 2 (mound 2A) and between mounds 2 and 3 (mound 2B). A more diffuse and difficult to interpret cluster of features lies between mounds 2A and 2B and mound 3.

Excavation has demonstrated that the mounds contain a complex structural sequence with several phases of reorganisation and rebuilding. Different phases of house construction can be conflated and some structures have had large sections of their stone walls removed. Surrounding the houses are complex sequences of layers of very varying consistency, magnetic response and water retention capacity. The surprising feature of the survey is therefore not the complexity of the anomalies visible but the fact that clear patterns are visible. The buildings visible probably represent a final phase of occupation prior to abandonment and a shift away from the machair. The interpretation outlined below is provisional, prior to further excavation, and any dimensions given are very rough estimates.

Mound 2 (Figure 14)

Mound 2 has a complex and extensive pattern of geophysical anomalies that have proved difficult to interpret (Figure 14) and excavation had already taken place on the mound in the two years that preceded the survey. A few features visible on the survey result from these excavations, notably the apparent gap in the enclosure wall. The interpretation of mound 2 depicted in Figure 14 is based on both the geophysical survey and the excavations. It would not have been possible to interpret the structures on the mound purely on the basis of the geophysical survey largely because of the complex sequence of building, rebuilding, robbing and midden deposition.

The principal buildings on mound 2 are S6 and S9. These represent the second and third houses in a sequence of three which provide the central focus of the occupation of this mound. Excavation revealed S6 (house 2) to be a substantial stone walled house, 19.3 m by 5.8 m internally, oriented east to west. It is vaguely visible on the resistivity and gradiometer survey as a diagonal trend in the anomalies pointing towards the corner of enclosure A. Excavation revealed S9 (house 3) to be a north-south oriented, stone-walled house, built on top of the east end of S6. It was 13 m by 6 m internally. This shows as an area of low magnetism as the house was filled with sterile wind-blown sand. The north wall is visible as a line of moderately high magnetism but the south wall is not at all clear. The high readings in the centre of the house indicate the position of the north wall of a secondary structure built into the abandoned house.

A structure S7 is visible on the gradiometer survey to the north of house S6 and this appears to run at an angle to S6. The south wall of this structure was discovered during the excavation but the west and north wall had been completely destroyed by later cultivation. S8 was a concentration of high readings on the south edge of the excavated trench. This coincides with some temporary structures built in the centre of house S6 but the anomalies continue across the south wall of the building which is not compatible with what was excavated. S10 is a structure recognised during the excavation but it is almost completely invisible in the survey because it was covered by the wall of enclosure A.

Outside the area excavated three obvious anomalies indicating possible structures can be identified:

- S11 is a large rectangular area, roughly 12 m by 5 m, defined by two parallel lines of high magnetism which run diagonally, northeast to southwest, from S10.
- S12 is a roughly square area, 7.5 m by 7.5 m, of high magnetism. Rabbit burrows in this area have produced Late Iron Age pottery and it is possible that, if this is a structure, we should be looking for a shape quite different to that of a rectangular building – the northeast corner does look rather curved.
- M1 is a large magnetic anomaly with an amorphous shape on the eastern edge of this mound. It would appear similar to anomalies on mound 2A that excavation demonstrated to be ash-rich middens.

Mound 2A (Figure 15)

The overall plan of anomalies on mound 2A indicates a roughly rectangular area of archaeological activity, 22.5 m long by 18 m wide (Figure 15). The initial interpretation (Hamilton and Sharples 1996) of the pattern within this area was to suggest that the high magnetic anomalies indicate structures and this was supported by the pattern of low resistance anomalies which appear to form a rectangular arrangement around the centre of the mound. However, excavation of the mound in 1999, 2000 and 2003 contradicted these interpretations. The highly magnetic features clearly represent midden dumps containing quantities of peat ash and slag (not from iron working). The principal domestic structures were located in a sequence to the south of the area excavated. These areas were not particularly clear on the survey, owing to the accumulation of sterile sand against the enclosure wall.

Mound 2B (Figure 16)

The overall plan of the geophysical anomalies on mound 2B indicates a rectangular area of archaeological activity, 20 m by 16 m, which has a distinct edge of low magnetic

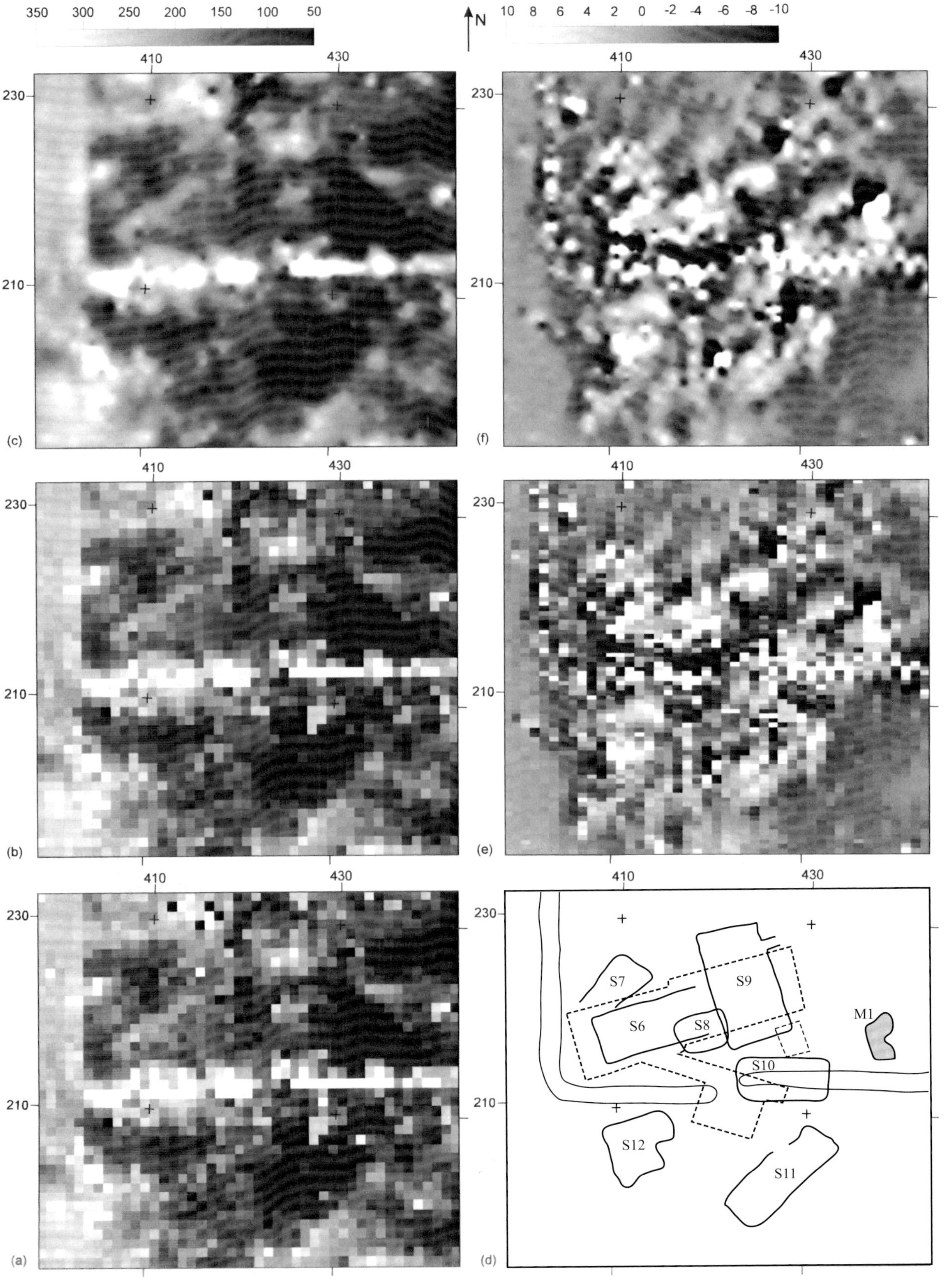

Figure 14. Mound 2: the geophysical data

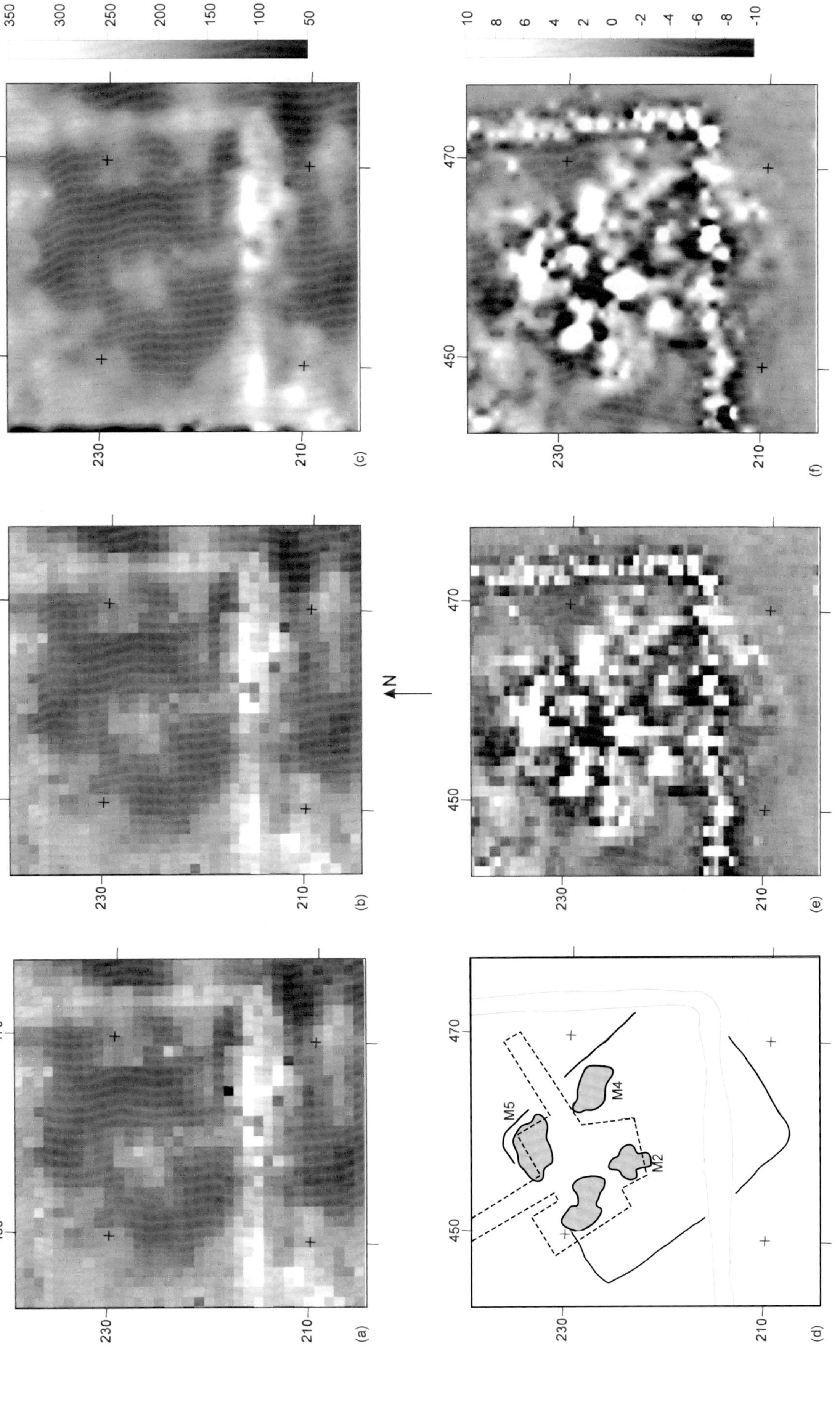

Figure 15. Mound 2A: the geophysical data

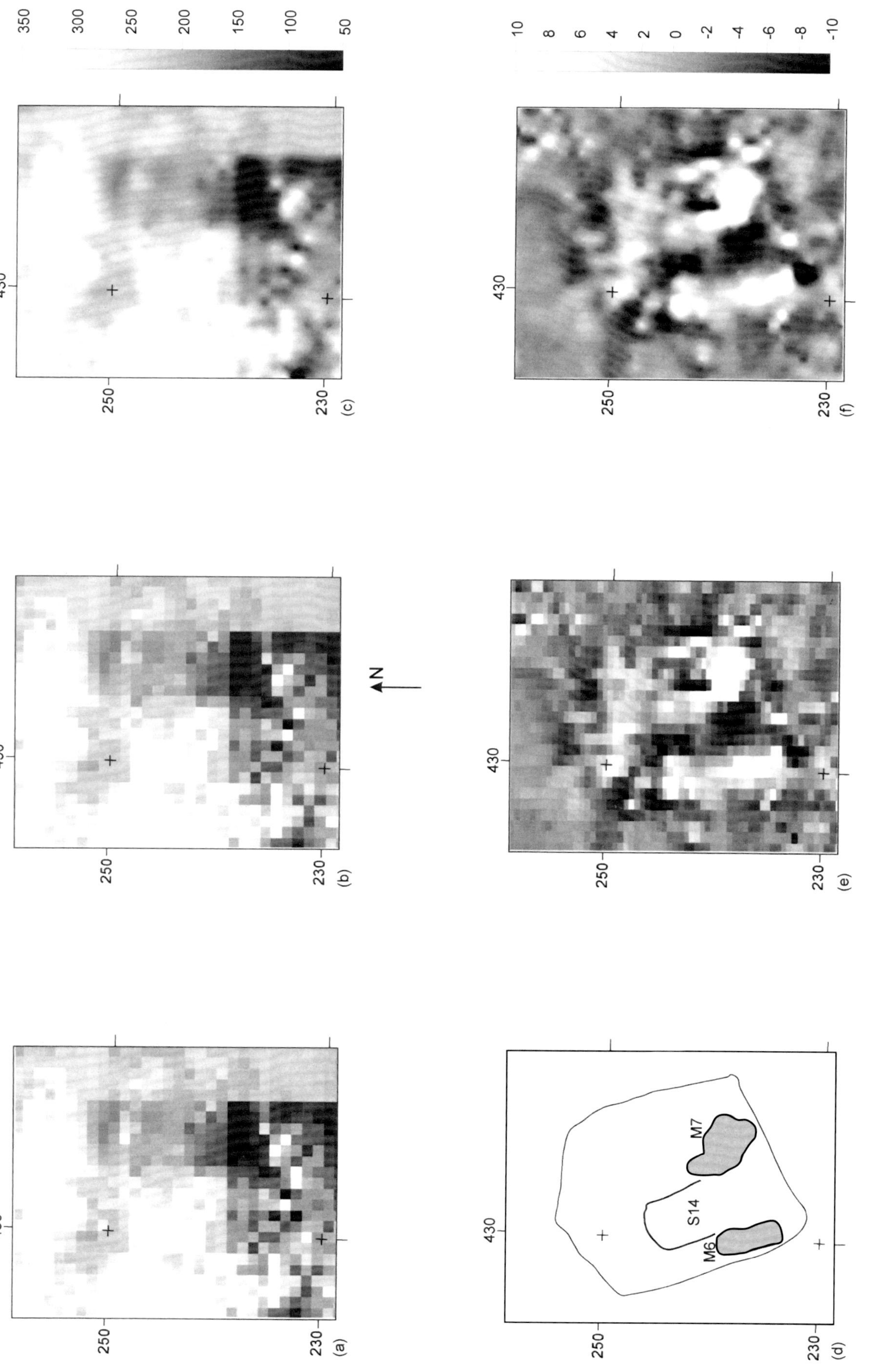

Figure 16. Mound 2B: the geophysical data

values (Figure 16). The patterns within were originally interpreted as indicating three buildings arranged in a quad with an open side to the south (Hamilton and Sharples 1996). These patterns were indicated by high magnetic anomalies of roughly rectangular form. The 'eastern house' was tested by a small, shallow excavation trench but this failed to identify any structural remains. Instead it revealed a thick peat-ash midden. The results of this trench confirm what was also revealed in the excavation of mound 2A, that many of the high magnetic anomalies indicate ash- and slag-rich midden. If this mound, which is similar in size to mound 2A, is similar in form then the principal structure (S14) will be placed in the centre and is represented by the rectangular low magnetic anomaly. The high magnetic anomalies (M6 and M7) probably represent middens on either side of the house.

Mound 3 (Figures 17 and 18)

Mound 3 is a much larger and less well-defined mound. Topographically it can be split into a north and south half and to the east of the southern half there is a scatter of features that includes at least one house. Figure 17 covers the southern half of the mound and the eastern periphery. Two of the strongest anomalies in this area were excavated specifically to test the results of the geophysical survey.

- S15 was a sub-rectangular feature, c. 8 m by 5 m, on the east side of the enclosure wall (A). This was defined on the gradiometer survey with positive walls and a neutral interior, aligned west-southwest to east-northeast. The resistivity survey showed this as an area of high resistance and suggests the building could extend a further 4 m to the east. The clarity of S15 made it an obvious candidate for test excavation (see chapter 6). A small trench 1 m by 5 m was excavated across the southern wall and, after the removal of only 0.3 m of topsoil and sand, a wall was located.
- S16 showed up as a minor feature on the gradiometer survey, an outline of high magnetic features, but as an area of significantly high resistance. Complete excavation of this structure revealed that the high resistance was a result of the infilling of the building with sterile wind-blown sand. The structure is a small kiln and barn complex, roughly 3.8 m by 4.6 m.
- S17 was a structure recognised in the southeast corner of the excavated area. This is visible on the gradiometer survey as an outline of high magnetic anomalies, approximately 6 m square.
- S18 was a similar anomaly lying immediately to the south of these structures. It appears to be another small ancillary structure.
- S21 is a rectangular arrangement of slight magnetic anomalies to the northeast of S16. This would not have been identified as a structure except for the observation of coursed stone walling in rabbit disturbance in this area.

Between S15 and S16 is a rather disorganised pattern of magnetic anomalies that probably indicate some structures are present but only two features stand out as interpretable buildings.

- S19 is a distinctive arc of high magnetic readings with a low centre and a gap oriented to the southwest. This gap is oriented on a very high magnetic anomaly just over a metre away. This could be a corn-drying kiln; the arc of masonry represents the bowl and the isolated high the fire at the end of the flue.
- S20 is a small rectangular feature immediately to the south of S19, which could be another ancillary building.

The northern half of mound 3 is much more difficult to interpret. It is partly obscured by the enclosure wall (A) and the excavations in 1995 also seem to distort the results. The principal high magnetic anomalies lie in the area to the south of the enclosure wall (A) and consist of two fairly unstructured blobs (Figure 17, M8 and M9). Excavation of the area around M9 indicates that this represents a midden deposit and it is possible that M8 is also a midden. The principal structure (S22) exposed by the excavations is not particularly visible and is at most represented by an area of low magnetism between the two middens. To the north of the enclosure on the mound there is a well-defined area of magnetic activity 17.5 m across and over 25 m long. Unfortunately no obvious patterns are visible in either survey and it is difficult to identify structures. S23 is a possibly structure, 7.5 m by 4 m, defined by a rectangular arrangement of low magnetic readings

Off-mound activity

A number of features are visible which do not seem to have any relationship to the archaeological features (Figure 12). A long linear feature, P, showing as mostly negative readings, could be a trench. This appears to continue across mound 2B to the eastern half of the enclosure. Within this feature are two 'iron spikes', the most prominent being at the western end. The lack of any obvious relationship with other archaeological features suggests this may be of relatively modern origin. The other two anomalies are indistinct, slightly positive magnetic areas, Q and R. The former has an 'iron spike' at the southern end. These are somewhat similar to the magnetic features on the west side of the settlement, M and N.

The resistivity survey (Figure 10) apparently shows evidence for structures (Figure 12, E) indicated by high resistance areas to the west of mound 3. These areas are not visible in the magnetic survey and test trenching revealed no archaeology in this area. It seems likely given the hummocky nature of the machair in this area that they indicate sterile sand accumulations.

One of the most visible features of the resistivity survey is a low resistance feature (Figure 10; 12, F) running from the east side of the enclosure wall, around the

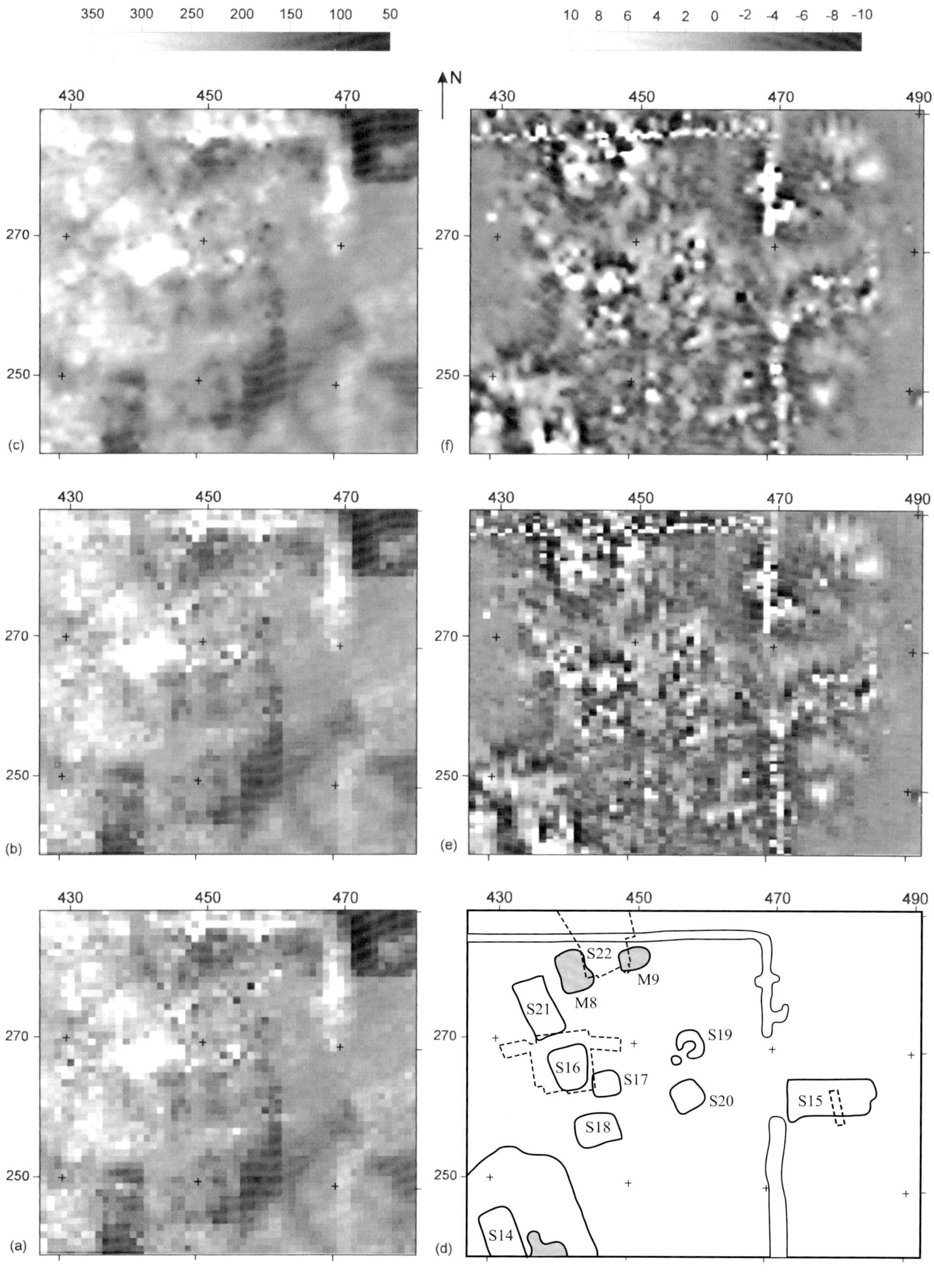

Figure 17. Mound 3 south: the geophysical data

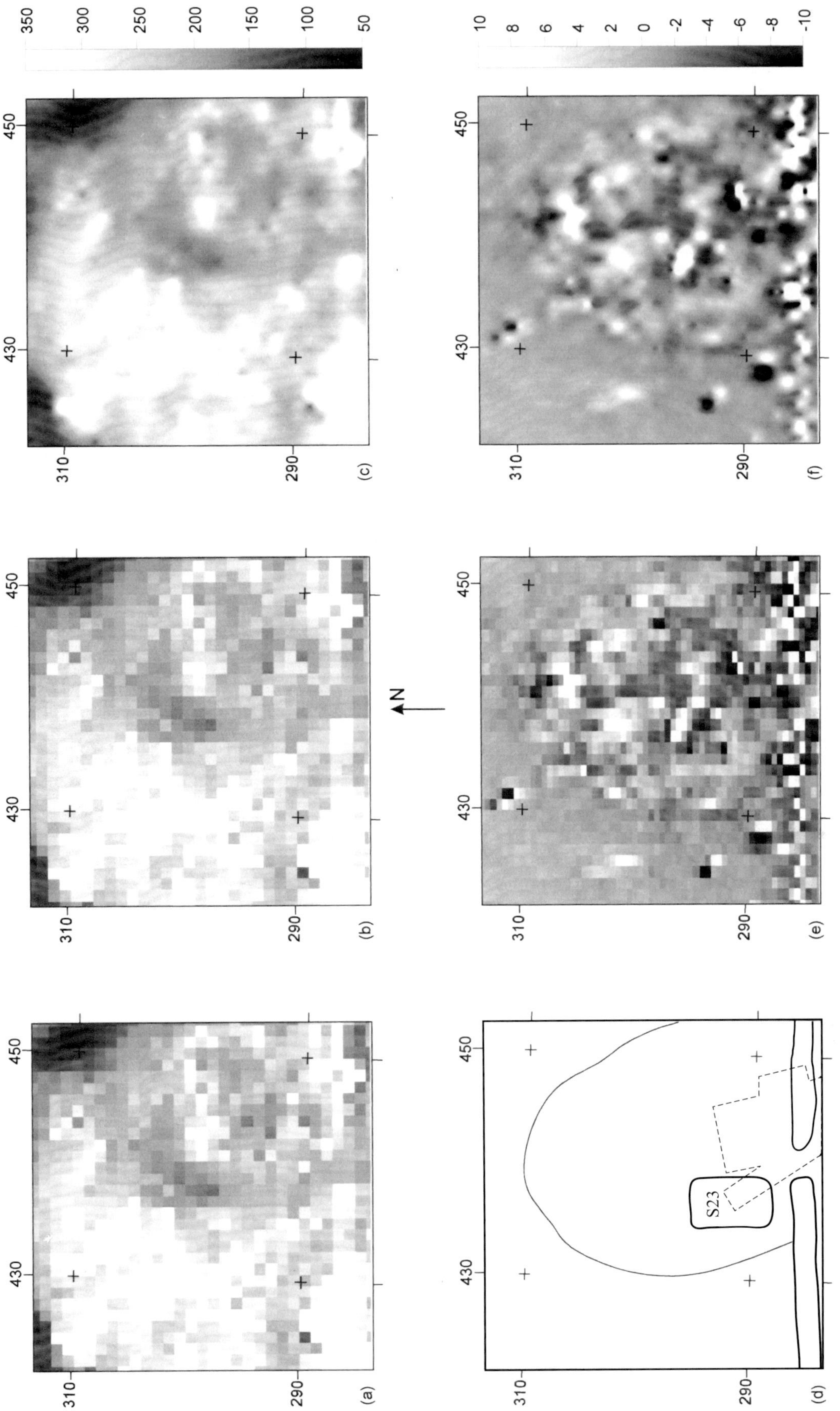

Figure 18. Mound 3 north: the geophysical data

northwest corner of the enclosure, round the north end of mound 3 and up to the northeast corner of the enclosure wall. This is not visible on the gradiometer survey. It may be connected to rainwater run-off from the archaeological deposits and the enclosure wall, and a similar feature was noted around mound 1.

Discussion

The geophysical and topographic survey of the mounds at Bornais has provided an invaluable resource for further work on the mounds and it still provides the clearest overall indication of the extent of the settlement. The organisation of the settlement into five clearly defined foci is particularly clear. It was obvious from the overall examination of the mounds that mounds 1 and 2 were separated by a large area of sterile ground but the relative isolation of mounds 2 and 3 required further exploration. It was almost immediately apparent that a considerable quantity of archaeology was present in the area between mounds 2 and 3 but the detail provided by the geophysical survey confirmed the presence of discrete concentrations of activity at mounds 2A and 2B and separated mound 3 into a well-defined northern half and much more ill-defined southern half, which spreads well beyond the upstanding mounds. It would have been impossible to define these features without the excavation of a large number of exploratory trenches and the input of resources way beyond those available to the project.

The geophysical survey has proved detailed enough to identify individual houses and other structures. Our initial testing of the survey results by excavation was very successful and produced a rather optimistic view that most anomalies were indications of buildings (Hamilton and Sharples 1996). However, further excavation has indicated that many anomalies reflect other archaeological activity such as middens containing highly magnetic peat ash and slag. This has transformed our interpretation of the occupation of mounds 2A and 2B, suggesting that they do not have the distinctive arrangement of buildings suggested earlier (Hamilton and Sharples 1996). However, further analysis of the survey results from mound 1 has clarified some of the earlier results and made it possible to identify structures not previously observed. The current analysis has identified 23 buildings. The identification of some of these buildings is dependent on the results of the excavation but these are only numbered on Figure 12 when they have a presence on the survey. Most of these structures appear to be rectangular houses but there were also some smaller buildings identified that are likely to be subsidiary structures; these are particularly common on the southern half of mound 3.

Geophysical survey has not been widely used on the Hebridean machair. The only equivalent survey was conducted at Bhaltos, West Lewis (Armit 1994), but on a smaller scale and with indifferent results. Atkinson attempted to use resistivity at Sollas, North Uist, but without success (Campbell 1991). The lack of comparable published sites means that in many respects the Bornais survey was ground-breaking and the interpretations largely tentative until tested by excavation. Furthermore the site cannot be closely compared with other sites on the Western Isles. The only excavated Norse settlements seem to be quite different: Cille Pheadair (Brennand, Parker Pearson and Smith 1998) is smaller, Drimore (MacLaren 1974) is probably smaller, but only partially excavated, and The Udal (Selkirk 1996) is more dispersed and includes features such as an enclosure (or fort) not visible at Bornais. The individual mounds at Bornais are comparable in size to the settlement excavated at Cille Pheadair (Brennand, Parker Pearson and Smith 1998). This suggests that these units might represent individual farms. If this is the case then we have a group of approximately five farms clustered together at Bornais.

The most famous Norse settlement in Scotland is Jarlshof on Shetland (Hamilton 1956). This started life as a single farmstead and appears to have grown over the centuries into a settlement consisting of perhaps four closely related households. Throughout the occupation the settlement was tightly clustered, with later buildings incorporating and overlying older structures. In total an area of approximately 60 m by 35 m was covered by structures: this is slightly larger than the area covered by mound 2 and mound 3 though equivalent in size to the area of mound 1. Most of the other well-known Norse settlements of the Northern Isles are also single farmsteads (even though some were substantially modified over the years): Pool, Orkney (Hunter, Bond and Smith 1993), Skaill, Orkney (Buteux 1997) Sandwick, Shetland (Bigelow 1985) and Underhoull, Shetland (Small 1966).

The only extensive settlement that has been comparatively well documented is that on the Brough of Birsay, Orkney (Hunter 1986; Morris 1996). This settlement consists of three elements: a densely packed and relatively nucleated settlement at the eastern point of the Brough, the church and its surrounding precinct, and a dispersed settlement that surrounds the latter two areas. The site has a chequered history of exploration, which has only gradually and belatedly been published. Much of the original work was directly linked to the display of buildings that visitors see today. Recent excavations (Hunter 1986; Morris 1996) have emphasised that much remains hidden below the turf and that many of the apparently unitary buildings have complicated and fractured histories. Nevertheless it is clear that this is a substantial settlement with many separate settlement foci. The full explanation for the development of this settlement has still to be written. It is clearly tied historically to the development of the Earldom of Orkney but much of the settlement appears to pre-date the historical events described in the Orkneyinga Saga. This implies the Brough was a significant population centre and presumably political centre from quite early in the settlement of the islands.

The very different nature of the landscapes of Birsay and Bornais makes it difficult to compare the two settlements. The presence of the church clearly differentiates the settlement at Birsay and provides it with a status (historical and archaeological) that is very different to that of the Bornais settlement. Nevertheless this is one of the few settlements of comparable size to Bornais outside of the urban contexts of York, Dublin and Waterford and the semi-urban context of Whithorn in southwest Scotland (Hill 1997). The spatial layout of these settlements is much more compact and the nature of the individual buildings is also very different to those found in the rural contexts of Birsay and Bornais. A more detailed comparison of Bornais and Birsay will be required on completion of the excavations but it is already clear that the size and layout of the Bornais settlement indicate an unusual settlement of considerable significance.

The most important result of the geophysical survey at Bornais has been to show that significant results can be obtained by this method of analysis. Previous work by Atkinson (Campbell 1991) and Armit (1994) had cast doubt on the effectiveness of this technique in the Western Isles but the Bornais survey confirms the potential indicated by Dockrill's (1986) work on Sanday in Orkney. Both the gradiometer and resistivity surveys have delimited the settlement and differentiated individual structural components. Taken together the two surveys provide an interpretable outline of the settlement at Bornais.

3 Methodologies

Excavation strategy – N Sharples

The original excavation strategy for Bornais was to dig exploratory trenches across the three substantial mounds. It was hoped (Parker Pearson and Webster 1994) that the excavation of these trenches would:

- Identify the latest structural phase.
- Locate buildings.
- Establish the depth of the stratigraphic sequence.
- Recover artefact assemblages that would allow us to characterise and to date the sequence of the occupation.
- Recover bone and carbonised plant assemblages for comparison with assemblages from other SEARCH sites.

The project began with the excavation of a 20 m by 2 m trench across the highest point of mound 2 in 1994. This mound was chosen because, at this point in time, it was the only mound to have produced clearly identifiable Norse pottery from surface collection. The excavations were sufficient to answer the general questions asked. However, the quality of the structures found and the depth of the associated deposits made it impossible to bottom the trench and it was only after seven seasons of excavation on this mound that the sterile sand that underlies the earliest deposits was exposed (Sharples 2003).

In 1995 the main focus for the excavation was mound 3 but a trench was also opened up on mound 2 and the mounds were surveyed (Sharples, Webster and Parker Pearson 1995). The trench on mound 3 was 10 m long and 2 m wide, cut across the centre of the mound, and was oriented roughly north-northwest to south-southeast (Figure 19). The trench immediately revealed a wall running roughly north to south across the trench. A subsequent expansion 4 m to the east and the excavation of two small test pits (Figure 20) revealed the south end of a north to south oriented building, 4 m wide. Field walking in the winter of 1994/1995 had recovered grass-marked Norse pottery from the surface of mound 3 and the excavation confirmed that this was a Norse settlement mound. Structures were located immediately below the turf and sand, and assemblages of animal bones and carbonised plant remains were recovered. Again it proved impossible to bottom the trench owing to the depth of the stratigraphy.

In 1996 the main focus for the excavation was mound 1, which surface collection had indicated was Iron Age in date, but excavation also continued on the area of mound 2 excavated in 1995 (Sharples 1996). It was hoped that the excavation of mound 1 and mound 2 would provide a continuous sequence of occupation from the Middle Iron Age through to the Medieval period, which would complement and continue the sequence established at Dun Vulan. However, Late Iron Age deposits on mound 2 proved elusive and the mound 1 occupation consisted of a building dated to the fourth to fifth centuries AD, with later Norse deposits on top. There was thus a break in the occupation between the Iron Age and Norse deposits. A geophysical survey was also undertaken in this year and, as discussed in the previous chapter, this transformed our understanding of the settlement. The survey clearly demonstrated that the area between mounds 2 and 3 was occupied and that evidence for settlement extended beyond the prominent mounds. The interpretation of the geophysical survey and the extent of the settlement were tested by two small trenches (E and G). One of these trial trenches (E) was located on the southeast periphery of mound 3 (Figure 19) and this trench is described fully in chapter 6.

At the end of 1996 we had a basic understanding of the settlement at Bornais. We were able to place it in the wider context of the township of Bornais where several excavations had occurred, notably Dun Vulan and Beinn na Mhic Aongheis (see above 2, 5) and into the general context of the settlement of the South Uist machair, which had now been completely surveyed (Parker Pearson 1996). It was clear that the settlement at Bornais provided a link between the Middle Iron Age settlement of Dun Vulan and the Late Medieval landscapes that survived to be mapped in the nineteenth century. However, it still had to be established that this sequence continued through the Viking colonisation and a more precise date for the shift from the machair to the inland site of Beinn na Mhic Aongheis was required. The geophysical survey had also revealed that this was a very large settlement, much larger than any of the settlements located by the machair survey and larger than most Norse settlements known from Atlantic Scotland.

Three years of work had also revealed that the site was being seriously damaged. Three threats were identified: rabbit burrowing, cattle trampling and cultivation. All three of these threats could now be demonstrated to be causing serious erosion and together they made this site one of the most severely threatened sites on the machair plain of South Uist (Parker Pearson 1996). It was clear that a more extensive excavation of Bornais was required.

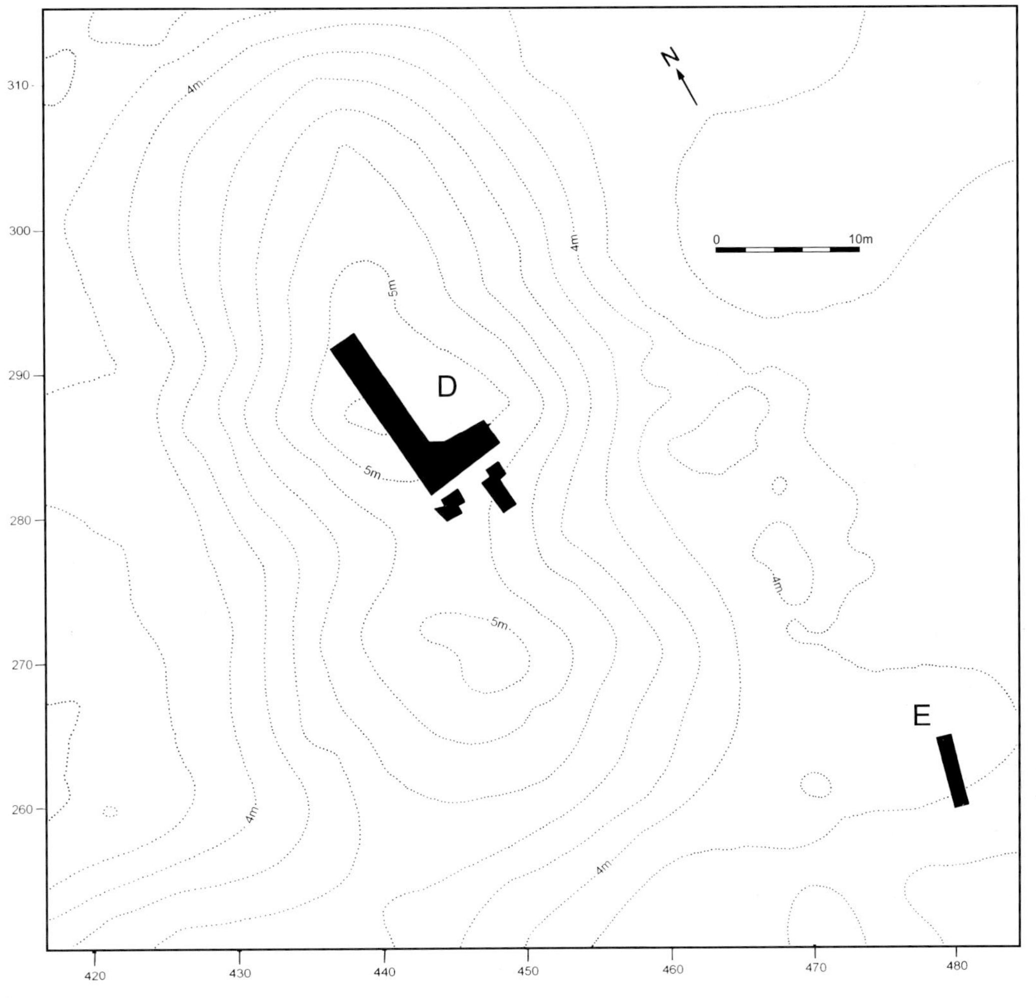

Figure 19. A plan of the mound 3 excavations in 1995 and 1996 (the isolated trench to the east)

Figure 20. Trench D looking from the south at the end of the 1995 excavations

Historic Scotland was approached for financial support and they agreed to continue to fund the excavation of the settlement. The research objectives framed in 1996/7 were:

- To test the hypothesis that the three mounds at Bornais formed a continuous long-term sequence of occupation.
- To find out when this sequence began and ended.
- To recover complete plans of the Norse houses, particularly those at risk from rabbits.
- To investigate the Late Iron Age building on mound 1.

In 1997 it was decided to excavate on all three mounds but this report will concentrate on the work undertaken on mound 3 (Sharples 1997). This mound was suffering the worst from rabbit damage and it was clear from the 1995 excavation that the floor layers associated with the final structure were being badly damaged. It was decided to completely excavate the structure, subsequently identified as a house, originally exposed at the centre of the mound. The final trench (D) was 12.5 m long by 6.6 m wide, with an extension 1.4 m to the east to examine an entrance passage (Figure 21). It was also decided to open up a second trench (F) at the south end of mound 3 to examine a feature that was highlighted by the geophysical survey (S16). Initially an 11 m by 2 m trench was opened (Figure 21). This located the expected structure and a new trench, 6.3 m by 6 m, was laid out to expose the principal structure. Unfortunately related structures to the south could not be examined as the southern boundary of the trench coincided with the edge of a field of oats. Both of these trenches provided the opportunity to examine complete Late Norse buildings (Figure 22). These were clearly the last structures to be occupied on this mound and would provide some indication of when the settlement was abandoned. At the end of the 1997 season the excavation of the house (trench D) was completed but the excavation of the building, clearly not a house, on the south side of the mound (trench F) required further work.

In 1998 Historic Scotland rejected our excavation proposal and no work was undertaken at Bornais (Sharples 1998a). However, the opportunity was taken to visit the site after the mounds had been cultivated and planted with barley. It was clear that this cultivation was causing damage and it was possible to show the visiting Inspector of Ancient Monuments disturbed structural remains and plough-damaged middens, and to recover artefacts, including important pieces of worked bone, that were lying exposed

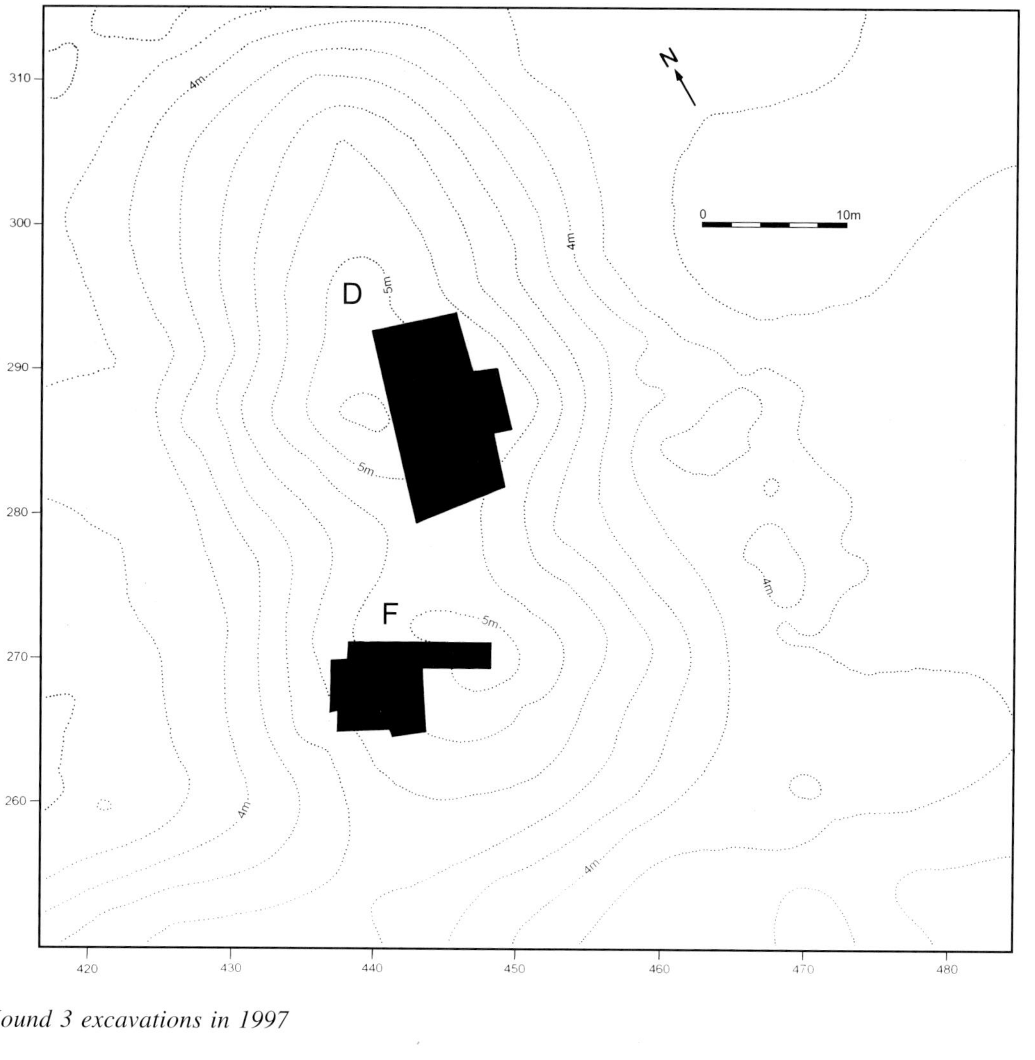

Figure 21. Mound 3 excavations in 1997

Figure 22. Trench D looking from the southwest at the end of the 1997 excavations

on the surface amongst the crops. The subsequent research proposal for work in 1999 was fully supported by Historic Scotland.

In 1999 four areas of the settlement were examined and the work on mound 3 was restricted to completing the excavation of the southern structure (Sharples 1999). The original trench (F) was reopened and extended to the south to create a trench roughly 8.4 m by 8.8 m (Figure 23), which exposed the full extent of the structure, a corn-drying kiln and barn (Figure 24). An extension, roughly 4 m by 2 m, was opened up to the west to examine the edge of the mound. This was extended to the west, by a detached trench excavated by JCB, which confirmed that this area was an archaeologically sterile sand dune. Another isolated JCB trench (K), to the northeast of the mounds, was excavated to explore a geophysical anomaly. Work on mound 3 was completed at the end of 1999. All the structural walls were left *in situ* but the floors and other deposits associated with the occupation of these buildings have been completely removed.

Further work was undertaken at Bornais in 2000 (Sharples 2000b), 2003 (Sharples 2003) and 2004. These excavations were restricted to the examination of mounds 2 and 2A and will be described in future volumes.

The stratigraphy in mound 3 can be divided up into the following units: D is the main trench, examined in 1995 and 1997; E the small trench dug to test the geophysical results in 1996; and F the second large trench opened up in 1997 and 1999. The main trenches are subsequently subdivided into:

DA EARLY HOUSE	FA PRE KILN/BARN SAND DUNE
DB ACCUMULATION	FB ADJACENT STRUCTURE?
DC MAIN HOUSE	FC KILN/BARN CONSTRUCTION
DD HOUSE FLOORS	FD KILN/BARN OCCUPATION
DE POST HOUSE DEPOSITS	FE KILN/BARN ABANDONMENT
	FF ASSOCIATED ACTIVITY
	FG MIDDEN ACCUMULATION

These blocks represent the principal spatial and structural divisions of the site stratigraphy. In trench D the divisions are arranged in a strict chronological sequence. In trench F the chronological relationships between some blocks were impossible to determine and the relationships are open. Complete site matrices are presented in Figures 25 and 26 and a list of all the contexts identified can be found in appendix 1. The main aim of the blocks is to provide a manageable structure for the description and discussion of the buildings and layers excavated or exposed and for the analysis of the material recovered from these contexts. In some cases the post-excavation analysis revealed that the blocks encompassed chronological change that would have been better separated out but this has relatively minor implications for the analysis and the blocks have not been revised.

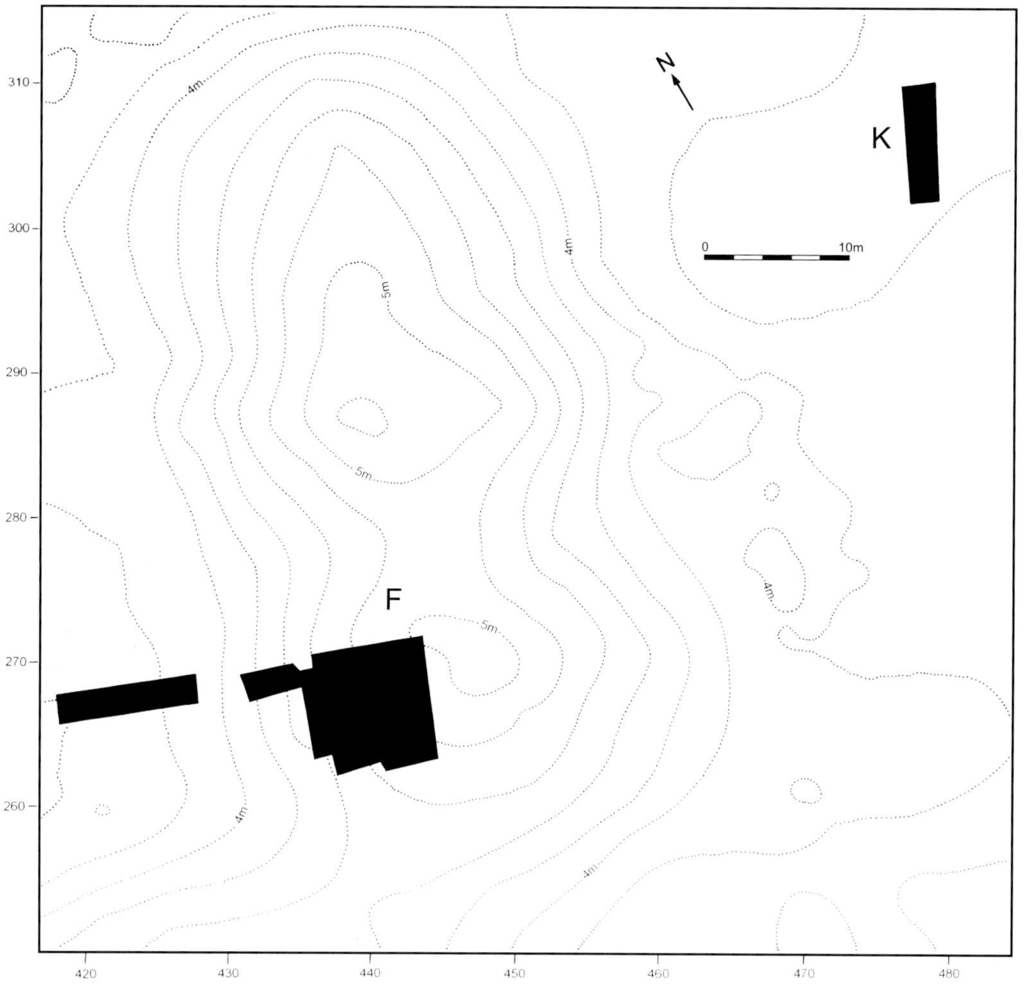

Figure 23. Mound 3 excavations in 1999

Figure 24. Trench F looking from the northwest during the 1999 excavations

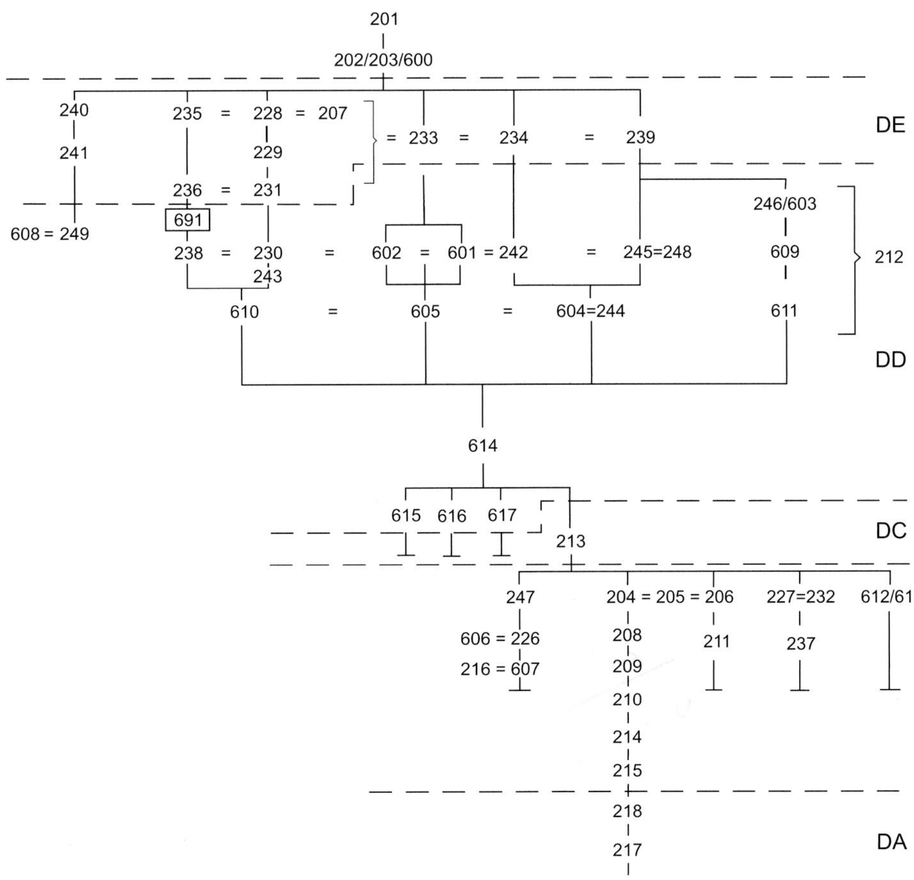

Figure 25. The Harris matrix for trench D

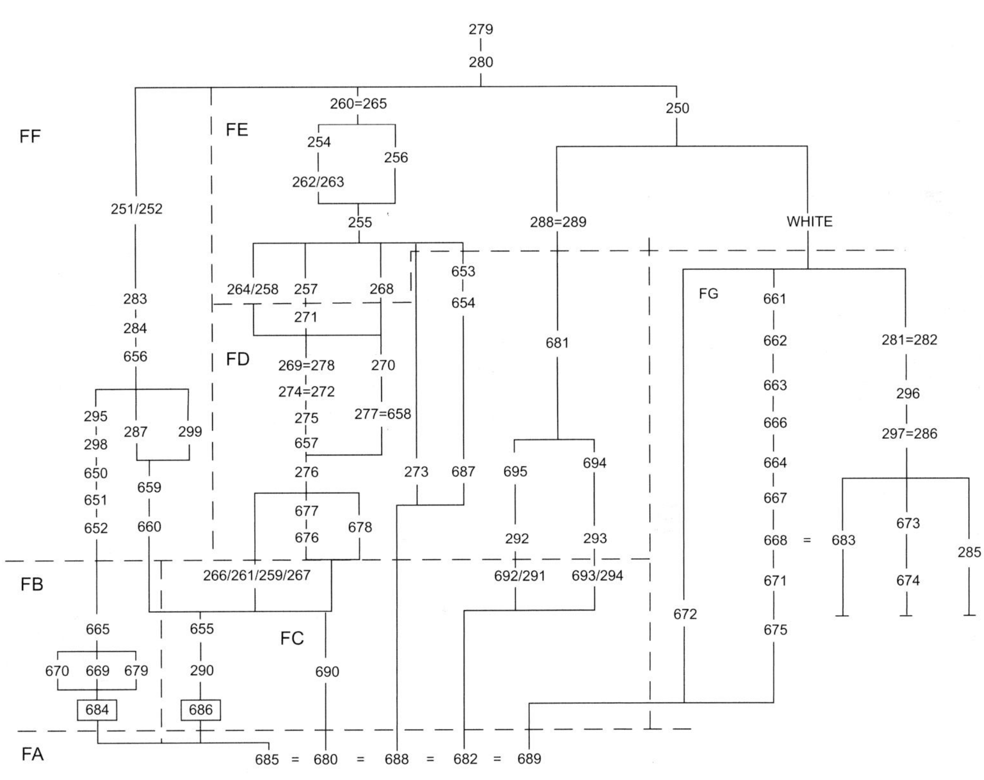

Figure 26. The Harris matrix for trench F

Sampling – N Sharples and H Smith

A number of different samples were taken for subsequent analysis and the overall research objectives behind this sampling strategy have been outlined in the introduction to this report. Routine sampling involved the removal of a two-bucket (or less when this was not possible) sample, which included all finds except those designated small finds, and a small (champagne glass) sample from every layer excavated. Floor layers were completely sampled on a 0.5 m by 0.5 m grid. The analysis of the small soil samples is discussed below. The large sample was transported to a water separation/flotation tank (Kenward, Hall and Jones 1980) where light material was collected as coarse and fine fractions (1mm and 300μm mesh sieves) and the heavy material as residue (above 1mm). This process was undertaken in a fashion that is standardised for all the sites excavated by the South Uist project.

The residues were transported to Cardiff for further analysis. All heavy residues were passed through a 10 mm mesh sieve and the artefactual and ecofactual material over 10 mm was removed, the number of items counted and bagged by finds category. Heavy residues (<10 mm) selected for further analysis were first sieved through a 0.5 mm mesh to remove fine dust particles and then sub-sampled for detailed analysis. The sub-sampling was done using a riffle splitter which creates samples by systematically halving the residues, creating fractions of 0.5, 0.25, 0.125, 0.0625 etc. The splitting was designed to reduce the residue to a size that could be sorted and recorded in about two hours. All the various sample fractions were bagged separately to enable further sampling. The sub-sample for sorting was first assessed for the percentage of marine shell. The residue was then examined systematically and all the material that was not stone or seashell was removed. The various categories of finds were counted and then bagged for subsequent analysis by specialists. The unexamined samples have been retained for future analysis.

The floor layers were the first group of samples examined at Bornais and as a result some methodological mistakes were made and we have subsequently revised our approach. The most obvious difference is that all the samples recovered from house floors 1 and 2 were examined. In subsequent years, for the kiln/barn floors discussed below for instance, alternate samples were sorted and examined to provide a chequer-board coverage of the floor. This reduced the number of hours required to undertake the analysis of this material whilst maintaining detailed coverage of the floor area.

A complete list of all the material recovered from sorting the residues is stored in the archive and will be made available on the internet in the near future.

Sediment analysis of floor layers – H Smith and P Marshall

Sediment samples were collected from the floors of the buildings on mound 3 for geochemical and magnetic analysis, including the measurement of total phosphorus (P), total nitrogen (N) and magnetic susceptibility (χ). The use of physical, chemical and magnetic analyses of sediments in the investigation of activities undertaken around settlements has been used in many studies (Entwistle and Abrahams 1997; Entwistle, Abrahams and Dodgshon 1998; 2000a; b; Middleton and Price 1996). More recently, there have been attempts at more broadly integrated studies of floor layers in order to reconstruct activities around settlements and within buildings (e.g. Bell 1990; Marshall and Smith 1999; Smith, Marshall and Parker Pearson 2001). Such integrated approaches, as adopted here, have employed geochemical analyses in conjunction with the study of micro-debitage distributions (ecofact and artefact remains; Metcalfe and Heath 1990; McGovern, Buckland, Savory, Sveinbjarnardottir, Andreasen and Skidmore 1993; Parker Pearson, Brennand and Smith 1996) and thin-section analysis of sediments from the floors (Boivin 2000; Matthews, French, Lawrence, Cutler and Jones 1996 and 1997; Milek this volume). The aim of this study was to assist in the interpretation of the two structures and, if possible, to assess spatial extent, intensity and nature of the activities taking place and influencing the formation of the floor deposits. These particular analytical techniques were selected because of the type of evidence they can potentially provide (i.e. character and origin of deposits).

All identified floor layers were sampled in detail within the house and kiln/barn structure on mound 3. In total, three floor layers were excavated within the house and two within the kiln/barn. Using the site grid, samples for geochemical and magnetic analysis were taken at 0.5 m intersections across the complete floor surfaces and any associated contexts such as hearths (Figure 27). It was hoped that these would complement the bulk samples, collected from units measuring 0.5 m × 0.5 m, in the investigation of activities undertaken within the buildings, including the degree of variation in the composition of the deposits. Where possible the complete depth of floor from a quadrant was sampled. This was undertaken in the hope that these samples would be more likely to contain material representing consistent use of an area for an activity, rather than samples from the floor surface that might have been the result of a 'one off' action (Metcalfe and Heath 1990).

For all samples, total phosphorus (P) and total nitrogen (N) were determined (based on the Kjeldahl digest (Allen 1989), and mass specific magnetic susceptibility (χ) was measured using a Bartington MS2 meter and MS2B dual frequency sensor (following the method of Gale and Hoare 1991), with results expressed as ($10^{-8}m^3kg^{-1}$).

Figure 27. Sampling the floors of the kiln/barn in trench F for phosphates and magnetic susceptibility

Soil micromorphology – K Milek

Four undisturbed block samples for micromorphological analysis were taken from the primary floor of the kiln/barn in trench F. The analysis of undisturbed soils and sediments in thin section provides detailed information about their mineralogical, organic and anthropogenic composition, internal organisation, and structure. The specific goals of thin section analysis were:

- To source the floor sediment based on its mineralogy and particle size distribution, to determine whether material had been brought into the structure and deliberately laid as a floor.
- To assess the interpretation that an open fire had been located at the entrance to the flue of the corn-drying kiln, based on the composition of the floor in this area, and any evidence that the original substrate had been altered by burning.
- To determine the types of fuels used to operate the kiln, by verifying the identification of peat ash and by identifying any other type(s) of fuel ash present in the floor deposit.
- To investigate the types of activities that took place in the building based on the anthropogenic inclusions in the floor, and to weigh this information against the interpretation that the structure was used for the storage and processing of cereals.

In addition to these main goals, micromorphological analysis was also used to provide information about post-depositional processes, such as bioturbation, the decomposition of organic materials, the diagenesis of anthropogenic materials (e.g. ash and bone) and pedogenesis. The technique was therefore an important complement to the bulk analyses that were conducted on the floor deposits.

The samples were taken using Kubiena tins sized 8.5 × 6.5 × 4 cm, following the method outlined by Courty, Goldberg and Macphail (1989). Thin sections were prepared at the McBurney Geoarchaeology Laboratory at the University of Cambridge. The samples were air dried and impregnated under vacuum with crystic polyester resin thinned with acetone, to which was added the catalyst methyl ethyl ketone peroxide. Once cured, blocks were thin sectioned following the procedure in Murphy (1986). Thin sections were analysed under petrological microscopes using plane polarised, crossed polarised, and oblique incident light, at magnifications ranging from ×1 – ×250. Micromorphological descriptions follow the internationally accepted terminology (Bullock, Federoff, Jongerius, Stoops, Torsina and Babel 1985). To make the data as accessible as possible, the more specialised micromorphological terms have been listed and defined in Table 1. Such terms are italicised the first time they occur in the text.

In thin section, it is often possible to distinguish

Table 1. Glossary of specialised micromorphological terms (following Bullock, Federoff, Jongerius, Stoops, Tursina and Babel 1985)

B-fabric:	the optical properties in crossed polarised light (i.e., birefringence) of the fine mineral material making up the groundmass.
Bridged grain microstructure:	a microstructure that is dominated by coarse mineral grains bridged by fine mineral material.
C/f ratio:	the ratio of coarse to fine mineral material, according to size categories set by the analyst (100 μm for the purpose of this analysis).
Crystallitic b-fabric:	a groundmass that exhibits a birefringence dominated by small grains of calcium carbonate.
Dotted fine mineral material:	fine mineral material which is not clean (i.e. limpid), but which contains an abundance of black silt-sized particles, which may be organic and/or mineral in origin.
Enaulic:	a term used to describe the related distribution of coarse and fine mineral material, in which fine mineral material is present in the form of aggregates situated between grains of the coarse mineral fraction.
Gefuric:	a term used to describe the related distribution of coarse and fine mineral material, in which fine mineral material forms bridges between grains of the coarse mineral fraction.
Monic:	a term used to describe the related distribution of coarse and fine mineral material, in which the coarse mineral fraction dominates and there is little or no fine mineral material.
Porphyric:	a term used to describe the related distribution of coarse and fine mineral material, in which coarse mineral grains are embedded in fine mineral material.
Rubified fine mineral material:	rounded to subrounded aggregates of clay-sized mineral material, which have well-defined boundaries, appear black in plane polarised light, have an undifferentiated b-fabric but appear dark reddish-brown in crossed polarised light (and are therefore probably microcrystalline), and reflect glittery, bright reddish-orange colours in oblique incident light. These optical properties are characteristic of fine mineral material that has been burnt (Courty et al. 1989), and have been observed in reference samples of burnt peat from South Uist.
Single grain microstructure:	a microstructure that is dominated by sand grains, with little or no fine mineral material.
Spongy microstructure:	a microstructure that is dominated by many interconnected, irregularly shaped voids, and in which clearly defined peds are absent.
Undifferentiated b-fabric:	a groundmass that exhibits no birefringence under crossed polarised light, either due to the presence of amorphous minerals, or due to masking by iron or manganese oxides. At Bornais, undifferentiated b-fabrics are due to the latter, with the exception of Vitrified Ash Type 4.
Vitrified ash:	rounded to subrounded aggregates of vesicular, slag-like material, thought to be produced by the melting of various minerals at high temperatures (>1000°C), including those silica- and phosphate-rich materials usually present in ash residues.
Vughy microstructure:	a microstructure that is dominated by irregularly shaped voids (vughs), and in which clearly defined peds are absent.

multiple layers within a stratigraphic unit that had been given a single context number in the field. As this was the case for the floor examined here (context 276), each microstratigraphic unit was given a letter suffix, and described. Each component or feature observed in thin section was semi-quantified on the basis of the percentage area it represented, averaged over at least ten fields of view, or, in the case of fine layers, averaged over the maximum possible. Visual percentage charts were used for this procedure. Those features which were more difficult to quantify with confidence – owing either to their small size or their potential masking by iron oxides – were allocated one of the broader frequency categories recommended by Bullock, Federoff, Jongerius, Stoops, Torsina and Babel (1985), rather than a percent value (e.g. phytoliths and faecal spherulites). While quantifying features in thin section, care was taken to avoid regions affected by bioturbation, such as worm channels, which were likely to contain intrusive material.

Microscopic globules of non-metallurgical slag that were observed in thin section were further analysed by electron microprobe in order to determine their composition and origin. Uncoverslipped thin sections were carbon-coated and analysed at the Electron Microprobe Laboratory, Department of Earth Sciences, University of Cambridge, under the direction of Dr. Stephen Reed. The vesicular globules to be targeted for analysis were first located using a polarising light microscope, and electron probe micro-analysis was then conducted on the selected globules using a Cameca probe Microanalyser, with a Link AN10000 energy-dispersive X-ray detector.

Pottery – A Lane and J Bond

The pottery was initially studied by Bond who followed the procedure used in studying the assemblage from The Udal, North Uist (Lane 1983). His description of this procedure is available in the site archive. This initial work produced a draft catalogue and discussion of the pottery excavated before 1998. Subsequent to this the whole assemblage was re-catalogued using his draft and adding the pottery excavated in 1999. This entailed some simplification of the original approach and in particular a revision of the fabric analysis.

The pottery from each context was counted, weighed, and divided into five categories – rims, bases, body sherds (sherds of at least 25 mm square area), miscellaneous sherds (misc.; small body sherds less than 25 mm squared), and platter. The separation of the platter sherds as a distinct category was undertaken because it was often possible to recognise such sherds even if they were of small size. Platters are pottery discs and therefore all the sherds are 'bases' – indeed some sherds are both rims and bases – so a separate category was necessary to avoid distorting the figures.

Bond initially subdivided the sherds according to quite small variations in fabric and this resulted in over 30 distinct categories. However, such fabric variations are meaningless in the Hebridean context where differences in colours, some surface variation and density of inclusions can be seen to vary on single vessels and sometimes on single sherds (Lane 1983, 83–84). The fabric series was consequently reduced to five groups, of which only four are present on mound 3, while retaining a different series for platter sherds although they have the same inclusions as the rest of the pottery.

Fabric groups

A: the most common fabric. A rough, gritty and hard fabric with quantities of Lewisian gneiss and other minerals. Surface finish is variable, with smooth, rough, wiped and grass-marked examples all being recorded. Sherds vary in thickness from 7–8 mm up to 18–20 mm, though most are between 8 and 12 mm; it is also found in all the possible colour variations, though most sherds in this fabric group are of grey or buff colouring.

B: a smoother, softer and less gritty fabric, though some of the variants assigned to this group have considerable quantities of quartz/quartzite as inclusions. Less commonly found with surface treatment, though examples do exist of grass-marking etc. Sherd thickness ranges from 5–14 mm, though most sherds are between 8 and 12 mm, and are found in a similar range of colours as fabric A.

C: a fine ware. A smooth, hard and shiny fabric, though considerable quantities of Lewisian gneiss can be used as an inclusion. Smoothed or burnished surfaces are common, though examples with only one treated surface are also common. Sherd thickness ranges from 3.5–7 mm, though most sherds are 4–5 mm, and are usually of a black or dark grey colour, though some sherds with buff-coloured patches have been recorded.

E: a fine ware. A smooth, hard and less commonly occurring fabric, distinctive by its thin walls (4–8 mm) and laminated fabric. Predominantly of grey/buff/reddish colour.

Platter 'fabrics'. The platter was subdivided into categories according to a variety of surface finish features and so is not strictly analysed by 'fabric'. It basically has the same clay and inclusions as the bulk of the assemblage (i.e. Lewisian gneiss) but is distinct in colour. The fabric is irregular and gritty and is subdivided by the presence/absence and quantity of grass-marking, though a few sherds, classed as P28 and P30 in the initial catalogue, had an unusually smooth and less gritty texture. Platter also has a variety of other surface treatment/finishes, such as fingernail impressions and stabbed or pierced holes; sherds range in thickness from 4–14 mm, and are commonly 4–7 mm or 8–11 mm; most are a light buff/red or grey colour, though a few darker examples were recorded.

Once sherds had been allocated to fabrics, they were then described according to any significant features of surface, form or construction. Most of the sherds are of small size and are difficult to allocate to particular forms. Likewise rim and base variation is slight and again may not indicate significant difference, e.g. rim-top variation from flat to slightly rounded occurs on the same vessel. Therefore only substantial differences have been recorded.

The vessel forms recognised in the Late Iron Age and Viking/Norse assemblages are:

Pre-Viking:	Bucket shape – straight-sided
	Shouldered Jar – rim fairly upright or flaring
Viking:	Convex Bowl – rim turned in to some extent
	Cup – small vessel with upright or inturned rim
	Steep-sided Bowl – rim and side fairly straight
	Platter – flat pottery disc

Additional distinctions were made according to the presence of round and/or sagging bases and the use of grass-marking. Construction techniques might also have been significant and were recorded when recognisable.

In the course of cataloguing the feature sherds (rims, bases, body sherds, platter and distinctive misc. sherds) measurements of thickness were made. As most of the assemblage was very fragmentary only a few rim and base diameters could be measured. A number of the initial diameter measurements were rejected by A. Lane as it is clear with such hand-made pottery that the shape of the vessels was irregular and therefore not amenable to the reconstruction of accurate diameters except where large pieces survive.

Surface treatment was noted as was the presence of sooting or organic encrustation on the inside and outside of vessels. An important feature was the presence of grass-marking though the distinction between organics in the fabric (i.e. organic tempering) and grass-marking (i.e. external) was not always easy to make. The use of organic temper was occasionally recognised though there is some difficulty in ascertaining how deliberate this is with small sherds. The occurrence of voids in the section of some of the sherds leaving the impression of organics may indicate organic tempering though whether this involved the addition of grass, chaff, or dung is not clear.

Other variations in surface treatment were occasionally noted:

- wiped
- organically wiped

- striated
- slurry-brushed
- rough
- smoothed
- finger-smoothed
- fingernail-impressed
- stabbed
- pierced
- cracked

The significance of these small variations in surface finish, for functional, cultural or temporal reasons, is not clear.

The colour of rims and bases was recorded in the catalogue for significant sherds and for other sherds when they seemed outside the normal colour range. The variety of colour exhibited by the assemblage from Bornais was in line with those recovered from The Udal (Lane 1983, 13–135) and was broadly speaking made up of the following colours:

- Black
- Grey
- Buff
- Brown
- Orange
- Pink
- Red

The above colours were represented in a variety of shades and tones too diverse to classify fully and instead the additional terms of 'dark' and 'light' were appended to the colour terms listed above. The multi-coloured nature of some of the sherds further reinforces the varied nature of the pottery, with some sherds having three to four different colours present. The colours show evidence for both reduced and oxidised firing conditions, but as these variations can often be seen on the same sherd (or on conjoining sherds) it seems likely that neither condition was the result of deliberate intention and instead results from the firing without proper air control on a hearth or open bonfire. Some colour variation may of course be due to subsequent exposure on the domestic hearth during cooking.

The blackening of parts of many of the sherds results from their use as cooking pots. The presence of sooting and/or carbonised residues and their position were noted in the catalogue.

Following the initial fabric classification by Bond a selection of sherds was examined by Tim Young, a geologist with experience of archaeological ceramics. He confirmed the view that the fabric variations were largely superficial and that all the examined sherds seemed to be of one general geological origin (cf. Lane 1983, 135–137). Some variation in organics was recognised but could not be observed throughout the assemblage. However the differences between the 'fine wares' and the general run of the fabric A and B sherds seem to be genuine though not based on inclusions. Some difference in finishing and perhaps firing may be the explanation but this may require future work to identify.

Fragmentation analysis – N Sharples

Fragmentation analysis was undertaken on bone and pot assemblages from a number of layers in mound 3. Unfortunately most of the contexts contained very few pieces of either bone or pottery large enough to warrant analysis and so the data available for comparative analysis is negligible. However, the available assemblages will provide data for future comparisons with the assemblages from the other mounds.

The methodology is similar to that used at Dun Vulan (Parker Pearson and Sharples 1999). All potsherds and all mammal bones above 10 mm were measured, but not fish bones, small mammals or bone artefacts. The finds from flotation samples were excluded as these would have increased considerably the numbers of small sherds from the house floors that had been heavily sampled and provided a biased comparison with other layers. The measurement data was limited to counting pieces that fell within 100 mm blocks. The data is presented as histograms and analysis is for the moment restricted to visual comparisons.

Artefact methodology – A Clarke, I Dennis, P Macdonald and A Smith

The artefact assemblage from this mound was limited and a complete catalogue is presented in appendix 2. The assemblage can be divided into four categories of material:

- coarse stone tools that were examined by A Clarke;
- the metalwork (exclusively copper alloys and iron, though lead is found on the other mounds at Bornais) that was examined by P Macdonald;
- the worked bone that was examined by A Smith;
- a small assemblage of flint that was examined by I Dennis.

The iron assemblage was X-rayed and a small number of finds were selected for investigative cleaning prior to examination. The preservation of the assemblage was poor and consequently the number of positive or detailed identifications that could be made was limited.

Slag and related materials – T P Young

The entire macroscopic (>10 mm) slag collection from mound 3 was examined (that from mound 1 has also been examined but is not reported on here), and representative materials from the fine sieving were also examined (the sub-10 mm sieved fines are described throughout this report as the microscopic slags). Data on the distribution by weight of slag material from both the coarse and fine sieved fractions was assembled for several key horizons, so that the spread of material with respect to various features could be determined. Detailed examination of examples of fine material from mound 3 was undertaken, including magnetic separation and examination under the SEM.

Analytical work was undertaken using the Philips PW 1400 X-ray fluorescence spectrometer (XRF) and the Perkin-Elmer Elan 5000A inductively coupled plasma – mass spectrometer (ICP-MS) of the Earth Sciences Department, Cardiff University. The electron microscope and microanalytical work was initially undertaken on the Cambridge Instruments S360 scanning electron microscope (with a Link Analytical Ltd. AN10000 energy dispersive X-ray analysis system) of the Earth Sciences Department, Cardiff University and later on the Camscan Maxim 2040 scanning electron microscope with Oxford Instruments energy-dispersive and wavelength-dispersive analytical systems of the Archaeology Section, HISAR, Cardiff University.

Carbonised plant remains – S Colledge and H Smith

The carbonised plant remains from 150 flotation samples were selected for examination. These comprised the floated coarse (>1 mm) and fine fractions (300 µm – 1 mm) for each sample, and also any charred remains that were found in the heavy residues (an estimate based on the sorted fraction). The coarse 'flots' were examined in their entirety for all but eight large samples. Because of the time-consuming nature of sorting it was considered necessary to sub-sample these so that only one half or one quarter of the total volume was examined. Appropriate calculations were then made to 'multiply up' the numbers of items in these sub-samples to produce the totals quoted in the list of taxa. Samples were examined using a low-powered stereo microscope at ×15–×80 magnification. Identifications were made using a modern seed reference collection. Identifications were often limited owing to poor preservation of much of the material. Details of modern habitats were obtained from reference sources such as Stace (1997), Pankhurst and Mullin (1991) and Clapham, Tutin and Moore (1989). The nomenclature is according to Stace (1997).

All identifiable items (with the exception of wood charcoal) were extracted from the 'flots': these included grains/seeds, chaff, nutshell, parenchyma (from vegetative storage organs, e.g. roots and tubers) and charred peat/dung/organic matter. A total of 23 taxa, represented by seeds/grains and chaff, were identified in the Bornais samples (Table 2). The samples were dominated by the grains and chaff (e.g. rachis internodes, floret bases and culm fragments) of domestic cereals.

The 'charcoal' density was measured for each sample, i.e. the ratio of the volume of charcoal in the 'flots' to the volume of sediment floated (cm^3/litre). Charcoal here refers to all charred plant material (e.g. seeds, chaff, parenchyma, etc.) and not just to charred wood. The values are given in the Tables associated with each block in chapters 4 and 5. The number of items per litre was also calculated for each sample.

Crop species

In the majority of cases taxa could only be identified at the generic rather than the species level, owing to the poor preservation of the plant remains. Cereals were represented by hulled barley (*Hordeum sativum*), common oat (*Avena* cf. *sativa*) and rye (*Secale cereale*), of which barley and oat were dominant. Initial scanning indicated that six-row barley was present (based on the ratio of straight (medial) to twisted (lateral) grains). The most likely identification of the oat grains in the samples is the common oat (*Avena sativa*); the presence of 'bristle oat', 'black oat' or 'small oat'(*Avena strigosa*), however, cannot be discounted. Wheat grains were not identified. Flax was the only crop plant other than the cereals found in the samples.

Wild plants

The number and diversity of wild taxa recovered from the samples were limited. The charred remains may be the result of the deliberate or accidental burning of plant remains that were present on site as a result of crop processing or other domestic activities involving the use of plant resources. The wild taxa represent plants that are found in cultivated fields, on disturbed and waste ground, and grassland and heath. The non-cereal plant material is likely to have arrived at the site through

Table 2. Plant species found on mound 3

Hordeum sativum
Secale cereale
Avena cf. *sativa*
Buglossoides sp.
Boraginaceae charred 'embroyos'
Caryophyllaceae
Chenopodium spp.
Compositae
Cruciferae
Carex spp. (/*Scirpus* spp.)
cf. *Fumaria* sp.
Bromus sp.
Lolium sp.
Phalaris sp.
Gramineae
Linum sp.
Plantago sp.
Polygonum /*Rumex* spp.
Ranunculus sp.
Rubus cf. *fruticosus*
Galium sp.
Solanaceae
Urtica sp.

deliberate collection (food, fuel, furnishings) or incidentally, either gathered in with the crops and other useful plants, or adhering to feet, clothing and animal fur, etc.

Wild plants possibly collected for food and fuel appear in the assemblage from Bornais. Edible material is represented by seeds of bramble (*Rubus* cf. *fruticosus*) and nutshell fragments (although only in one sample). Wild plants that might have been eaten as leafy vegetables, could possibly be represented by seeds of the cabbage family (Cruciferae).

Heather (*Calluna vulgaris*), which is represented by seeds/seed capsules, might have been collected for use as fuel or furnishings. Historically heather was often used for bedding, thatching, ropes and brushes, whilst the tips were used to produce a yellow dye (Beveridge 1911). Seeds of grasses (*Phalaris* sp., *Lolium* sp., *Bromus* sp.) and sedges (*Carex* spp.) may represent other plants that would be useful as flooring, roofing etc. and might have been deliberately collected. The parenchyma fragments (which were not identified further) may represent resources that were deliberately collected, such as edible roots and tubers; they may, however, merely indicate that certain plants (e.g. cereals, grasses and sedges) were gathered by uprooting. Historically, sedge roots (specifically glaucous sedge, *Carex flacca*) were used for thatching (Walker 1764) and for making fish nets and tethers (Beveridge 1911) and as temporary thatching while grass (specifically bent grasses, *Agrostis* sp.) was used for making sacks, ropes and mats (Beveridge 1911).

Plants commonly found in arable fields or areas of disturbed or waste ground may be represented by taxa identified as gromwells (*Buglossoides* cf. *arvense*), goosefoots (*Chenopodium* spp.), knotgrasses/docks (*Polygonum/Rumex* spp.) and buttercup (*Ranunculus* sp.), whilst seeds of plants included in the pink family (Caryophyllaceae) and cabbage family (Cruciferae) may also represent areas of cultivated and waste ground. Taxa that occur less frequently in the Bornais samples, but occur in similar areas, include plantain (*Plantago* sp.), cleavers/bedstraw (*Galium* sp.), nettle (*Urtica* sp.) and fumatory (cf. *Fumaria* sp.). Some of these taxa have preferences for lighter sandy soils (i.e. gromwell) and others occur in damp or well-drained ground.

Taxa indicative of grassland and heathland areas are represented by seeds of grasses and sedges, and also knotgrasses/docks, plantain and buttercup. Certain of these taxa, for example many of the sedges, are often associated with areas of damp ground. Although no longer typical weeds of cultivation, these may represent relic weeds of cultivation, possibly indicating areas or pockets of damp arable ground (Jones 1988; van der Veen 1992).

Charcoal – R Gale

The quantity of charcoal recovered from the complex programme of environmental sampling was relatively small in comparison with the charred plant remains and, although charcoal-rich contexts and layers were recorded during the excavation, none of the flotation samples produced particularly large quantities of charcoal. These samples often contained small fragments from narrow ericaceous stems. A total of 30 samples was selected for identification. In addition to the main flotation sampling programme, charcoal was collected by hand during the excavation of the site. These samples frequently included larger fragments of charcoal that clearly derived from non-ericaceous wood and, although not directly comparable with the bulk soil samples, they have been included in the current analysis in order to obtain a comprehensive evaluation of wood resources employed/available on the island.

Identification was undertaken:

1. To indicate the character of the firewood and type of wood used.
2. To establish spatial and temporal differences in the deposition of fuel wood species.
3. To obtain environmental evidence.

The charcoal was generally firm and well preserved. The samples were prepared for identification using standard methods (Gale and Cutler 2000). The anatomical wood features were examined using a Nikon Labophot-2 microscope at magnifications up to ×400 and matched to reference slides of modern wood. When possible, roundwood diameters were recorded but since the volume of wood is considerably reduced during charring, possibly by as much as 40% (Gale and Cutler 2000), these measurements will not correspond to the wood's original dimensions.

Classification follows that of *Flora Europaea* (Tutin, Heywood *et al.* 1964–80). Group names are given when anatomical differences between related genera are too slight to allow secure identification to genus level. These include members of the Ericaceae (heathers), Salicaceae (*Salix* and *Populus*) and *Picea* and *Larix*. Where a genus is represented by a single species in the British flora this is named as the most likely origin of the wood, given the provenance and period, but it should be noted that it is rarely possible to name individual species from wood features.

Mammalian bone – J Mulville

The majority of the animal bone was retrieved by hand collection and sieving through a 10 mm mesh on site. A number of bulk samples were also taken for flotation. Material from the flotation residues was sorted and recorded separately. Unless otherwise stated the discussion is concerned solely with the hand-collected material.

The animal bone was identified using the reference collection at the Faunal Remains Unit at the University of Southampton. Sheep and goat were distinguished using the criteria described in Boessneck (1969), Kratochvil (1969) and Payne (1969 and 1985) for a restricted suite of elements: dP_4, distal humerus, distal metapodii, distal tibia, astragalus, calcaneum and horncores. Where distinction between the two species was not possible, fragments were classified under a single heading of sheep/goat. Rib and vertebral fragments, except the atlas and axis, were only assigned to size categories as either 'cattle-size' or 'sheep-size'. Distinction between red and fallow deer followed criteria noted by Lister (1996).

Fragments were recorded using a combination of Davis's (1992) 'restricted suite of bone' method and Serjeantson (1991) zoning method. Thus only a pre-determined set of elements were recorded: all the long bones, the occipital condyle, zygomatic arch, calcaneum, astragalus, patella, navicular cuboid, isolated incisors, lower premolars and molars, ribs when the head was present, vertebrae when over 50% of the centrum was present, and atlas and axis when over 50% of the total bone was present. Horncore and antler were recorded when over 50% of the circumference was present or the tip. In order to avoid multiple counting of very fragmented bone, over 50% of at least a single zone had to be present. For long bones the zones followed Serjeantson zones; for the smaller bones (astragalus, calcaneum, phalanx, pig metapodial, navicular cuboid or patella) over 50% of the element had to be present.

The total number of fragments (NISP) was calculated for all species and minimum number of individuals (MNI) for the most common taxa. As the recording method indicates which zones are present on each bone, the minimum number of each element present (MNE) could be calculated. From this it was possible to estimate the minimum number of individuals (MNI) that must have been present on site to form the bone assemblage recovered. NISP counts tend to be biased towards the larger species as larger bones suffer greater fragmentation and produce higher counts and the use of MNI counts reduces this bias. The percentage survival of each element was also calculated following Brain (1981), where the maximum number of each element present is expressed as a percentage of the most frequently occurring left or right element (i.e. the number expected if all the skeleton was present).

The calculation of MNE from the most abundant zone is an attempt to reduce the effects of fragmentation. However, if bone is fragmented to a size that is less than half a zone, it will not be counted, thus more fragmented material becomes under- rather than over-represented using this method.

Wear stages were recorded for dP_4s, P_4s and permanent molars of the domestic species using Grant (1982) and grouped into age stages following the methods of Halstead (1985), Payne (1973) and O'Connor (1988). Deer tooth eruption and wear were recorded using a modified version of Grant (1982) and the animals grouped following O'Connor (1988). The fusion stage of post-cranial bones was recorded and related age ranges taken from Getty (1975).

Measurements were taken on cattle, sheep/goat, pig and horse bones, following von den Driesch (1976), Davis (1992) and Payne (1969). Those taken on pig teeth followed Payne and Bull (1988) and for horse teeth followed Levine (1982). Measurements were compared with those listed in publications of other contemporary sites and will be published in future volumes.

Bird bone – J Cartledge

The bird bones were identified with the aid of the comparative collections at the University of Sheffield and my own. Ribs and vertebrae are included in the unidentified count. An attempt was made at identification of all the other bird bones. This is so that where a particular species is only represented by a single bone, it is not excluded on the basis that it falls into the wrong bone category. The Hebridean sites often produce a wide range of species, some of which are only represented by a few or single bones. Minimum number of individuals was calculated using the humerus, the most frequently occurring bone. Only those bones that could be assigned a family or species were recorded in detail. The other bones (mainly the shaft fragments of long bone missing their proximal and distal ends) were counted as unidentified. The identified long bones were recorded in six categories – complete, proximal end, proximal end and shaft, fragment, distal end, distal end and shaft. There was a visual assessment of the age range with three categories Juvenile, Sub-adult and Adult (a possible fourth category, Neonatal, was not used). Butchery marks and signs of pathology were recorded. Condition of the bone was recorded as was burning and the presence of gnawing.

Fish bone – C Ingrem

A considerable quantity of fish bone was recovered from the fine sieving of the house floors of mound 3. This floor material was originally analysed as the author's MA dissertation at the University of Southampton. The research design was therefore aimed at gathering the maximum information from the fish assemblage as was possible in the given time. Fish bones recovered from intervening layers and from trench F were recorded at a later date using the same methodology. For the purposes of this report all of the material has been combined and analysed as a whole.

The fish bones were identified and recorded with the aid of the comparative collection of the Faunal Remains Unit at Southampton University, and the unpublished manuscript of Lepiksaar (1981). When necessary, the remains were examined using a low power (x10) binocular microscope. Identification and recording were limited to a selected suite of the more robust elements which would allow species level identification and the calculation of body part representation; this forms the basis for the basic fragment count or number of identified specimens

(NISP). The elements selected were the vomer, pre-maxilla, maxilla, dentary, articular, opercular, otolith, hyomandibular, anterior abdominal vertebrae (AAV), cleithrum, supracleithrum, post-temporal, posterior abdominal vertebrae (PAV) and caudal vertebrae (CV). The unidentified material was not quantified owing to its fragmentary nature.

The proportion of an element represented by each fragment was recorded as < 25%, 25–50%, 50–75% and >75% according to completeness. Vertebrae and otoliths are the exception: these were only recorded if more than half of the element was present. Where possible, elements were sided. Only fragments which had been both sided and were more than 50% complete have been used in the calculation of the minimum number of elements (MNE). The minimum number of individuals (MNI) was determined according to the frequency of the most numerous element derived from one side of the body.

The state of preservation was recorded as good, medium and poor. The incidence and location of butchery marks were noted according to the categories of Barrett (1997). Similarly, evidence of damage caused by gnawing, burning and digestion were all recorded. Measurements were taken where possible and generally follow the guidelines of Morales and Rosenlund (1979); however, additional measurements were devised during recording. The total length of cod was calculated according to the method of Rojo (1986). In addition, size was visually categorised with the aid of the reference specimens. In the interests of comparative studies the visual size categories follow those used by Cerón-Carrasco (1999) as follows: very small (<150 mm), small (150–300 mm), medium (300–600 mm), large (600–1200 mm) and very large (>1200 mm).

The fish assemblage is comprised of three categories of material:

- all the fish bone recovered by hand collection (>10 mm)
- material from the samples that is over 10 mm,
- and a fraction of the material from the samples that is between 10 mm and 1mm.

For the purposes of this report, the material is divided into that over 10 mm and that under 10 mm; when discussing species representation, these will be analysed separately in order to overcome, investigate and illustrate the effects of recovery methods on species and body part representation. In order to compensate for fractionation of the <10 mm material, estimated totals are often used when discussing species and body part representation; where this occurs it is stated in the text and tables. This estimated total was also used to calculate the density of identified bone per litre of soil.

Marine shell – N Sharples

Large quantities of marine shell are present in the occupation layers of the Bornais settlement, far too many shells to make total recovery possible or in any sense desirable. The strategy used to assess the quantity and species variation was threefold (Evans 1973):

- All species were recovered from the flotation samples and counted.
- Species other than limpets or winkles were recovered whenever they were observed during excavation.
- When particularly large and dense shell layers were excavated a large sample was taken (this did not occur on mound 3).

The basic analysis of the shells involved counting to assess species variation. For the common species (limpets and winkles) and for other gastropods only the apices were counted but for other species rarely found such as clam, razorshells and oysters, numbers were so few and the shells so fragmented that the presence of any part of the shell was sufficient to be counted.

Large samples of winkles and limpets were also assessed for diseases and where a large sample (>100) of complete limpets was available, these were measured. Both of these features provide some indication of the condition of the coast from which the shellfish originated. The shape of the limpet is directly related to the degree of wave action as it dictates the size of the muscle required to hold the limpet in place (Evans 1973). A low flat shell comes from near the low-water mark whereas a high conical shell comes from near the high-water mark. The size of the shell may also indicate patterns of exploitation. The opportunity was taken to examine some of the Dun Vulan shells to provide comparative size samples of limpets from a settlement close to the seashore.

Crab – J Light

Samples of crab shell were extracted from the below 10 mm flotation residues from soil samples floated to extract carbonised plant remains.

Identification of crab shell elements is problematic. Carapace fragments can be difficult to pinpoint taxonomically unless the sculpture and ornament is particularly distinctive. Crab limbs comprise diverse skeletal elements. Upon disarticulation of crab exoskeleton, chelae (commonly called claws or pincers) are more persistent than other limb components. These are most frequently encountered in fossil assemblages, even in high-energy deposits, which rarely yield recognisable carapace remains. Another difficulty concerns the inter-generic similarities within families' of elements such as the chelae. Finally, one crab species can exhibit eight distinctive chelae: male and female, cutting claw and crushing claw, with the possibility of the latter claw types occurring on either 'hand' during the life of an individual crab (Collins 1999).

All samples of crab shell extracted from soil samples were examined microscopically. Most of the material from mound 3 came from the house floors but there were a few midden layers and other occupation deposits with significant assemblages.

4 Trench D

The excavation of the northern area of mound 3 (Figure 28) focused on the exposure of a house (DC) and the associated occupation deposits (DD). The house lay in the centre of the mound and other than some abandonment deposits (DE) was the last feature to be constructed and occupied in this area. The only attempt to explore the deposits underlying this structure occurred in the 1995 exploratory trench. The north end of this trench (Figure 29) was excavated to a depth of 0.58 m and revealed, after the removal of a sequence of layers (DB), an earlier building (DA).

The early house (DA) – N Sharples

The early house was represented by two walls (Figure 28; 30, 217), which appear to meet at a corner just beyond the eastern edge of the excavated area. The N-S wall was clearly truncated in the trench but a feature filled with yellow sand may have been a stone hole. If this stone hole marks the position of the wall then the wall appears to be turning a corner and would define a structure roughly 3.6 m wide. The E-W wall appears to be turning outwards, just as it enters the north section, and if this is the case then it indicates the presence of an entrance facing north.

Medium-sized water-rounded stones, on average 0.4 m long, 0.3 m wide and 0.15 m thick were used to construct the wall and two courses of these stones were exposed. The excavation ceased with the exposure of a brown sand (218), which was confined to the interior of the house. This layer had a relatively flat surface and probably represents a floor layer. Probing suggests that more courses of walling may be hidden by the unexcavated floor deposits but it is very unlikely that a wall much more substantial than that of the later structure (DC) ever existed. The surface of this layer had a distinctive mottling that, subsequent observations suggest, may be the result of cattle trampling (Figure 29). As this was not realised at the time no detailed recording of the phenomenon was undertaken.

Other than four bones (three sheep, one cattle) and two potsherds (weighing 42g) no finds or samples were recovered from the house or the associated floor layer. The two potsherds are undiagnostic body sherds. One could be a Late Iron Age plain ware form but it is more likely that they are both of Viking/Norse date. A crushed sheep skull was observed underlying a flat stone that lay flush with the floor.

Sand accumulation (DB) – N Sharples

Approximately five layers (Figure 30) could be defined between the floor of the underlying house and the deposits associated with the house (DC). Immediately over the DA floor was a pale yellow sand with occasional lenses and patches of brown (215). A radiocarbon date (OxA-10274) was obtained from a cattle bone in layer 215. This produced a date of 1004±32 bp, which when calibrated indicates that this occupation layer was deposited between cal AD 980–1160 (95% probability). Above this was a dark grey sand (214) restricted to the east side of the excavated area. Clearly visible in the section but not projecting into the excavated area was a row of three to four stones and a whalebone which suggests the presence of a structure immediately to the east of the excavated area. A complementary but stratigraphically later layer of brown sand (210) was restricted to the west side of the trench. A radiocarbon date (OxA-10273) was obtained from a sheep bone in layer 214. This produced a date of 1065±35 bp which when calibrated indicates that this occupation layer was deposited between cal AD 890–1030 (95% probability). These occupation deposits were sealed by a thick layer of pale yellow sand (209), with frequent minor changes of colour. Above this was a brown sand (208) with lenses of both darker and lighter brown sand.

The final layer was a homogeneous brown sand (204/205/206) which covered the whole of the trench and which appeared to be the layer into which the main house (DC) was built. This layer (206) was removed at the south end of the trench to expose a slightly different brown sand (211). The 1997 excavation exposed a large area of this brown sand around the main house. The layer was homogeneous around the north, south and west of the main house. Exploration of this area was limited to a 1m wide slot dug to the north of the house wall (Figure 28) and this trench only involved the removal of approximately 0.20 m of brown sand (227, 232). Further excavation of this layer was restricted to an area behind the north wall of the house (237) and an area to the west (612/613), which was excavated to check that there was no blocked western entrance. In neither area was the brown sand removed to expose an earlier layer.

The deposits to the east of the house were potentially more varied. Cleaning of the east side of the house revealed a sequence of three layers. The lowest appears

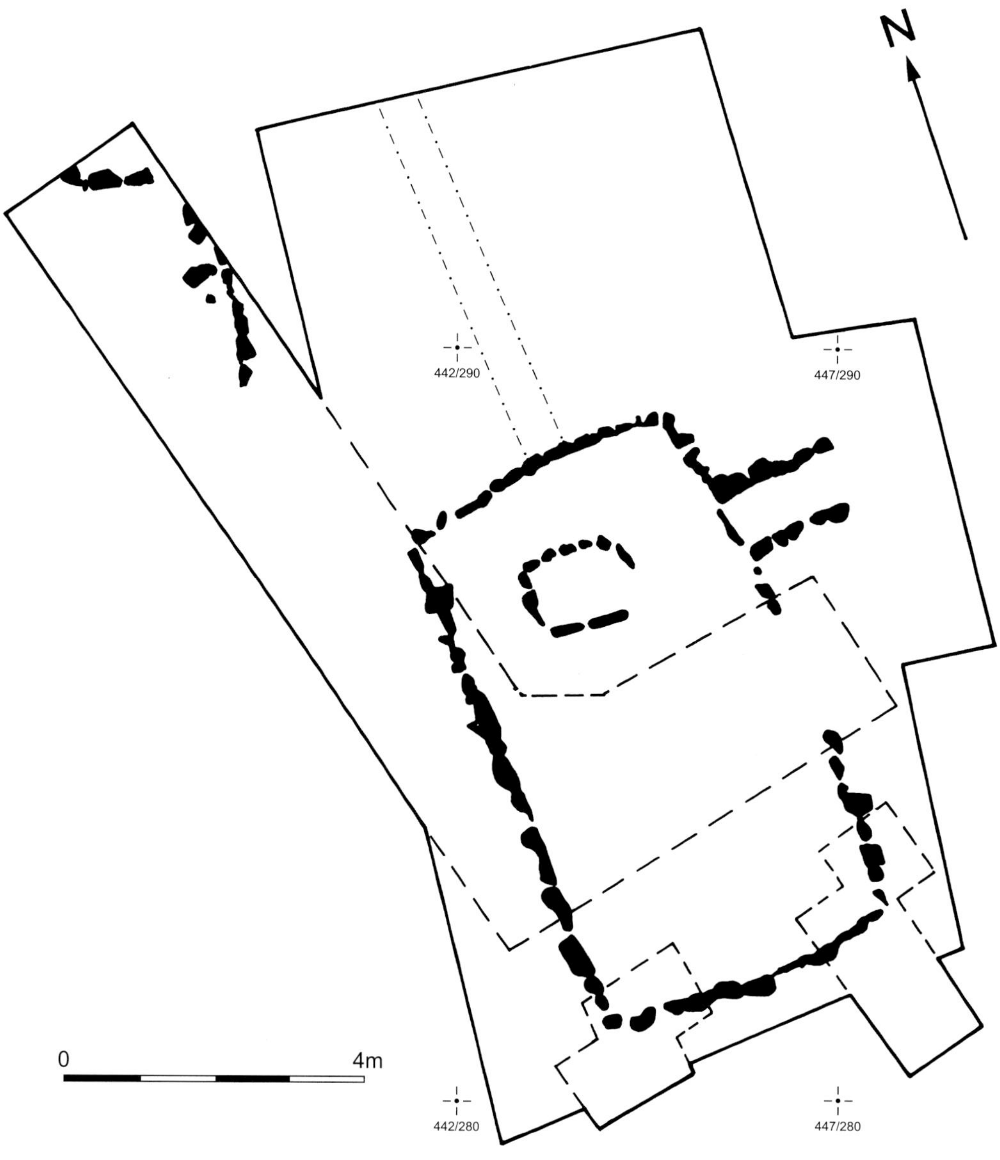

Figure 28. General plan of the trenches dug in 1995 and 1997 showing the main structural features (note these buildings are not contemporary)

to be a light grey sand (216/607) which occurs under most of the floor of the house. This was overlain by a red-orange clayey sand (226/606) which underlay the east side of the house. The layer immediately below the house was a shell midden (247), restricted to the southeast corner but similar to an unexcavated concentration around the entrance.

Sampling – N Sharples

Eight samples, 175 litres of soil, were taken and processed from the DB contexts: 208, 210, 211, 214, 227, 232, 247, 606, and the material from below 10 mm was sorted for three samples from contexts 227, 232 and 606. The material from above 10 mm was limited, consisting of small quantities of fish bone (an average density of 0.2 pieces per litre), bone (0.3 pieces per litre), pottery (under 0.1 pieces per litre) and marine molluscs (limpets had an average density of 0.9 individuals per litre, winkles an average density of 2.5 individuals per litre) and occasionally slag. The richest sample was from context 606: this had the highest densities of fish, mammal bone and pottery and dense concentrations of shellfish, though the highest concentrations of limpets came from 232 and winkles from 208.

The material from below 10 mm contained large quantities of fish (227 produced 108 pieces per litre, 232 produced 133 pieces per litre and 606 produced 233 pieces per litre) that were similar in density to the samples from the floor of the house. The sample from 232 has a very

Figure 29. A view of the structure found at the base of the 1995 trench

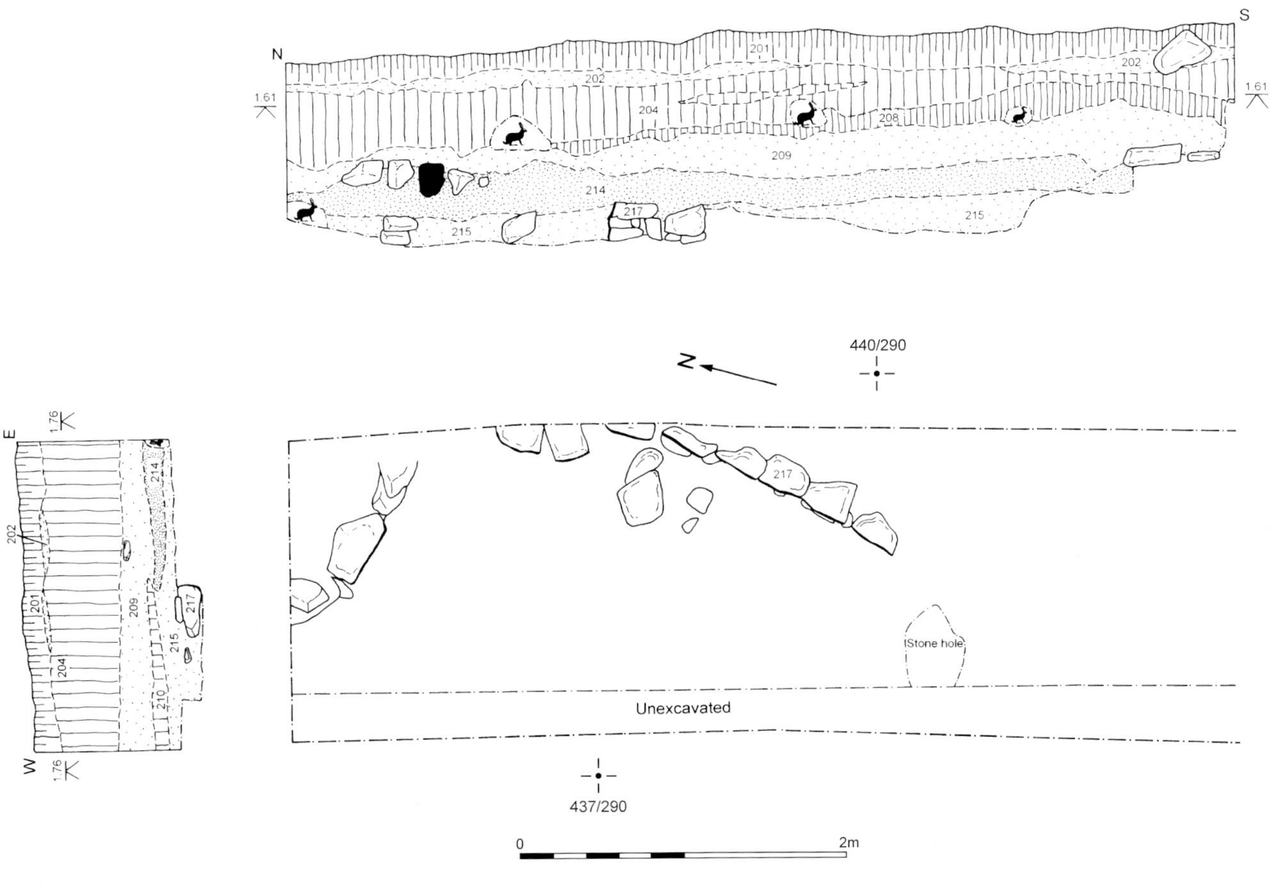

Figure 30. A plan and the sections for the north end of the 1995 trench

high density of unburnt bone (136 pieces per litre) and the other two have above average densities. The only other feature of note was the sizeable quantity (27 fragments) of eggshell found in context 606.

Pottery – J Bond and A Lane (Figure 31, 32; appendix 3)

The distribution of material from these layers is fairly uninformative (Table 3). None of the contexts had a large assemblage but in general the brown sand layers surrounding the later house (DD), and the layers which underlay this house, have the more substantial assemblages.

Most of the assemblage shows signs of fairly heavy activity, with small (misc.) sherds predominating (48%) – especially if it is considered that many of the feature sherds – the rims, bases, platters and the fine wares – were also of misc. size. The presence of associated sherds in some contexts suggests that these had been deposited at the same time, especially the bases from 612 and 226, and the platters from 237 and 227/232. Average sherd weight shows a significant difference between the contexts excavated in 1995 and those excavated in 1997. This directly reflects the systematic sieving of the latter contexts. It is clear that small sherds were likely to be missed in the layers excavated in 1995. The average sherd weight in the DB category is 7.8g.

The majority of sherds were thick-walled (9–13 mm), though a number of medium wall thickness (6–9 mm) were recovered and also a number of very thick-walled (13–17 mm) examples were occasionally recovered. A proportion of the vessels are manufactured with thinner walls (3–6 mm), classed as fine wares, and these sherds appear to be from small vessels. Unfortunately, owing to their thinner walls, these fine ware sherds are more fragmented and often only appear as misc. sherds.

No fine ware sherds and, with one exception, no platter sherds were recovered from the lower layers in this sequence, 214, 210, 209 and 208. Thick-walled open bowl forms dominate these layers. Apart from the one sherd in 209, platter begins in the brown sand surrounding the house 204/205/206 and is present in quantity in 211, 227, 232 and 237.

The angle/slab technique of construction was the only technique recognized. Most of the sherds recovered are fabric A, but all the other fabrics are represented by a few sherds. Grass-marking occurs and is most commonly a feature of sagging bottomed vessels (and platters), though sparse organic impressions are more widespread throughout the whole assemblage. Wiping or smoothing of the vessel exteriors was sometimes noted, and was especially common on the fine wares.

Convex or open-mouthed bowls, with round or flat rims, are the only recognisable vessel form, apart from the platter discs, in the assemblage (Figures 31 and 32). The fine wares are usually of convex form, with round rims, and flat or sagging bases. No definite examples of everted rims were found in these pre-house levels.

Twenty-five rims (6%) were found and these have a fairly random distribution. Only four vessel diameters are measurable anywhere in the mound 3 assemblage and all four are in this context group. One rim diameter of 200 mm was measurable from a straight-sided vessel (Figure 32, 3). Two basal diameters were measurable from context 208. One sagging base has a diameter of 310 mm (Figure 31, 4), another a diameter of 160 mm (Figure 31, 5). Another sagging base bowl has a diameter of 150 mm (Figure 31, 20); while another can be estimated

Table 3. Pottery from the DB layers listed by context in stratigraphic sequence

context	weight	sherds	rim	base	body	misc.	platter	fine	Ave. Wght.
204/205/206	293	42	3	3	8	21	7	13	6.98
227/232	316	67	2	7	4	30	24	2	4.72
247	173	43				41	2	8	4.02
612/613	596	53		38	3	7	5	2	11.25
208	492	24	1	5	8	10			20.50
237	239	39	2	3	3	21	10	7	6.13
226/606	126	37	3	15	2	17		1	3.41
216	29	5	1			2	2		5.80
211	192	42	4	1	4	18	15	2	4.57
209	100	9	1		3	4	1		11.11
210	306	30	2	10	1	17			10.20
214	389	26	6	2	6	12			14.96
Total	3251	417	25	84	42	200	66	35	7.80

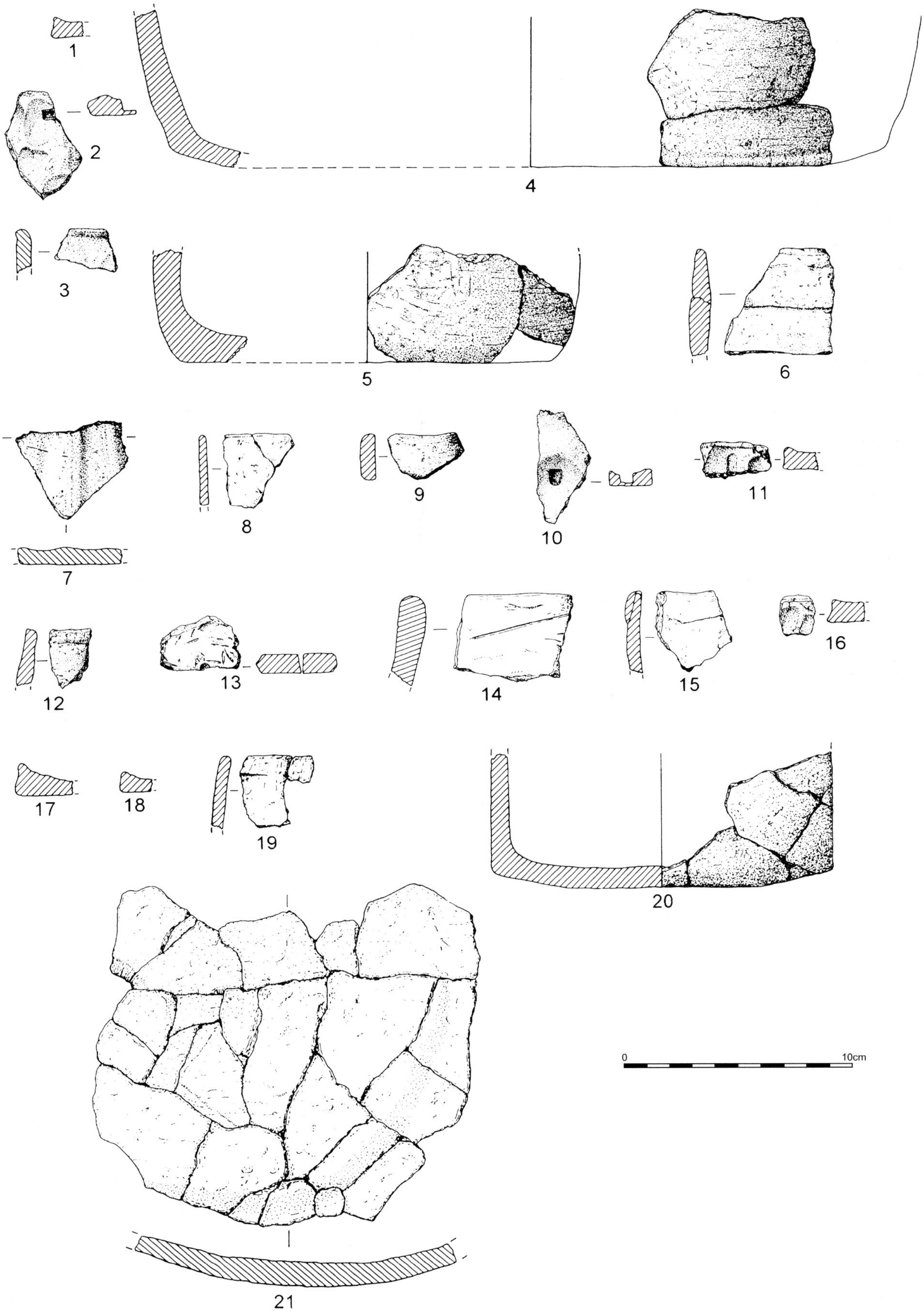

Figure 31. The pottery from DB contexts

as 200 mm in diameter though none of the wall angle survives (Figure 31, 21). Eighty-four base sherds (20.1%) were found and there is a notable concentration in contexts 612 and 226. These concentrations are likely to represent *in situ* breakage.

Sixty-six platter sherds (15.8%) were identified but no diameters were measurable. They are all medium or thick types. Most have fingered interiors, stabbed examples are rare, and very few are pierced. The use of a square-sectioned implement for the creation of the stabbed holes (Figure 31, 2 and 10) is unusual and was found in a restricted group of platters in contexts 204, 209 and 211. It is uncertain whether the use of square holes is a temporal variation or the result of individual variability. Platter sherds with this feature are likely to be from three different vessels.

Many of the sherds show signs of sooting, blackening or carbonised residues, which may indicate their use in cooking, and this includes both the platter and the fine ware sherds. A white deposit was recognised on some sherds but has not been positively identified.

Some chronological variation may be recognisable in these layers.

- The lower pre-house contexts 214, 210 and 208 only have thick-walled bowl forms.
- One sherd of platter appears in context 209 and platter subsequently occurs in most contexts of the pre-house layers above this. Platter sherds are particularly common in contexts 211, 227, 232 and 237.
- There are no definite everted rims in the pre-house deposits.
- There is no evidence for Late Iron Age residual material in any of these layers.

Artefacts – A Clarke, P Macdonald and A Smith

This block produced four pieces of worked bone, five pieces of iron, two stone objects and five flints (Table 4). Most of the objects were found in the brown sand layers that surround the house and which are probably contemporary or slightly earlier than its construction. The collection was disparate consisting of a comb tooth plate (Figure 33, 1061), two bone handles (Figure 33, 1065 and 1066) made from hollowed sheep metapodials, a miscellaneous collection of iron objects (Figure 33, rove 1226; Figure 33, holdfast 1325; nail 1227; bar 1326; plate fragment 1225) which are largely structural fittings, a small whetstone (Figure 33, 1434) and a fragment of steatite bowl (Figure 33, 1513) that joins another fragment (1509) from the house floor 2. The only distinctive early object was a fragment of a comb side plate (Figure 33, 1438) from brown sand 210.

Carbonised plant remains – S Colledge, R Gale and H Smith

Three flotation samples were examined from contexts 227, 232, and 247 (Table 5). These contexts are poor

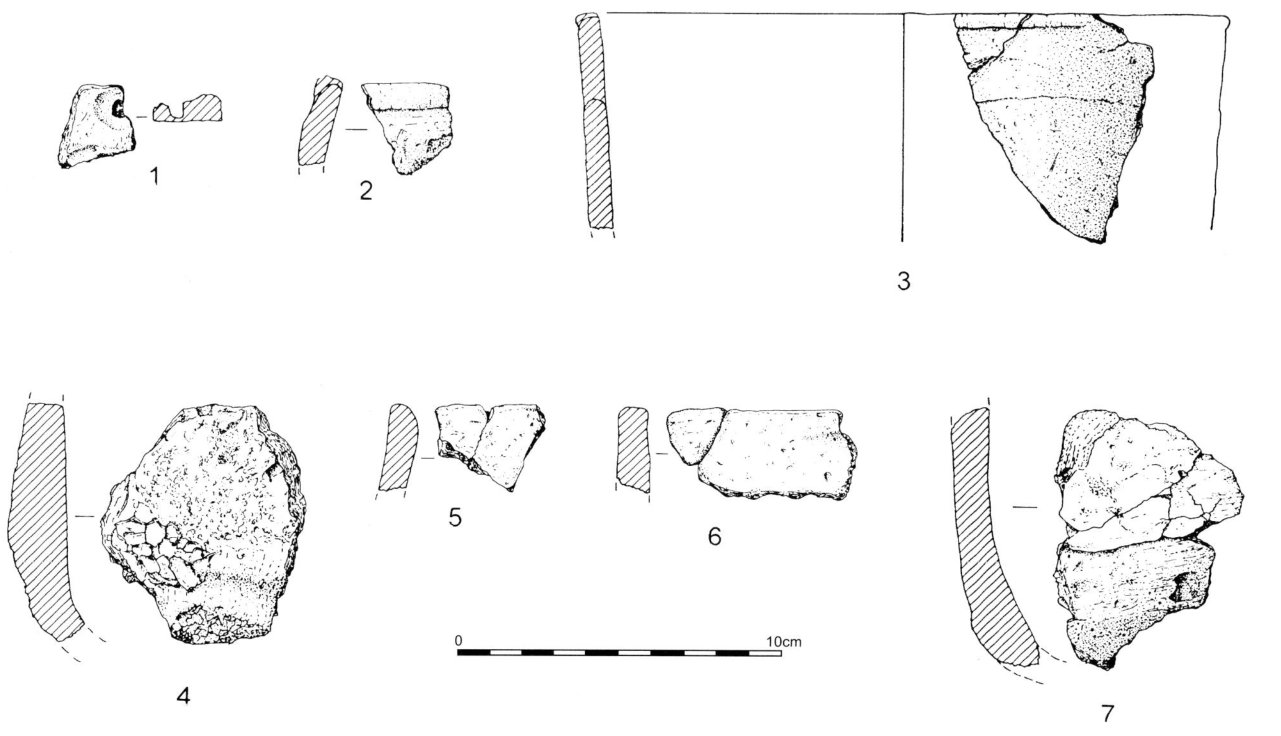

Figure 32. The pottery from DB contexts

Table 4. Artefacts from DB

	Bone/Antler		Iron					Stone		
Context	**Handle**	**Comb**	**Rove**	**Holdfast**	**Nail**	**Bar**	**Plate**	**Flint**	**Whetstone**	**Bowl**
204	2		1							
205								1		
227/232				1		1				
237										1
216/607		1							1	
211					1			4		
210		1					1			
Total	2	2	1	1	1	1	1	5	1	1

with very low densities of cereals and weed seeds per litre of soil. Barley is the most commonly identified cereal but oats and rye are present in all the samples. Flax is present in two samples. Small fragments of hazel and narrow stems from a member of the heather family were recorded in samples from 227 and 247, respectively. The heather family was also identified from handpicked charcoal from context 210 (Table 70).

Animal bone – C Ingrem, J Mulville and J Cartledge

The animal bone assemblage from DB was the largest from any of the stratigraphic units on mound 3, contributing 45% of the NISP, though the overall numbers are still small in relation to the material recovered from the other mounds. The assemblage comes from a range of different contexts with no one context contributing more than 18% of the total (Table 6). The final brown sands contained a large group of material but the lower contexts 209, 210, 214 and 215 were also rich in bone. It should be noted that the latter contexts were largely excavated by shovel and therefore small mammal bones might have been missed. However, the sheep and sheep/goat fraction from DB is larger (51%) than for the carefully excavated floor layers. Analysis of the gnawing and butchery evidence indicates that bone from the lower layers tended to be both more heavily butchered and gnawed than the bone in the upper layers. Very few bones were burnt.

Cattle, sheep/goat and pig were present, as was a fairly broad selection of other animals: dog, cat, horse, red deer, otter and some intrusive rabbits. This is an unusually rich collection for mound 3. The horse bones include a foetal metapodial, from 214, vertebra and a number of loose teeth: an adult incisor from 232, and a deciduous incisor, from 208. The presence of an articulated dog foot (metapodials and toes) and a skull fragment in 209 suggests the disposal of at least part of a complete skeleton. There were also a couple of dog toes and a vertebra in 237 and two further vertebrae in 204. The cat was represented by loose teeth and an axis. At least two red deer are present; they are represented by fragments of limb bones, mostly from the right-hand side, with a vertebra and skull fragments also present. These animals are mostly young with evidence of three neonatal bones which could have all come from a single individual. Red deer are found in many of the other contexts but elsewhere the species is represented either by antler or bones from the extremities that might have been attached to skins.

Two bird bones were identified from these layers: an ulna from a mature black-back gull in 227 and a digit from sub-adult cormorant in 237.

A small quantity (n=135) of fish bones was recovered from these layers. The majority of the identified bones from the >10mm samples belong to cod but hake is also well represented and when the estimated NISP is calculated for the <10mm samples, herring becomes dominant (Table 7). Table 8 shows the anatomical representation of the large gadid fish recovered from >10mm material. Both cranial and axial elements are represented and a consideration of the number of times that an element occurs in the body suggests that vertebrae are under-represented. In contrast, the estimated anatomical representation for herring and whiting in the <10mm material suggests that cranial elements are under-represented (Table 8).

Marine shell – N Sharples

Winkles dominate the assemblage from DB providing 73% of the total quantities of shells recovered from the samples (Table 9). Only two layers (214, 227) had assemblages with limpets dominant and these were both layers with low densities of shells. Only three other species were recorded and crab was present in only one sample (227).

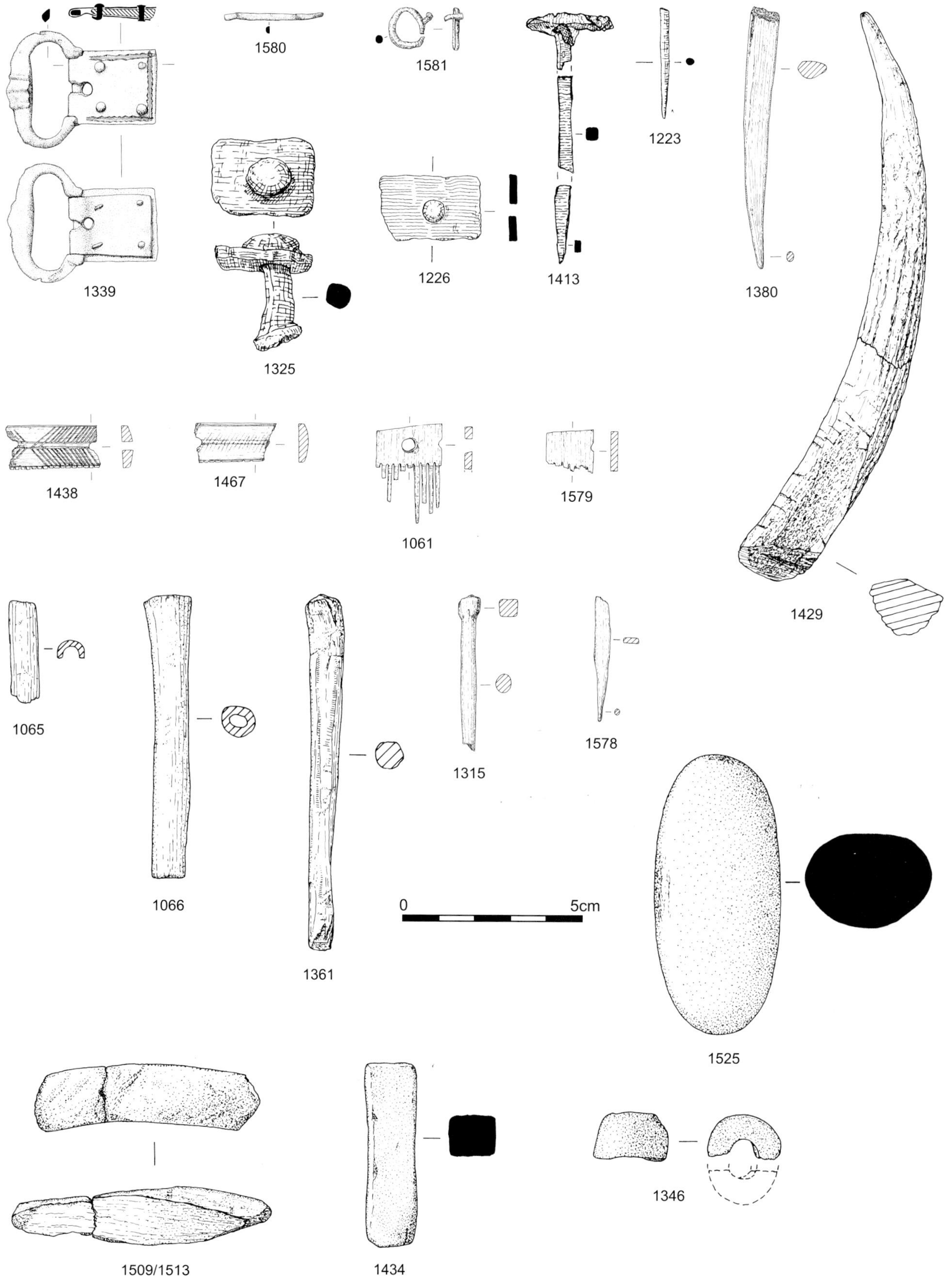

Figure 33. The artefacts found in trench D: 1339, 1580 copper alloy; 1325, 1581, 1226, 1413 iron; 1525, 1509/1513, 1434 stone; all the others bone and antler

Table 5. The charred plant remains from DB

sample number	context		volume floated (litres)	volume of charcoal (cm^3)	charcoal density (cm^3/l)	*Hordeum sativum* - grains	*Secale cereale* - grains	*Avena* cf. *sativa* - grains	Cereal indet - grains	Cereal/Gramineae - culm frags (?)	Cereals per litre of soil	Caryophyllaceae (several species)	*Chenopodium* spp.	Cruciferae (several species)	*Carex* spp. (/*Scirpus* spp.)	cf. *Fumaria* sp.	Gramineae Indet (various spp)	*Linum* sp.	*Polygonum*/*Rumex* spp.	Cereals per litre of soil	Indet/unident specimens	wood charcoal	dung/peat/organic frags
5750	**227**	**DB**	20	3.4	0.2	7	2	9	x		0.90		1	1					1	0.15	x	x	x
5771	**232**		19	2.4	0.1	18	1	2	x		1.11	1	1	1	1		1	1	1	0.37	x	x	x
5818	**247**		14	1.8	0.1	19	1	3	x		1.64	3			2	2	1	4		0.86	x	x	x
	Total		53	7.6		44	4	14	0	0	1.17	4	2	2	3	2	2	5	2	0.42			

Table 6. Animal bone NISP from DB

Unit	CTX	Sheep/Goat	Sheep	Cattle	Pig	Dog	Cat	Horse	Red deer	Otter	Total
DB	204/205/206	31		19	3	2			2		57
	227/232	3	10	14							27
	247	5	1	3	1						10
	612/613	1		2							3
	208	27	1	26	3				2	1	60
	237	1	5	5		2					13
	216	2									2
	226			2							2
	211	10		2			1		1		14
	209	18		5		4		1	3		31
	210	14		13	4	2			1		34
	214	25	1	8	4			1	1		40
	215	14	1	15	3				1		34
DB Total		151	19	114	18	10	1	2	11	1	327
		46%	6%	35%	6%	3%	<1%	1%	3%	<1%	

Discussion – N Sharples

This group of contexts is probably the least coherent of all the stratigraphic blocks from mound 3. It clearly represents a sequence of activities and the radiocarbon dates suggest these layers formed over a relatively long period of time, possibly long enough to cover a major change in the development of the ceramic record – the appearance of platter. The alternating sequence of light and dark brown sand layers probably indicates periods when human activity and, in particular, house construction alternate with periods of abandonment, or relative inactivity, in this part of the mound. It is certainly the case that the final brown sand contexts were closely associated with the construction, and possibly the use of, the final house (DC) and there is therefore a chronological overlap between the top of DB and the succeeding block DC.

The contexts have produced a reasonably substantial quantity of animal bone, pottery and small finds, though the lack of intensive sampling meant that the fish bone and carbonised plant assemblages were not very substantial. The absence of platter from the lowest layers has already been noted and it is also important to note the absence of definitely everted rims and decoration from any of these contexts. This is the best evidence from mound 3 that these formal traits have a chronological significance but this observation will have to wait for the analysis of the

Table 7. Fish bone from DB

a. > 10 mm samples (NISP): b. < 10 mm samples (estimated NISP).

	216a	226a	227a	227b	232a	232b	237a	247a	606a	606b	612a	613a	Total
Herring				16		56				48			120
Eel				32									32
Whiting						8							8
Pollack					2		1	1				1	5
Saithe								1					1
Cod	1	1	11		2		7	7	6		9	6	50
Hake		2	9				6	2			1		20
Ling							5	2					7
Large gadid			1		12		6	2	1	4	1	1	28
Medium gadid								1					1
Ballan wrasse			1										1
Mackerel					1								1
Flatfish						8							8
Total	1	3	22	48	17	72	25	16	7	52	11	8	282

Table 8. The anatomical representation of major fish species from DB

Species in over 10mm material (NISP) and under 10mm, shaded (estimated NISP).

	Pollack	Cod	Hake	Ling	Total	Herring	Whiting	Total
Premaxilla		6	1		7			
Maxilla	1	3	2	2	8			
Dentary			2		2			
Articular	1	8			9			
Hyomandibular		2			2			
Opercular		1			1			
Cleithrum					0			
Supracleithrum		3	1		4			
Posttemporal		2			2			
AAV	1				1			
PAV	1	15	5	4	25	32		32
CV	1	10	9	1	21	88	8	96
Vert.frag.								
Total	5	50	20	7	82	120	8	128
%	6	61	24	9	100			

AAV = anterior abdominal vertebra
PAV = posterior abdominal vertebra
CV = caudal vertebra

Table 9. Marine shell from DB

Context	No of samples	Litres	Limpet	Winkle	Flat periwinkle	Iceland cyprine	Common mussel	Crab
205						1		
208	1	30	31	217	1			
210	1	28	14	19				
211	1	30	40	72				
214	1	25	11	6				
227	1	20	5				1	+
232	1	19	37	71				
247	1	14	7	32	1			
606	1	9	17	29				
Total			162	446	2	1	1	

material from mounds 2 and 2A to be confirmed. The animal bone assemblage was dominated by sheep but included a much wider range of species than the other blocks. This included prime meat bones from red deer, which is the only evidence for the consumption of venison rather than the use of antler and skins.

The main house (DC) – N Sharples

The house was a strikingly unimpressive structure (Figure 34). It was defined by a revetment wall (213) of normally two, but occasionally three, courses, 0.25 m high and with a stretch of approximately 1.6 m of the wall missing in the centre of the east side. The stones used were of small to medium size, 0.5 m by 0.3 m, and had been smoothed by water (Figure 35). The structure defined was 4.0 m wide and 7.2 m long internally and was oriented roughly north to south (Figure 36). It had a single east-facing entrance that opened into the centre of the northern half of the building (Figure 35). The entrance was defined by two walls that created a passage approximately 0.65 m wide and 1.7 m long. The transition from the passage to the interior was marked by a threshold stone and a drop to the floor level of 0.10 m.

No post holes were located inside the walls and there is no positive evidence for the nature of the superstructure. The absence of a large amount of tumble inside the house

Figure 34. A view of the house in trench D near the end of the 1997 excavation

Figure 35. A view of the entrance to the house under excavation

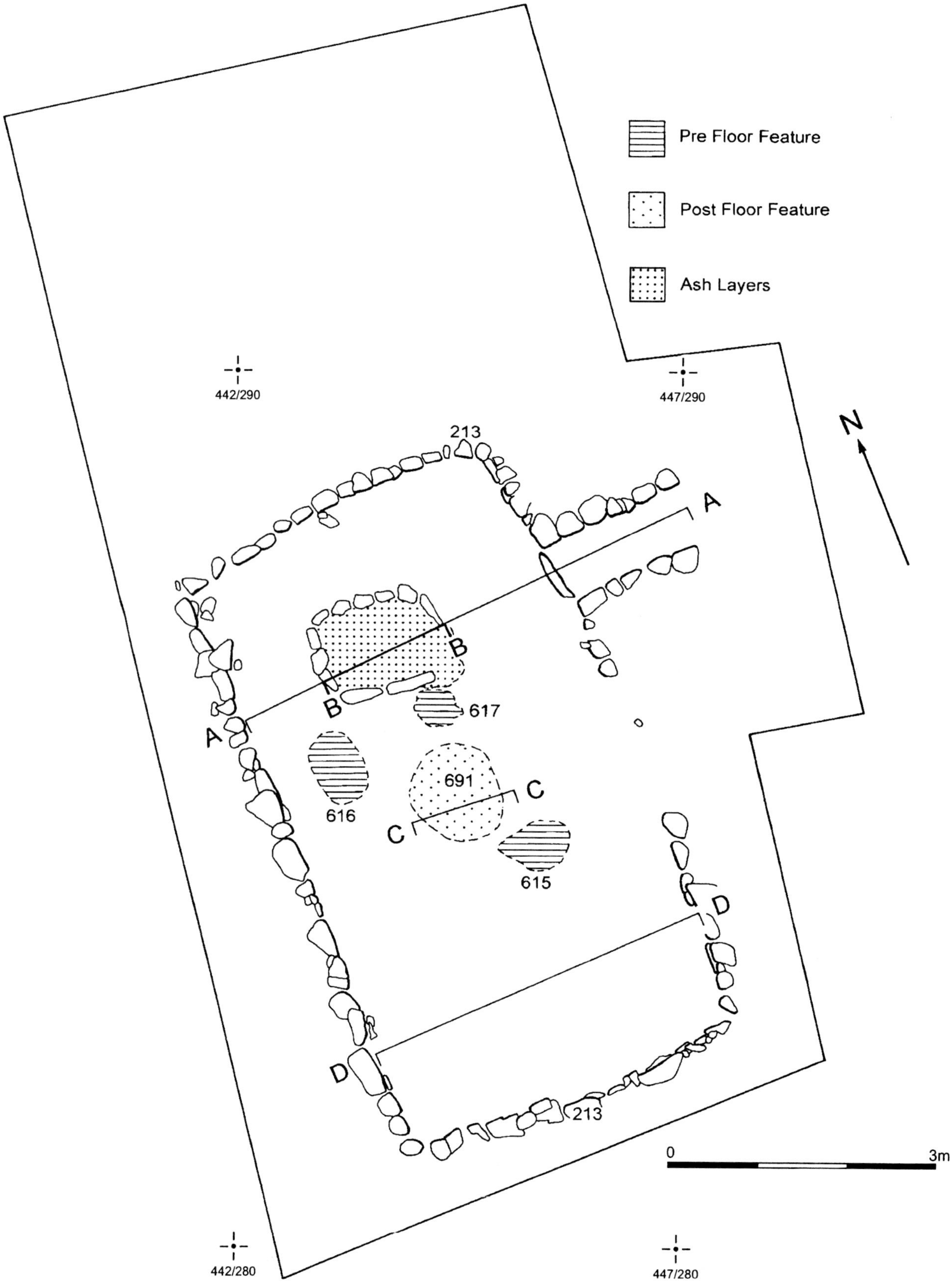

Figure 36. A plan of the house showing features found in and under the floor level and the location of the sections in Figure 37

and the relatively uniform low height of the wall suggests that this might have been the original height of the stone walls. The alternative is to assume a substantial and uniform lowering of the wall. If the walls are more or less intact then it suggests that the wall core was made of turf and that the surviving stone revetment supported an internal timber superstructure. No evidence for the extent of this turf wall was found and there was no eaves drip gully such as that found around house 007 at Cille Pheadair (Brennand, Parker Pearson and Smith 1998). A detailed discussion of the possible form of this building is provided in chapter 11.

The house floors (DD) – N Sharples

The occupation of the house is represented by:

- Three thin charcoal layers that cover the area within wall 213 (Figure 37).
- Three features cut into the underlying stratigraphy and sealed by the floor layers.
- A stone-lined hearth (Figure 38) and associated ash dump.
- A single floor layer in the passage.

Unfortunately the excavation of these contexts was not perfect. The initial trial excavation removed the upper two floor layers (as layer 212) before their significance

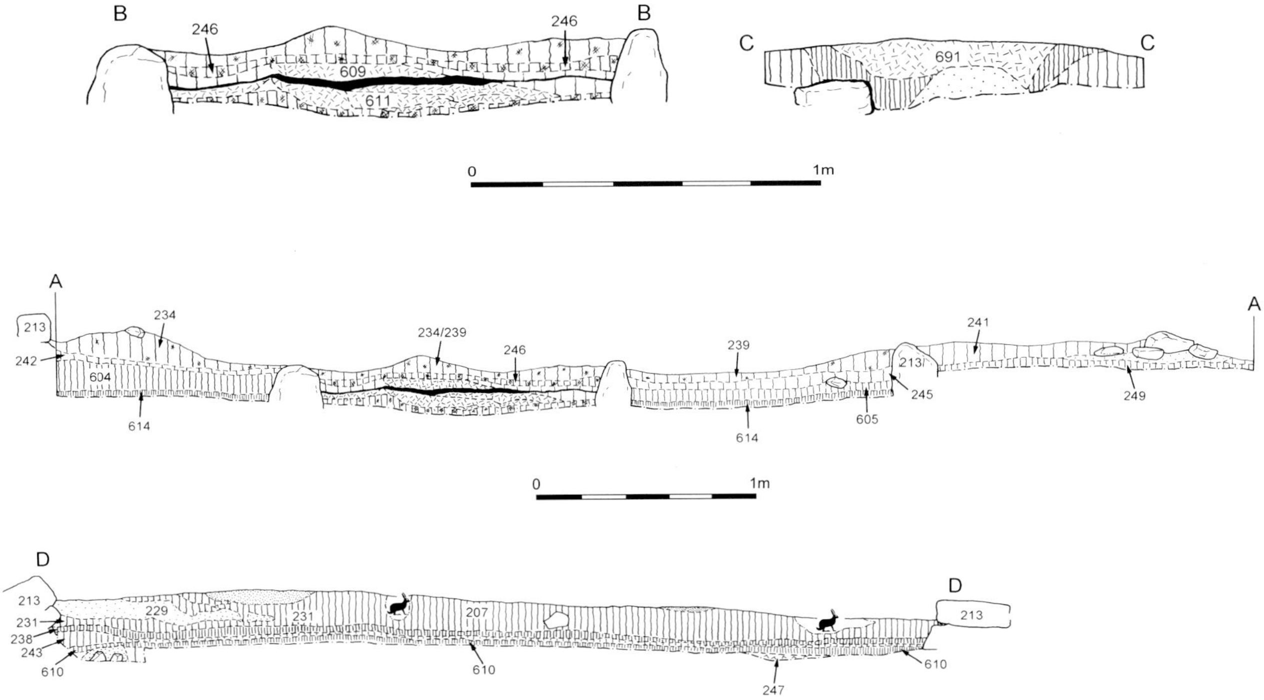

Figure 37. Sections through the house floors

Figure 38. A view of the hearth with the ash fill, half sectioned

was understood. This means that both the later floor layers have a strip of unsampled deposits with no data across the centre of the house. The understanding of the floor layers is also inhibited by serious rabbit disturbance of the southern half of the house floor. The excavation of the sub-floor features was partial and incomplete owing to time constraints.

Two of the sub-floor features (615, 616) were filled with very dark brown clayey sand (615, 616). One (617), which was close to the hearth, was filled with very dark brown sand flecked with orange clay (617). Only the first two were excavated and both pits, though of slightly different shape, had the same dimensions, up to 0.80 m long and 0.58 m wide and about 0.10 m deep.

The lowest floor layer was a black charcoal-flecked sand (614), which covered most of the interior. A radiocarbon date (OxA-10292) was obtained from a single carbonised grain of oat from sample square 8045 (Figure 39a). This produced a date of 590±50 bp, which when calibrated indicates that this occupation layer was deposited in the period cal AD 1290–1440 (95% probability). Another radiocarbon date (OxA-10304) was obtained from a single grain of oat in sample square 8077 (Figure 39a). This produced a date of 660±50 bp, which when calibrated indicates that this occupation layer was deposited in the period cal AD 1270–1410 (95% probability). It proved difficult to identify this floor at the southern end of the house but it is not clear if this

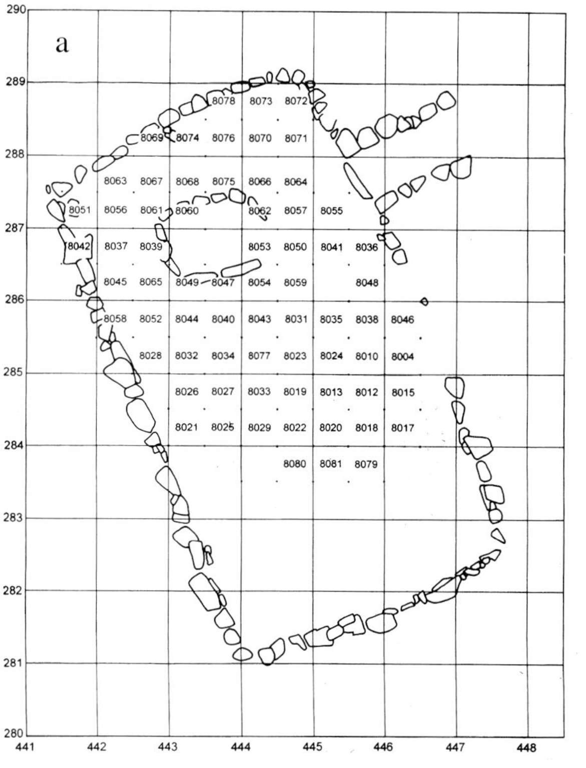

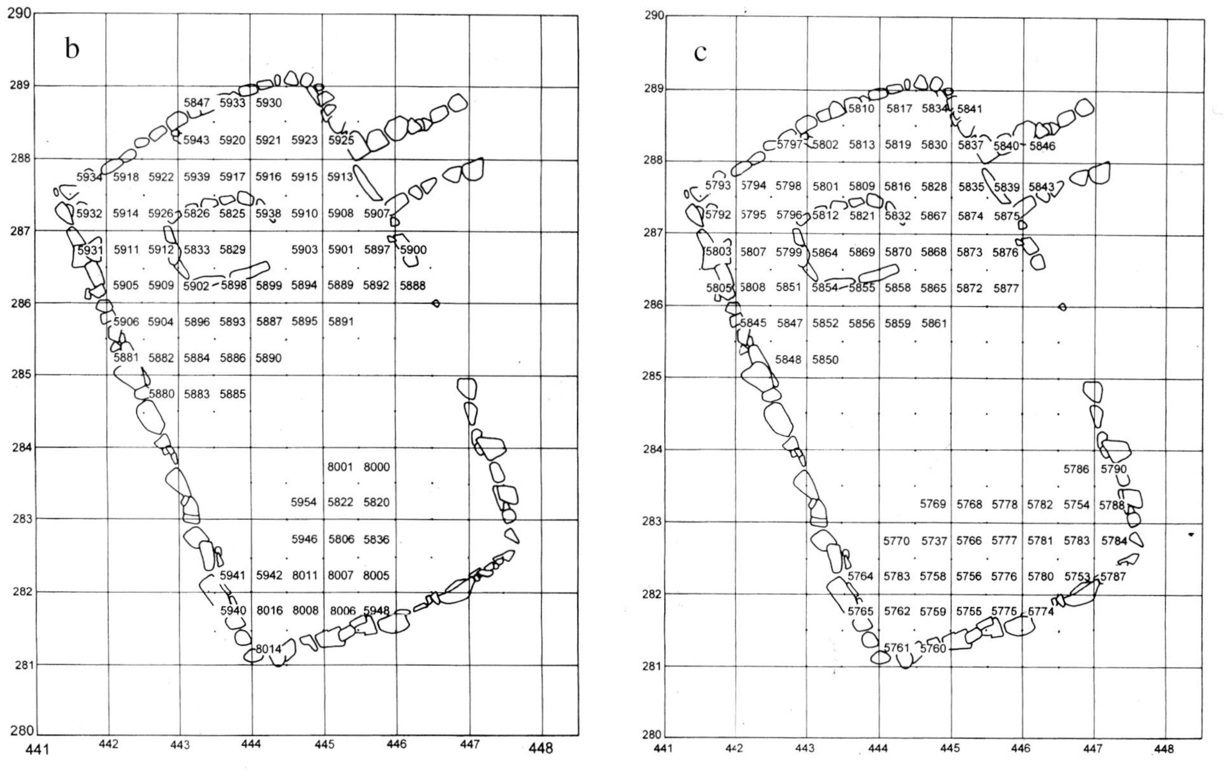

Figure 39. Plan of sample squares; a) floor 1, b) floor 2 and c) floor 3

was due to the extensive rabbit damage in this area or because it was not present.

The second floor was another thin layer of black charcoal-flecked sand. The south part of the house was numbered 610, the northeast 605 and the northwest 604/244; a central strip was removed as 212 in 1995. A radiocarbon date (OxA-10275) was obtained from a single carbonised grain of barley from sample square 5906 (Figure 39b) in context 604. This produced a date of 880±32 bp, which when calibrated indicates that this occupation layer was deposited around cal AD 1030–1250 (95% probability). Another radiocarbon date (OxA-10291) was obtained from a single grain of oat in sample square 5909 (Figure 39b) in context 604. This produced a date of 580±70 bp, which when calibrated indicates that this occupation layer was deposited in the period cal AD 1310–1450 (95% probability). The former date appears to be too early and may indicate residual material incorporated in the floor.

The upper floor layer was a layer of brown sand with charcoal flecks. This was numbered 238 in the SW corner, 230 in the SE corner, 602 in the centre east, 601 in the centre west, 245 in the NE and 242 in the NW. This layer was separated from the underlying floor by a thin wedge of yellow sand (243) in the SE corner of the house. Incorporated within this floor layer was a dump of shells (248) in the extreme NE corner of the house. In the passage the occupation of the house was represented by a single layer of charcoal-flecked, dark brown sand (249/608).

In the centre of the north half of the house was a hearth edged with upright stones (Figure 38). This was rectangular with a slightly out-curved east end. The stones used were medium-sized water-worn cobbles 0.4 to 0.5 m long, 0.3 to 0.4 m deep and 0.1 to 0.2 m thick. The fill of this hearth overlay a charcoal-rich sand that was similar to the floor layers. The hearth fill was excavated as three separate layers (Figure 37). At the bottom was brown sand with charcoal and orange clay flecks (611), over this was a layer of mixed orange clay and charcoal patches (609) and above this was a dark sand with a lot of charcoal (246/603).

In the centre of the house to the south of the hearth was a circular deposit of yellow clayey sand (691). This appears (Figure 37) to be the fill of a pit 0.95 m wide and 1.12 m long. The central fill was a bright yellow ash but the area around the edge of the pit was a more mixed brown/yellow sand. A mound of white sand had been placed on the bottom of the pit prior to it being infilled. This pit cut all the floor layers and may well be connected with the abandonment of the house.

Sampling – P Marshall, H Smith and N Sharples

Two hundred and fifty-eight samples, 2363 litres of soil, were taken as bulk samples and processed from the DD contexts: 86 from floor 3 (top), 74 from floor 2, 69 from floor 1 (bottom) and 29 from other contexts, 160 of these samples had the below 10 mm residue sorted. It was felt that the amount of rabbit disturbance undermined the integrity of floors and so only five samples from this floor had their fine residues (below 10 mm) examined.

The residue from the above 10 mm sort produced the usual material; fish bone (an average density of 0.24 pieces per litre), bone (also 0.24 pieces per litre), pot (0.17 pieces per litre), and marine molluscs, with a few samples producing charcoal and BOM (burnt organic material). The lowest floor appears to have the densest quantity of material for all categories and the non-floor contexts, largely the hearth and passage layers, produced the least material.

The standard range of material was recovered during

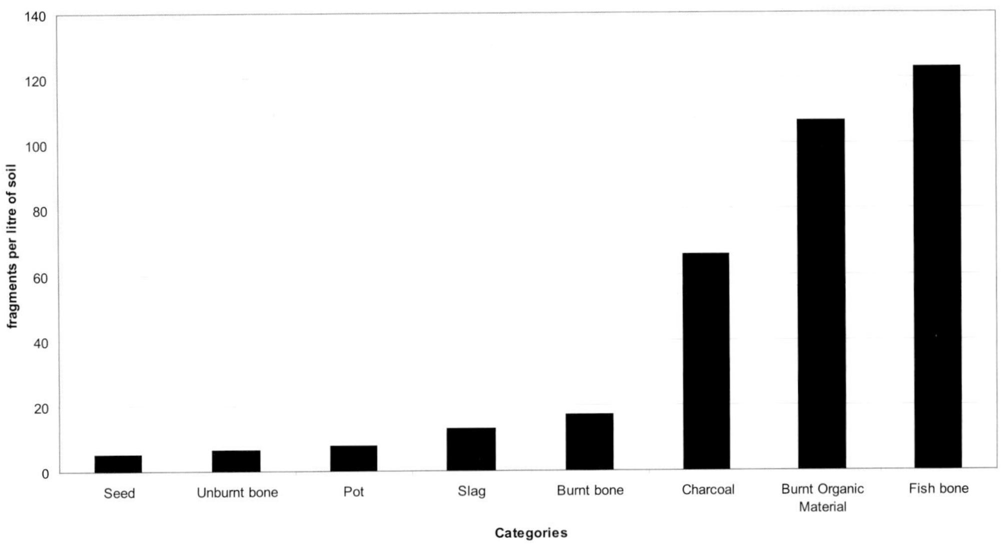

Figure 40. A comparison of the average densities of material from the house occupation deposits

the sorting of the below 10 mm residue. Burnt bone, fish bone and charcoal was present in all samples and BOM was present in all but one sample. Unburnt bone was present in 94% of the samples, pot in 86% and slag in 80%. The average densities of the main materials present are shown in Figure 40. Fish bone was the most common material found and has a particularly high density in floor 1 (191 fragments per litre of soil). The lowest densities were in floor 3 but only a small number of samples were examined and these may be unrepresentative. The four categories that follow this in density, BOM, charcoal, burnt bone and slag (non-metallurgical) are all debris from a fire and presumably indicate the source for most of the floor deposits was ash produced by the hearth and redistributed across the interior of the house. The remaining categories of material, pot, unburnt bone and seed, are probably the result of domestic activity and food consumption in the house. Unburnt bone was common in floor 2 whereas pot, like fish bone, was more common in floor 1 and also had high densities in the hearth. Despite the low average densities, in isolated samples seed occasionally occured in very large numbers.

Floor 1

Total phosphorus concentrations in the lower house floor range from 1036–5731 mg/kg, with an average of 2490 mg/kg. The distribution of P (Figure 41) is mostly uniform, with a spread of the higher concentrations in the central area of the floor. P concentration is also high in the north of the house, away from the areas of burning, and this may represent the build-up of organic waste at the junction between wall and floor, where areas are less frequently cleaned. Lower values occur around the edge of the building and especially along the western edge of the floor (1218–1440 mg/kg). The pattern shown in phosphorus is mostly mirrored by the concentration of nitrogen (Figure 41). Values range from 162–1592 mg/kg, with an average of 838 mg/kg. Slightly lower values occur in the northern area of the floor and generally around the perimeter of the building (e.g. 263–573 mg/kg). Although nitrogen is not commonly included in geoarchaeological studies, owing to its more transient nature, the similarity in distribution of both P and N is to be expected, as both are likely to be derived from the deposition or accumulation of organic materials.

Magnetic susceptibility values (χ) vary from 53–913 ($10^{-8}m^3kg^{-1}$) with an average of 226 ($10^{-8}m^3kg^{-1}$). The distribution of χ is shown in Figure 41. There is an area of enhanced χ to the east of the stone-lined hearth spreading towards the entrance area (605–622 ($10^{-8}m^3kg^{-1}$)) and a second area in the southern part of the house floor, immediately to the south of the central hearth (508–913 ($10^{-8}m^3kg^{-1}$)). Lower values are found in the north-western and southeastern areas of the floor and mostly around the edges of the building.

The distribution of the material from sorting the above 10 mm fraction is depicted in Figure 41. In contrast to the distribution of bone recovered from the fine fraction, the bone of larger size has a peripheral distribution, concentrating along the east side of the house. The most substantial quantities occur in the middle of the east side, though generally numbers are higher around the hearth in the north half of the building. The east half of the building also produced the bulk of the marine shell, with two separate concentrations in the south and north half of the building. The northern concentration is by far the larger concentration and extends along the north wall. The fish bone is more evenly spread across the floor with a single large sample immediately to the south of the hearth. The pottery is slightly more complex with significant differences between the north and south halves of the building. In the north the most substantial concentrations occur to the north of the hearth with very little from the rest of the area. In the south half of the building there is a more even distribution of medium density samples across the interior.

The distribution of the material recovered from sorting the fine fraction (<10mm) is depicted in Figure 42. The fragments of unburnt mammal bone are most obviously concentrated at the south end of the building, whilst fish bones are concentrated around the hearth. There are subsidiary concentrations of both these materials around the edges of the floor. The burnt materials display similar patterns in their distribution. Carbonised seeds are concentrated in and to the south of the hearth, whilst charcoal is concentrated around the hearth (especially to the east) and to the south of the doorway, with subsidiary concentrations along the western edge of the floor. Burnt bone fragments are concentrated in the hearth. Burnt organic matter (BOM), pot and slag show concentrations in the northeastern area of the floor, though slag also has a high density in one sample in the south end of the building.

Floor 2

Total phosphorus concentrations in the middle house floor range from 691–5514 mg/kg, with an average of 2142 mg/kg. The distribution of P (Figure 43) is mostly uniform, although in general the higher values occur in the central (to the east of the hearth) and southern part of the house, and the lower values to the north and west. The pattern shown in phosphorus is mostly mirrored by the concentration of nitrogen (Figure 43), as it was in the case of the lower house floor. N values range from 425–1526 mg/kg, with an average of 859 mg/kg.

Magnetic susceptibility values (χ) vary from 48–590 ($10^{-8}m^3kg^{-1}$) with an average of 142 ($10^{-8}m^3kg^{-1}$), lower than the earlier floor. The distribution of χ is shown in Figure 43. There is an area of enhanced χ in the northern area of the floor, to the east of the hearth (169–305 ($10^{-8}m^3kg^{-1}$) and the higher values in the range also occur towards the south of the building.

The distribution of P, N and χ shows enhanced values to the east of the kerbed hearth and towards the entrance

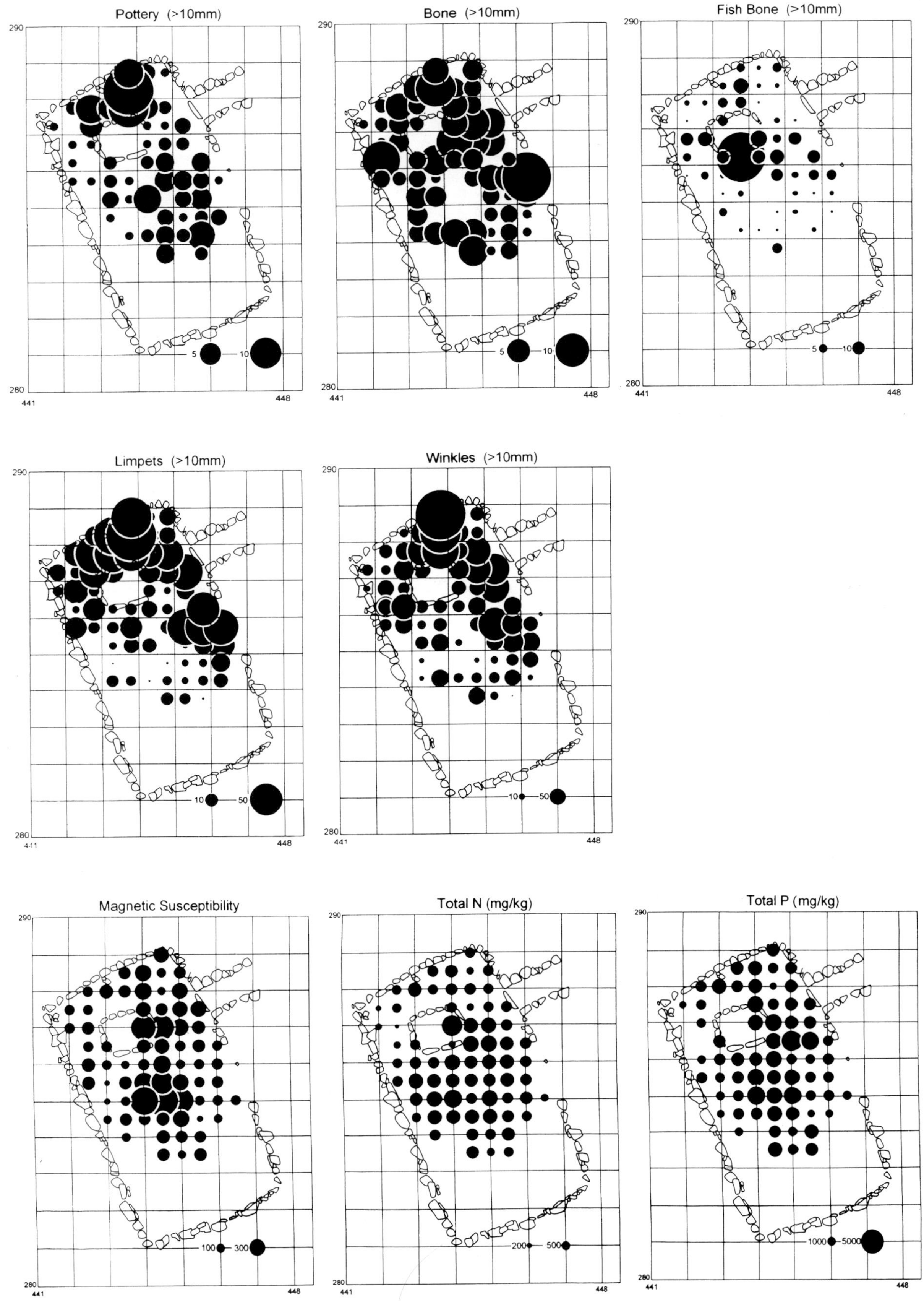

Figure 41. Floor 1: distribution maps of the material recovered (number of fragments) during sieving through a 10 mm mesh and the results of the chemical analysis of the soil

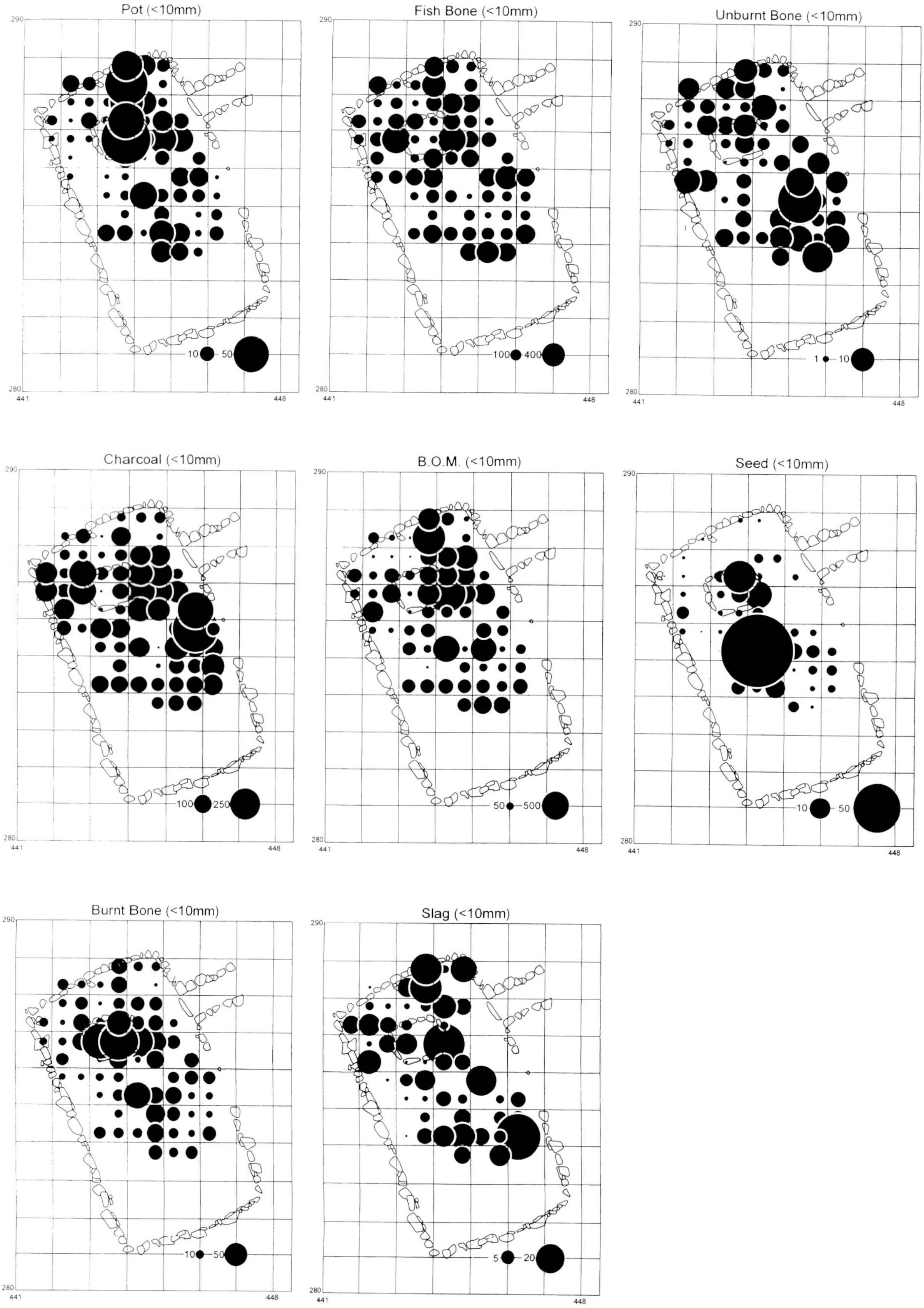

Figure 42. Floor 1: distribution maps of the material recovered (number of fragments per litre of soil) from sorting the below 10 mm residues

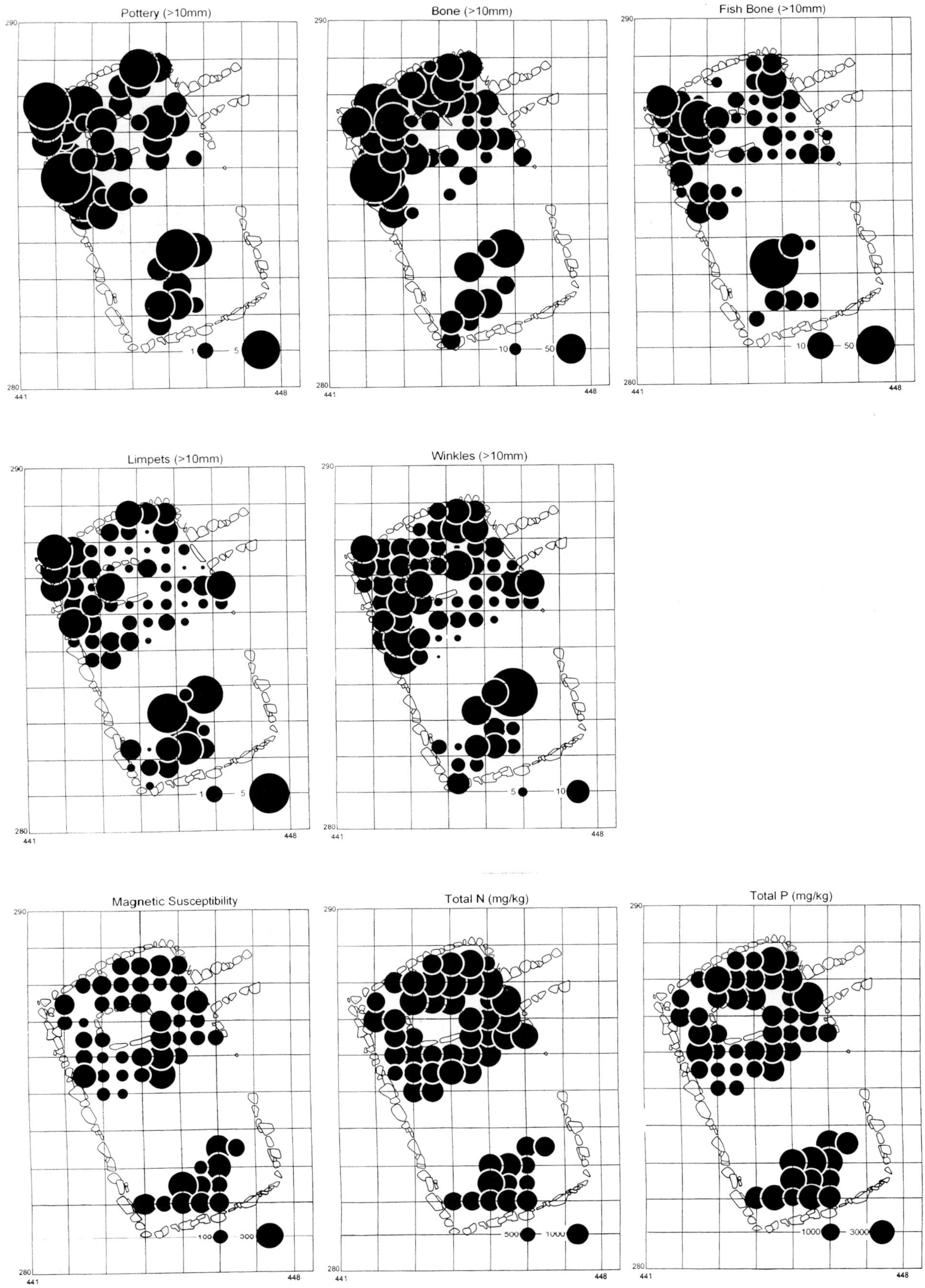

Figure 43. Floor 2: distribution maps of the material recovered (number of fragments) during sieving through a 10 mm mesh and the results of the chemical analysis of the soil

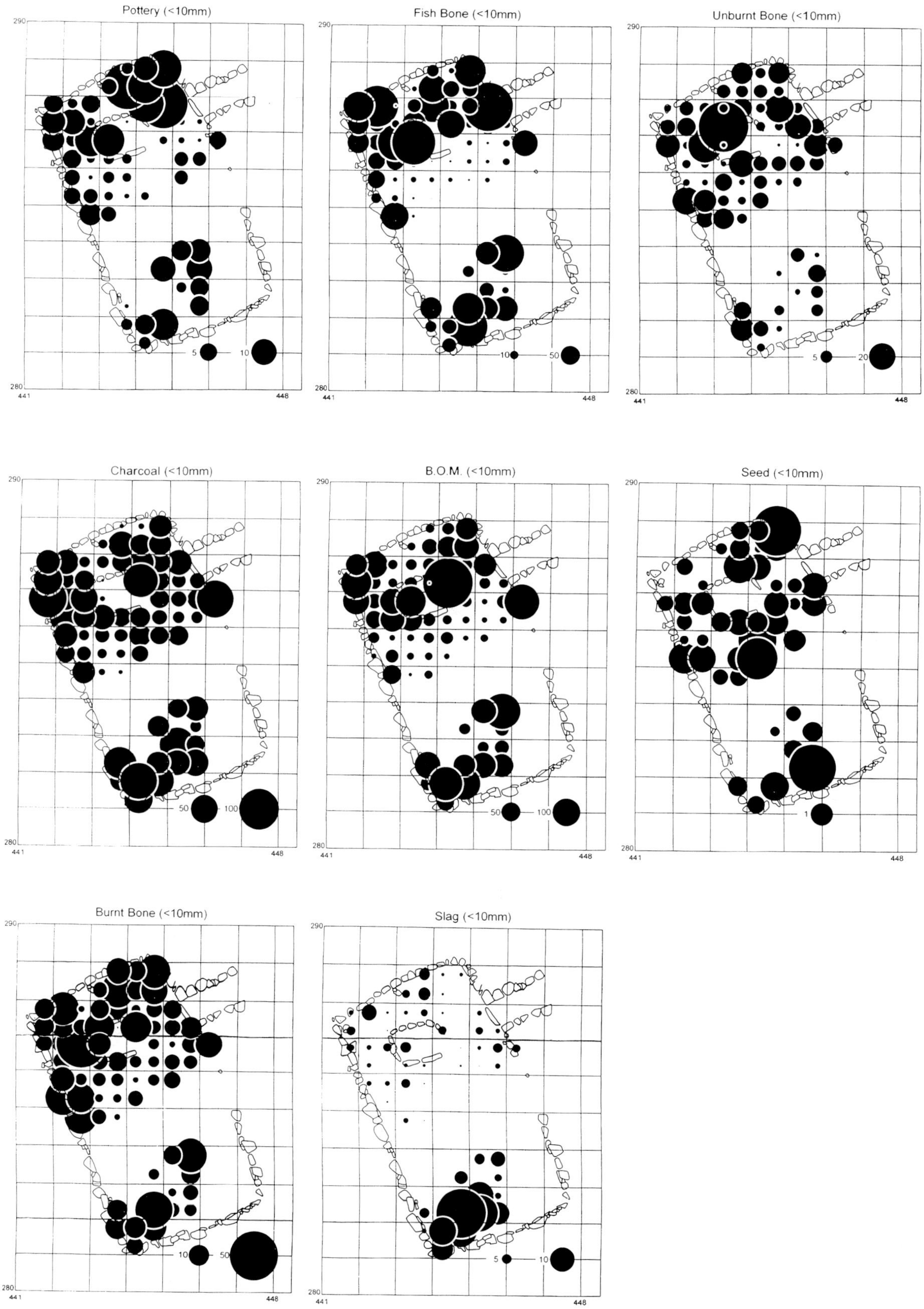

Figure 44. Floor 2: distribution maps of the material recovered (number of fragments per litre of soil) from sorting the below 10 mm residues

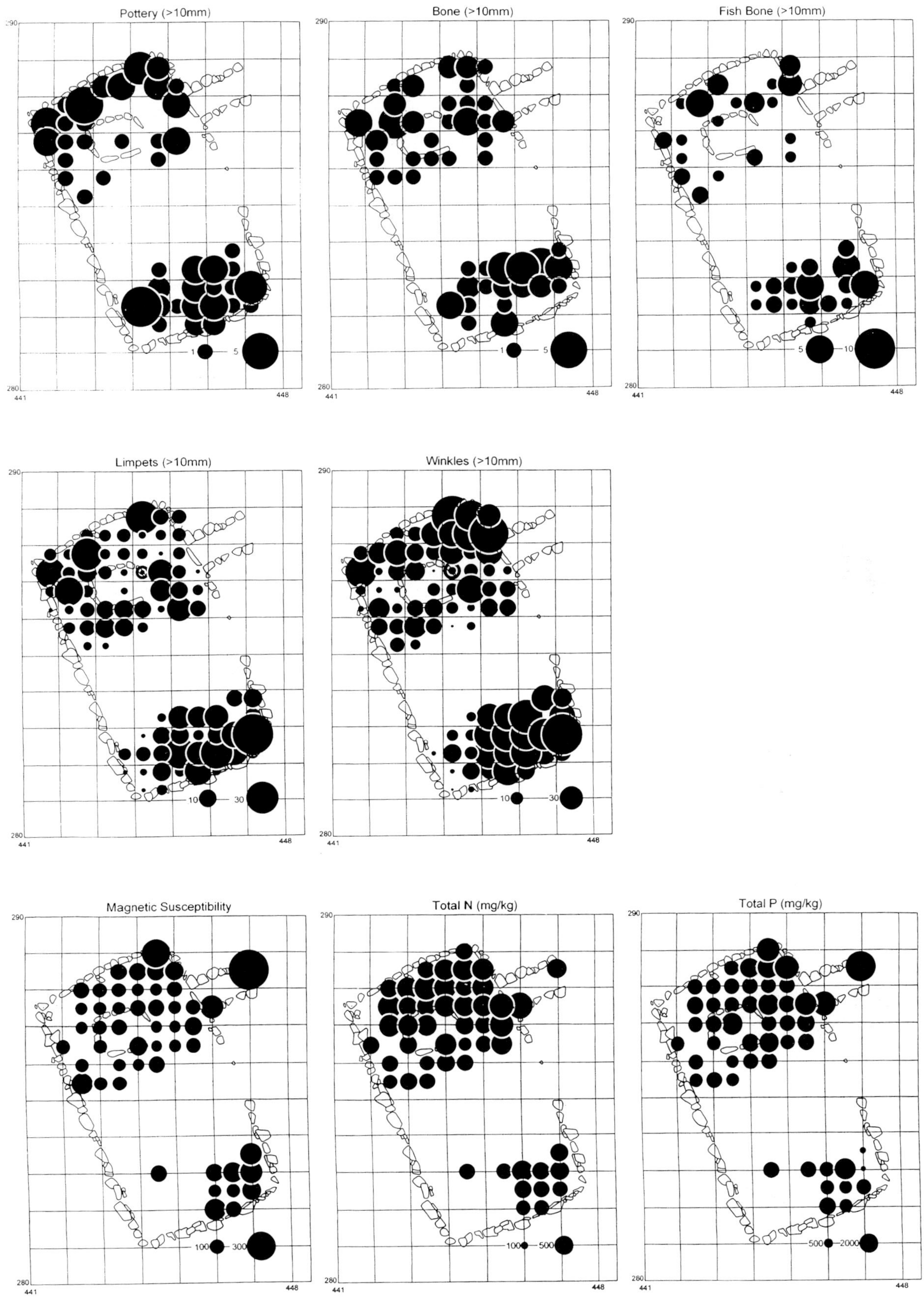

Figure 45. Floor 3: distribution maps of the material recovered (number of fragments) during sieving through a 10 mm mesh and the results of the chemical analysis of the soil

to the house. This may represent ash raked away from the hearth and swept or trampled towards the entrance or the deliberate deposition of the peat ash as a floor constituent.

The distribution of the material from sorting the above 10 mm fraction is depicted in Figure 43. The pottery fragments are peripheral, as they are in the fine fraction, but in contrast to the fine fraction the major concentration is along the west side of the north half of the building. This is also where most of the large fragments of fish bone came from and some of the samples with high densities of bone, though these also have a northeast concentration. There is a significant difference between the distribution of the winkles and limpets. The winkles are fairly evenly distributed across the north half of the building but the limpets are concentrated along the west side and at the south end.

The distribution of the material recovered from sorting the fine fraction (<10mm) is depicted in Figure 44. The burnt bone, charcoal and BOM have fairly similar distributions with a large concentration in the southwest corner of the house and one either side of the hearth. The slag distribution has a concentration in the southwest corner but densities are very low throughout the north end of the building. The distribution of carbonised plant remains is, however, quite different with concentrations in the centre of the house and in the northeast corner. Unburnt bone is generally found around the hearth whereas the fish bone is widely distributed across the north with concentrations in the south end as well. Pottery is also concentrated in the northeast and to a lesser extent the northwest corners of the house.

Floor 3

Total phosphorus concentrations in the upper house floor range from 227–4265 mg/kg, with an average of 1588 mg/kg, showing lower concentrations than the earlier two floors. The distribution of P (Figure 45) is mostly uniform, with slightly higher concentrations in the northern and eastern area of the floor, towards and spreading out of the entrance. Lower values occur in the western and southern area (e.g. 227–1287 mg/kg). The pattern shown in phosphorus is mirrored by the concentration of nitrogen (Figure 45), as before. Values range from 122–1305 mg/kg, with an average of 729.18 mg/kg. Higher values occur in the northern area of the floor and lower values in the western and southern area of the floor (e.g. 474–641 mg/kg).

Magnetic susceptibility values (χ) vary from 56–587 ($10^{-8}m^3kg^{-1}$) with an average of 118 ($10^{-8}m^3kg^{-1}$). The distribution of χ is shown in Figure 45. Higher values occur in the northern area of the floor and around the entrance and passage (202–586 ($10^{-8}m^3kg^{-1}$)), which mirrors the distribution of P and N. The occurrence of higher χ and P values together indicates concentrations of ash in these locations and could represent trampling and/or sweeping of ash out of the house.

The distribution of the material recovered from the above 10 mm fraction is shown in Figure 45 (the below 10 mm residues were not sorted). The distributions emphasise the importance of the south end of the building which produced large quantities of most material. In the north the high density samples have a very peripheral distribution, particularly along the north wall. Bone is found closer to the hearth with slightly increased densities in the northeast corner and between the hearth and the entrance. Fish bones are less common and only a couple of samples to the north and east of the hearth have above average densities. Winkles are found throughout the north half of the building with a concentration in the northeast and southwest corners. Limpets are less common but have slight concentration adjacent to the corners of the hearth.

Measurements – N Sharples

Sufficient animal bone and pottery were present in the samples taken from three floor layers in block DD to provide reasonable comparative samples (DD/1 397 bones, 104 potsherds; DD/2 377 bones, 94 potsherds; DD/3 202 bones, 76 potsherds). The pottery assemblage as a percentage of the animal bone assemblage was respectively 26.1% (DD/1), 24.9% (DD/2), 37.6% (DD/3) and 28% for all three floor layers. This is a higher percentage than that present in the overlying fill layers (DE) and a much higher percentage than the contexts in block FG (occupation layers on the west side of the kiln/barn). It suggests that house floors have a higher ratio of pot to bone than other fill layers and this is confirmed by analysis in other trenches (though some midden layers have exceptional pottery concentrations). This may result from a reduction in the quantity of bone present in a nominally clean domestic environment but it may also represent the increased breakage and loss of ceramics owing to activities around the domestic hearth.

The size distribution of the pottery and bone from these floors is depicted in Figure 46 and it is clearly very similar for all three layers. The mode for all three floors is 20–30 mm for both bone and pot though it is noticeable that the DD/2 pot mode is not as clearly defined as it was in the other floors. Over 90% of the bone is smaller than 60 mm. The DD/2 bone assemblage is slightly better preserved than that of the other floors but it is only a very slight difference. There is slightly more variability in the pottery assemblage; DD/3 had the most abraded assemblage, DD/1 had the lowest proportion of small sherds but is otherwise similar to DD/2.

Pottery – J Bond and A Lane (Figure 47; appendix 3)

The distribution of the pottery associated with the occupation of the house is summarised in Table 10. The pottery from the pre-floor pit 615 included one small, very fine, rim probably from an everted rim form (Figure 47, 34)

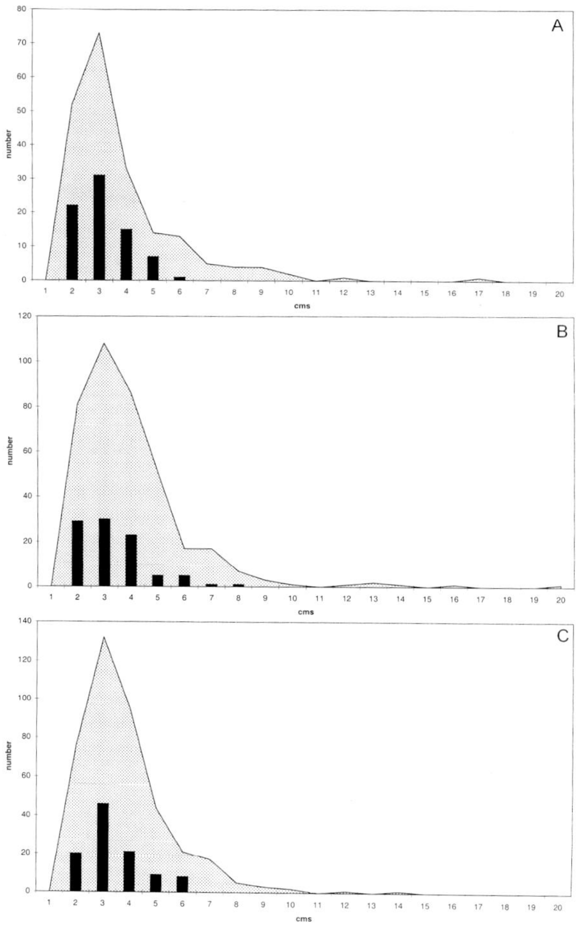

Figure 46. The size distribution of the pottery (line) and bone (column) from the house floors: A floor 3, B floor 2, C floor 1

and this is likely to be the earliest definite everted rim. The base sherds from this pit were also slightly unusual in that they have deep surface cracking on their basal surface.

Floor 1

The lower floor assemblage contains open and convex bowls, with flat and sagging bases, fine wares and platters (Figure 47, 18–24). Only angle/slab construction was noted. Many of the sherds show signs of sooting. The A fabric is the predominant type, with c. 66% of sherds being of this fabric, though two sherds of the less common D fabric were also recovered and four of uncertain A/D fabric. The fine wares account for 8.4% of all sherds and the platters 16%. The 59% of sherds classified as misc. would be increased if the small feature sherds were also included in this total, and it is clear that the house floor has seen considerable trampling activity. This latter point is reinforced if the rarity of conjoining sherds is also considered along with the average weight of 4.8g.

The distribution of the miscellaneous sherds and the diagnostic sherds is shown in Figure 48. There is no obvious pattern to this material other than to highlight the northeast corner of the structure where there is a concentration of both miscellaneous and diagnostic sherds. Diagnostic sherds also tend to be more common in the southern half of the structure, which may indicate this area was less heavily trampled or cleaned than the area around the hearth.

The rims are clearly from five different vessels, two A fabric rims from open mouthed forms (Figure 47, 23 and 24), a smaller C fabric everted rim (Figure 47, 22), an E fabric everted rim vessel (Figure 47, 19), and one small sherd of uncertain form, though possibly everted (Figure 47, 20). No vessel diameters were recoverable from either the rims or the bases, though no sherds appear to be unusually large or small.

The base sherds, all A fabric, are mostly sagging with grass-marked and/or cracked exteriors, though a few flat base sherds and one slightly footed base sherd were also recovered. The sagging bases were clustered in two main concentrations, one at either end of the floor, though individual sherds were found in other areas. The main cluster, in the northeast corner of the house (Figure 39, 8071, 8072 and 8073), contained two bases classed as slightly sagging and four sagging, which is slightly over 26% of all the bases recovered, whilst the second smaller cluster, at the south end of the floor (Figure 39, 8015 and 8020), contained four sagging bases; all the bases show signs of cooking. The bases are evenly divided between medium, thick and very thick types. It is difficult to reconstruct vessel profile from the basal sherds recovered, but it is likely that only convex and/or open mouthed bowls are present.

The body sherds are mostly of A fabric and thick, though medium examples are also present. Most of the body sherds could not be used to reconstruct vessel form, though many were noted as being curved/convex. Only a few sherds have signs of finishing, such as smoothed or wiped exteriors. Many of the A fabric body sherds show signs of sooting, as do the fine ware sherds. The fine wares account for c. 25% of body sherds, and appear to be from vessels of a similar form to the common sherds, though smaller and finer. The fine ware sherds appear across most of the floor, but there is a cluster, on the east side of the house (Figure 39, 8004, 8013, 8024 and 8038), with nearly 50% of all fine ware sherds in this area.

The platters are the normal types with a slight bias towards thick types, though medium examples are nearly as common. The one platter rim is the usual in-angled flat form, very thick at the rim, but narrower towards the centre. This sherd, like many of the platter sherds, has signs of sooting, from blackening of both surfaces, and also an off-white residue on its exterior and on its broken section, though this latter feature is not common. This sherd has a fingered interior, which is fairly common, and also has fingernail impressions, which is less common, but not that unusual. One sherd has a stabbed hole and none are pierced. Stabbed or pierced holes represent

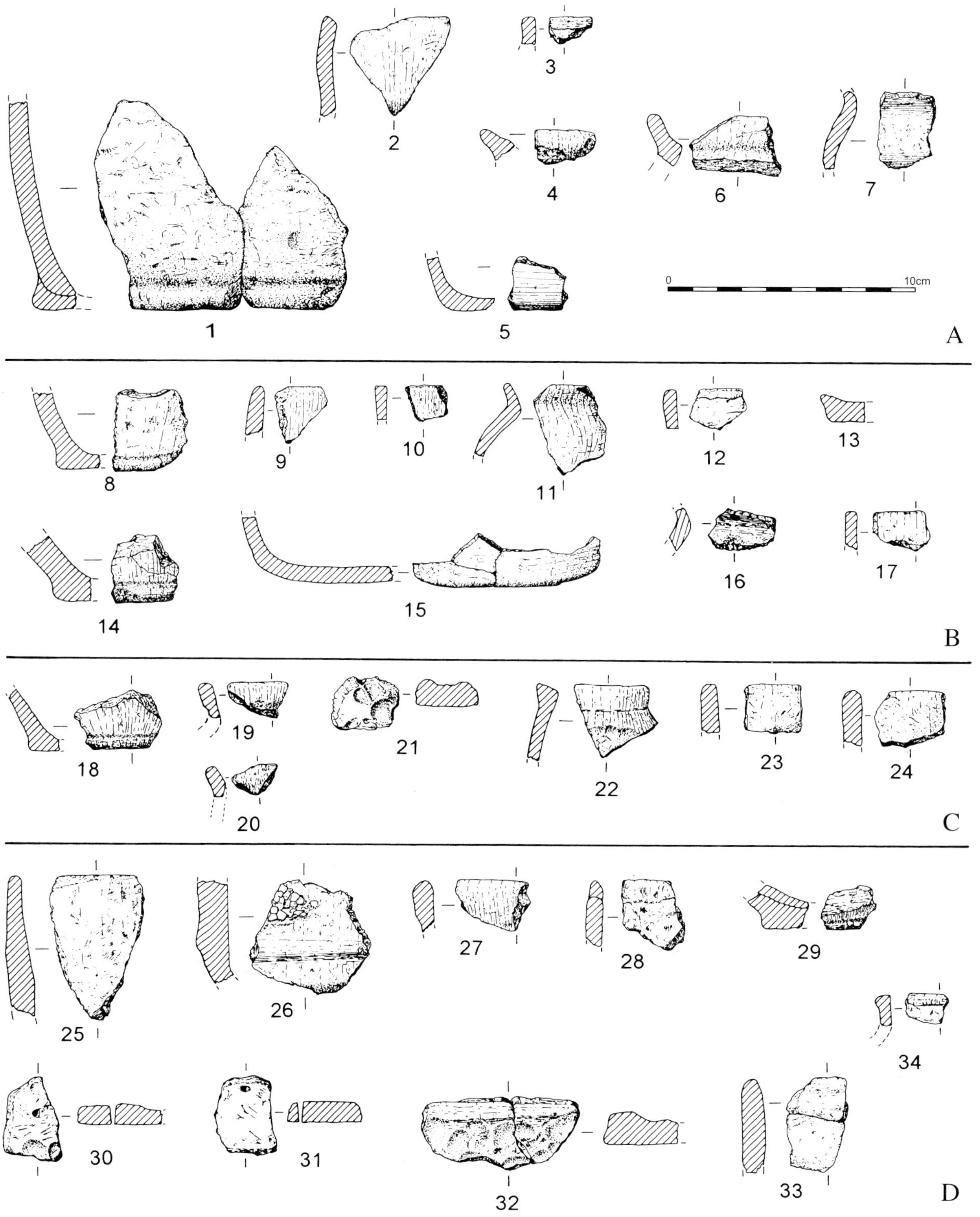

Figure 47. The pottery from house occupation contexts: A floor 3, B floor 2, C floor 1, D miscellaneous contexts

a weak point in the platters and it has been noted in other contexts that the platters sometimes fracture across such holes. The platter sherds were concentrated in two main clusters: five sherds were found at the north end of the house (Figure 39, 8069, 8070, 8074 and 8076), whilst the second cluster, which lay to the south of the hearth (Figure 39, 8032, 8033, 8034 and 8077), had seven sherds. There were another seven sherds from unlocated samples. It is possible, despite the apparent mixture of platter thickness found in the two clusters, that the platter sherds represent one vessel from each, as it is likely that variability in individual platters was considerable.

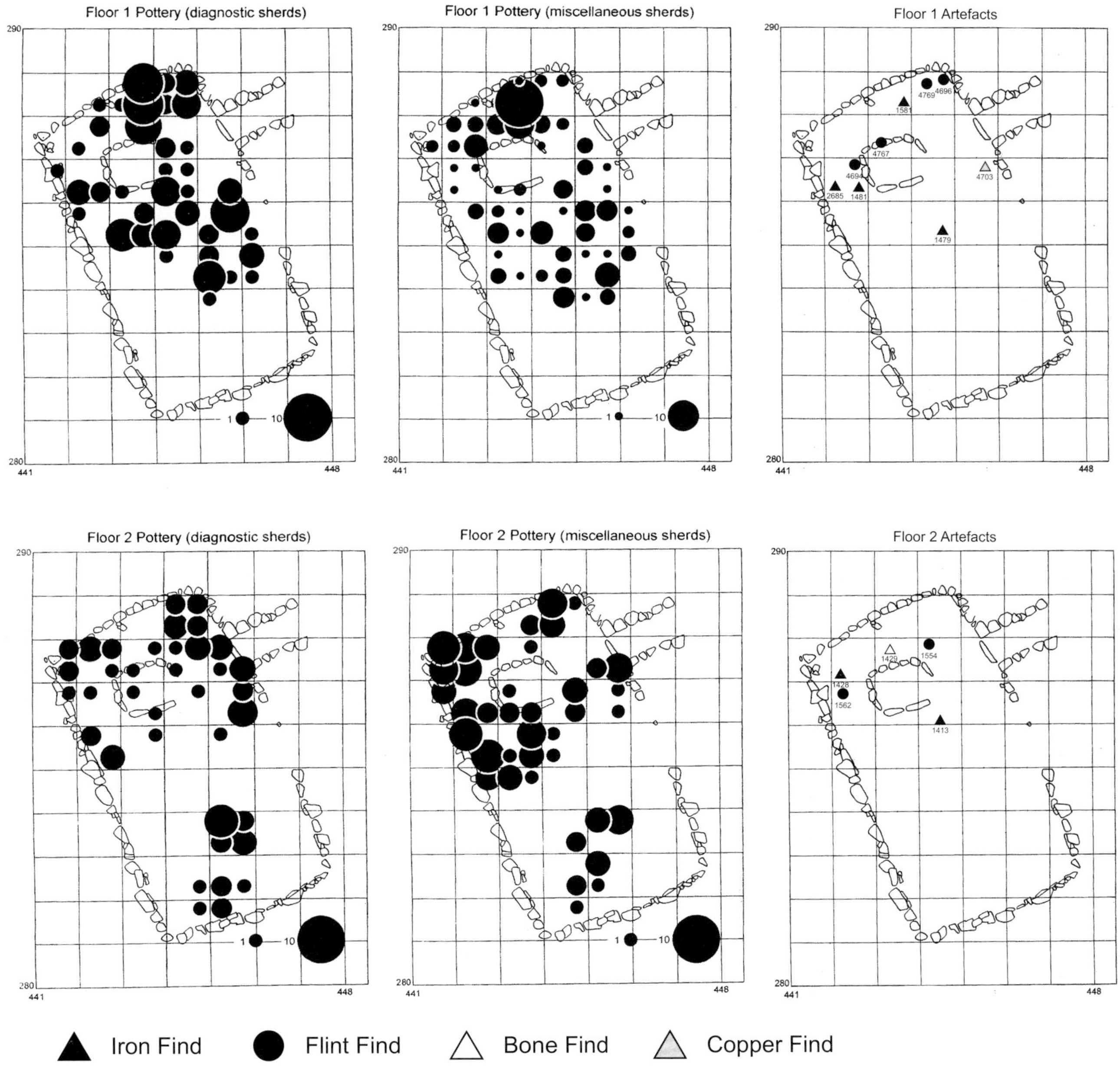

Figure 48. The distribution of the diagnostic sherds, miscellaneous sherds and artefacts from house floor one on the top and house floor two at the bottom

Floor 2

The diagnostic sherds from the middle floor include flat bases, some with grass-marking, as well as fine and well-finished, sagging bottomed fine ware vessels and platters (Figure 47, 8–17). The rims and bases are mostly very small so there are few clear indications of the size of the vessels. Many of the sherds have blackening or sooting and appear to have been used for cooking, and again this includes some of the platter sherds. Many of the sherds survived as small or misc. size fragments (54%) and this, combined with the lack of conjoining sherds suggests considerable trampling. Average sherd weight is 4.5g.

The distribution of the miscellaneous sherds and the diagnostic sherds is shown in Figure 48. This shows quite a distinctive pattern, with most of the larger diagnostic sherds concentrated on the east side of the house whereas the smaller miscellaneous sherds are concentrated on the west side of the house. The southern end of the house, which was only partially sampled, seemed to have relatively large quantities of both miscellaneous and diagnostic sherds. It is difficult to understand the significance of this pattern but perhaps it reflects the manner in which the house floor was swept clean.

The rims include three of flat form, from open mouthed and convex bowls (Figure 47, 10, 12 and 17), a round one, from a convex bowl (Figure 47, 9), and one everted rim (Figure 47, 11).

Between the middle and upper floor was a thin wedge

Table 10. Pottery from DD

context	weight	sherds	rim	base	body	misc.	platter	fine	Ave. Wght.
212	291	42	4	2	3	32	?1	?2	6.93
249	7	4				4			1.75
246/603	6	2				1	?1		3.00
609	36	5		2		3			7.20
611	12.9	2	1	1					6.45
Floor 3	616	160	6	10	16	100	28	15	3.85
243	270	41	3	1	2	5	30		6.59
Floor 2	921	206	11	19	24	111	41	9	4.47
Floor 1	1251	262	5	23	37	155	42	19 +3?	4.77
615	42	5	1	2		1	?1	1	8.40
Total	3452.9	729	31	60	82	412	141	49	4.74

of yellow sand (243) in the southwest corner of the house. This layer contained a large assemblage of 30 platter sherds, with the remaining eleven from more 'normal' vessel types (Figure 47, 28–32). The other sherds were all classed as A fabric, with two rolled, round rims, an irregular rim, a rounded base with a cracked and grass-marked exterior, and two wiped body sherds.

The platter sherds include three inward-angled rims of which two are conjoining (Figure 47, 32). The other rim is from a medium/thick vessel (7 to 10 mm), as are most of the other sherds, with blackening of the rim and exterior surface. The paired rims are very thick, (but vary from 10 to 15 mm, as do six of the other sherds), have cracked exteriors and fingered and fingernailed interiors. These two rims appear to be from a platter of very large diameter. There is very light blackening on part of the rim and the interior surface. Though not visible on the rims, some of the very thick sherds have grass-marked exteriors and, though not certain, it is likely that they derive from a single vessel, whilst the other rim is considered to have derived from the same vessel as the thinner platter sherds. Of the thinner sherds, three have pierced holes (Figure 47, 30, 31) and one has a stabbed hole visible, whilst five have blackening on their exteriors. All the platter sherds are of a similar colour and texture, and the thickness variation is such that all could possibly derive from a single disc.

Floor 3

The upper floor assemblage contains slightly sagging-based bowls, everted and round rims, of both the common fabric and the fine wares, and platters (Figure 47, 1–7). Except for a cluster of A fabric sherds from 230, the rest of the sherds are mostly of misc. or near misc. size (average weight 3.85g) and show high levels of activity on this floor. E fabric seems to be more common on this floor.

Two rounded rims came from a single convex bowl (Figure 47, 1–2), with a slightly sagging base, and cracked exteriors. A number of body sherds, from probably the same vessel, were recovered in the southwest area of the floor (230). This vessel is A fabric and of medium to thick type and had been used for cooking. The other diagnostic rims are from everted rim vessels, one worn example of medium thickness A fabric (Figure 47, 7), and the remaining two rims of E fabric (Figure 47, 4, 6). These latter rims are unusual in some of their features, especially the use of fingered impressions around the exterior of the rim and upper body, which also have fine striations present, from wiping with organic matter, such as clumps of grass. The rim and the associated body sherds all shows signs of sooting, though its interior is fairly clean. Similar E fabric sherds were recovered from all across the floor, except the area from which the A fabric vessel cluster was located (230 and 601). In this area a single sherd of the other fine fabric, C fabric, was recovered.

The platter is mostly thick, without stabbed or pierced holes and infrequently fingered, and not showing much sign of sooting. It is possible that all these sherds originated from a single disc. They were spread across four of the six areas of the floor, and were absent from the area containing the A fabric cluster (230 and 601).

The hearth produced some sherds but most are small and undiagnostic. The two base sherds from 609 are conjoining sherds from a sagging-based, common fabric cooking vessel and it is thought that they were deposited accidentally during use and, whilst the majority of the broken vessel was removed, these two sherds were left. The passage fill (249) had a few tiny sherds that do not provide any useful data. There is one unusual rim from a convex bowl in 212, which was thicker than the normal fine wares (Figure 47, 27) and this layer also produced a base with a linear ridge on the exterior wall (Figure 47, 26) and a rounded rim from an open bowl (Figure 47, 25).

- The house floors DD were striking for the small size of their sherds with an average weight of 4g and a distinct infrequency of rim (3.5%) and base sherds (8.3%).
- Platter remained a significant feature of all the floors (17.7%).
- Everted rims form a significant percentage of the rims though the tendency of these sherds to break at the neck means they are almost certainly under-represented.

Artefacts – A Clarke, P Macdonald and A Smith

This block produced seven pieces of worked bone, eleven pieces of iron, two copper alloy objects, two stone objects and eight flints (Table 11). Most of the objects came from the house floors; floor 3 produced eight objects, floor 2 six objects and floor 1 ten objects. Floor 1 produced a fragment of a comb side plate (Figure 33, 1467), two iron structural fittings (rove 1481, nail 1479), an iron ring (Figure 33, 1581), an amorphous iron fragment (2685), a copper alloy sheet fragment (4703) and four flints. Most of these objects were located either to the west of the hearth or in the northeast corner. Floor 2 produced a fragment of antler waste (Figure 33, 1429), iron nails (Figure 33, 1413, 1428), a fragment of a steatite bowl (Figure 33, 1509), that joins another fragment in block DB, and two flints. Most of these objects were located around the hearth. Floor 3 produced two bone pins (Figure 33, 1315 and 1380), a bone point (Figure 33, 1578), a copper alloy brooch pin or strip (Figure 33, 1580), three iron structural fittings (rove 1323, plate 1582, strip 1583) and one flint. The iron plate and strip and a bone pin came from the area around the hearth but the flint, the rove and a pin came from the south end of the house. The earlier excavation of the floor (212) produced a possible iron dress pin (Figure 33, 1223). The passage produced a comb tooth plate (Figure 33, 1579) and a fragment of iron plate (1584) and the sand layer, 243, a faceted cobble (Figure 33, 1525) and a pin blank (1361). Other than a general tendency to concentrate around the hearth, there is no strong pattern to the distribution of objects on these floors (Figure 48). Most of the objects are broken fragments or insignificant pieces and it seems likely that they represent accidental losses during the occupation of the house.

Carbonised plant remains – S Colledge and H Smith

Thirty-one flotation samples were examined from floor 1, 34 from floor 2, one from floor 3 (it was felt there was a greater chance of contamination in this floor layer), 10 from the hearth and another three from associated contexts (Tables 12, 13, 14). Barley was present in all the contexts but not in the high densities present in the kiln/barn (see chapter 5). Oats and rye were very poorly represented compared to the kiln/barn. Flax was present in most of the samples and these included some very rich samples

Table 11. Artefacts from DD

context	Bone/Antler					Iron							Copper alloy	Stone		
	Comb	Pin	Tool	Pin blank	Tine off-cut	Pin	Rove	Nail	Ring	Plate	Strip	Unknown	Objects	Flint	Bowl	Cobble tool
212						1								1		
249/608	1									1						
Floor 3		2	1				1			1	1		1	1		
Floor 2					1			2						2	1	
243				1												1
Floor 1	1						1	1	1			1	1	4		
total	2	2	1	1	1	1	2	3	1	2	1	1	2	8	1	1

Floor 3 = 230/238/242/245/248/601/602
Floor 2 = 604/605/610
Floor 1 = 614

Table 12. The charred plant remains from house floor 1 (DD)

sample number	context		volume floated (litres)	volume of charcoal (cm^3)	charcoal density (cm^3/l)	*Hordeum sativum* - grains	*Hordeum sativum* - rachis int frags	*Secale cereale* - grains	*Secale cereale* - rachis frags	*Avena* cf. *sativa* - grains	Cereal Indet - grains	Cereal/Gramineae - culm frags (?)	Cereals per litre of soil	*Buglossoides* sp.	Caryophyllaceae (several species)	*Chenopodium* spp.	Cruciferae (several species)	*Carex* spp. (/*Scirpus* spp.)	cf. *Fumaria* sp.	*Bromus* sp.	*Lolium* sp.	*Phalaris* sp.	Gramineae Indet (various spp)	*Linum* sp.	*Plantago* sp.	*Polygonum*/*Rumex* spp.	*Ranunculus* sp.	*Rubus* cf. *fruticosus*	Solanaceae	Wild seeds per litre of soil	Indet/unident specimens	wood charcoal	dung/peat/organic frags
8012	**614**	**DD/1**	8	1.0	0.1	13				10	x		2.88											1		1				0.25		x	x
8017	**614**		2	0.5	0.3	6					x		3.00																	0.00			
8019	**614**		6	4.6	0.8	73		2		34	x		18.17			6								42	4					8.67	x	x	x
8020	**614**		8	1.2	0.2	14				4	x	x	2.25			1								5		1				0.88		x	x
8021	**614**		4.5	1.0	0.2	9					x	x	2.00			1					1			1						0.67	x	x	x
8024	**614**		12	5.0	0.4	104		1		34	x	x	11.58			1		2	1					124						10.67	x		x
8027	**614**		15	2.2	0.1	27		2		1	x	x	2.00			2		3						2		3				0.67	x		x
8029	**614**		8	1.6	0.2	26	1	6		11	x		5.50			1		1						14						2.00		x	x
8031	**614**		9	3.0	0.3	70				8	x	x	8.67			3	1	1						80						9.44	x	x	
8032	**614**		14	0.5	0.0	10				2	x		0.86																	0.00		x	
8036	**614**		15	1.0	0.1	14				2	x		1.07											1		4				0.33	x	x	
8038	**614**		10	2.6	0.3	13				2	x	x	1.50				1	1						2		2				0.60	x	x	x
8039	**614**		5	0.3	0.1	13				9	x		4.40											1						0.20		x	
8042	**614**		5	0.3	0.1	7					x		1.40					1								1				0.40		x	x
8045	**614**		15	5.8	0.4	179				37	x	x	14.40		8	13		12						33		4	1			4.73		x	x
8049	**614**		9	0.8	0.1	14		5		5	x		2.67					1						2		2				0.56		x	x
8050	**614**		11	3.4	0.3	49		2		29	x		7.62		1			2				1		3		2				0.86	x	x	
8052	**614**		12	2.8	0.2	27		1		5	x		2.75			1								2		1				0.33	x	x	x
8054	**614**		10	3.8	0.4	67		8		25	x	x	10.00		2	6		3					1	9		2	1			2.40	x	x	
8055	**614**		10	2.0	0.2	40		5		16	x	x	6.10							1	1									0.20	x	x	x
8060	**614**		6	0.2	0.0	23				2	x		4.17					1								1				0.33		x	
8062	**614**		8	2.4	0.3	30		3		8	x		5.13		1	3		2		1				4		1				1.50	x	x	x
8064	**614**		7	1.6	0.2	16					x		2.29					1						1		1				0.43	x	x	x
8067	**614**		12	1.4	0.1	18		1		2	x		1.75										1							0.08	x	x	x
8070	**614**		8	1.6	0.2	12				3	x		1.88			3								1		2				0.75	x	x	x
8072	**614**		10	6.0	0.6	25		4		1	x		3.00			2	2			1				2		2		1		1.00	x	x	x
8074	**614**		16	2.8	0.2	21		5		6	x		2.00			1		1					1	1		3				0.44	x	x	x
8075	**614**		16	2.6	0.2	25		2		17	x		2.75		1			1					1	4		2				0.56	x	x	x
8077	**614**		21	18.6	0.9	570	19	4		259	x	x	40.57	1	20	13	13	1		1			3	2250		25			1	110.86	x		x
8078	**614**		16	8.0	0.5	59	3	3		4	x		4.31			4		3						1		3	1			0.75	x	x	x
8080	**614**		10	0.8	0.1	9		2		2	x		1.30										1	4		1				0.60	x	x	x
	Total		318	89		1583	23	56	0	538			6.92	1	33	61	17	37	1	4	2	1	8	2590	4	64	3	1	1	8.89			

Table 13. The charred plant remains from house floor 2 (DD)

sample number	context		volume floated (litres)	volume of charcoal (cm^3)	charcoal density (cm^3/l)	*Hordeum sativum* - grains	*Hordeum sativum* - rachis int frags	*Secale cereale* - grains	*Secale cereale* - rachis frags	*Avena* cf. *sativa* - grains	Cereal Indet - grains	Cereal/Gramineae - culm frags (?)	Cereals per litre of soil	Caryophyllaceae (several species)	*Chenopodium* spp.	Cruciferae (several species)	*Carex* spp. (/*Scirpus* spp.)	cf. *Fumaria* sp.	*Bromus* sp.	Gramineae Indet (various spp)	*Linum* sp.	*Plantago* sp.	*Polygonum*/*Rumex* spp.	*Ranunculus* sp.	*Rubus* cf. *fruticosus*	*Galium* sp.	*Urtica* sp.	Cereals per litre of soil	Indet/unident specimens	wood charcoal	dung/peat/organic frags	root/tuber frags	? heather
5882	**604**	**DD/2**	16	3.0	0.2	54		2		6	x		3.88		1		1				1							0.19	x		x		
5883	**604**		15	0.8	0.1	12				3	x		1.00				1				2							0.20					
5886	**604**		18	1.2	0.1	8				5	x		0.72			2	2			2	3	1						0.56		x	x		
5887	**604**		10	2.2	0.2	36		4		21	x		6.10	5	5						8		1					1.90	x	x			
5896	**604**		13	0.8	0.1	7		1		7	x		1.15		1													0.08		x	x		
5898	**604**		12	2.2	0.2	34		1		11	x	x	3.83		4													0.33	x	x	x		
5906	**604**		21	5.2	0.2	51		10		1	x		2.95	1	1		2				5		4					0.62	x	x	x		
5909	**604**		15	3.4	0.2	72		4		10	x		5.73		1					2	19		2					1.60	x	x	x		
5911	**604**		16	4.2	0.3	39	1	3		9	x		3.25						2		2							0.25	x	x	x		
5918	**604**		13.5	1.8	0.1	15				7	x		1.63		1													0.07	x	x	x		
5926	**604**		16	4.0	0.3	26		1		6	x		2.06								1				1			0.13	x	x	x		
5939	**604**		12	2.4	0.2	12				4	x		1.33	1														0.08	x	xx	x		
5891	**605**		3	0.8	0.3	5				1	x		2.00				1				3							1.33		x			
5892	**605**		6	1.4	0.2	5				2	x		1.17								2		1					0.50		x			
5894	**605**		10	1.6	0.2	25				7	x	x	3.20	1						1	6		1					0.90	x	x	x		
5900	**605**		3	0.4	0.1	6				1	x		2.33			1												0.33		x			
5901	**605**		9	0.6	0.1	6				4	x		1.11	1		1												0.22		x		x	
5907	**605**		9	1.4	0.2	24		1		7	x		3.56				1			1	2							0.44	x	x			
5910	**605**		6	1.0	0.2	5				4	x		1.50								1							0.17		x	x		
5913	**605**		8	1.0	0.1	9		1		4	x		1.75															0.00		x	x		x
5916	**605**		9	2.0	0.2	24		1		8	x		3.67	1	1						1		3					0.67		x	x		
5920	**605**		9.5	1.0	0.1	19		2		2	x	x	2.42		1		1						1					0.32	x	x	x		
5923	**605**		14	2.0	0.1	28		3		16	x		3.36	1		1				1	5		1					0.64	x	x	x		
5929	**605**		6	1.4	0.2	13				2	x		2.50		1		1				4							1.00		x	x		
5930	**605**		6	3.2	0.5	15		1		5	x		3.50								1							0.17	x	xx	x		
5932	**605**		14	10.2	0.7	33	2	5		3	x		3.07								2		4					0.43	x	xxx	x	x	
5806	**610**		10	1.2	0.1	19				3	x		2.20	15		1	1	1			3		3					2.40		x			
5820	**610**		10	1.2	0.1	17		1		1	x		1.90															0.00	x	x	x	x	
5941	**610**		8	0.8	0.1	10		1		1	x		1.50	1	1		1				2							0.63					
5945	**610**		16.5	3.6	0.2	26		7		1	x		2.06	2	1		3		1		4		2	1				0.85	x	x	x		
8001	**610**		7.5	2.0	0.3	8		1		5	x		1.87				2									1		0.40	x	x			
8005	**610**		4	0.2	0.1	7					x		1.75															0.00					
8011	**610**		17	2.2	0.1	19				10	x		1.71	51			4				1		1				3	3.53	x	x	x		
8016	**610**		7	4.0	0.6	6				2	x		1.14	1			2				1		1					0.71	x	xxx	xxx		
	Total		370	74		695	3	50	0	179			2.51	81	19	6	23	1	3	7	79	1	25	1	1	1	3	0.68					

Table 14. The charred plant remains from contexts associated with the occupation of the house (DD)

sample number	context		volume floated (litres)	volume of charcoal (cm^3)	charcoal density (cm^3/l)	*Hordeum sativum* - grains	*Hordeum sativum* - rachis int frags	*Secale cereale* - grains	*Secale cereale* - rachis frags	*Avena* cf. *sativa* - grains	Cereal Indet - grains	Cereal/Gramineae - culm frags (?)	Cereals per litre of soil	Caryophyllaceae (several species)	*Chenopodium* spp.	Cruciferae (several species)	*Carex* spp. (/*Scirpus* spp.)	cf. *Fumaria* sp.	*Bromus* sp.	Gramineae Indet (various spp)	*Linum* sp.	*Polygonum/Rumex* spp.	*Ranunculus* sp.	Wild seeds per litre of soil	Indet/unident specimens	wood charcoal	dung/peat/organic frags	root/tuber frags	? heather
5825	**609**	**DD**	4	6.4	1.6	159	1			47	x	x	51.75	11	12	1	2	1			33	11		17.75	x	x	x	x	
5833	**609**		4	1.0	0.3	80		2		34	x	x	29.00		1						2	1		1.00		x			
5944	**611**		15	9.0	0.6	223	3	1		59	x	x	19.07	10	21	132	1	2	2	1	562	52		52.20	x	x	x		x
8006	**611**		8	min	0.0	8							1.00	1		9					8			2.25					
5812	**246**		4.5	0.6	0.1	5				3	x		1.78									1		0.22		x	x		
5815	**246**		8	1.0	0.1	12				3	x		1.88											0.00		x	x		
5821	**246**		4	0.8	0.2	24				6	x		7.50	1	1						1			0.75					
5832	**246**		3.5	1.2	0.3	8				10	x		5.14								2			0.57		x	x		
5864	**603**		2.5	0.8	0.3	8				3	x		4.40								1			0.40		x			
5871	**603**		3	0.8	0.3	4		1		2	x		2.33								1			0.33		x	x		
8082	**615**		13.5	2.0	0.1	20				9	x		2.15				1				4	1		0.44	x	x	x		
5804	**243**		13	0.8	0.1	6		2		5	x		1.00				1							0.08		x	x		
5831	**248**		17	19.0	1.1	105	1	3		20	x		7.59		6		3				1	2	1	0.76	x	xxx	x		
5847	**601**	**DD/3**	11	0.4	0.0	4				5	x		0.82									1		0.09			x		
			111	43.8		666	5	9	0	206			7.98	23	41	142	8	3	2	1	615	68	1	8.14					

in floor 1. Floor 1 had the highest average densities of all three crops and the single sample from floor 3 had the lowest density.

The distribution of sample densities from floor 1 are plotted on Figure 49 (top). A consistent pattern is the concentration of material in the centre of the house, well to the south of the hearth. This comprised high densities of barley as well as the highest density of flax seeds found on mound 3. The only other concentration of note was to the west of the hearth where a high density of barley and flax seeds were present.

The distribution of samples from floor 2 are plotted in Figure 49 (bottom). The distribution of cereals shows a fairly consistent pattern across the floor with a slightly higher density in the top half of the house. The distribution of wild seeds is different; a couple of samples in the southern half of the house produced higher densities than any other samples, though the numbers are low. These concentrations consisted of several species of Caryophyllaceae. The flax seeds in contrast are found around the hearth. The distribution of charcoal is distinctive. The highest densities are found in the three corners of the building (northeast, northwest and southwest; the southeast corner was too disturbed to sample). This distribution presumably indicates the central areas of the floor were kept clean.

Two of the most productive samples from the site were associated with the hearth; 5825/609 had the highest density of cereals in trench D and 5944/611 had large quantities of barley, oats, Cruciferae and flax. These deposits are very similar in composition to those from the house floors and suggest that the hearth may be a possible source for the material found on the house floors.

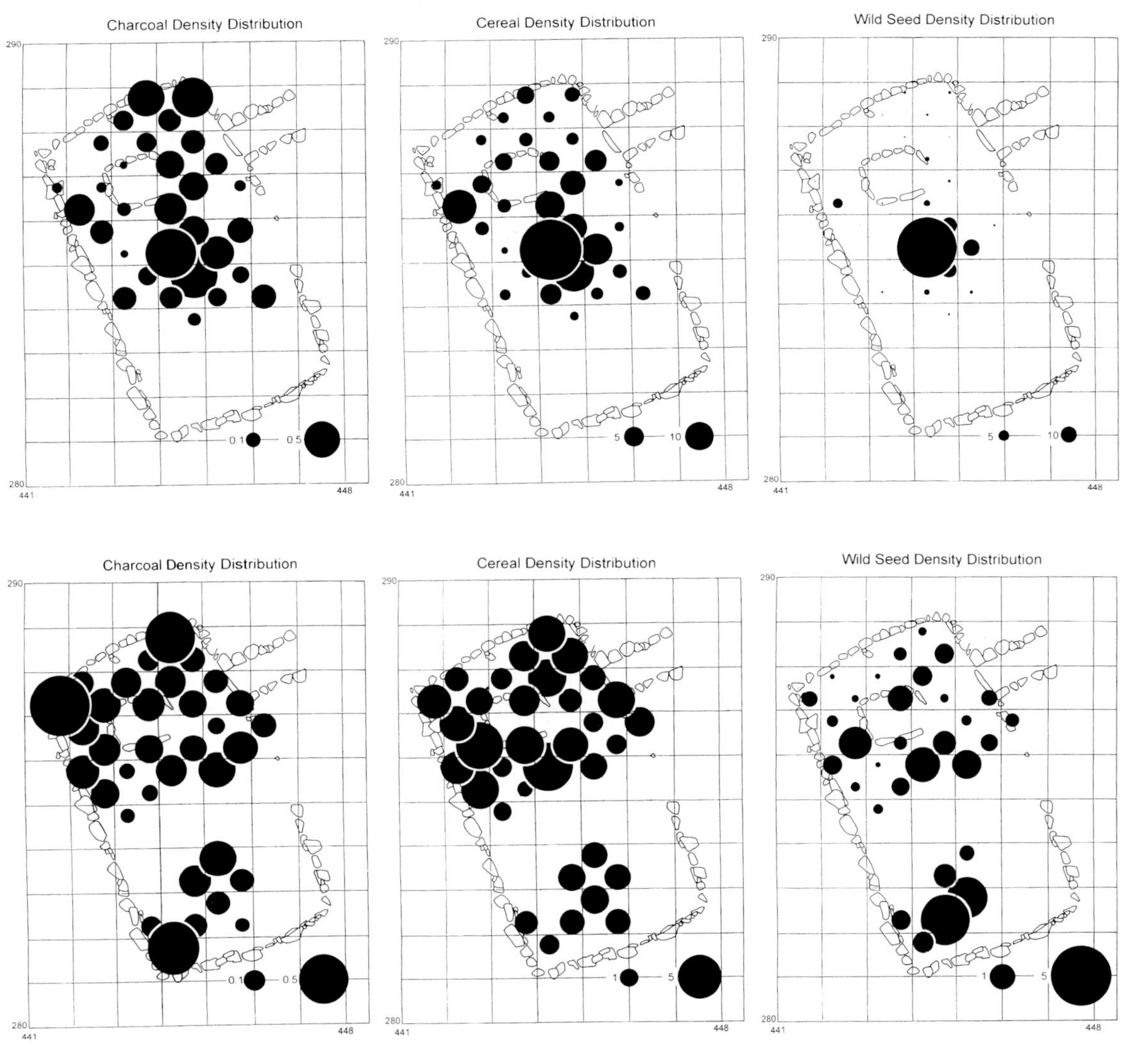

Figure 49. The distribution (number per litre of soil) of the carbonised plant remains in house floor 1 top and house floor 2 bottom.

Charcoal – R Gale

The charcoal was examined from a total of 22 samples from the floor layers (Table 70): 12 flotation samples from floor 1; seven flotation samples from floor 2; one flotation sample and two handpicked samples from floor 3. A single handpicked sample was examined from occupation deposits on the floor of the entrance passage (context 249) and a flotation sample from the bottom of the hearth (context 611). Charcoal fuel debris from the domestic use of the hearth was scattered across the floor of the house but tended to accumulate more densely around the base of the walls and in corners.

On the lowest floor (Figure 49, Table 70), the highest frequency of charcoal was concentrated in an area just south of the hearth and in the north-east corner of the house; deposits were also common in the intervening area (between the hearth and the entrance passage). None was recorded from the southern end of the building. The charcoal examined was obtained from sample squares close to the periphery of the interior of the structure. Ericaceous stems occurred in 11 of the 12 samples examined. Hazel was recorded in sample 8036, on the south side of the entrance passage, and in sample 8056/8063, in the northeast corner. Oak was identified from sample 8034 to the south of the hearth. Thus, in the early phase of the house, wood fuel appears to have consisted predominantly of heather with occasional use of hazel and oak.

The distribution pattern of charcoal on the middle floor (Figure 49, Table 70) varied considerably in comparison to that of the lower floor. Hotspots were focused in the northeast, northwest and southwest corners (the southeast corner was not examined) and a more general scattering occurred around the hearth and central southern areas. Charcoal was examined from contexts 604 (north-east quadrant), 605 (northwest quadrant) and 610 (south-west quadrant). Heather was common to each context. Hazel was recorded from context 604 and willow or poplar from context 605. Birch was present in three of the four samples examined from context 610 (southwest quadrant) but was not recorded from elsewhere in the house during this phase.

A single flotation sample, 5808, was examined from the northwest corner of the upper floor (Table 70) and contained spruce or larch. Handpicked samples of birch were also obtained from this level.

The two samples examined from occupation deposits included a single piece of spruce or larch, recovered from the lowest layer of the hearth (611) and a handpicked sample from context 249 (Table 70), from the floor of the entrance passage, provisionally identified as heather (the poor condition of this material prevented a positive identification).

Animal bone – J Mulville and J Cartledge

The animal bone assemblage from DD was the second largest assemblage from any of the stratigraphic blocks on mound 3, contributing 21% of the bones identified (Table 15). The assemblage is largely derived from the three house floors; floor 1 produced 44 identifiable bones, floor 2 produced 38 bones and floor 3 produced 33 bones. These layers are all potentially roughly equal in density of bones as a portion of the two upper floors were removed as 212 in 1995. The bones from floor 2 are more heavily gnawed than the bones from either floor 1 or 3. Floors 2 and 3 have an identical level of butchery but those from floor 1 show much less evidence for butchery.

The assemblage is dominated by the usual domestic species: sheep/goat make up 52%, cattle 35% and pig

Table 15. Animal bone NISP from DD

context	Sheep/ Goat	Sheep	Cattle	Pig	Dog	Horse	Red deer	Seal	Whale	Total
212	10		8	1		1				20
249	1									1
Floor 3	8	7	15	2					1	33
243	2	4	12				1	1		20
Floor 2	14	8	11	4						38
Floor 1	16	10	9	7	1			1		44
Total	51	29	55	14	2	1	1	2	1	156
	33%	19%	35%	9%	1%	1%	1%	1%	1%	

Floor 3 = 230/238/242/245/248/601/602

Floor 2 = 604/605/610

Floor 1 = 614

9%. Other species present include dog, horse, red deer, seal and whale. Seal is represented by a very young tibia found in the same context, 243, as a loose seal tooth, and a single, first toe from floor 1 in the house (614) which has been gnawed by a canid. These are the only occurrence of this species from mound 3.

Twelve bird bones were identified from these layers: three from a common/herring gull, a gannet, a guillemot, two guillemot/razorbill, a skylark, a song thrush, a golden plover and two domestic fowl (Table 74). Most of these came from floor 1 (five bones) and floor 2 (four bones) and there was only one from the final floor and one from the hearth layers.

Fish – C Ingrem

The house floors produced the bulk of the identified fish remains (n=2,307, 75%) from mound 3. Cod dominate the >10mm material (Table 16) but herring are the most frequent species overall, even without accounting for the effects of fractionation (Table 16). The fish remains from the floor layers constitute an assemblage of sufficient size to warrant more detailed analysis of taphonomy, species representation, body part representation and surface modifications.

Taphonomy

Almost all (98%) of the fish remains from the floor layers were well preserved with only a small proportion categorised as moderately preserved. In addition, three-quarters of the bones are more than 75% complete. A small proportion of bones recovered from the floor layers and one from the hearth display evidence of having been gnawed in the form of tooth marks or crushing; it was not, however possible to discern the agent responsible (Table 17). The majority of affected bones belong to herring and cod. Several herring bones and a few bones belonging to other species display evidence of burning; the majority are from the primary floor and a smaller number came from the second floor (Table 17).

Two herring bones from the primary floor layer display evidence of butchery in the form of cut marks (Table 17). A posterior abdominal vertebra has a cut mark in the transverse plane and a caudal vertebra in the sagittal plane. A few cod bones from the floor layers and one from a pit also displayed evidence for butchery: five supracleithra possess marks in the transverse plane; of these one is a chop mark and the remaining four cut marks. Four posterior abdominal vertebrae also display butchery marks in the transverse plane. Only one other species displays evidence of butchery; a premaxilla belonging to hake has been chopped through mid-way along its length.

Representation

Table 18 shows the number of identified bones according to feature from the >10mm and <10mm material respectively and it is clear that most of the of the bones are from the floor layers, particularly the primary and secondary floors. Cod make up almost half of the >10mm material with hake the next most numerous species followed by pollack and ling. The <10m material is dominated by herring which constitutes 92% of the identified material according to raw NISP. Whiting and saithe, the next most numerous species, are comparatively scarce (Table 18). The estimated NISP in <10mm material (Table 19) suggests that approximately 4,458 identifiable fish bones are present and confirms the predominance of herring which again represents 92% of the estimated total.

The minimum number of individuals has been calculated for cod from the floor layers (Table 20) but was not attempted for hake owing to the limited sample size. This suggests that a minimum of six cod are represented in the remains from the primary floor and three from both the second and upper floors. Owing to the virtual absence of elements other than vertebrae belonging to herring, it was only possible to obtain a rough estimate of MNI by simply dividing the estimated number of vertebrae recovered by the average number in the body. This suggests that a minimum of 66 herrings were recovered from the primary floor and 68 from the second floor (Table 21).

The herring remains from the floors are comprised almost entirely of vertebrae with very few cranial or appendicular elements (Tables 21, 22). Cod and hake remains appear to be dominated by vertebrae with head and appendicular elements also present (Table 22). However, when the number of times that an element occurs in the body is considered, a different pattern is visible for cod (Figure 50). The premaxilla is the best represented element in the remains from the primary floor followed by the dentary with vertebrae relatively under-represented. Vertebrae are better represented in the remains from the second floor, particularly those from the anterior abdominal region although the vomer and premaxilla are the best represented elements. Vertebrae are poorly represented in the deposits from the upper floor compared to cranial elements, with the maxilla the best represented element; the supracleithrum and posttemporal bones which come from the appendicular region are also better represented than vertebrae.

Size

According to comparisons made with reference specimens almost all the herring bones from the floor layers were derived from fish between 150–300 mm in length (Table 23). A relatively small number were from larger individuals between 300–600 mm, and a few were from fish below 150 mm. The bones of cod, hake and ling are predominantly from large individuals between 600–1200 mm, those of saithe are from large (600–1200 mm) and small fish (150–300 mm), and those of whiting small or very small (<150 mm). During recording it was noted that most of the small category herring were only slightly below 300 mm.

Table 16. Fish bone from DD

a. > 10 mm samples (NISP): b, < 10 mm samples (estimated NISP)

	212a	249a	249/608b	246/603a	246/603b	609b	611a	Floor 3a	Floor 3b	243a	Floor 2a	Floor 2b	Floor 1a	Floor 1b	615a	615b	Total
Tope														4			4
Herring			140		6	2			100	1		3767		3673		104	7793
Salmon												9					9
Sea trout					1							8	1				10
Salmonid												28		44			72
Eel												20		16			36
Conger eel								2				16					18
Whiting			2						1			50		34			87
Pollack	1		8	1				6			4	6	10	28			64
Saithe	1							3			5	20	5	62			96
Cod		1	2	3			1	36		7	95	14	74	48	1		282
Haddock								1									1
Hake	3						1	10		5	11		35		1		66
Ling	1							5		2	7		12				27
Large gadid				2				18	1		24	14	24	4	1		88
Medium gadid			8		4			3			2	24	4	14			59
Small gadid			2									54	1	78			135
Gadid								1				16					17
Sea bream								1									1
Scad														8			8
Sparidae												1		16			17
Corkwing Wrasse														8			8
Labridae												14		16			30
Labridae ?														8			8
Mackerel												4					4
Stickleback												4					4
Flounder											1	8					9
Flatfish														20			20
Total	6	1	162	6	11	2	2	86	102	15	149	4077	166	4081	3	104	8973

Table 17. The taphonomy of the fish bones in the house floor deposits (DD)

	Primary floor			Second floor			Third floor			Pit		Hearth
	butchery	gnawing	burning	butchery	gnawing	burning	butchery	gnawing	burning	butchery	burning	gnawing
Herring	2	21	19		15	7		2			1	1
Salmonid		1										
Conger eel								1				
Whiting									1			
Pollack		1						1				
Saithe					1							
Cod	4	1	1	3	2		2	5		1		
Hake					2		1		1			
Ling					2							
Gadidae						1						
Large gadid	1	1										
Medium gadid	1				1							
Small gadid			2									
Labridae?			1									
Total	8	25	23	3	23	8	3	9	2	1	1	1

Table 18. Floor layers (DD): species representation of fish bones according to context

a. > 10 mm samples (NISP); b. < 10 mm samples (raw NISP).

	Primary floor		Second floor		Upper floor		Hearth		Passage layer		Pit		Shell dump	Yellow sand	Total
	below	above	below	above	below	above	below	above	below	above	below	above	above	above	
Tope	1														1
Herring	678		937		56		8		31		13			1	1724
Salmon			3												3
Sea trout		1	2				1								4
Salmonid	6		4												10
Eel	3		4												7
Conger eel			1			2									3
Whiting	9		16		1				1						27
Pollack	4	10	3	4		7		1	1						30
Saithe	10	5	7	5		4									31
Cod	7	74	5	95		36		4	1	1		1		7	231
Haddock						1									1
Hake		35		11		13		1				1		5	66
Ling		12		7		6								2	27
Large gadid	1	24	3	24	1	18		2				1			74
Medium gadid	4	4	6	2		2	1		1				1		21
Small gadid	12	1	12						1						26
Gadidae			2			1									3
Scad	2														2
Sparidae	2		1			1									4
Corkwing wrasse	1														1
Labridae	1		3												4
Labridae?	1														1
Mackerel			1												1
Stickleback			1												1
Flounder			1	1											2
Flatfish	2														2
															0
Total	744	166	1012	149	58	91	10	8	36	1	13	3	1	15	2307

Measurements of other species were also taken and these are listed in the archive. The only species and element that provided sufficient measurements, and for which regression equations are available to calculate total length, are cod premaxillae. Using the method of Rojo (1986), this confirms that the majority of cod fall into the large category, although a few are small and a few very large (Table 24).

Temporal and spatial analysis

The primary and secondary floor layers produced similar quantities of identified fish bones and are similar in terms of species representation (Tables 16, 18). The assemblages are dominated by herring with small proportions of cod, hake and other gadids. Apart from herring and gadids, other species are represented in the >10mm material only by a single flounder bone which came from the

Table 19. Floor layers (DD): projected species representation according to context in <10 mm material (estimated NISP)

	Floor 1	Floor 2	Floor 3	Passage layer	Pit	Hearth	Total
Tope	4						4
Herring	3673	3767	100	140	104	8	7792
Salmon		9					9
Sea trout		8				1	9
Salmonid	44	28					72
Eel	16	20					36
Conger eel		16					16
Whiting	34	50	1	2			87
Pollack	28	6		8			42
Saithe	62	20					82
Cod	48	14		2			64
Large gadid	4	14	1				19
Medium gadid	14	24		8		4	50
Small gadid	78	54		2			134
Gadidae		16					16
Scad	8						8
Sparidae	16	1					17
Corkwing wrasse	8						8
Labridae	16	14					30
Labridae?	8						8
Mackerel		4					4
Gasterostidae		4					4
Flounder		8					8
Flatfish	20						20
Total	4081	4077	102	162	104	13	8539
%	*48*	*48*	*1*	*2*	*1*	*<1*	*100*

Table 20. Cod: minimum number of elements and individuals from floor layers

	Primary floor			Second floor		
	Left	Right	Midline	Left	Right	Midline
Vomer			2			4
Premaxilla	3	6		3	3	
Maxilla	1				1	
Dentary	1	1		1		
Articular		1		1	1	
Hyomandibular				1		
Opercular		1				
Supracleithrum		1		1		
Posttemporal	1	1			3	
AAV			5			13
PAV			25			24
CV			21			31
MNI	6			3		

Table 21. Herring: estimated minimum numbers of elements and individuals from floor layers

	Primary floor			Second floor
	Left	Right	Midline	Midline
Articular		8		
Hyomandibular	8			
AAV			144	103
PAV			1612	1252
CV			1855	2344
Total	8	8	3611	3699
MNI	66			68

Table 22. Cod and herring body part representation in floor layers (raw NISP)

	Primary floor		Second floor		Upper floor	
	Cod	Herring	Cod	Herring	Cod	Herring
Vomer	2		4		2	
Premaxilla	10		8		3	
Maxilla	2		1		5	
Dentary	5		4		2	
Articular	4	1	3	2	1	
Hyomandibular		2	1		1	
Opercular	1		2	1		
Cleithrum		1	1			
Supracleithrum	1		1		2	
Posttemporal	2		3		3	
Otolith	1				1	
AAV	5	27	14	29	3	1
PAV	26	288	24	327	6	11
CV	21	358	33	578	6	44
Total	81	678	100	937	36	56

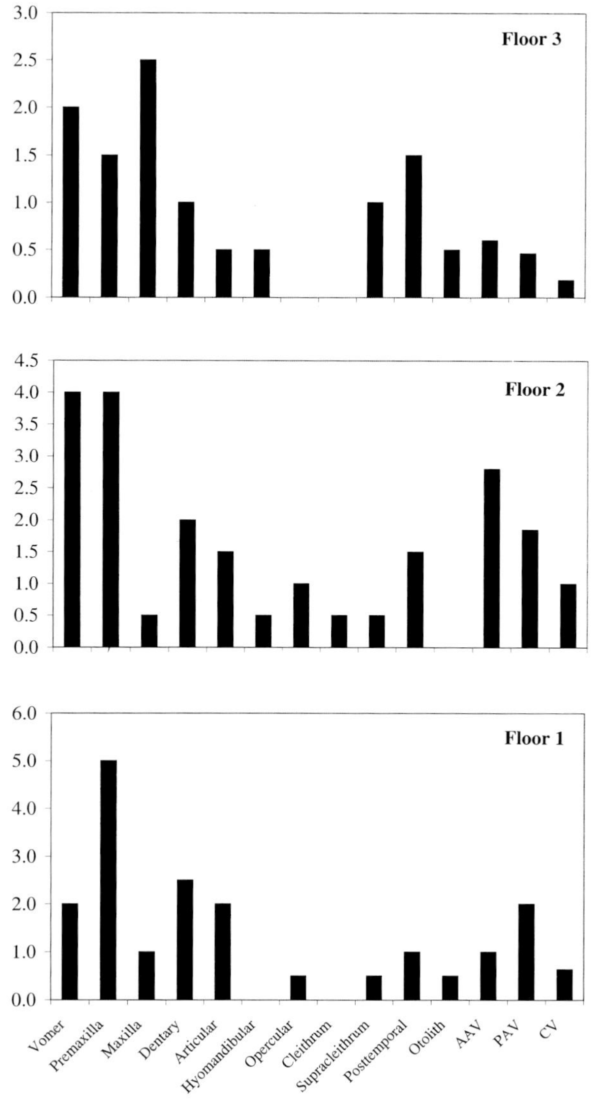

Figure 50. Cod body part representation on the house floors

Table 23. Size of major fish species from floor deposits (DD)

	V. large	Large	Medium	Small	V. small
Herring			119	1584	16
Whiting			1	19	7
Pollack		18	6	6	
Saithe		11	5	10	5
Cod	1	198	27	2	1
Hake		48	1		
Ling	4	23			
Total	5	298	159	1621	29

Table 24. Cod: total length

Hm (mm)	TL (mm)	Size category
1.95	153	Small
1.97	154	Small
2.22	166	Small
15.2	819	Large
15.3	824	Large
15.5	834	Large
15.6	839	Large
17.6	940	Large
18.1	965	Large
18.7	995	Large
18.9	1005	Large
19	1010	Large
19.8	1050	Large
20.1	1066	Large
20.9	1106	Large
22.9	1206	Very Large

Hm = maximum height (Morales and Rosenlund measurement 2)
TL = total length

second floor; a variety of species are represented in the <10mm material but are only present as trace taxa. The density of fish bones is also similar for the primary and second floor; the former produced an estimated 6.7 identified fish bones per litre of soil, the latter 5.6 per litre of soil.

Bones were recovered from most areas of the floors (Figure 51) although the numbers are variable. The area with the highest quantity on the primary floor is fairly centrally located whilst another area with large numbers was located on the western side. Areas of moderate quantities occur primarily on the northern and southern edges but are also scattered around the centre. The highest quantity of identified fish bone on the second floor was found in the southern area. In the northern area high and moderate quantities were clustered to the west of the hearth with more isolated samples located in the northeast corner and in the centre of the east side.

Marine shell – N Sharples

Winkles dominate the assemblage from DD providing 74% of the total quantities of shell recovered (Table 25). This figure is remarkably consistent for all three floors (3–75%, 2–77%, and 1–73%). Almost all the shells came from the floor layers and this is a direct reflection of the amount of sampling that was undertaken on these layers (only samples with shells and with an accurate record of the quantity of soil sieved are counted). Almost half of the shells were recovered from the lowest floor and this accurately reflects the increased density of shells on this floor layer. The large number of samples taken also resulted in a large number of other species being recorded. However, these never make up more than 1% of the total from the block. After winkles and limpets the most

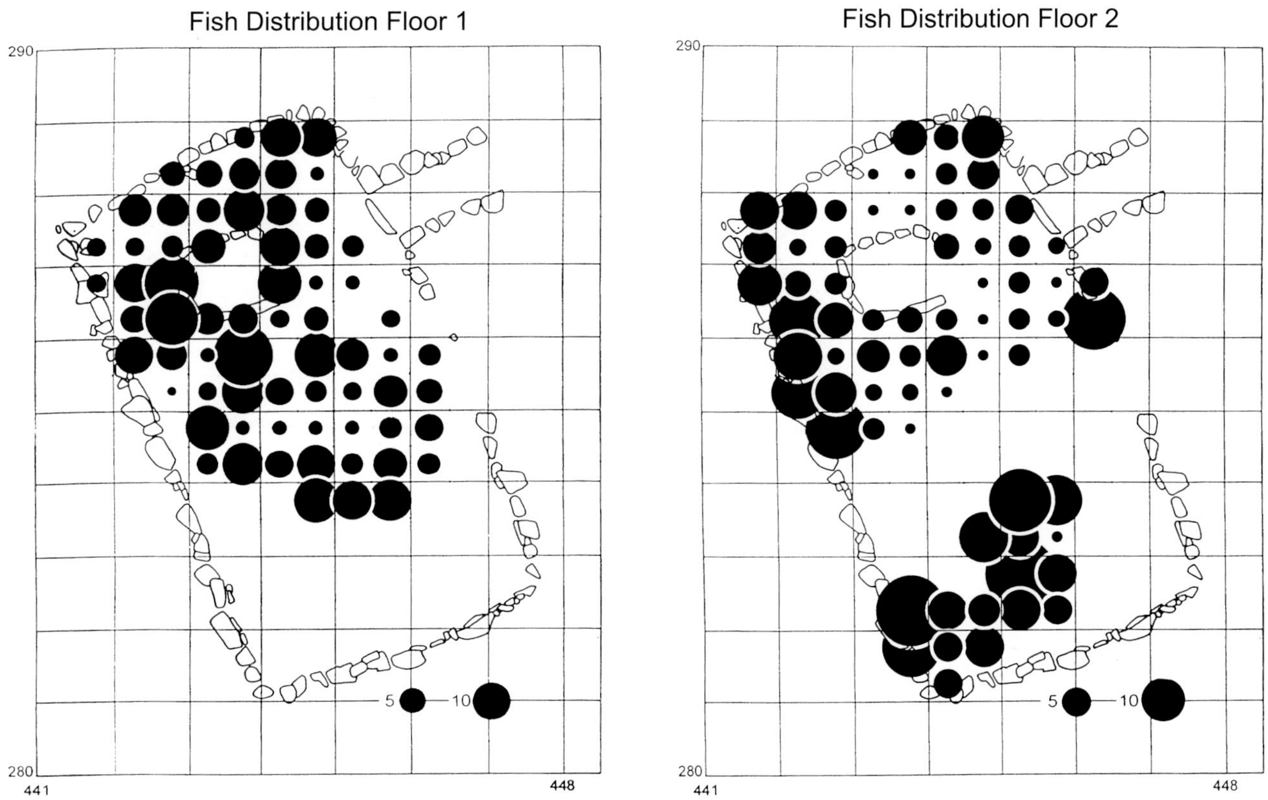

Figure 51. The distribution of the identified fish bones on the house floors

Table 25. Marine shell from DD

Context	No of samples	Litres	Limpet	Winkle	Flat periwinkle	Rough periwinkle	Dog whelk	Common whelk	Scallop	Mussel	Grey topshell	Razor	Crab	Crab	Crab	Crab
														Liocararcinus	C. maenas	Cancer sp.
212	1	20	11	52	1		1									
249	8	22.5	97	220	4											
608	3	13	19	59												
246	3	16.5	6	25												
603	2	5.5	2	2							1		+			
609	3	9	2	2	2											
611	3	28.5	5	61	1											
DD/3	82	731.5	675	1819	28	2	7			2	1				+	
243	1	13	6	29						1	4					
DD/2	74	732	838	2785	39	2	10	1	2	4	3	2	+	+	+	+
DD/1	63	637	1479	4400	45	4	8	2	1	9			+	+		
Total			3140	9454	120	8	26	3	3	16	9	2				

common species are flat periwinkles and to a lesser extent dog whelks; the more appetising bivalves, such as scallops, are still very rare discoveries. Crab was present as isolated pieces in context 603 and floor 3 and in larger numbers in floors 1 and 2.

Discussion – N Sharples

The detailed analysis of the two principal floors will be presented in chapter 11 so it will only be necessary to briefly summarise the information from the house occupation. The presence of two to three distinct floors in the house is unusual and has not been observed in the houses excavated at Cille Pheadair. Unfortunately no samples were taken for soil micromorphology so we cannot provide a definite interpretation of these floor levels. The assumption is that the floors were deliberately created by the redeposition of material from the hearth and from the discard or accidental loss of material from activities undertaken inside the house. This is certainly the best interpretation of the material found in the floors. The relatively large assemblages of pottery and bone are heavily fragmented indicating trampling *in situ*. Most of the pottery is heavily sooted which would suggest that it was used for cooking though serving food straight from the pot is also to be expected. The animal bone consists of prime meat bones that represents food consumed inside the house.

The largest and most important assemblages are of fish bones and carbonised plant remains. Both assemblages were derived from extensive flotation of the floor layers and indicate material largely invisible to the occupants of the house. The carbonised plant remains confirm the impression that much of the floor layer derives from the hearth, as the samples from inside the hearth are very similar to those from the floor. The samples are dominated by barley and flax. Several samples have large quantities of flax seeds and these would indicate the importance of this crop to the inhabitants of the settlement. The fish bones are likely to be the waste from food consumption and the large numbers present give a good indication of the importance of this foodstuff. Herring was the dominant species and appears to have come into the house as prepared fillets with the heads removed. In contrast cod was largely recognised through the presence of head bones and it seems likely that the heads were being consumed, perhaps in some form of stew.

The relative absence of small finds is interesting particularly as large numbers of finds have been recovered from many of the other house floors excavated at Bornais and Cille Pheadair. It may indicate the relative wealth of the inhabitants but it may also reflect a change in the nature of depositional practice.

The house abandonment deposits (DE) – N Sharples

The final layers in the house consisted of a brown sand up to 0.16 m thick that infilled the house (Figure 37). It was a fairly homogeneous layer, with patches of white, wind-blown sand streaked through it, and was almost identical to the brown sand found outside the wall (DB). In the south this fill layer was divided in two; to the southeast 235 overlay 236, to the southwest 228 overlay 231 (split by white sand layer 229). In the south central part of the house the fill was 207/212 and in the north central 233. In the northeast it was numbered 239, in the northwest 234. The passage was infilled with a comparable brown sand layer (241), which was overlain by rabbit-disturbed deposits (240).

Sampling – N Sharples

Six samples, 87 litres of soil, were taken and processed from the DE contexts: 228, 231, 233, 234, 239, 241 and the residue from below 10 mm was sorted from all but 241.

The material from above 10 mm was very limited consisting of small quantities of fish bone (an average density of 0.06 pieces per litre), mammal bone (0.1 pieces per litre), pottery (0.09 pieces per litre) and marine molluscs (limpets 1.9 individuals per litre, winkles 3.9 individuals

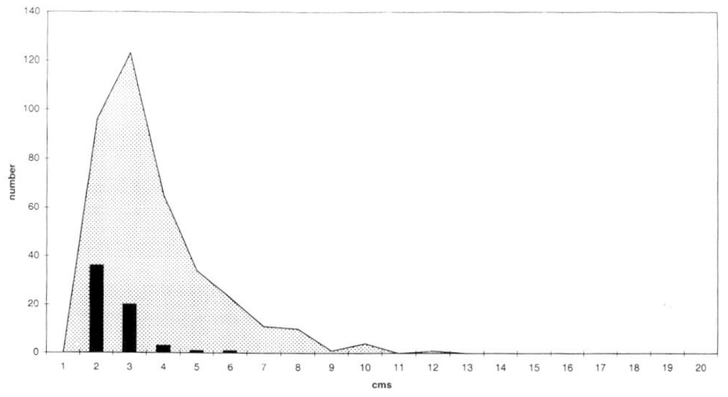

Figure 52. The size distribution of the pottery (line) and bone (column) from the DE contexts

per litre). These densities are all lower than the densities of material from the house floors except for the marine molluscs, which have, on average, higher densities in this block. This high density is due to the large numbers of shells present in 239, which also produced the highest density of pottery. Context 228 produced the highest densities of both fish and animal bone.

The material from below 10 mm contained quantities of unburnt and burnt bone and slag that are generally within the range of the samples from the underlying house but the quantities of seed, charcoal and pot are lower. This may be because the latter are more susceptible to erosion and would have been naturally destroyed.

Measurements – N Sharples

The assemblage from DE had a much smaller proportion of pottery than the floor layers (only 16.6% of the bone assemblage). The bone assemblage has a mode of 20–30 mm and the curve is very similar to the assemblage from the house floors with over 90% of the pieces smaller than 60 mm (Figure 52). The pottery assemblage is not as well preserved as the assemblage from the house floor with the mode occurring between 10–20 mm. The similarities of the bone with the house floors may be because this material represents the decay of the house itself and the increased destruction of the ceramics represents their greater susceptibility to erosion through weathering.

Artefacts – J Bond, A Clarke, A Lane, P Macdonald and A Smith

The sherds of pottery from DE are similar to those found in the floors below (Table 26, Figure 53, appendix 3). Most sherds are small and uninformative (average 4.9g). Miscellaneous sherds form 57% of the assemblage and indicate its fragmented nature. Conjoining sherds are rare though small clusters of similar sherds at the northern end of the house (234 and 239) may be significant. These clusters were of fine wares, which are largely absent from the southern end of the house.

Table 26. Pottery from DE

context	weight	sherds	rim	base	body	misc.	platter	fine	Ave. Wght.
207/228/235	311	60		7	8	41	4	1	5.18
233/234/239	369	78	6	9	7	40	16	21	4.73
231/236	61	13	2	2		5	4		4.69
240	9	1	1					1	9.00
Total	750	152	9	18	15	86	24	23	4.93

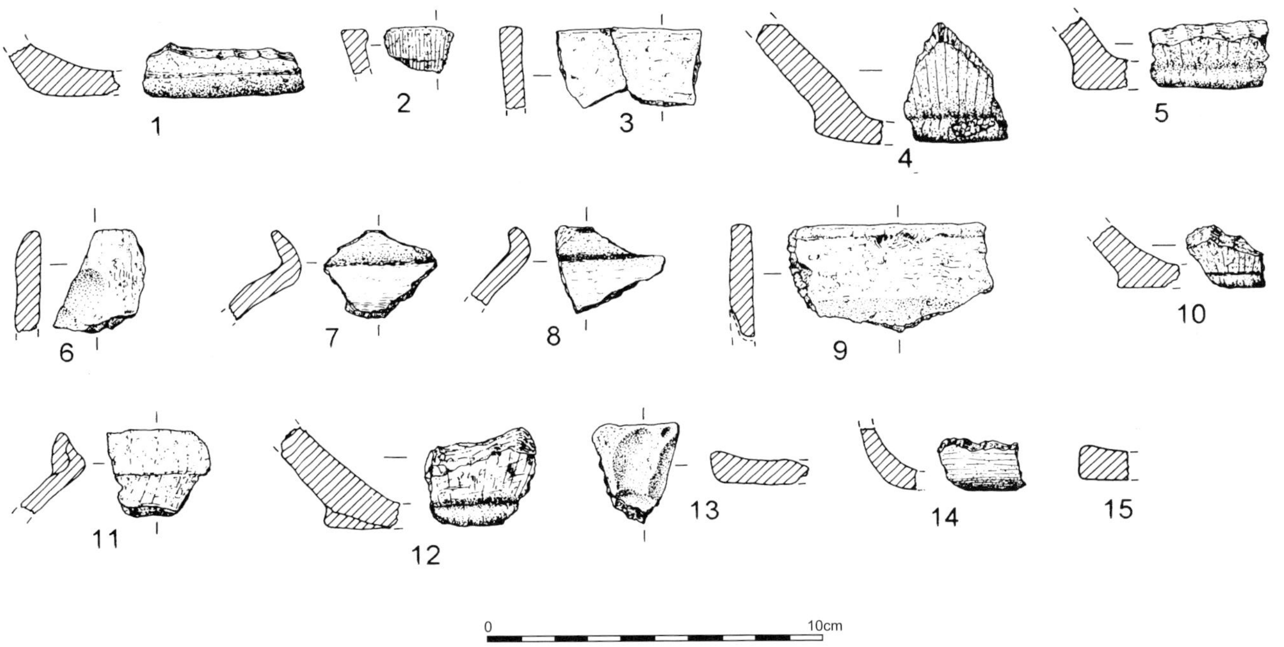

Figure 53. The pottery from the DE contexts

Table 27. Artefacts from DE

Context	Copper alloy		Iron	Stone	
	Sheet	Buckle	Rove	Flint	Sp whorl
207				2	
228			1		
234		1			1
240	1				
total	1	1	1	2	1

Most vessels have medium/thick walls but a few thin and medium sherds, from the fine wares, are also present. Grass-marking is rare, except on platters. Smoothing or wiping of vessel exteriors occurs and is also found on the interior surface of some of the fine fabric vessels.

- The sherds are from convex bowls, open-mouthed bowls and everted rim vessels.
- The nine rims are a mixture of round, flat and everted forms. No diameters were reconstructable.
- Sooting and blackening appears common, and this includes significant numbers of the platter sherds.

This block produced two copper alloy objects, one piece of iron, two flints and one stone object (Table 27). A steatite spindle whorl (Figure 33, 1346) and the copper alloy buckle (Figure 33, 1339) came from the northwest corner of the house, an iron rove (1310) from the southwest corner and a very fragmentary sheet of copper alloy (1353) from the passage. The buckle is a significant object and its position in an abandonment deposit may indicate deliberate deposition to mark the end of the life of the house.

Carbonised plant remains – S Colledge, R Gale and H Smith

Five flotation samples were examined from this block (Table 28). Barley and oats were present in all samples; rye and flax, however, occurred less frequently in these contexts. The densities of charcoal/taxa for these samples were amongst the lowest recorded in mound 3 contexts;

Table 28. The charred plant remains from DE

sample number	context		volume floated (litres)	volume of charcoal (cm^3)	charcoal density (cm^3/l)	*Hordeum sativum* - grains	*Secale cereale* - grains	*Secale cereale* - rachis frags	*Avena* cf. *sativa* - grains	Cereal indet - grains	Cereals per litre of soil	Caryophyllaceae (several species)	*Chenopodium* spp.	Cruciferae (several species)	*Carex* spp. (/*Scirpus* spp.)	*Linum* sp.	*Polygonum*/*Rumex* spp.	Wild seeds per litre of soil	indet/unid specimens	wood charcoal	dung/peat/organic frags	root/tuber frags
5751	**228**	**DE**	23	3.0	0.1	19	5		2	x	1.13	1		1		2	1	0.22		x	x	
5767	**231**		14	1.8	0.1	11	1		6	x	1.29		1			1	1	0.21		x	x	
5773	**234**		15	0.6	0.0	8	1		3	x	0.80				1			0.07		x		
5772	**235**		9	0.1	0.0	1			1	x	0.22				1			0.11		x		
5784	**239**		16	2.0	0.1	12	3		5	x	1.25					1		0.06	x	x	x	
	Total		77	8		51	10	0	17		1.01	1	1	1	2	4	2	0.14				

Table 29. Animal bone NISP from DE

context	Sheep/Goat	Sheep	Cattle	Pig	Red deer	Total
207/228/235	7	1	7	1	2	18
233/234/239	5	2	4	2		13
231/236	3	5	8			16
240			1			1
241	3		1			4
Total	18	8	21	3	2	52
	35%	15%	40%	6%	4%	

Table 30. Fish bone from DE

a. > 10 mm samples (NISP): b. < 10 mm samples (estimated NISP)

	207a	228a	228b	231a	231b	233a	234a	234b	235a	235b	236a	239a	239b	Total
Herring			96		24			12		2			112	246
Sea trout ?					4									4
Argentine?								4						4
Eel													16	16
Pollack				1							1			2
Saithe						1								1
Cod	2	2				5	1		2		6	3		21
Haddock		1												1
Hake	5	2				3					1			11
Ling											1	1		2
Large gadid	3			2	4	4					1			14
Medium gadid		1												1
Total	10	6	96	3	32	13	1	16	2	2	10	4	128	323

Table 31. Marine shell from DE

Context	No of samples	Litres	Limpet	Winkle	Flat periwinkle	Rough periwinkle	Grey topshell	Dog whelk	Razor	Great scallop	Oyster	Crab
228	1	23	10	23					3	1	1	+
231	1	14	5	23								
233	1	9	1	8								+
234	1	15	9	23	4		1	1				+
239	1	16	134	207	1			1				
241	1	10	11	55	1	1						
Total			170	339	6	1	1	2	3	1	1	

there were no obvious concentrations of plant remains. A single sample of ericaceous charcoal was identified from context 234 (Table 70).

Animal bone – C Ingrem, J Mulville and J Cartledge

The animal bone assemblage from DE (Table 29) was dominated by the three main species; sheep/goat make up 50%, cattle 40% and pig 6%. This is a high percentage of cattle compared to other units. Other species were limited to two fragments of red deer. Only 8.5% of the assemblage has been gnawed which is perhaps surprising for an abandonment deposit. It supports the idea that the house on mound 3 was one of the last structures to be occupied at Bornais and that once it was abandoned there were no people, and more significantly no dogs, around to gnaw the bones. Five per cent of the bones showed evidence for butchery.

Nine bird bones were identified: a common/herring gull, a great black-back back gull, a gannet, two dunnock, two domestic fowl, a teal and a turnstone.

A small quantity (n= 82) of fish bones was recovered from this block (Table 30). They comprise mainly herring, cod and hake with the former dominant when estimated NISP is considered. Cod and hake from the >10mm material are represented by elements from all parts of the body whereas herring from the <10mm samples is represented solely by posterior abdominal and caudal vertebrae.

Marine shell – N Sharples

Winkles dominate the assemblage from DE providing 66% of the total quantities of shells recovered (Table 31). The largest quantity of shells came from a sample from the northeast corner of the house (239). Other species were rare but it is noticeable that the context from the southwest corner of the house (228) produced three razor shells, a Great scallop and an oyster. These may indicate someone having a snack in the abandoned house. Crab was present in three contexts (228, 233, 234).

Discussion – N Sharples

The final block of deposits almost certainly represents the abandonment and decay of the house. The brown soil is almost identical to the brown sand outside the walls of the house and this suggests that the deposits inside the house derive from the erosion and redeposition of the external deposits after the abandonment of the house. If this interpretation is correct, this indicates that almost all the material found in this block could derive from the turf walls of the house and is therefore contemporary with or earlier than the construction of the house. The only find that this probably does not explain is the copper alloy buckle, which could well be a placed deposit associated with the abandonment of the house. It is noticeable that there were no collapsed stones in the interior, possibly indicating that the walls were never any higher, and that there were no obvious mounds to mark the position of the walls, which suggests that the remains of the turf walls were systematically removed, probably to be dumped on the field surrounding the settlement.

5 Trench F

The excavation of the southern area of mound 3 (Figure 54) was focused on a feature identified by the geophysical survey, which turned out to be an agricultural building with an attached corn-drying kiln (FC, FD), infilled with sterile wind-blown sand (FE). Excavation of the surrounding deposits was limited but included an area in the southeast corner of the trench (FF) and a trench to the west of the structure (FG). Both areas exposed sterile wind-blown sand (FA) into which the structure had been built and in the southeast corner evidence for another structure, lying immediately to the east of the house, was exposed (FB).

The pre-kiln/barn sand dune (FA) – N Sharples

Excavation in a variety of areas in the trench exposed an underlying light grey sand, which is believed to represent a sand dune that has accumulated largely through natural processes. This sand dune was given various numbers, depending on where it was exposed; in the southeast corner it was 685, under the building's floor it was 680, under the kiln it was 682, under the fill of the west entrance it was 688 and under the midden in the western extension it was 689. In no area was any attempt made to systematically excavate this layer so it is possible that earlier deposits underlie the wind-blown sand. No finds were recovered but during the micromorphological sampling of the building's floors (FD) the underlying sand was also examined and described (see below 98).

An adjacent structure (FB) – N Sharples

Excavations in the southeast corner of the trench revealed a deep pit (684) against the east section (Figure 55). This was at least 3 m long; it extended up to 0.6 m into the trench and was over 0.9 m deep. There is every indication that it was deeper immediately east of the area excavated. On the lower edge of the pit were three discrete contexts: a red-brown sand (669), a compact dark brown sand (670) and a loose red-brown sand (679). The rest of the pit was infilled with a homogeneous light brown sand (665).

Sampling – N Sharples

Two samples, 6 litres of soil, were taken and processed from FB contexts 669 and 670. The only material recovered in any quantity from the above 10 mm sort were marine molluscs, limpets in particular. The below 10 mm sort produced high densities of unburnt bone but low densities of all other materials including slag. Eggshell was present in both samples.

Artefacts – J Bond, A Lane and P Macdonald

The ceramic assemblage from FB was small and not very diagnostic (Table 32). Sherds with sooted and blackened exteriors were frequent. Sherd size (average weight 7g) is larger than that in the house floors, DD (c. 4g). One platter rim of expanded wedge shape appeared in context 665, confirming a Norse period date for the associated material.

An iron knife (Figure 56, 1887) was found in the fill of the construction pit (665).

Animal bone – C Ingrem, J Mulville and J Cartledge

A small quantity (n=14) of identifiable animal bones was recovered from these deposits (Table 33). This assemblage was dominated by sheep/goat. Cattle and pig were also present but no other species. Two bird bones were identified in the fill of the pit (665): both were

Table 32. Pottery from FB

context	weight	sherds	body	misc.	platter	Ave. Wght.
670	8	1	1			8.00
669	13	3	1	2		4.33
665	56	7	4	2	1	8.00
Total	77	11	6	4	1	7.00

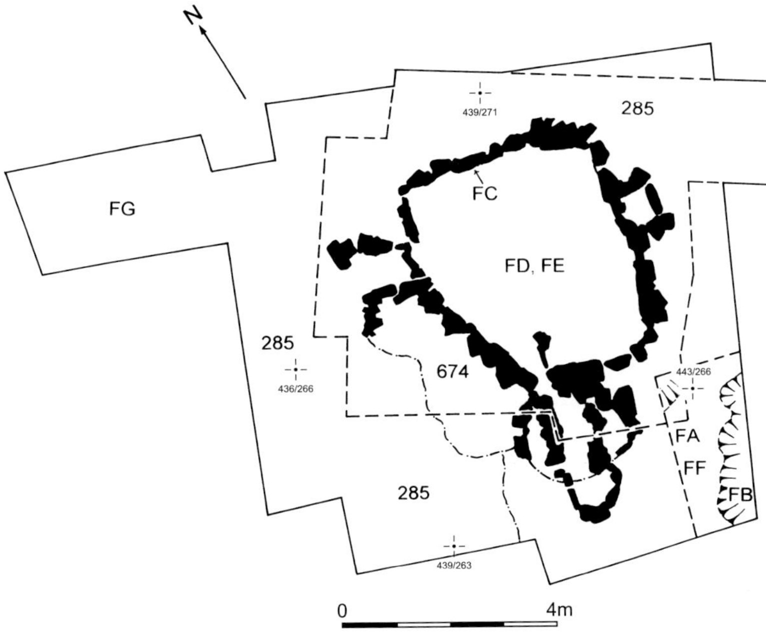

Figure 54. General plan of the trenches dug in 1995 and 1997 showing the location of the different stratigraphic blocks

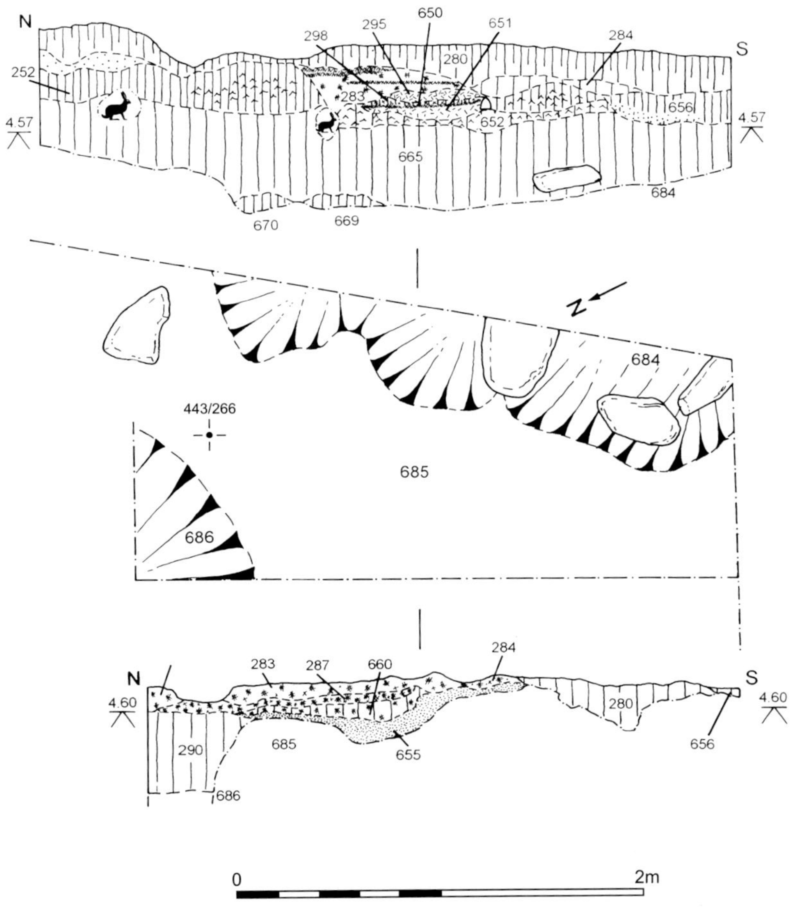

Figure 55. The area excavated in the southeast corner of trench F showing in plan the construction pits (FB/684, FC/686) and in section the later occupation deposits (FF)

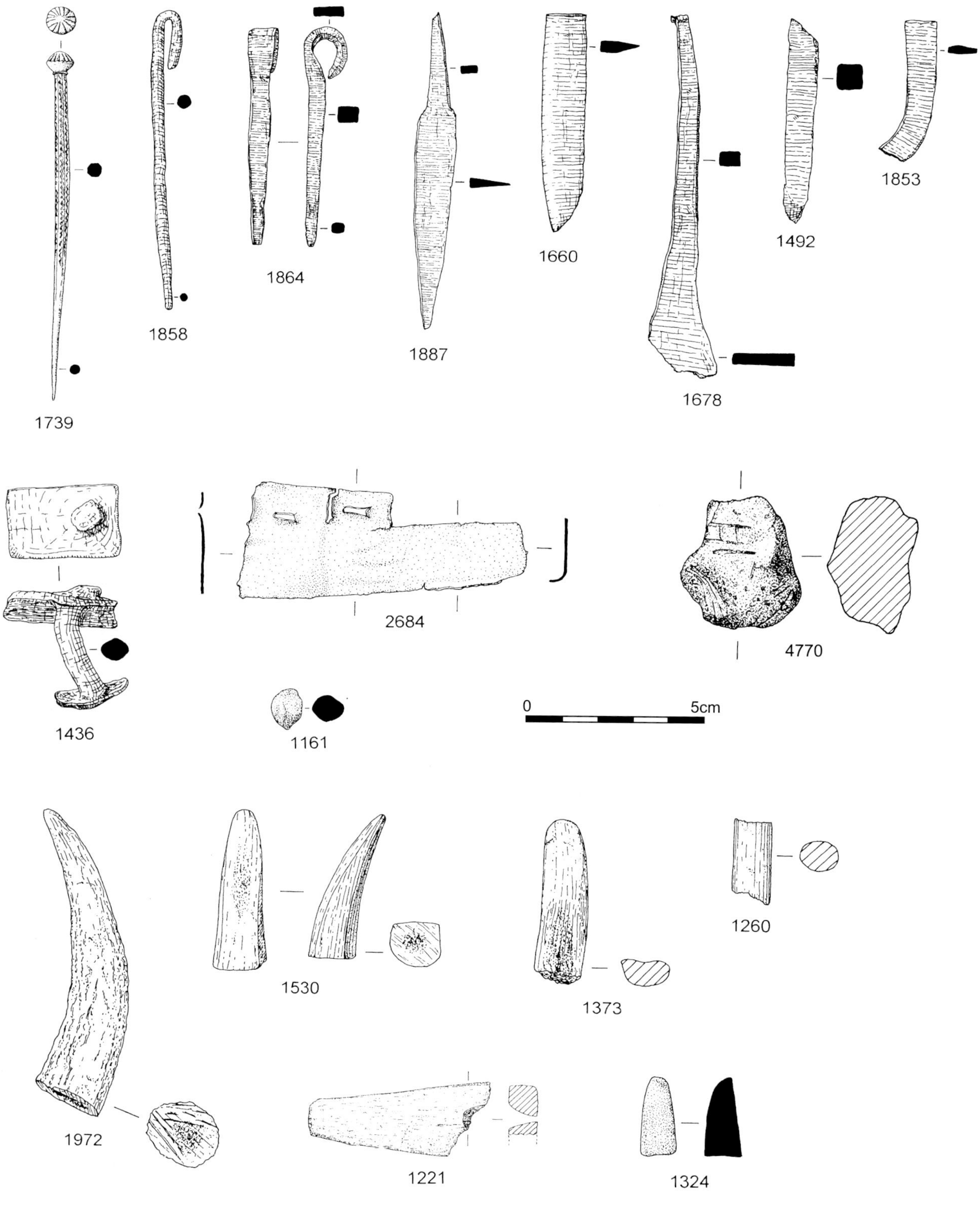

Figure 56. A selection of the most important artefacts recovered from trenches E and F. In the top half the artefacts are all iron except 1739, 2684, 1161, which are copper alloy and 4770, which is clay. In the bottom half of the figure all the objects are bone/antler except 1324, which is stone.

Table 33. Animal bone NISP from FB

context	Sheep/Goat	Cattle	Pig	Total
665	10	2	1	13
669	1			1
total	11	2	1	14
	79%	14%	7%	

Table 34. Fish bone from FB

a. > 10 mm samples (NISP); b. < 10 mm samples (estimated NISP).

	665a	669b	670a	Total
Herring		24		24
Pollack	3			3
Saithe	2			2
Cod	4		1	5
Hake	5			5
Ling	1			1
Large gadid	3			3
Megrim?	1			1
Total	19	24	1	44

Table 35. Marine shell from FB

Context	Sample	Litres	Limpet	Winkle
669	1	5	36	4
670	1	1	1	0
total			37	4

common/herring gull. A small number of fish bones (44) were recovered from the FB contexts (665, 669 and 670). Herring dominated the assemblage from 669 but the assemblage from 665 included a variety of species (Table 34) with cod and hake as the most dominant species.

Marine shell – N Sharples

This is the only block in mound 3 where limpets dominate the assemblage, providing 90% of the total quantity of shells recovered (Table 35). These shells come from a single small sample from a layer (669) placed at the bottom of the construction pit, which also contained a fish bone assemblage. It may represent either a single meal for one of the people working on the construction or perhaps a food offering left as part of the construction process.

Discussion – N Sharples

It seems likely that this pit is a construction pit for a building lying to the east of the structure excavated but, though a few slabs were present, there was no evidence for a wall. The ceramics indicate a Norse date for the feature. The knife was the only complete knife from mound 3 and its presence in the fill (665) suggests that it was a deliberately placed offering. The ecological assemblage though small included a limpet dump.

The kiln/barn construction (FC) – N Sharples

The structure revealed by the excavation is a sub-rectangular building 3.80 m by 4.60 m (Figures 54, 57). It has a principal entrance on the west side, a ventilation hole directly opposite this, on the east side, and attached to the south side is a corn-drying kiln. The northeast, northwest and southeast corners are all well defined but the southwest corner is by-passed by a wall which runs from the west entrance to the passage of the corn-drying kiln.

Excavation in the southeast corner of the trench (Figure 55) revealed that the building was constructed in a pit (686) excavated into an area of blown sand (685). A layer of grey sand (655) on top of 685 may indicate the turf line prior to the construction of the house. The pit appears to have been located on the edge of the sand dune such that the top of the east wall of the building was level with the surface of the sand dune, whereas the west wall protruded some distance above the pit, and had to be backed by dumped organic rich sand (not excavated). The only area of the pit excavated was around the southeast corner and in this area it was filled with a

Figure 57. A view of the kiln/barn from the north with floor 1 exposed

nondescript brown sand (290). A patch of brown sand (690) underlying the walls in the northeast corner of the building may also be related to its construction. Two separate brown sand layers (291, 294) were identified around the corn-drying kiln and these probably represent an attempt to create a compact and stable ground surface around the structure.

The walls of this building (Figure 58) were very well preserved particularly on the south (266) and east (261) sides, where six to seven courses standing 1.0 m high were the norm. The stones used in the construction of the east wall (261) were roughly 0.4 m by 0.15 m. Vertical columns and horizontal lines of stones were noticeable. The principal stones used in the south wall (266) were slightly smaller and included a distinct group of smaller stones used to fill in irregular gaps between the larger stones. Horizontal and vertical building lines were more difficult to identify. There was a straight join between the two walls with the south wall (266) tucked behind the east wall (261).

The west wall (267) is much scrappier in construction (Figure 59). The constant threat of a major collapse, exacerbated by a rabbit burrow that ran underneath the wall for most of its length, meant that the basal course was not fully exposed. Four to five courses were present, standing up to 0.95 m high. A variety of stones were used, ranging from some of the largest slabs in the wall (0.65 m by 0.13 m) to small stones (0.5 m by 0.08 m).

The wall to the north of the west entrance was very badly preserved with only two to three courses surviving up to 0.6 m high. On the north side of the entrance a large block, 0.65 m by 0.45m, was clearly placed to give stability to the corner. A series of noticeably small stones were used to continue the wall face across the entrance and thus block it. These rested on a sand layer which infilled the lowest 0.25 m of the passage. There was a suggestion that this wall may have been a facing put in front of the original wall but this possibility was not explored.

The north wall (259) was better preserved than the west wall but was still not as good as the east and south walls. The stones used were roughly 0.4 m by 0.2 m and normally five courses survived up to 0.85 m high. There is a suggestion that the wall was built in columns and horizontal courses similar to the east wall but these are not so well defined. The east end of this section of wall had several courses that had clearly slumped forward.

The west entrance was a passage 1.60 m long and 0.60 m wide (Figure 60). The floor of the passage was level with the old ground surface outside the building but involved a step down into the interior, which was revetted by a line of three stones. Flanking the entrance passage on the outside was a short stretch of walling. That to the south of the entrance was a wall approximately 0.8 m long. To the north of the entrance only a single large stone marked the line of the revetment. The ventilation hole on the east side consisted of a recess 0.57 m wide by 0.78 m deep. Access was stepped 0.24 m above the floor level and a single stone 0.6 m high acted as a back slab.

The kiln to the south of the building appears to have two phases (Figure 61). The final L-shaped kiln structure cut through an earlier bowl-shaped kiln that was only partially exposed as it was decided not to destroy the later kiln walls (Figure 62). Two arcs of walling to the east (692) and west (693) of the later passage were exposed. Excavation was restricted to the removal of the upper 0.4 m of fill (292, 293) between the passage and the original walls. This exposed a full arc on the east side and about half an arc on the west side and indicates the original bowl was at least 1.60 m in diameter and was joined to the main structure by a passage approximately 0.5 m long. About three courses were exposed on

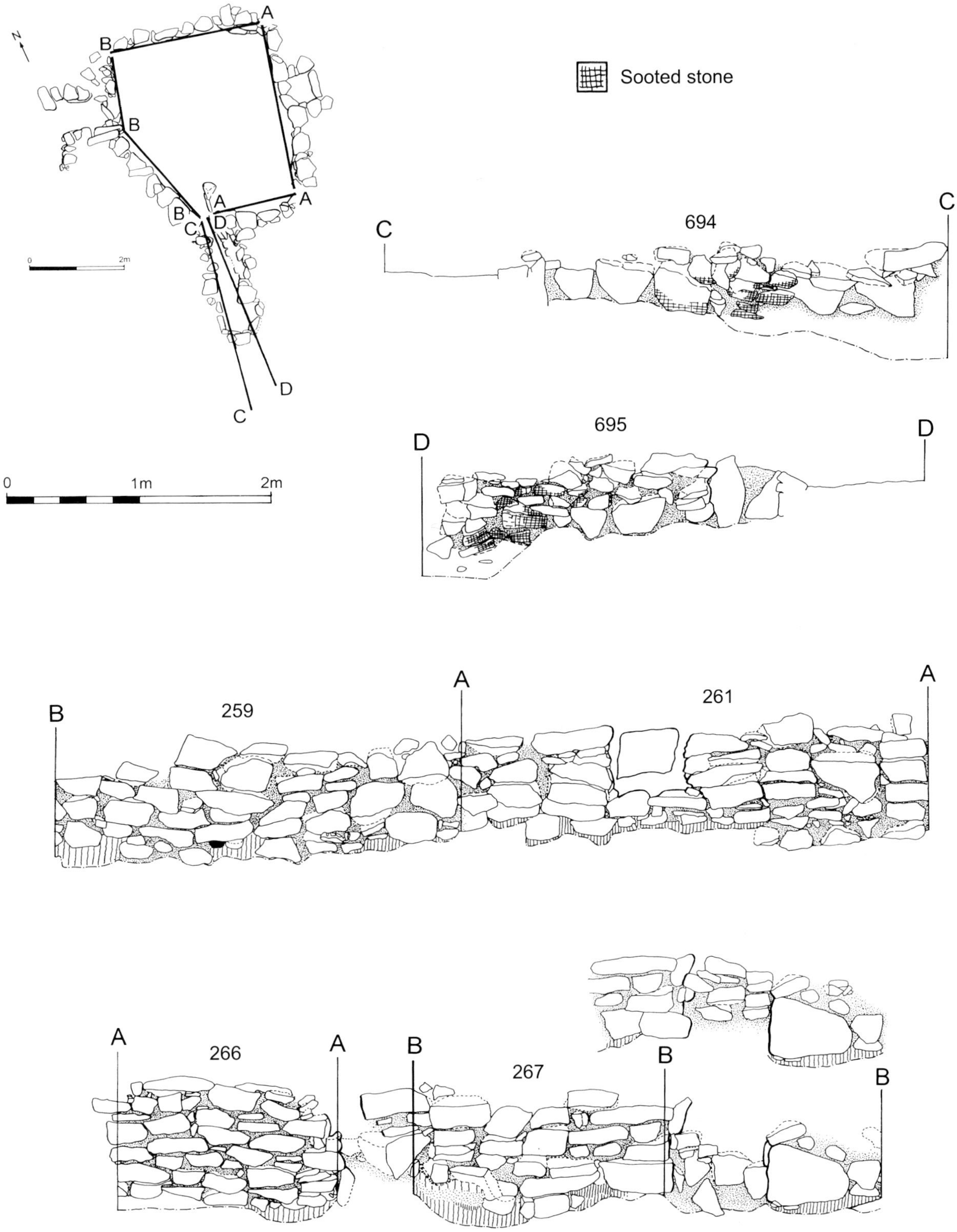

Figure 58. Elevations of the walls of the kiln/barn

Figure 59. The west wall of the kiln/barn. The loose sand at the base of the wall is a rabbit burrow

Figure 60. The blocked entrance to the kiln/barn with the winnowing hole in the background

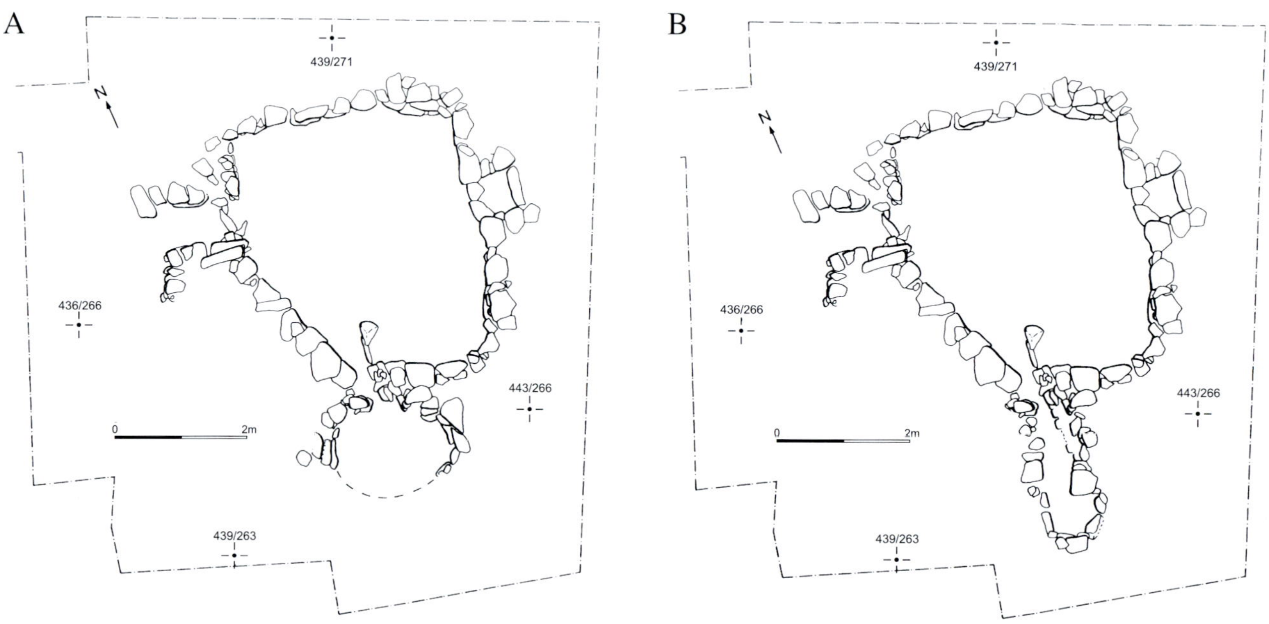

Figure 61. A. A plan of the first phase of the kiln/barn. B. A plan of the second phase of the kiln/barn

Figure 62. A view of the kiln after the earlier phase had been partially exposed and the later kiln/barn infilled

Figure 63. The kiln with the final phase fully exposed

the east side and these seemed to be set back, suggesting that the walls were opening out as they rose up.

The later kiln was defined by a passage (694, 695) 2.65 m long, measuring from the basal course, with a small bowl at the south end (Figure 63). The entrance of the passage was 0.60 m wide and when originally exposed in 1997 it still had one unstable, *in situ* lintel, approximately 1.0 m above the ground level. Two stones carry the line of this passage 0.65 m into the interior of the building (Figures 57, 64), but there was also a low sill separating the flue from the interior. At its narrowest point 0.8 m from the entrance, the passage was 0.20 m wide and roughly 1.65 m from the entrance it widened to 0.50 m. The height of the walls declines from 0.65 m at the entrance to 0.50 m at the end. These walls are constructed from a very ill-assorted collection of cobbles (Figure 58) and the structure created was very unstable. The passage near the entrance is largely coursed masonry and this is particularly true of the east side. As one moves towards the end of the passage, orthostats become more common. The bowl was 0.80 m by 0.60 m and constructed using three rather fine slabs.

Many of the stones of the passage were partially covered by soot. This started not at the entrance to the passage but just inside the entrance (Figure 58) and was most extensive on the stones between 0.5 m and 1.0 m before disappearing completely by 1.4 m.

Figure 64. The kiln looking from the inside of the barn

Table 36. Pottery from FC

context	weight	sherds	body	misc.	platter	Ave. Wght.
290	28	8	1	7		3.50
655	4	1			?1	4.00
291	14	3			2+?1	4.67
Total	46	12	1	7	4	3.83

Table 37. Animal bone NISP from FC

context	Sheep/Goat	Cattle	Pig	Total
655		1		1
690			1	1
290	2	1		3
total	2	2	1	5
	40%	40%	20%	

Table 38. Fish bone from FC in >10 mm samples (NISP)

	290
Pollack	1
Cod	4
Hake	1
Ling	1
total	7

Artefacts – J Bond, A Lane and P Macdonald

The ceramic assemblage from FC was small and not very diagnostic but platter and possible platter occurred in two contexts (291, 655; Table 36) confirming a Norse date. Average sherd size is fairly small (3.8g) suggesting trampling of sherds.

An iron object that may be either a buckle, or pennanular brooch pin or a loop-headed spike (Figure 56, 1864) was found in the pit fill (290). This is quite a large object and, like the knife in FB, it may be a deliberately placed offering. It is worth noting also the position of the copper alloy pin (1739) that is recorded as unstratified. This was found during the re-excavation of the trench backfill at the beginning of the 1999 excavations lying in a rabbit nest near the east wall of the kiln/barn. The most likely source of the object is from deposits behind the adjacent wall through which the rabbit had burrowed.

Charcoal – R Gale

Handpicked birch charcoal was collected from context 290 (Table 70).

Animal bone – C Ingrem, J Mulville and J Cartledge

A very small quantity of identifiable bones was recovered from these deposits; five bones of cattle, sheep and pig (Table 37), three bird bones, a great black–backed gull, a gannet and a curlew (the only one found on mound 3) and seven fish bones, of which four belong to cod whilst herring is notably absent (Table 38).

Discussion – N Sharples

The building that dominates trench F is clearly not a house; it is too small and the presence of the distinctive kiln suggests it was associated with agricultural activities, which certainly included drying cereals. Similar, though not identical, structures are known in the eighteenth and twentieth century vernacular architecture of the island and these structures will be discussed in chapter 11. The most distinctive feature of the kiln is that it does not appear to lie underneath the roof of the building. There is no evidence for an extension of the building beyond the south wall from which the kiln extends and it seems likely that the roof rested on the revetment wall that defines the interior of the building.

The roof partitions the building into an external area where the drying of crops took place and an internal area where the kiln fire was lit but which was otherwise unconnected with the drying of crops. The structure has another important feature that suggests that the interior was connected with crop processing. This is the 'ventilation hole', which was situated in the east wall, opposite the entrance in the west wall. This feature is best interpreted as a winnowing hole, which, when open, would have created a through draft that enabled the removal of chaff and weeds from threshed grain. This arrangement of door and winnowing hole is a common feature of buildings in the Highlands and Islands. The use of this building for both the drying and winnowing of grain clearly suggests it is closely connected with crop processing. It also possible that crops were stored in the southeast corner of the building and therefore the building will henceforth be referred to as the kiln/barn.

The kiln was clearly substantially remodelled during its life and this suggests it had a relatively long period of use. The barn was built as a semi-subterranean structure with access on the flat to the west but with the roof resting on the ground surface to the east. Only a small part of the foundation pit was excavated but it is noticeable

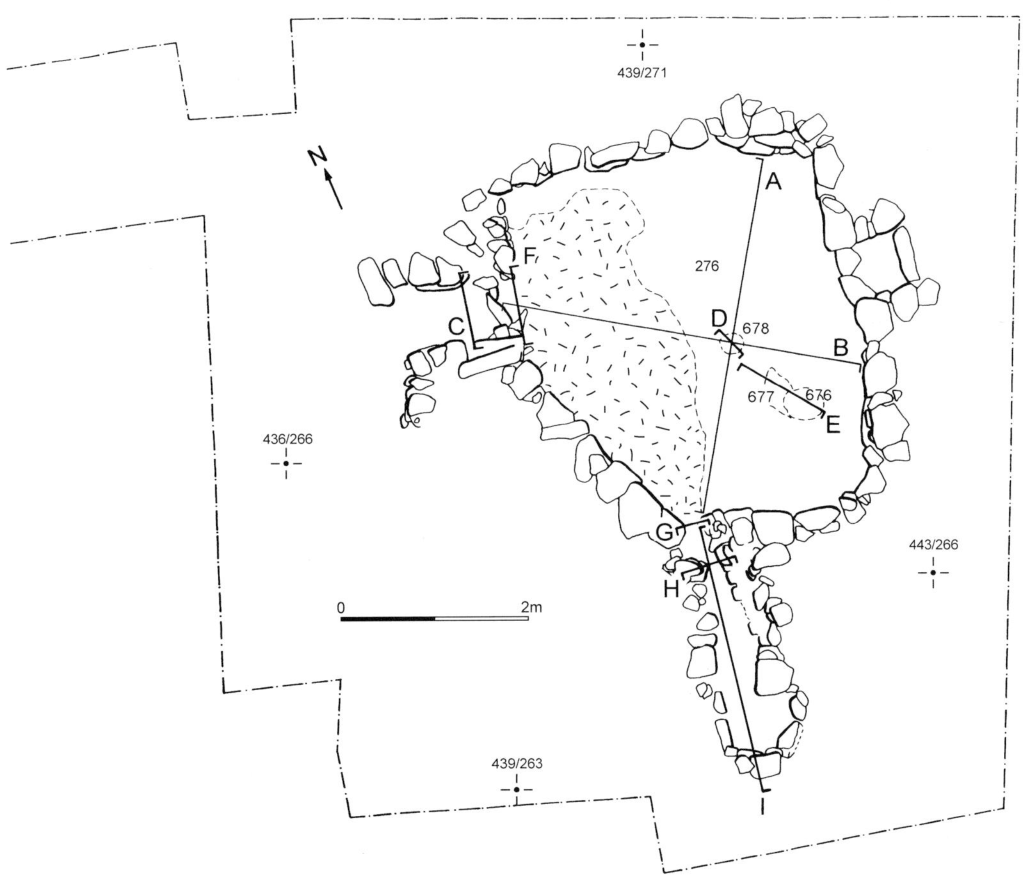

Figure 65. A plan of the kiln/barn showing the position of the sections in Figure 66 and the location of the underlying contexts and the extent of the more compact ash spread within layer 276

that, like the adjacent pit FB, this produced a significant iron object and, though the identification of the function of this object is problematic, it may well be a deliberately placed object.

The occupation of the kiln/barn (FD) – N Sharples

The occupation of the kiln/barn was represented by two almost continuous floor layers which were separated by layers of sand that might have been deliberately dumped as part of the major structural modification of the kiln noted above. Several discrete contexts were also noted both below the primary floor and between the two floor layers and there was evidence for a hearth in the mouth of the kiln. The floor layers were intensively sampled and samples were also taken from most of the discrete contexts. These provide a substantial assemblage of ecological data related to the use of the kiln/barn. The lowest floor layer was also examined using soil micromorphology and this provides important information on the formation of this floor deposit.

The lowest floor layer was a compact red-orange sand with charcoal flecks (276, Figure 65). This was particularly hard and compact along the west edge of the interior. It was separated from the overlying floor by a soft brown sand (275) and a thin layer of white sand (274/272). The upper floor was a compact red-brown sand with charcoal flecks (269). These layers covered most of the interior of the structure though there was a gap between the northern edge of 269 and wall 259. Radiocarbon dates were obtained from single grains of oat from both floors. The lowest floor produced a radiocarbon date (OxA-10278) from sample square 8629 (Figure 66). This produced a date of 563±33 bp, which when calibrated indicates occupation in the period cal AD 1300–1440 (95% confidence). A second radiocarbon date (OxA-10305) came from sample square 8633 (Figure 66). This produced a date of 705±50 bp, which when calibrated indicates occupation within cal AD 1220–1400 (95% confidence). The upper floor produced a radiocarbon date (OxA-10276) from sample square 5964 (Figure 66). This produced a date of 537±34 bp, which when calibrated indicates occupation within cal AD 1320–1440 (95% confidence). A second radiocarbon date (OxA-10277) came from sample square 5971 (Figure 66). This produced a date of 521±32 bp which when calibrated indicates occupation within cal AD 1320–1450 (95% confidence). The significance of these dates is discussed in chapter 8.

The earliest deposits inside the kiln/barn interior were three small features 676, 677, 678 that could be defined as dumps quite separate from the overlying floor (Figures 65, 67). 678 lay near the centre of the building whereas 676 and 677 were in the southeast quadrant. 678 was a charcoal-flecked sand in a very shallow scoop 0.03 m deep, 0.24 m long by 0.20 m wide. 677 was a charcoal-flecked patch of sand, 0.4 m long by 0.24 m wide and 0.05 m thick, which overlay 676, an orange sand 0.44 m long by 0.32 m wide and 0.07 m thick; neither appeared to be in a negative feature. Lying between 276 and 275 was a patch of charcoal-rich sand (657). Within 269 was

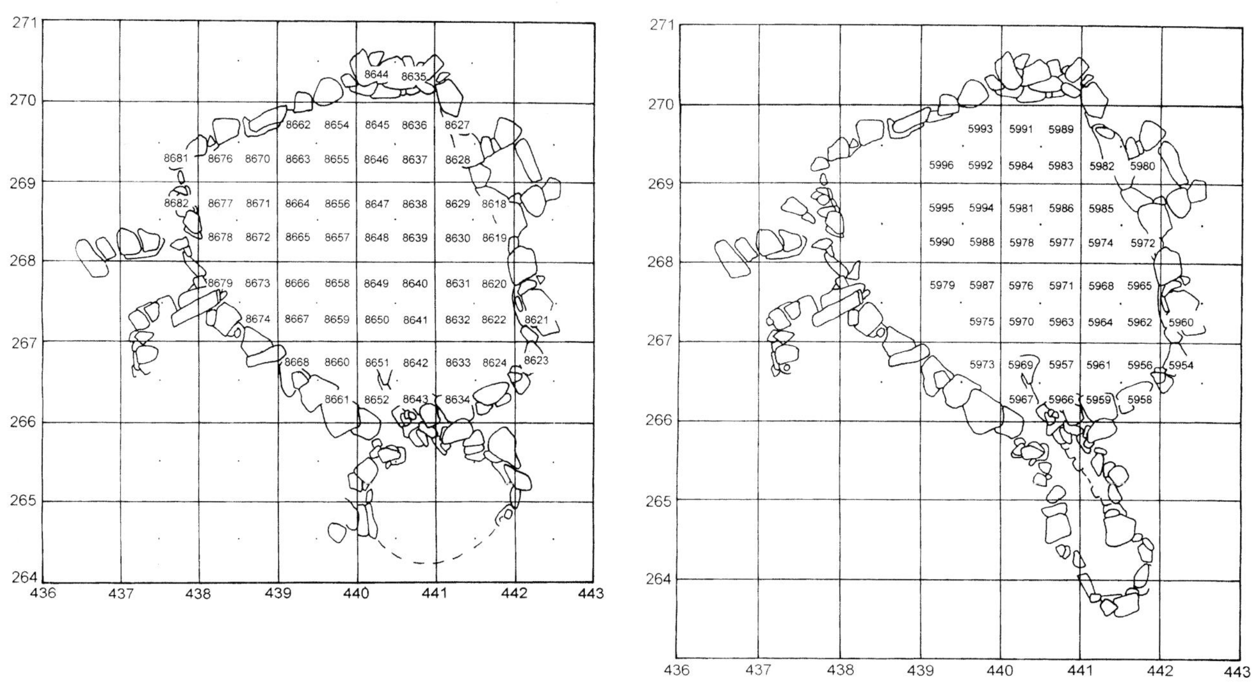

Figure 66. A. Plan of sample squares, floor 1. B. Plan of sample squares, floor 2

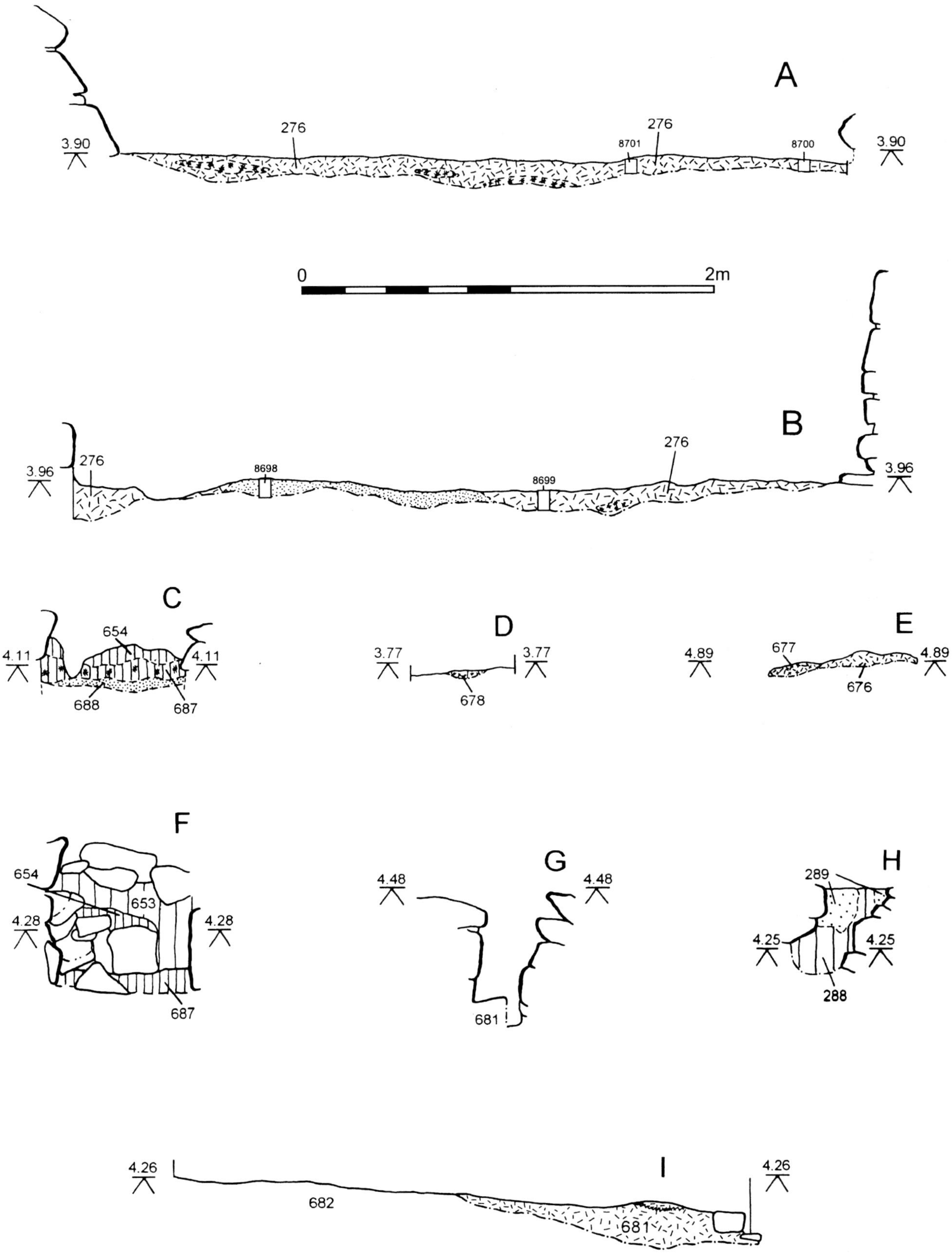

Figure 67. Sections associated with the occupation of the kiln/barn. The location of the soil micromorphology samples are indicated on sections A and B.

a charcoal layer (278), 0.52 m by 0.4 m and lying on top of it was another patch of charcoal (271), 0.6 m by 0.2 m.

The area around the entrance to the kiln was characterised by intense burning. There was a distinctive orange sand (681) within the passage (Figure 67). This reached a maximum thickness of 0.20 m at the entrance to the passage. At the top a thin charcoal line was observed which separated out an upper layer of yellow-orange sand. These were not given separate context numbers. The deposits inside the flue (the kiln passage) were separated from those outside by two stones. Outside the lowest deposit was a charcoal layer (277/658) that was overlain by an orange sand (270). These layers were defined on the east side by two upright stones that continued the line of the passage into the interior.

The wind-blown sand fill of the ventilation hole came down onto a compact brown sand (273). In contrast the west entrance was deliberately infilled with rubble and there is evidence, in the form of collapsed stones, for a formal revetment closing off the entrance passage. The floor of the passage was dark red-brown sand (687), which lay directly on the underlying pale grey sand (688). Above this the passage was filled with rubble that can be separated into two layers, a dark brown sand (654) overlain by a pale brown sand (653, Figure 67).

Soil micromorphology – K Milek

Four micromorphological samples were taken from the primary floor of the structure (context 276), from sections exposed along the two main axes of the building (Figure 67). This ensured that several different floor areas were sampled, including a spread of peat ash on the western side of the structure, the area adjacent to the mouth of the flue, and the centre of the floor. The samples incorporate three main sediment types: the natural dune sand below the structure, the layer of peat ash that spread between the mouth of the flue and the entrance on the west side of the structure, and the mixed ash and sand that represented the bulk of the floor. A summary of the sampling location and sediment type(s) captured by each micromorphology sample is provided in Table 39 and Tables 40 and 41 contain a summary of the features observed in thin section.

Natural dune sands

The natural dune sand at the bottom of sample 8698 was very well sorted medium sand (250–500 µm) containing c. 30% quartz, c. 30% feldspars, c. 30% calcium carbonate (shells and other marine bodyforms), c. 5% amphibole, c. 2% clinopyroxene, and trace amounts of other minerals, including olivine and polycrystalline quartz. It is significant that both the size and mineralogy of the natural sand below the structure differed from the sand component embedded in the peat ash in the floor deposit. These differences, and their possible interpretation, will be discussed in more detail below.

The natural dune sand had a *single grain* microstructure, with c. 5% localised intergrain micro-aggregates composed of fine organo-mineral material. These micro-aggregates were brown to dark brown in plane polarised light, with a *dotted* aspect, containing up to 50% silt and fine organic fragments under 10 µm in size. The birefringence of this fine organo-mineral material (i.e. its optical properties under crossed polarised light) was *crystallitic*, reflecting the dominance of fine crystals of calcium carbonate embedded in the groundmass. There was, however, a locally *undifferentiated* b-fabric, where the birefringence of the groundmass was masked by iron oxides, rendering it opaque in crossed polarised light. In oblique incident light, this fine organo-mineral material reflected colours ranging from reddish-brown to bright yellowish-orange and included aggregates of *rubified fine mineral material*. This is a category of material only found in archaeological contexts, since it represents burnt fine mineral material, and is therefore not a term used by Bullock, Fedoroff, Jongerius, Stoops, Tursina and Babel (1985). Here, it is defined as clay-sized mineral material,

Table 39. Summary of soil micromorphology sample locations, and their major macro- and mesoscopic characteristics

Sample	Location of Sample	Summary of Macro- and Mesoscopic Characteristics
8698	Compact peat ash at western side of structure.	Sterile sand capped by 6 cm of peat ash, which contained six internal horizons, each distinguished by different proportions of sand, ash and pore space.
8699	Compact brown sand in centre of structure.	Mixed sand and aggregates of ash; no internal horizonation, but gradual increase in density towards top of sample.
8700	Compact brown sand at south end of structure, adjacent to mouth of flue.	Mixed sand and aggregates of ash containing four internal horizons, each distinguished by different proportions of sand, ash and pore space.
8701	Compact brown sand in south central part of structure.	Mixed sand and aggregates of ash containing four internal horizons, each distinguished by different proportions of sand, ash and pore space.

Table 40. Summary of features observed in thin sections 8698, 8699, 8700 and 8701: microstructure, porosity and coarse mineral component

				Structure			Coarse Mineral Material (>100 µm)					
Thin Section	Microstratigrapic Unit	Layer Thickness	Lower Boundary of Microstratigraphic Unit	Microstructure	$C/f_{(100\ \mu m)}$ Related Distribution	$C/f_{(100 \mu m)}$ Ratio	$CaCO_3$ (shell and bodyforms)	Quartz	Feldspar	Amphibole	Other Minerals	Fine:Medium Sand Ratio
8698	276.a	7 mm	Clear	Vughy	Porphyric	70:30	■	■■■	■■■	■	■	75:25
	276.b	12 mm	Clear	Spongy	Porphyric	60:40	■	■■■	■■■	■	■	75:25
	276.c	8 mm	Sharp	Spongy	Porphyric	70:30	■■	■■■	■■■	■	■	50:50
	276.d	17 mm	Irregular	Spongy	Porphyric	60:40	■	■■■	■■■	■	■	75:25
	276.e	4 mm	Irregular	Spongy	Porphyric	70:30	■■	■■■	■■■	■	■	50:50
	276.f	7 mm	Sharp	Spongy	Porphyric	50:50	■	■■■	■■■	■	■	75:25
	Natural dune sand	13 mm	Bottom of thin section	Single grain	Monic; enaulic	93:7	■■■	■■■	■■■	■	■	30:70
8699	276.g	67 mm	Bottom of thin section	Bridged grain	Gefuric	80:20	■■■	■■■	■■■	■	■	30:70
8700	276.h	20 mm	Clear, undulating	Vughy; spongy	Porphyric	50:50	■	■■■	■■■	■	■	75:25
	276.i	15 mm	Clear	Spongy	Porphyric	80:20	■■■	■■■	■■■	■	■	30:70
	276.j	3 mm	Clear	Vughy; spongy	Porphyric	50:50	■	■■■	■■■	■	■	75:25
	276.k	30 mm	Bottom of thin section	Bridged grain	Gefuric	90:10	■■■	■■■	■■■	■	■	30:70
8701	276.l	20 mm	Clear	Bridged grain	Gefuric	85:15	■■■	■■■	■■■	■	■	30:70
	276.m	10 mm	Irregular	Spongy	Porphyric	70:30	■■	■■■	■■■	■	■	50:50
	276.n	4 mm	Undulating	Single, bridged grain	Monic; gefuric	97:3	■■■	■■■	■■■	■	■	30:70
	276.o	30 mm	Bottom of thin section	Spongy	Porphyric	65:35	■■	■■■	■■■	■	■	50:50

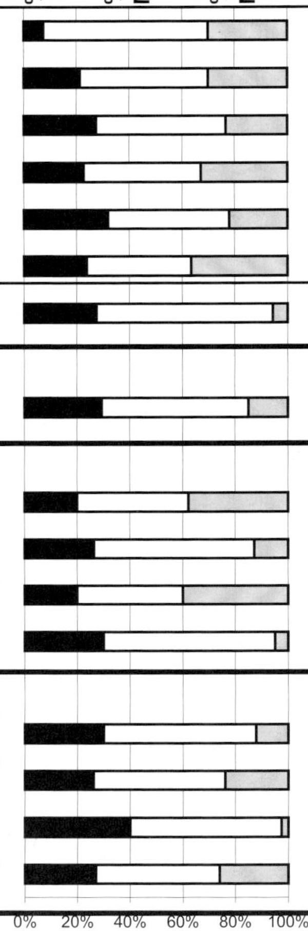

Frequency class refers to % area (following Bullock et al. 1985): - trace amount (<1%); ■ very few (1-5%); ■■ few (5-15%); ■■■ frequent (15-30%)

Table 41. Summary of features observed in thin sections 8698, 8699, 8700 and 8701: fine mineral component, organic component and other anthropogenic inclusions

Thin Section	Microstratigaphic Unit	Nature of Fine Mineral Material (PPL)	Colour of Fine Mineral Material (OIL)	Birefringence Fabric (XPL)
8698	276.a	Grey; dark brown; dotted	Yellowish-orange; orangy-red	Crystallitic; locally undifferentiated
	276.b	Grey; dark brown; dotted	Yellowish-orange; orangy-red	Crystallitic; locally undifferentiated
	276.c	Grey; dark brown; dotted	Yellowish-orange; orangy-red	Crystallitic; locally undifferentiated
	276.d	Grey; dark brown; dotted	Yellowish-orange; orangy-red	Crystallitic; locally undifferentiated
	276.e	Grey; dark brown; dotted	Yellowish-orange; orangy-red	Crystallitic; locally undifferentiated
	276.f	Grey; dark brown; dotted	Yellowish-orange; orangy-red	Crystallitic; locally undifferentiated
	Natural dune sand	Brown; dotted	Yellowish-orange; orangy-red	Crystallitic; locally undifferentiated
8699	276.g	Brown; dotted	Reddish-brown; yellowish-orange	Crystallitic; locally undifferentiated
8700	276.h	Brown; dotted	Reddish-brown; yellowish-orange	Crystallitic; locally undifferentiated
	276.i	Brown; dotted	Reddish-brown; yellowish-orange	Crystallitic; locally undifferentiated
	276.j	Brown; dotted	Reddish-brown; yellowish-orange	Crystallitic; locally undifferentiated
	276.k	Brown; dotted	Reddish-brown; yellowish-orange	Crystallitic; locally undifferentiated
8701	276.l	Brown; dotted	Reddish-brown; yellowish-orange	Crystallitic; locally undifferentiated
	276.m	Brown; dotted	Reddish-brown; yellowish-orange	Crystallitic; locally undifferentiated
	276.n	Brown; dotted	Reddish-brown; yellowish-orange	Crystallitic; locally undifferentiated
	276.o	Brown; dotted	Reddish-brown; yellowish-orange	Crystallitic; locally undifferentiated

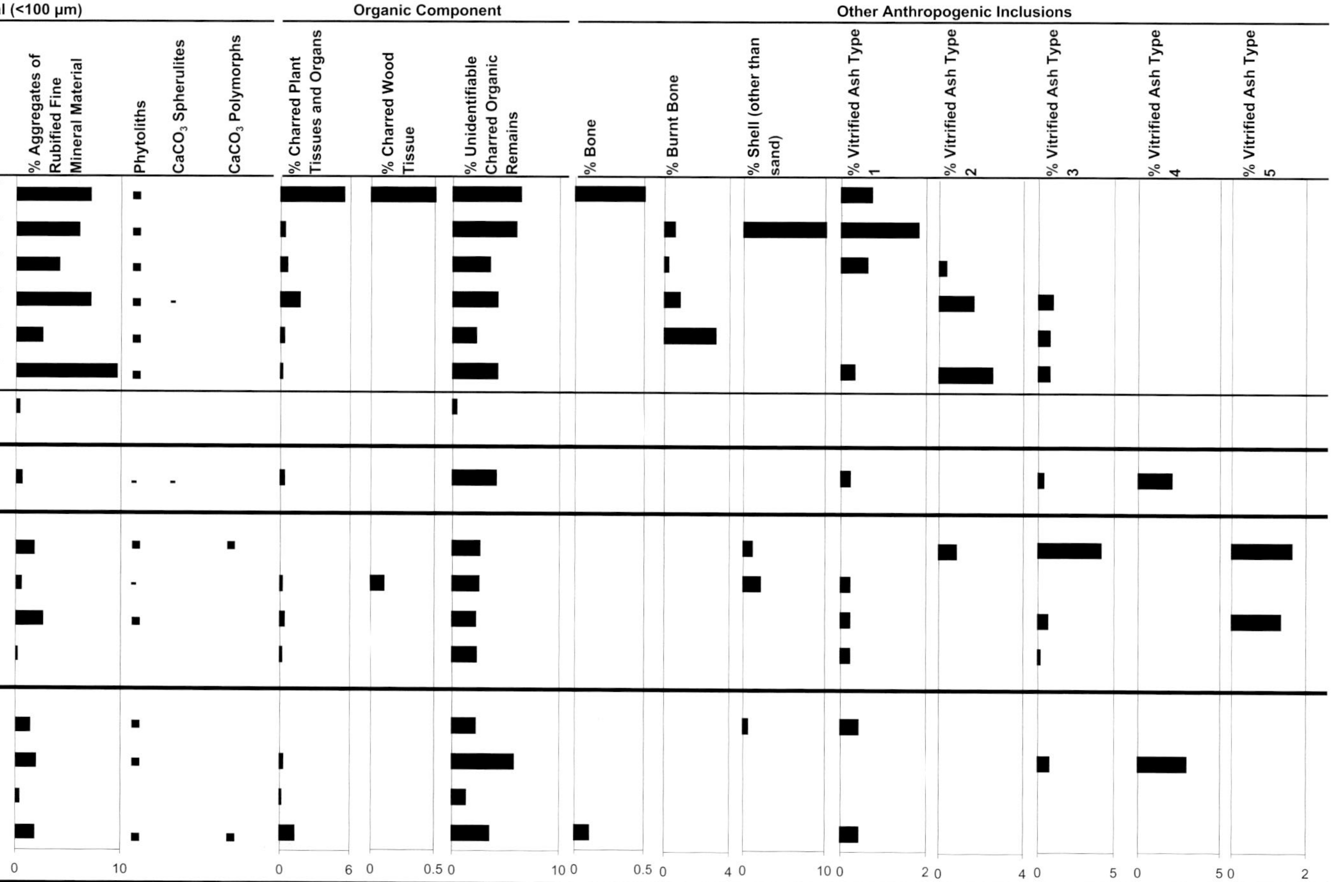

Frequency class refers to % area (following Bullock et al. 1985): - trace amount (<1%); ■ very few (1-5%); ■■ few (5-15%); ■■■ frequent (15-30%)

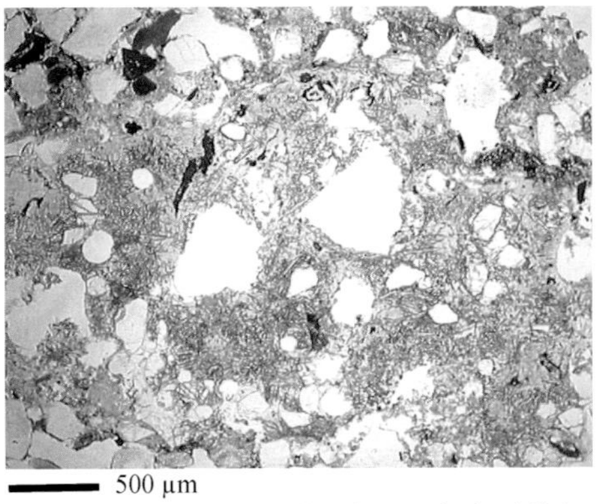

1 Vitrified ash Type 4 in plane polarised light, showing the amorphous yellow fabric (probably phosphatic) with acicular crystals.

2 Vitrified ash Type 4 in partially crossed polarised light, with the characteristically low order birefringence of the acicular crystals.

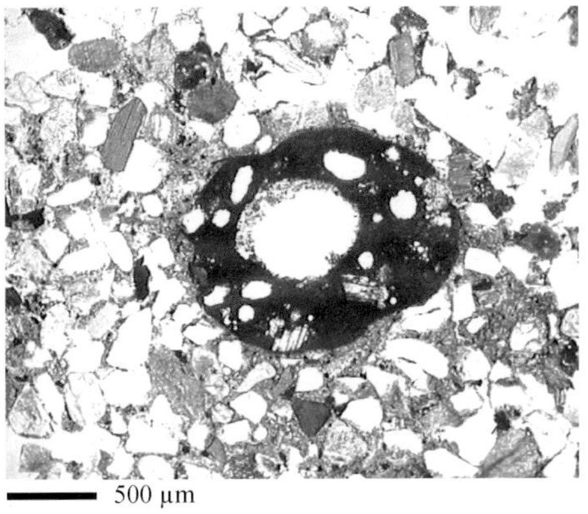

3 Vitrified ash Type 1 in plane polarised light.

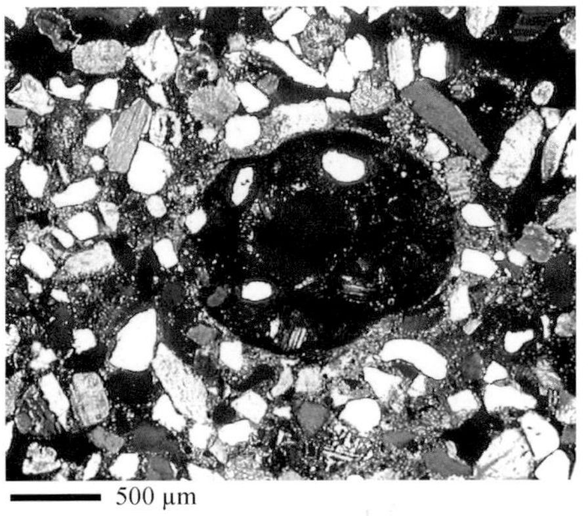

4 Vitrified ash Type 1 in crossed polarised light.

5 Burnt bone in plane polarised light.

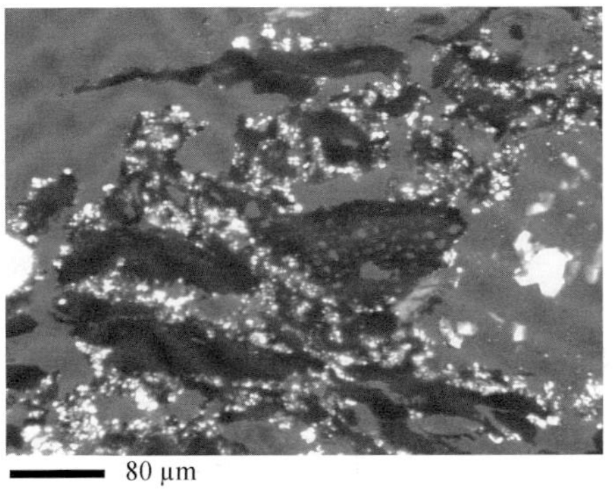

6 Dung ash in partially crossed polarised light, showing faecal spherulites.

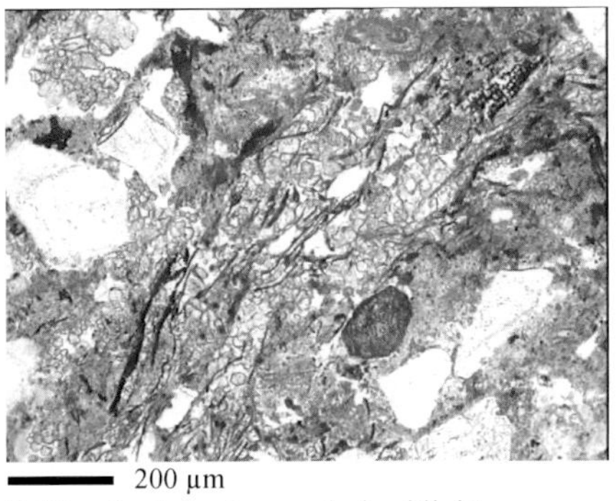

7 Wood ash in plane polarised light.

8 Wood ash in partially crossed polarised light, showing *in situ* calcitic crystals.

Figure 68. The soil micromorphology plates

which appears black in plane polarised light and dark reddish-brown in crossed polarised light (and is therefore probably microcrystalline), and reflects a glittery, bright reddish-orange colour in oblique incident light. Rubified fine mineral material is a common component of the peat ash layer above, and since most of the fine mineral material in the natural dune sand is present in the form of localised clusters of intergrain aggregates (soil fauna excrements), it was undoubtedly worked downwards by soil fauna.

Context 276: The peat ash deposit

Above the natural dune sand in sample 8698 was a thick layer of sandy loam that had been identified as peat ash in the field. This deposit had been spread between the mouth of the flue of the corn-drying kiln and the entrance on the west side of the structure, and was thought to potentially represent a deliberate attempt by the occupants of the site to create a more stable, compact surface in this part of the floor. In thin section, this deposit was composed of six distinct layers, each of which had slightly varying proportions of sand, fine organo-mineral material and pore space. These variations in composition affected the colour of each layer to the naked eye, with lighter layers representing those with relatively higher proportions of sand, and darker layers representing those with relatively higher proportions of fine organo-mineral material.

In contrast to the 'shelly' dune sand below, the sand component of context 276 contained only 10% shell sand (c. 5% of the total visible area in thin section), the dominant size of the sand was fine rather than medium, and the amphibole grains were frequently marked by a dark reddish-brown alteration rim that would appear to be a product of burning.[1] This fine, relatively shell-free sand embedded in the peat ash is likely to have been a component of the original peat. The sandiest layers within 276 (e.g. 276.c and 276.e) contained a slightly higher proportion of shell sand and the medium-sized sand fraction, indicating that they were derived from the natural dune sand.

The fine mineral material in these layers was grey to dark brown in plane polarised light, and had a dotted aspect, containing up to 50% inclusions of black silt-sized particles, many of which were finely fragmented charred organic remains. Other silt-sized inclusions embedded in this fine material were phytoliths, diatoms, and calcium carbonate spherulites of the type frequently found in herbivore dung (Canti 1999), some of which were clustered around fragments of charred plant material (Figure 68.6). Also embedded in the fine mineral material were silt-sized calcite grains, which were responsible for the crystallitic birefringence fabric that characterised the groundmass. An undifferentiated b-fabric was present in areas where the groundmass was heavily masked by iron oxides. Discrete aggregates of rubified fine mineral material were present in frequencies of up to 10%, representing about one quarter of all of the fine organo-mineral present in these layers. It is this rubified mineral material, and the oxidised iron throughout the groundmass, which creates the overall appearance of orange and reddish colours that are typical of South Uist peat ash.

Within the matrix of fine mineral material were also embedded charred organic remains and other inclusions that can be attributed to human activity within the structure (Table 41). Most charred organic remains were unidentifiable but in sample 8698 it was possible to identify leaves, stems, petioles and seeds of herbaceous plants, as well as possible moss (?) sporangium and leaves (Marco Madella, pers. comm.). A fragment of wood charcoal in layer 276.a was identified as belonging to the Betulaceae family (Lydia Zapata, pers. comm.), which includes species such as alder (*Alnus*), hazel (*Corylus*) and birch (*Betula*). A low shrub form of birch, such as *Betula nana*, is considered to be a likely candidate.

Relative to the other samples taken from context 276, the peat ash layers in sample 8698 contained the highest number of anthropogenic inclusions. These included burnt bones (<5%; e.g. Figure 68.5), one small fragment of unburnt bone, a large shell fragment, and various types of non-metallurgical slag (globules < 4mm in size eg. Figures 68.1 to 68.4). In total, five different types of non-metallurgical slag were distinguished on the basis of their optical characteristics (see Table 42), although all were characterised by rounded to subrounded shapes and vesicular microstructures. Microprobe analysis determined that the globules of Types 1–3 were composed predominantly of silica (c. 40–45%), iron (c. 15–20%) and calcium (c. 15–20%), as well as a smaller proportion of potassium, aluminium and magnesium (all < c. 8%). The acicular crystals in Types 2–4 were identified as augite, a clinopyroxene ($Ca(Mg,Fe)Si_2O_6$), which typically forms in basic, rapidly cooling environments. All of these

Table 42. Summary descriptions of the various types of 'vitrified ash' or 'non-metallurgical slag'

Type	Colour in PPL	Colour in OIL	Birefringence	Microstructure	Inclusions
1	Black	Dark grey	Undifferentiated	Vesicular	Fine sand
2	Black	Dark grey	Crystallitic and/or acicular	Vesicular	Fine sand
3	Grey and/or greyish brown	Light grey	Crystallitic	Vesicular	Fine sand
4	White, yellow and/or grey	Light grey to brownish grey	Crystallitic and/or acicular	Vesicular	Fine sand
5	Very pale yellowish brown	Pale yellow	Isotropic and weakly crystallitic	Vesicular	None to very few

elements were available in the peat ash and the lenses of dune sand, and their relative concentrations are within the ranges noted in other studies of vitrified sands and ashes (e.g. Evans and Tylecote 1967; Folk and Hoops 1982). The globules were evidently formed by the localised high-temperature vitrification of the phytoliths, siliceous and calcareous sands, iron oxides and calcareous ash crystals that were abundant in context 276.

Interpretation and discussion

A whole of suite of micromorphological characteristics, and comparison to experimentally burnt South Uist peat, combine to confirm that the portion of context 276 captured in sample 8698, on the west side of the structure, was composed predominantly of peat ash. The aggregates of rubified fine mineral material, as well as the general reddish aspect of the groundmass in reflected light, represent iron-rich mineral material that has been oxidised at high temperatures (Courty, Goldberg and Macphail 1989; Ulery and Graham, 1993). The presence of phytoliths, diatoms, and charred plant tissues in this layer is also typical of peat ash, and it is likely that the peat ash in sample 8698, which contains an abundance of identifiable plant organs, was produced by the burning of an upper peat deposit, rather than a lower, well-humified peat, in which the cell structure of most plant tissues would be decomposed. Also typical of South Uist peat is the significant quantity (up to 10%) of fine, wind-blown sand. Since the sand embedded in the reference samples and in the peat ash in sample 8698 is finer and less calcareous than the dune sand, it probably represents the wind-blown component of the original peat, which formed prior to the full development of the shelly sands on the west coast of the Outer Hebrides.

In contrast to the peat ash, there were higher proportions of shell and medium-sized grains in the two sandier lenses (276.c and 276.e), which are likely to be thin spreads of the calcareous, medium-sized sandy floor material covering the rest of the structure (see below). The successive deposition of peat ash and thin layers of coarser, more calcareous sand from other parts of the floor is not consistent with the hypothesis that the floor on the western side of the structure had been deliberately laid. The fine lensing, and the variable nature and composition of the mineral component, support a scenario in which fuel ash was periodically raked out from the mouth of the corn-drying kiln, and in which calcareous sands moved around the interior of the structure by scuffing and trampling.

While peat ash was certainly the dominant fuel residue present in sample 8698, the presence of charred wood tissue and localised concentrations of calcium carbonate spherulites, a distinctive crystal form that frequently occurs in herbivore dung (Canti 1999), indicate that both wood and dung were occasionally burnt as well. The low but persistent frequency of burnt bone embedded in the peat ash is also significant. The association of burnt bone and ash is usually considered to be a characteristic of domestic ash deposits, and it is therefore possible that the fire in this structure was at least occasionally used for cooking and/or for the burning of food waste.

Context 276: The main floor deposit

Samples 8699, 8700 and 8701 were taken from the central and southern parts of the floor, which appeared in the

Table 43. Summary of the goals, methods and results of the micromorphological analysis

Research Question	Method Employed	Micromorphological Results	Resolution
Deliberate floor construction?	Mineralogy and grain size compared to the natural sand below.	Mineralogy identical to the natural sand, except within aggregates of peat ash, due to the windblown sand component of the peat itself.	Floor was not deliberately laid, but gradually accumulated during the use of the structure.
Fire at the mouth of the flue?	Composition of the floor in this area, and evidence for alteration of the original substrate by burning.	In this location there was a significantly higher concentration of vitrified ash than in other parts of the floor.	A fire had been located at the mouth of the flue.
Types of fuel used?	Composition of ashes, based on their calcareous, siliceous, charred organic and rubified mineral components.	Predominantly peat ash, but also localised concentrations and small aggregates of wood and dung ash.	Peat was the dominant type of fuel used, but dung and wood were also used.
Function of the building?	Types and quantity of anthropogenic inclusions.	Anthropogenic inclusions dominated by ash and charred plant remains, with a smaller quantity of burnt bone.	The interpretation of the building as a barn for the storage and processing of cereals is corroborated. Cooking may also have taken place within the building, perhaps to make use of the fire when it was lit for drying grain.

field to be a compact brown sand. In thin section, the grain size, shape, and mineralogy of these sandy deposits were very similar to the natural dune sand below the structure, and had clearly been derived from them.

These calcareous sands were bridged by fine organo-mineral material that was brown in plane polarised light, and had a dotted aspect, containing 40–50% black, silt-sized mineral and organic fragments. It appeared brown, reddish-brown and yellowish-orange in oblique incident light, the latter colour indicating the presence of iron oxides. In crossed polarised light, this material exhibited crystallitic birefringence, but was locally undifferentiated where iron oxides had masked the b-fabric. A low but consistent number of phytoliths and aggregates of rubified fine mineral material were also present. These characteristics have much in common with the peat ash described above, indicating that most of this fine mineral material consists of peat ash that has been raked or trampled across the calcareous, sandy floor. In addition to peat ash, a small cluster of calcium carbonate spherulites associated with charred plant residues in sample 8699 indicates the presence of a least a small quantity of dung ash. Samples 8700 (especially 276.h) and 8701 (especially 276.o) also contain low but significant quantities of calcite (Figures 68.7, 68.8), which is the dominant component of wood ash (Wattez and Courty 1987).

In addition, all three samples contain aggregates and lenses of material similar in every way to the peat ash deposit (e.g. lens 276.j). Compared to the calcareous, sandy fabric that dominates the floor, these aggregates and lenses have a significantly higher proportion of fine mineral material and aggregates of oxidised iron, a higher proportion of fine sand grains, and a much lower proportion of shell sand – all of which points to the origin of this material in the peat ash deposit on the west side of the building. Some layers within samples 8700 and 8701 contained higher quantities of peat ash aggregates (276.h, 276.m and 276.o), which seemed to have been partially reworked into the surrounding sandy matrix, probably by bioturbation. Evidence for bioturbation came from the presence of two partially infilled worm channels in sample 8701, the very rare soil fauna excrement in sample 8700, the very rare granule of biogenic calcium carbonate (produced by earthworms) in samples 8699 and 8700, and the destruction of all internal horizonation in sample 8699.

Like the peat ash deposit, the organic component of the floor deposit consisted of charred organic remains, most of which were unidentifiable organic residues – those without any surviving cell structure. Charred plant tissues and organs were present only in frequencies of less than or around 1%, and of these, only one herbaceous stem and one possible moss (?) leaf could be identified. In general, the organic remains in these samples were much more poorly preserved and more highly fragmented than those in the thicker peat ash layer in sample 8698. This is likely to be a product of mechanical disturbance, first by the movement of this charred material, along with small quantities of peat ash, across the floor by raking and/or trampling, and later by bioturbation.

The suite of other anthropogenic inclusions in the floor deposit differed significantly from the peat ash deposit. Burnt bone was completely absent, and unburnt bone was present only in trace amounts in sample 8701. Bones that were rounded to subrounded in shape, precisely the same size as the sand grains (100–250 μm) and clearly part of the sand skeleton rather than embedded in peat ash, were interpreted as relics and were not counted when quantifying bone inclusions of anthropogenic origin. Two such relict bone fragments were present in sample 8701, and one in sample 8700. Rounded and subrounded vesicular aggregates of non-metallurgical slag were present in all of the samples taken from the floor deposit, the highest concentration occuring in the uppermost layer (276.h) of sample 8700.

Interpretation and discussion

The floor layer (276) was clearly composed of a mixture of the natural dune sand below the structure and the peat ash that dominated the upper 48 mm of sample 8698. There is no evidence that the mineral material making up the floor had been imported into the structure or deliberately laid as a floor. Instead, the lens of peat ash and the layers containing higher frequencies of peat ash aggregates suggest that the floor deposit developed *in situ*, through the raking and trampling of ash debris into the natural dune sand.

It is significant that there is an especially high quantity of non-metallurgical slag in sample 8700. This sample was taken at the south end of the structure, adjacent to the mouth of the flue of the corn-drying kiln. The fact that this sample contains a high quantity of non-metallurgical slag can be attributed to its close proximity to the fire that is likely to have been located at the mouth of the flue when the corn-drying kiln was in use.

Sampling – P Marshall, N Sharples and H Smith

Ninety-eight samples, 900.1 litres of soil, were taken and processed from the FD contexts: 32 from the upper floor, 54 from the lower floor, and twelve from other contexts. Seventy of these samples had the below 10 mm residue sorted.

The assemblage from the above 10 mm sort was very impoverished. It included only occasional occurrences of fish bone (an average density of 0.02 pieces per litre), mammal bone (0.09 pieces per litre), pot (only 4 pieces in total), and even the marine molluscs were quite sparse (limpets 0.15 individuals per litre, winkles 0.22 individuals per litre). However, the lower floor was unusual in producing substantial quantities of both slag and coprolite. The densities of most material were slightly higher in the upper floor with only limpets denser in the lower floor.

It was decided during the sorting of the below 10 mm residues from the upper floor that it was necessary to

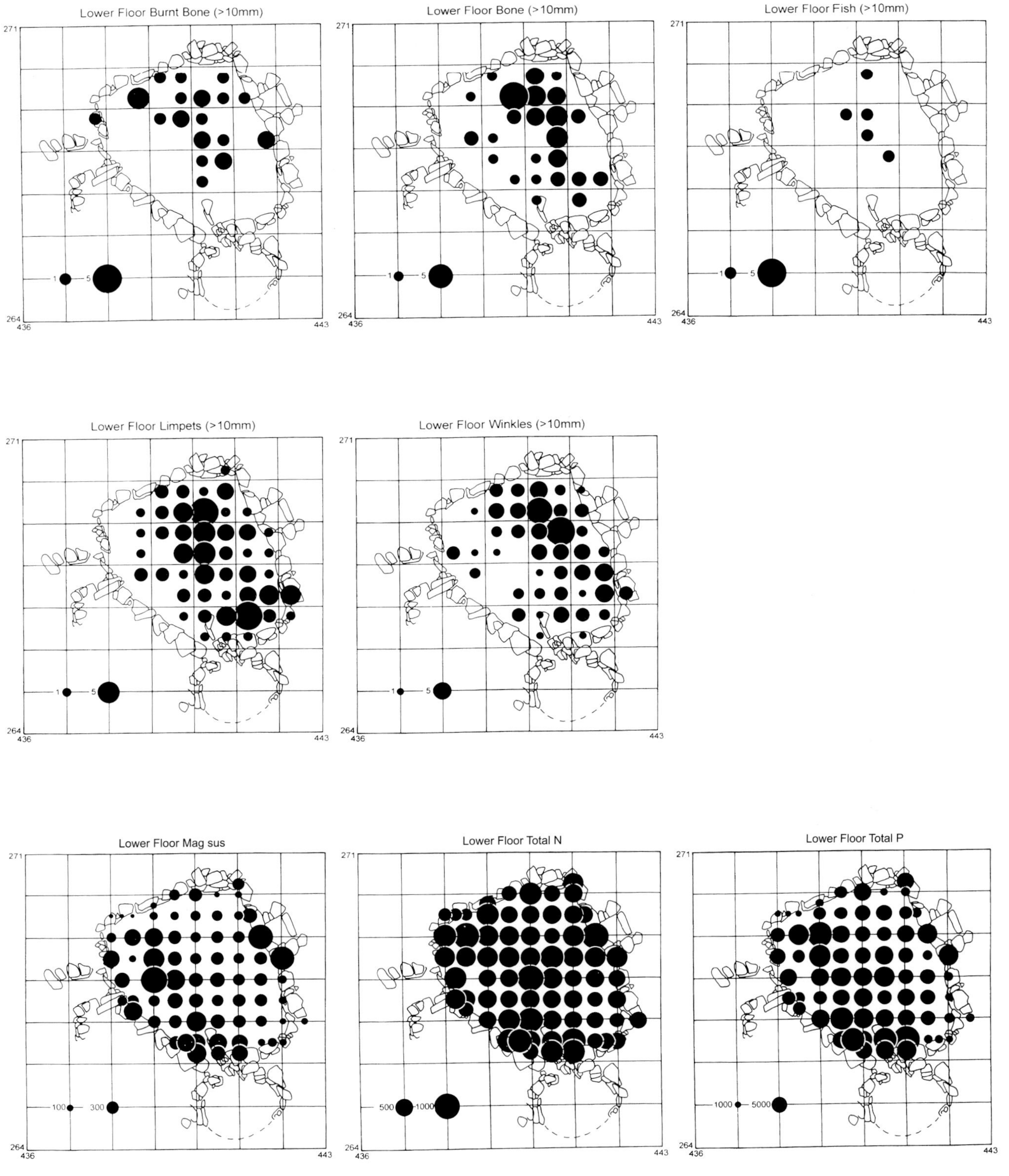

Figure 69. Distribution maps of the material recovered (number of fragments) from floor 1 during sieving through a 10 mm mesh and the results of the chemical analysis of the soil

reduce the number of samples sorted, from that point on only 50% of the floor samples were sorted. This reduced the post-excavation costs but still provided sufficient information for an analysis of the horizontal patterning. As part of the post-excavation processing the barn floor samples were floated for a second time in the laboratory to increase the recovery of carbonised plant remains. This reduced considerably the quantities of charcoal and seed found during sorting of the residues.

Both floors have very similar contents in the below 10 mm residues and seem to have been formed and used in an identical manner. Only two categories of material, slag and BOM, were found in 100% of the samples; pot (and seed, owing to second flotation) were absent from over 50%. The only categories of material which regularly had densities above 100 pieces per litre were BOM and slag, and the latter in particular had a very dispersed distribution with some samples producing very large quantities of material. These samples were generally much poorer in cultural material than the samples from the house floors and are characterised by large quantities of small slag and BOM fragments.

Floor 1

Total phosphorus is generally very high across the whole of the lower barn floor (Figure 69), with values ranging from 927 – 12,573 mg/kg, with an average of 4920 mg/kg. The lower concentrations are found towards the southeast corner (1235 – 1655 mg/kg) of the building and the far northwest corner (927 – 994 mg/kg). The highest concentrations are found around the entrance to the kiln flue itself (9319 – 12,573 mg/kg), and also in the northwestern area of the floor, which corresponds with greater accumulation of ash in the floor layers in this location. The pattern shown in phosphorus is mirrored by the concentration of nitrogen (Figure 69). Values range from 258 – 978 mg/kg, with an average of 561.46 mg/kg, which are lower than the N values in all three house floors. A cluster of high values located around the flue entrance (789 – 907 mg/kg) corresponds with the thick ash deposit.

Magnetic susceptibility values (χ) vary from 45 – 1146 ($10^{-8}m^3kg^{-1}$) but are generally high compared to the house floors, with an average of 335 ($10^{-8}m^3kg^{-1}$). The distribution of χ is shown in Figure 69. A cluster of high values corresponds with the high concentrations of phosphorus and ash around the flue entrance (456 – 702 ($10^{-8}m^3kg^{-1}$)), although higher values occur in the northwest of the floor (608 – 1146 ($10^{-8}m^3kg^{-1}$)) and northeast of the floor (918 – 1000 ($10^{-8}m^3kg^{-1}$)). Enhanced values of χ are consistent with an area of burning or the presence of materials resulting from such activities, i.e. ash.

The high values of P and N around the flue entrance correspond with the very thick ash deposits at this point and probably reflect the concentration of elements through burning of organic materials (see discussion). This interpretation is supported by the distribution of magnetic susceptibility levels in this area.

The microdebitage from the floor of the kiln/barn was not as common as from the house floors (note that the charcoal and carbonised plant concentrations are misleading as these samples were refloated in Cardiff). Only the slag occurred in large quantities and the source of this material is discussed in detail by T Young (see chapter 10).

The distribution of the material from sorting the above 10 mm fraction is depicted in Figures 69 and 70. The BOM and slag is concentrated in the southwest in front of the entrance to the kiln and this contrasts with the burnt bone which is found in the north and east. Fish bone and mammal bone have a more central distribution in the north half of the building and this is comparable to the distribution of shellfish, though limpets also have a significant concentration along the south wall. The

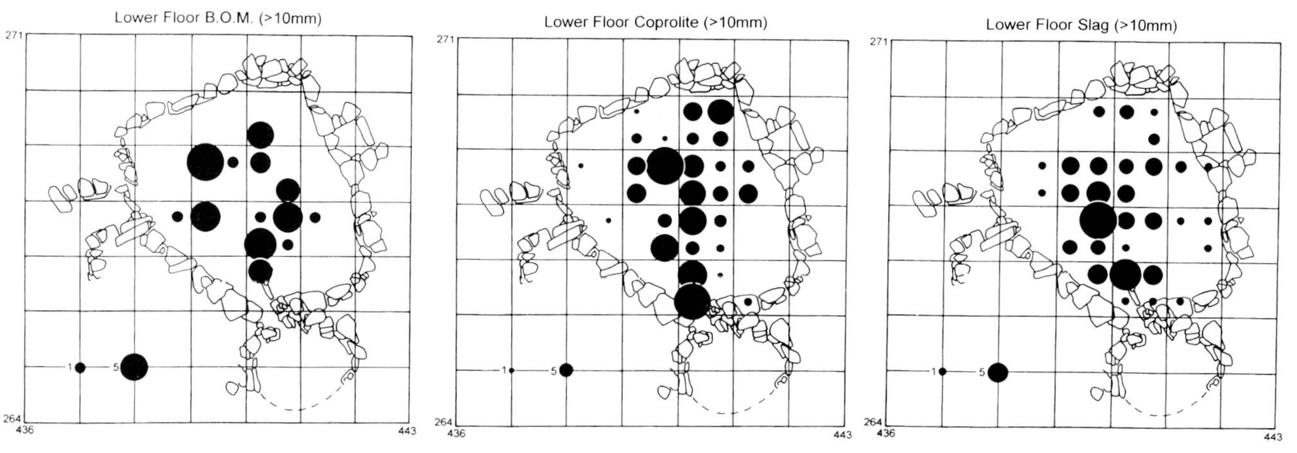

Figure 70. Distribution maps of the material recovered (number of fragments) from floor 1 during sieving through a 10 mm mesh

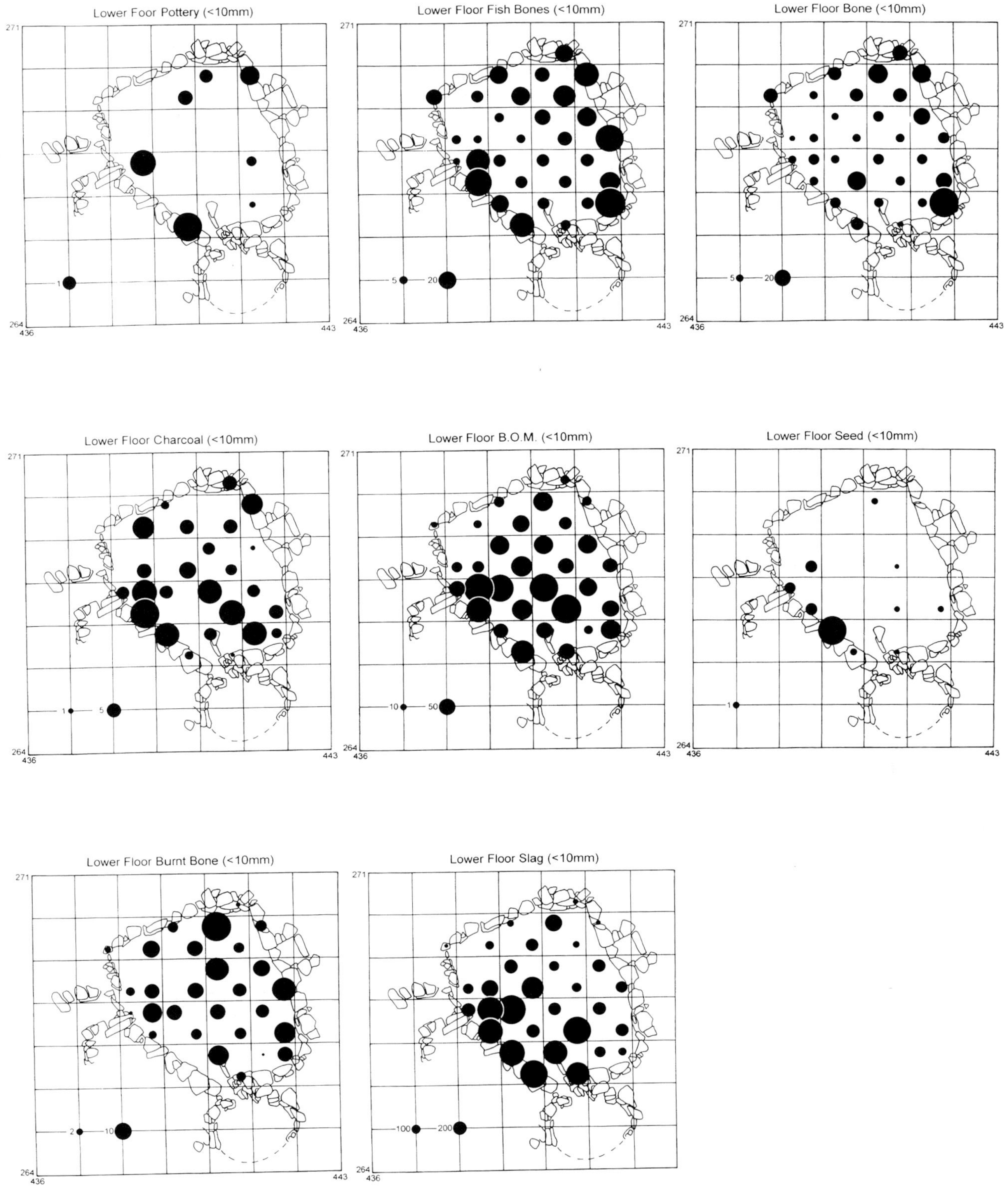

Figure 71. Distribution maps of the material recovered (number of fragments per litre of soil) from floor 1 during sorting of the below 10 mm residues

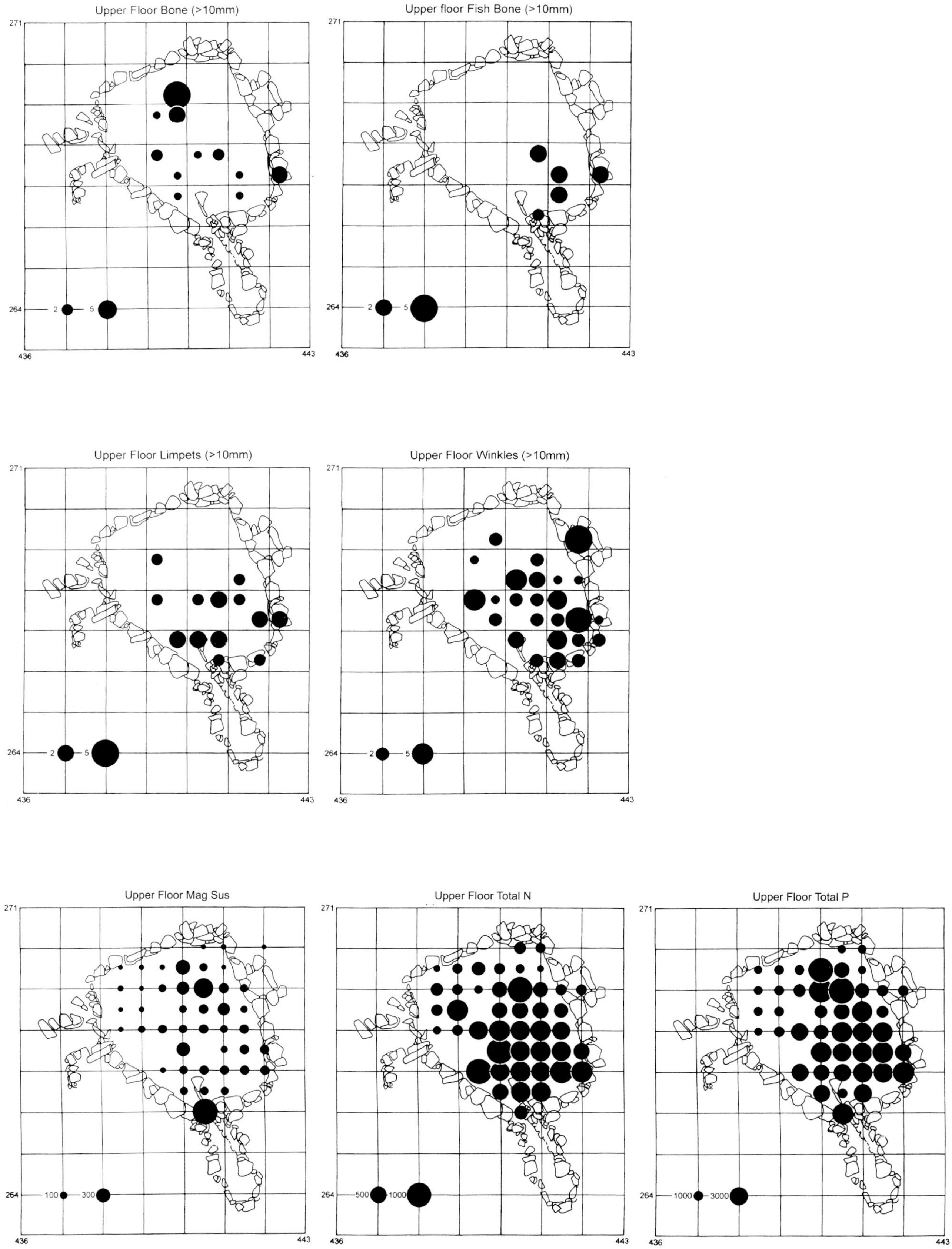

Figure 72. Distribution maps of the material recovered (number of fragments) from floor 2 during sieving through a 10 mm mesh and the results of the chemical analysis of the soil

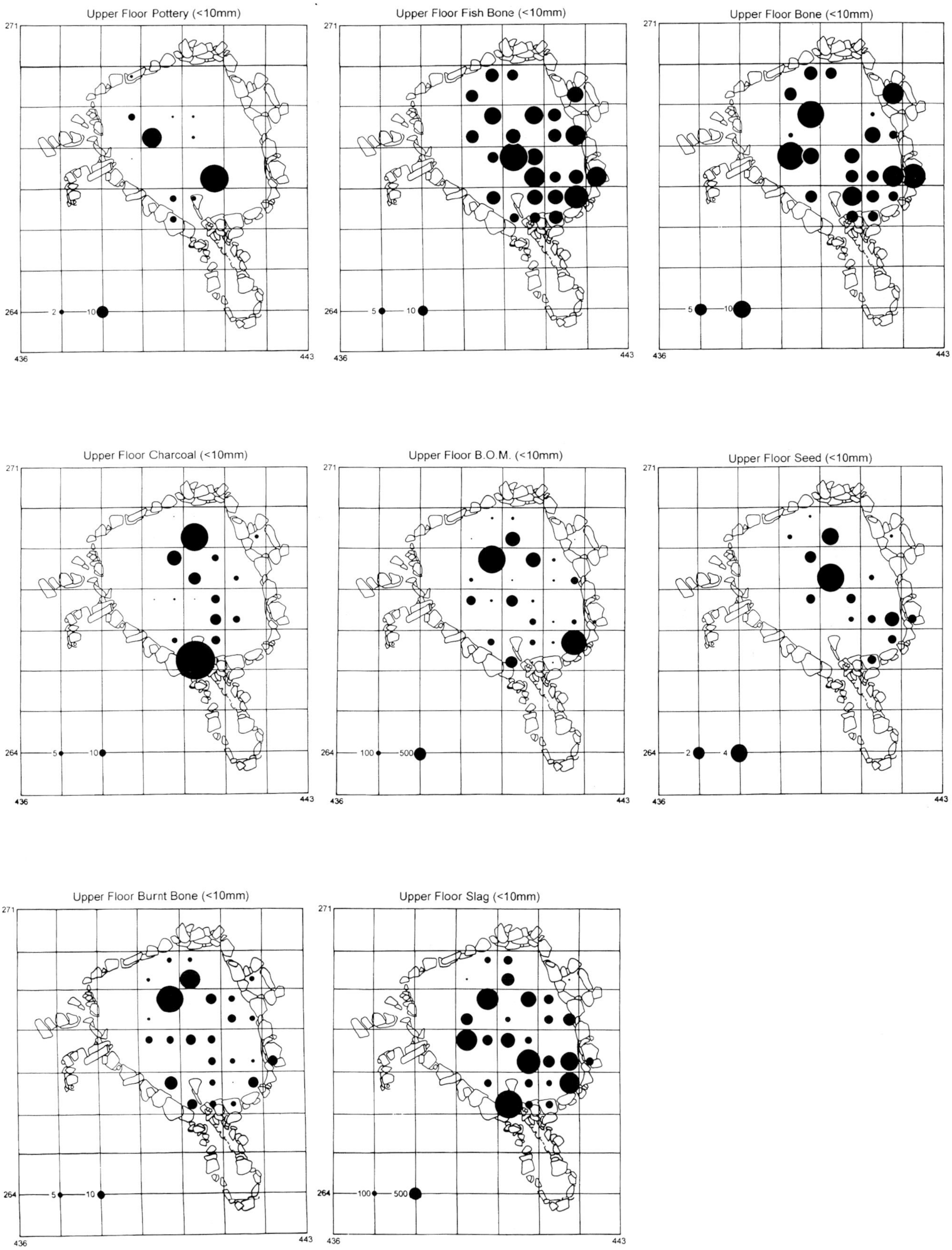

Figure 73. Distribution maps of the material recovered (number of fragments per litre of soil) from floor 2 during sorting of the below 10 mm residues

coprolite fragments have a rather peculiar distribution, which concentrates in the centre of the building.

The distribution of the material recovered from sorting the fine fraction (<10mm) is depicted in Figure 71. Most of the burnt material (BOM, slag, charcoal and carbonised plant remains) was concentrated on the west side of the kiln/barn between the entrance and the flue. This is only to be expected, as the source for most of this material would have been the fire lit in the flue and removal of the ashes was through the entrance. The exception is the burnt bone, which shows a tendency to favour the east side. This pattern repeats the pattern of the above 10 mm residues and suggests that the burnt bone did not derive from accidental burning in the flue. Most of the other materials have fairly peripheral concentrations, suggesting they only survived around the edge of a floor that was regularly cleaned.

Floor 2

Total phosphorus concentrations in the upper floor range from 691 – 5514 mg/kg, with an average of 2325.39 mg/kg, lower than the earlier floor but similar to the lower and middle house floors. The distribution of P (Figure 72) is mostly uniform, with a spread of the higher concentrations in the central and southern area of the floor. Two areas of lower values occur in the northwestern area (719 – 1105 mg/kg) and along the northern edge of the floor (691 – 722 mg/kg). The pattern shown in phosphorus is mostly mirrored by the concentration of nitrogen (Figure 72), as it was in the case of the lower barn floor. Values range from 95 – 1054 mg/kg, with an average of 476 mg/kg, which are lower than the N values in the earlier floor or the three house floors. The higher values in the range occur in the southern and central area of the floor, but the lower values spread from the northwest to the northeastern area (95 – 325 mg/kg).

Magnetic susceptibility values (χ) vary from 47 – 864 ($10^{-8}m^3kg^{-1}$) with an average of 147 ($10^{-8}m^3kg^{-1}$). The distribution of χ is shown in Figure 72. There is an area of enhanced χ in the northern area of the floor (239–529 ($10^{-8}m^3kg^{-1}$)) but the highest value is next to the entrance to the kiln (864 ($10^{-8}m^3kg^{-1}$)). As with P and N, an area with lower values appears in the northwest of the floor (53 – 108 ($10^{-8}m^3kg^{-1}$)).

The distribution of the material from sorting the above 10 mm fraction (Figure 72) is rather sporadic as very little material other than shell was recovered. Most of the shell is found in the south and west of the floor with very little in the northeast corner. There is a small concentration of animal bones in the centre of the northern half of the building and the only fish bones come from the southeast corner

The distribution of the material recovered from sorting the fine fraction (<10mm) is depicted in Figure 73. The patterns are not nearly as clear as they are in the lower floor. The burnt material is not obviously concentrated in the area adjacent to the flue. Although one large charcoal concentration and a much less significant slag concentration were located in this area, most of the concentrations of burnt bone, BOM and carbonised plant remains were found in the centre of the north half of the building. Unburnt bone also shows a concentration in this area but the fish bone is more widely dispersed across the south and east of the building. Pottery was rare and concentrated in two squares.

Artefacts – J Bond, A Lane and P Macdonald

None of the ceramics found in FD were very diagnostic (Table 44). There was one possible platter sherd in 275 and a bodysherd with angled construction joins in 276. The bodysherds had blackened and sooted exteriors.

Three iron objects were found in these deposits. Two nails, one (1836) from the brown sand (275) between the floors, and one (1875) from the lower floor (276), and a fragment of strip (Figure 56, 1853), also from the lowest floor. This is a surprisingly limited number of objects compared to the numbers found in the house floors (DD).

Carbonised plant remains – S Colledge, R Gale and H Smith

Twenty-six flotation samples were examined from floor 1, 14 from floor 2 and nine from associated contexts (Tables 45, 46 and 47). Both floor layers had particularly high densities of barley, oats and rye, much higher than the house floors. Flax, however, occurred infrequently,

Table 44. Pottery from FD

context	weight	Sherds	base	body	misc.	platter	Ave. Wght.
275	9	1				1?	9.00
276	110	13	1	2	10		8.46
293	5	1			1		5.00
654	6	3			3		2.00
653	8	1		1			8.00
687	3	4		3	1		0.75
Total	141	23	1	6	15	1	6.13

Table 45. The charred plant remains from the lower floor of the kiln/barn (FD)

sample number	context		volume floated (litres)	volume of charcoal (cm^3)	charcoal density (cm^3/l)	*Hordeum sativum* - grains	*Hordeum sativum* - rachis int frags	*Secale cereale* - grains	*Secale cereale* - rachis frags	*Avena* cf. *sativa* - grains	Cereal indet - grains	Cereal/Gramineae - culm frags (?)	Cereals per litre of soil	*Buglossoides* sp.	Boraginaceae - charred embryos	Caryophyllaceae (several species)	*Chenopodium* spp.	Compositae	Cruciferae (several species)	*Carex* spp. (/*Scirpus* spp.)	cf. *Fumaria* sp.	*Bromus* sp.	Gramineae indet (various spp)	*Linum* sp.	*Plantago* sp.	*Polygonum*/*Rumex* spp.	Wild seeds per litre of soil	indet/unid specimens	wood charcoal	dung/peat/organic frags	root/tuber frags
8619	**276**	**FD/1**	7	0.8	0.1	24				16	x		5.7														0.00		x	x	
8622	**276**		9	4.4	0.5	119		24		244	x	x	43	3	2	1	3		3							4	1.78		x	x	
8623	**276**		3	0.4	0.1	10		1		15	x		8.7														0.00		x	x	
8627	**276**		1.65	0.8	0.5	14	1	1	1	8	x	x	15		1	1	1									2	3.03		x	x	
8629	**276**			11.5		199	2	18	3	83	x			1			6							1		4			x	x	x
8631	**276**		14	7.4	0.5	208	5	25	3	167	x		29	6		2	1							1		2	0.86	x	x	x	
8633	**276**		15	6.8	0.5	156		12	2	131	x		20		1						1					4	0.40		x	x	
8635	**276**		3	0.6	0.2	7		1		6	x		4.7														0.00	x	x	x	
8637	**276**		27	8.6	0.3	141	1	21		97	x		9.6	15												2	0.63	x	x	x	
8639	**276**		27	11.5	0.4	279	3	117	6	263	x	x	25	9			5		1							2	0.63	x	x	x	
8641	**276**		10	6.4	0.6	146		36	1	118	x		30	8			2									1	1.10	x	x	x	
8643	**276**		7	6.6	0.9	149	3	14		129	x		42	2													0.29		x	x	
8645	**276**		17	10.4	0.6	249	1	23		235	x	x	30	10	2		3		3					6		9	1.94	x	x	x	
8647	**276**		25	18.0	0.7	440	3	118		314	x	x	35	21			6		4							8	1.56	x	x	x	
8649	**276**		24	18.0	0.8	437	6	124	6	377	x	x	40	22	2		4		4						1	5	1.58		x	x	
8651	**276**		20	30.0	1.5	709	13	148	4	636	x		76	11			6									3	1.00	x	x	x	
8655	**276**		28	14.0	0.5	370	1	22		130	x		19	28												3	1.11		x	x	
8657	**276**		16	5.6	0.4	85		20		104	x		13	2	1											2	0.31		x	x	
8659	**276**		11	11.5	1.0	241	2	57		87	x		35	10	5					1				1			1.55		x	x	
8662	**276**		8	1.8	0.2	38	1	6	7	21	x	x	9.1				2					2	1			4	1.13		x	x	
8664	**276**		17	6.0	0.4	132		16		76	x		13	4												5	0.53	x	x	x	
8666	**276**		15.5	20.0	1.3	594	15	9	4	315	x		60	2		4	13		2	1						29	3.29	x	x	x	
8670	**276**		5	2.2	0.4	35		2		35	x		14														0.00		x		
8672	**276**		6	2.6	0.4	133	4	1		35	x		29							1							0.17		x	x	
8678	**276**		5	2.2	0.4	38		3		25	x		13					1	1								0.40		x	x	
8682	**276**		1	1.2	1.2	16				12	x		28				1										1.00		x	x	
	Total		322	209		4969	61	819	37	3679			30	154	14	8	53	1	18	3	1	2	1	9	1	89	1.10				

Table 46. The charred plant remains from the upper floor of the kiln/barn (FD)

sample number	context		volume floated (litres)	volume of charcoal (cm^3)	charcoal density (cm^3/l)	*Hordeum sativum* - grains	*Hordeum sativum* - rachis int frags	*Secale cereale* - grains	*Secale cereale* - rachis frags	*Avena* cf. *sativa* - grains	Cereal indet - grains	Cereal/Gramineae - culm fragments (?)	Cereals per litre of soil	*Buglossoides* sp.	Boraginaceae - charred embryos	Caryophyllaceae (several species)	*Chenopodium* spp.	Cruciferae (several species)	*Carex* spp. (/*Scirpus* spp.)	cf. *Fumaria* sp.	Gramineae indet (various spp)	*Linum* sp.	*Polygonum*/*Rumex* spp.	*Ranunculus* sp.	Wild seeds per litre of soil	indet/unid specimens	wood charcoal	dung/peat/organic fragments
5956	**269**	**FD/2**	7	7.2	1.0	49		8		133	x		27.14		1	1	1	2			3		1		1.29		x	xxx
5957	**269**		6	2.8	0.5	18	1	9		45	x		12.17												0.00		x	
5959	**269**		5	1.0	0.2	3	1			5	x	x	1.80												0.00		xxx	
5960	**269**		7	6.0	0.9	43		8		109	x		22.86	2		2				1					0.71		x	x
5964	**269**		15	12.5	0.8	103		30	3	189	x		21.67	1	3	1		1				1	2		0.60		x	x
5965	**269**		6	3.0	0.5	28	1	7		51	x		14.50		1		1						1		0.50	x	x	
5971	**269**		12	12.5	1.0	134	4	10	3	226	x		31.42	1		2	3	2				1	2		0.92		x	
5973	**269**		8	20.0	2.5	170		16	2	322	x		63.75	14	2		8	2					4		3.75	x	x	x
5974	**269**		7.5	6.6	0.9	37	13	6	4	95	x		20.67	1	1	2	5						1		1.33		x	x
5978	**269**		10	7.8	0.8	112		7		188	x		30.70	1			3								0.40		x	x
5986	**269**		6	5.4	0.9	40	12	4		73	x		21.50	1	1	1					1				0.67			x
5987	**269**		4	2.8	0.7	23	1	3		58	x		21.25					1			1				0.50			x
5990	**269**		4	4.0	1.0	29	2	3		82	x		29.00		2		1								0.75	x	x	x
5994	**269**		2	14.0	7.0	58	10	2	2	326	x	x	199.00	2		4	2		2					2	6.00		x	x
	Total		100	106	19	847	45	113	14	1902	0	0	29.36	23	11	13	24	8	2	1	5	2	11	2	1.03			

Table 47. The charred plant remains from deposits associated with the use of the kiln/barn (FD)

sample number	context		volume floated (litres)	volume of charcoal (cm^3)	charcoal density (cm^3/l)	*Hordeum sativum* - grains	*Hordeum sativum* - rachis int frags	*Secale cereale* - grains	*Secale cereale* - rachis frags	*Avena* cf. *sativa* - grains	Cereal indet - grains	Cereal/Gramineae - culm frags (?)	Cereals per litre of soil	*Buglossoides* sp.	Boraginaceae - charred embryos	Caryophyllaceae (several species)	*Chenopodium* spp.	Cruciferae (several species)	*Carex* spp. (/*Scirpus* spp.)	*Lolium* sp.	Gramineae indet (various spp)	*Polygonum*/*Rumex* spp.	*Urtica* sp.	Wild seeds per litre of soil	indet/unid specimens	wood charcoal	dung/peat/organic frags
5967	**270**	**FD**	0.5	7.2	14.4	19	1	1	3	192	x		432.00	1	2		4					3		20	x	x	x
5993	**272**		5	3.6	0.7	17	8	2	2	45	x	x	14.80			2						2		0.8		x	
5996	**272**		9	7.0	0.8	41	21	3	5	117	x	x	20.78		2	2	4					1		1	x	x	x
5980	**273**		4	2.4	0.6	18	2	2	1	14	x		9.25		1	1							1	0.8		x	x
5984	**278**		0.5	2.0	4.0	15	5			39	x		118.00									1		2	x		x
8683	**657**		0.5	0.0	0.0					1	x		2.22											0			
8685	**658**		1	5.4	5.4	56		3		185	x		244.00	13			1					2		16	x		
8708	**681**		10	40.0	4.0	588		36		920	x		154.40	252				4		4	4	4		27			x
8709	**681**		8	2.0	0.3	26				27	x		6.63	21			1	1	1					3		x	
	Total		38	69.6		780	37	47	11	1540	0	0	62.81	287	5	5	10	5	1	4	4	13	1	8.7			

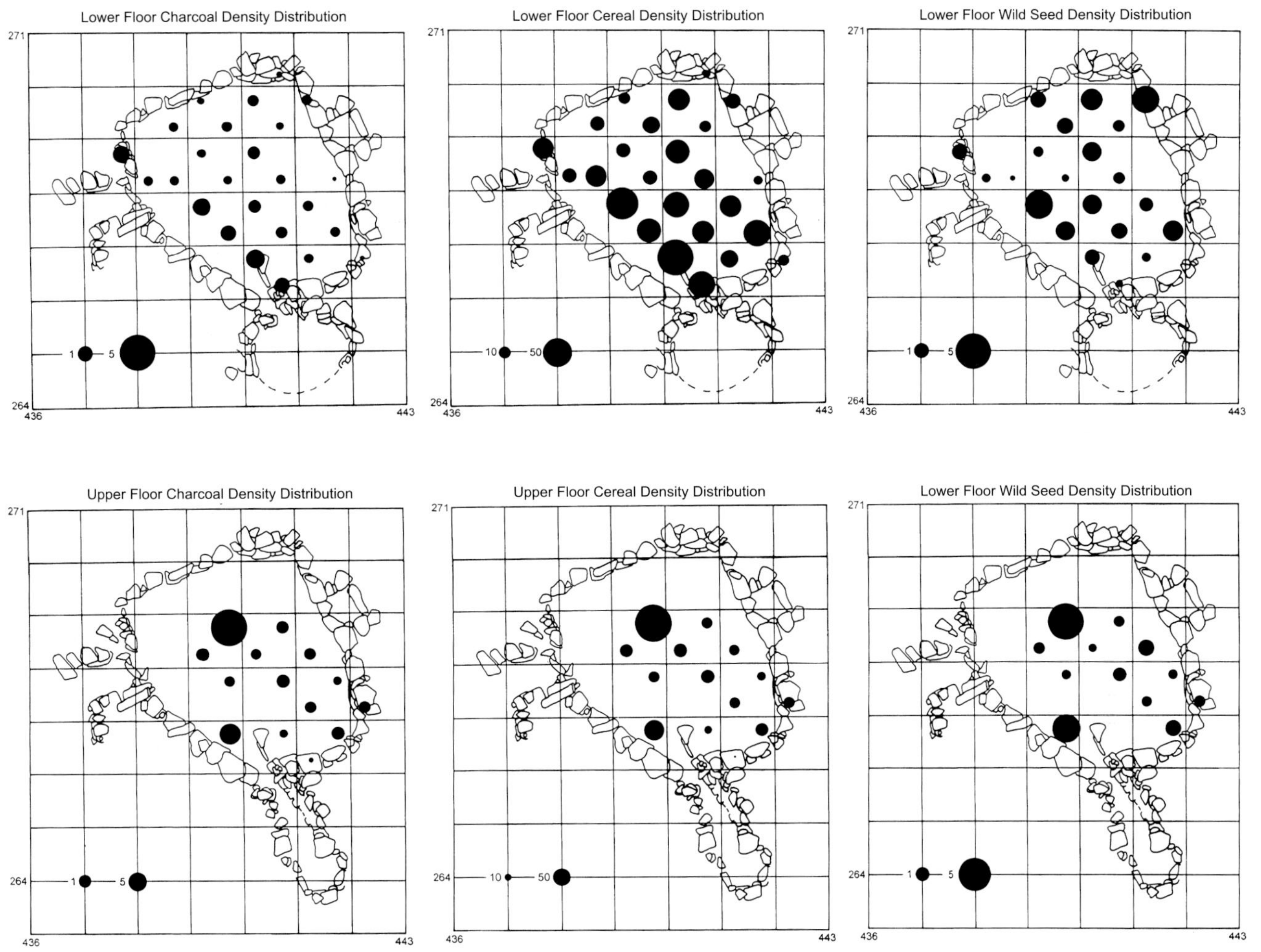

Figure 74. The distribution of different plant species from the lower (top) and upper (bottom) floor of the kiln/barn

Table 48. Animal bone NISP from FD

context	Sheep/ Goat	Cattle	Pig	Red deer	Small mammal	Total
269	1	1				2
272	1					1
276	7	3	1	1	1	13
687	3					3
total	12	4	1	1	1	19
	63%	21%	5%	5%	5%	

with small numbers of seeds in very few samples. Both floors had similar densities of cereals, but floor 1 had particularly high densities of barley, whereas floor 2 had high densities of oats. The highest densities were associated with the samples from discrete contexts, most of which were ash dumps in or in front of the flue to the kiln. Samples 5967/270, 8685/658 and 8708/681 had the highest densities of cereals from mound 3.

The distribution of the crop remains on the floors is depicted in Figure 74. Cereal grains, in particular barley grains, are concentrated along the southwest wall between the flue and the entrance. Oats are more scattered throughout the deposits but in the southwest corner there is a concentration of grains. Wild taxa have a different distribution and only one sample on the west side had relatively high numbers of seeds. Another sample with a high density was located in the northeast corner, an area which otherwise had very low densities of carbonised plant remains. Knowledge of the distribution in the upper floor is limited by the location of the samples analysed. Sample 5994, which is located in front of the entrance, had a high density of charcoal and cereal grains. Most of the remaining material came from samples along the centre of the building. There was one outlying sample (5973), located against the south wall, which had a high density of barley and wild taxa.

The distribution of charcoal on the upper and lower floors of the kiln/barn are shown in Figure 74. Charcoal was more abundant on the lower floor with a greater density of deposits along the southwest wall between the flue and the entrance. Three flotation samples were examined from the lower floor layer (276) (Table 70).

The processed samples, however, were rather small. From the northeast quadrant, sample 8636 included alder, birch and hazel, and birch was also recorded in sample 8651 at the southern end of the kiln. Sample 8657 contained only heather. Charcoal in a flotation sample from context 293 was identified as juniper.

Animal bone
– C Ingrem, J Mulville and J Cartledge

A small quantity (n=19) of identifiable animal bones was recovered from these deposits (Table 48). This assemblage is dominated by sheep/goat. Cattle and pig are also present and one red deer phalanx. Most of the bones came from the lower floor (276). A relatively low proportion of the bones have been gnawed and two bones have evidence for butchery. Several fragments of antler from 276 probably all derive from a single shattered tine.

Eleven bird bones were identified in these layers: a domestic fowl, three goose, a puffin, two from a cormorant and four from a rock dove. The rock dove bones were found in 292 and possibly represent the remains of an articulated group. Similarly the goose bones were all found in the first floor (276) along with the domestic fowl. Only one puffin bone came from the upper floor. The two cormorant bones were split between the sand 272 and 293.

A significant quantity (n=216) of fish remains were recovered from FD, the majority coming from the lower floor and a smaller amount from the upper floor. The latter produced a higher density (1.93 identified bones estimated per litre) than did the lower floor (0.79 identified bones estimated per litre). Cod and hake are both present but almost all of the remains are herring, even without considering the effects of fractionation (Table 49). When estimated NISP is considered for the <10mm material it

Table 49. Fish bone from FD

a. > 10 mm samples (NISP); b. < 10 mm samples (estimated NISP)

	269a	269b	272b	273b	276a	276b	676b	678b	681a	681b	Total
Herring	1	162	4	6	4	761	16	3		32	989
Salmonid						1					1
Eel						8					8
Pike					1						1
Whiting						1					1
Saithe				1							1
Cod	1				1	1					3
Hake	1				1						2
Ling	3										3
Large gadid					2				1		3
Medium gadid					1						1
Large gadoid	1										1
Mackerel		2									2
Sea bream		8									8
Total	7	172	4	7	10	772	16	3	1	32	1024

Table 50. The anatomical representation of major fish species from the kiln/barn occupation (FD)

	Herring		Cod		Hake	Ling
	above	below	above	below		
Vomer		2				
Maxilla		16				
Dentary	1					
Articular		16				
Opercula	1					
Cleithrum		1	1			
AAV		45	1			
PAV	3	425		1	1	
CV		471			1	3
Vert. Frag.		8				
Total	5	984	2	1	2	3

is clear that the herring assemblage is dominated by posterior abdominal and caudal vertebrae although some cranial elements are present (Table 50). At least 17 individual herrings are represented by vertebrae whereas only eight are represented by cranial elements.

It is interesting that this is the only area where cranial elements belonging to herring are found in significant numbers. The sample size as represented by NISP is small and it is difficult to estimate the proportions in which cranial elements and vertebrae were originally present because of the likely effects of taphonomic bias. Cranial and appendicular elements are more fragile and therefore more prone to the effects of fragmentation and density-related preservation than vertebrae; they are therefore unlikely to survive in equal numbers to vertebrae. However, the virtual absence of cranial elements in other areas and phases of the site where preservation is similar suggests that herring were generally present in a decapitated form. The presence of cranial elements here suggests that this may be the area where heads were removed, probably prior to curing. Evidence for a kiln suggests that the curing process may have involved smoking.

Marine shell – N Sharples

Winkles dominate the assemblage from FD but compared to most of the other productive blocks they are less dominant, providing only 58% of the total quantity of shells recovered (Table 51). Most of the material from this block comes from samples taken from the lower floor with the remaining assemblage dominated by the samples from the upper floor. In the upper floor winkles have a dominance comparable to other contexts but in the lower floor they are clearly only slightly more common than limpets. Other shellfish species were found in the lower floor and it is noticeable that most of these were of the more edible bivalves: three scallop shells and two mussel shells. Only one crab fragment was present in the upper floor.

Discussion – K Milek, N Sharples and H Smith

Two floors were identified inside the kiln/barn and these can be equated with the two phases of kiln construction, though it was not possible to establish this stratigraphically. Other than the floors, the main context was a mound of orange sand in the flue of the kiln and several distinctive thick spreads of ash around the entrance of this flue. These deposits were thought to indicate the location of the fire used to operate the corn-drying kiln and this view is supported by thin section analysis. The micromorphology sample taken close to the mouth of the flue contained a significantly higher proportion of non-metallurgical slag than the other samples, and this is likely to be due to its proximity to the fire.

Soil micromorphological analysis of the lowest floor indicates that this accumulated gradually by the periodic raking out of peat ash from the mouth of the flue towards the western entrance of the building. It was also spread in lesser quantities elsewhere on the floor – probably by a variety of means, such as raking and trampling – where it accumulated as fine lenses, or as aggregates in the natural calcareous sands that had formed the original floor surface of the building. These aggregates were then reworked by bioturbation, and the percolation of rain-water, which translocated some of this ashy material and deposited it in the form of coatings around and bridges between the sand grains.

The fuel ash that has accumulated in this structure is predominantly peat ash, and much of this ash actually shows evidence for *low* temperature burning – particularly the survival of partially charred plant tissues and organs, which would have been completely ignited at temperatures over 480ºC, and the survival of phytoliths and diatoms, which begin to lose structural water at around 800ºC. The vitrification of silicate sands and phytoliths normally requires temperatures close to 1000ºC, but in the presence of fluxing agents such as K (abundant in wood ash and potassium feldspar grains) and CaO (abundant in shell sand), the fusion of the siliceous material within the floor deposits could have occurred at temperatures as low as 800°C or even 500°C, if exposed to that temperature for several hours. Domestic hearths are usually operated at c. 300–500°C, but temperatures of 800–1000°C are within the effective operating temperature range of hearths and kilns (McDonnell 2001). It is therefore very likely that in the normal operation of the fire used to heat the air of the corn-drying kiln, temperatures occasionally reached 800°C

Table 51. Marine shell from FD

Context	No of samples	Litres	Limpet	Winkle	Flat periwinkle	Common whelk	Scallop	Mussel	Crab
269	27	187.6	19	56					+
272	2	14		2					
273	1	4		8					
275	1	7.5	1	1	1				
276	51	657.7	104	125	3	1	3	2	
681	1	8		2					
total			124	194	4	1	3	2	

or higher, and caused the localised vitrification of the ash and sand at the base of the fire. In addition to peat, and occasionally wood, thin section analysis showed that dung was occasionally burnt in this structure as well.

Both floors were systematically sampled for phosphorus, nitrogen and magnetic susceptibility, the floor was completely floated for the recovery of carbonised plant remains and a sample of the residues was sorted for the recovery of micro-residues. All of this sampling was based on a grid that enabled the analysis of the distribution of the different materials. The quantities of pottery, artefacts, fish and large mammal bones were negligible from all of the deposits and clearly indicate the depositional activities were quite different to those in the house.

On the lower barn floor, phosphorus and magnetic susceptibility values are generally very high across the entire floor, as compared to the upper kiln/barn floor and house floors on mound 3. For example, the average phosphorus value for the lower barn floor is approximately twice the value for the upper barn floor and the house floors. These high values may reflect the burning of organic materials resulting in the enhancement of magnetic susceptibility and the concentration of elements such as phosphorus.

The distribution of the micro-residues on the lower floor shows concentrations of material likely to have derived from the fire, i.e. charcoal, slag and burnt organic material, around the entrance to the flue and along the southwest wall towards the entrance to the barn. This is particularly clear in the distributions of the material from sorting residues below 10 mm and from the analysis of the carbonised plant remains recovered by flotation. The larger fragments appear to be more widely distributed. Some cereals (such as oat) might have been dried by holding them over the fire (graddaning) and accidental combustion during this process may explain the high densities of cereal grains on the floor. However, it should be noted that oats are not concentrated around the flue. The bones of mammals, fish and shellfish do not have the same pattern as the burnt material and neither do the fragments of coprolite. The larger pieces tend to be scattered across the centre of the floor in very low numbers whereas the smaller pieces occur in concentrations around the periphery. The distribution suggests the structure was regularly cleaned with only small fragments around the edge surviving to create concentrations. The few larger bones in the centre may indicate the last use of the structure was not cleaned out.

The upper floor shows high values for phosphorus, nitrogen and magnetic susceptibility away from the entrance, on the south and east side. Higher concentrations occur around the flue entrance, but these are not as distinctive as the earlier floor. The distribution of micro-residues from the upper floor are not nearly as clear as those from the lower floor and this is probably a reflection of the very low quantities of material present in this floor. The carbonised plant remains recovered by flotation are much reduced in numbers and indicate a concentration in the centre of the building and much less emphasis on the area around the flue. The lower quantities suggest that the level of parching had declined in this later phase.

The evidence from all the deposits in this building supports the interpretation that the structure was closely associated with processing of crops and that it can legitimately be called a kiln/barn. Activities associated with the structure include drying outside in the kiln bowl, and probably threshing and winnowing of the crops inside the building (or outside in good weather). However, other activities can also be identified. Animal bones indicate people were eating in the building and the burnt bones may indicate they were cooking, though the low numbers indicate these were snacks rather than meals. Of more importance is the fish bone assemblage. This was slightly different to that from the house in containing bones from the skull of the herrings. These bones may indicate that the fish in this structure were not fully processed for consumption and were present not because people were consuming them but because they were being processed. It is possible they were being smoked at the same time as the grain was being dried.

The abandonment of the kiln/barn (FE) – N Sharples

Above the floor the initial fill of the kiln/barn can be split into three different areas. On the north side of the structure was a cluster of slabs (264) that tipped down into the floor from north to south. They were surrounded by a soft brown sand (258). In the northwest corner of the structure was a dark grey sand (257) and around the southwest corner there was a brown sand (268). The collapsed stone work is interesting as it suggests the northern wall collapsed soon after the structure was abandoned. However, this wall survived to over 0.8 m high and it may be that the stones represent a collection of good building stones stacked against the wall of an abandoned building. Covering the layers of tumble inside the barn was a thick deposit of clean white sand (255) which was also found in the kiln (288/289) (Figure 66). This probably represents wind-blown sand accumulating inside the abandoned structure.

Sometime after the accumulation of the wind-blown sand had half filled the kiln/barn, a small structure was built against the northwest corner of the building (Figures 75, 76, 77). An arc of walling was constructed from the original west entrance to a point half-way along the north wall, creating a structure approximately 2.8 m by 3.0 m. The new wall was approximately 0.9 m thick and had a distinct inner and outer wall face with white sand between the two. The inner face (262) was constructed of large slabs up to 0.71 m × 0.21 m × 0.27 m, and two courses survive to a height of 0.44 m. The outer face (263) consisted of much smaller stones, on average 0.3 m × 0.7 m

Figure 75. A general view of the structure built after the abandonment of the kiln/barn, from the north

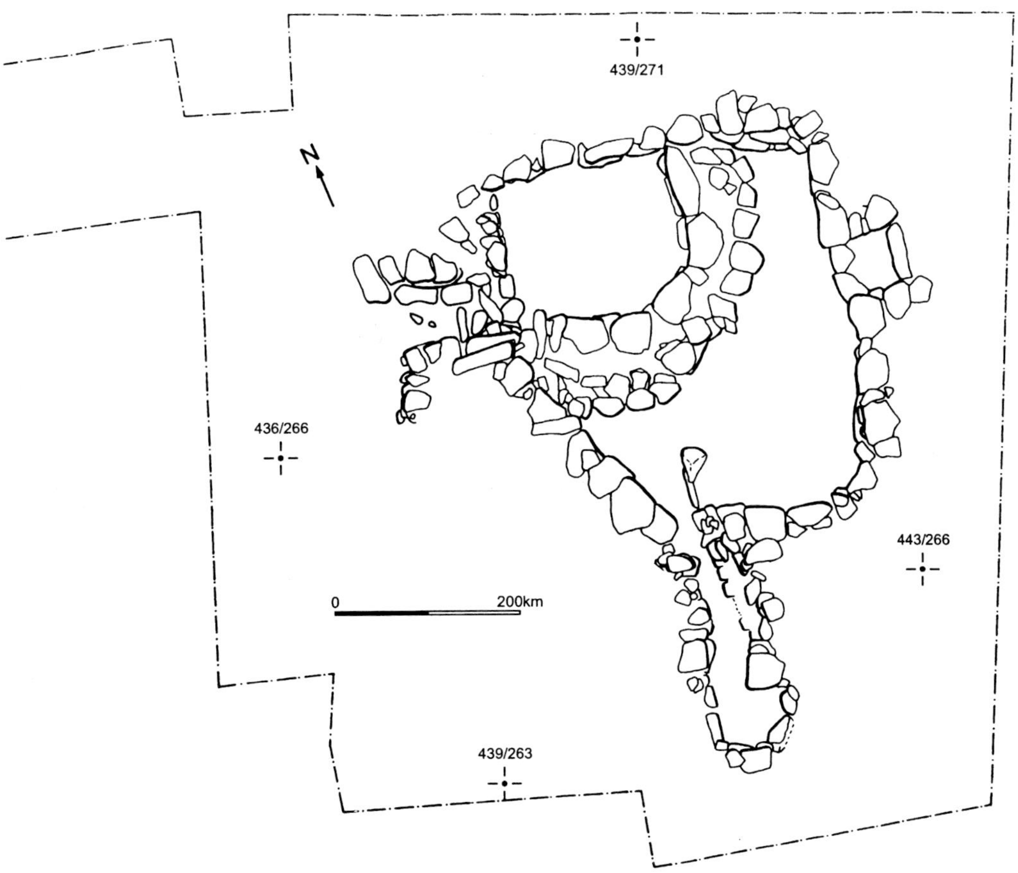

Figure 76. A plan of the secondary structure built into the kiln/barn

Figure 77. A view of the secondary structure from the west

Table 52. Animal bone NISP from FE

context	Sheep/ Goat	Sheep	Cattle	Pig	Red deer	Whale	Total
255	15	3	6	5	2	1	32
257	2		1	1			4
265	1						1
268				1			1
total	18	3	7	7	2	1	38
	47%	8%	18%	18%	5%	3%	

× 0.29 m, and again two courses survived to a height of c. 0.33 m.

No floor level was identified that could be associated with this structure and there was no collapse from the walls. The white sand into which the structure had been cut was covered with identical white sand (254) presumably again the result of wind-blown deposition. Outside the structure a layer of brown sand (256) covered the wind-blown sand and this could be a surface through which the structure was dug. The brown sand was covered by another sterile wind-blown sand layer (250, 260 and 265), which completed the infilling of the building.

Sampling – N Sharples

One sample (9.5 litres of soil) was taken and processed from FE, context 288. The sample contained low densities of most materials (appendices 1 and 2).

Artefacts – J Bond, A Lane and P Macdonald

The only ceramics from this block come from context 255 and comprised 32 sherds, weighing 170 g (an average weight of 5.3g). There were 24 miscellaneous sherds, seven body sherds and one base sherd. Three sherds were classed as fine wares and seven sherds were of pre-Viking wares. This was an unusual assemblage, which has a number of sherds with tongue and groove construction and one sherd from a shouldered jar. These are likely to be Late Iron Age in date and one small bodysherd with an applied zigzag cordon is definitely Iron Age. The miscellaneous sherds include two thin sherds which may be broken from everted rim vessels and have fabrics of probable Norse date. The context clearly includes intrusive material and it seems likely that this results from confusion in the post-excavation process. This is the only context from mound 3 with any evidence for LIA material and is best ignored.

One fragment of iron bar (Figure 56, 1492) was found in the white sand (255).

Charcoal – R Gale

Small pieces of birch charcoal were recovered by hand from the white sand (288) that had accumulated inside the abandoned structure.

Animal bone – C Ingrem, J Mulville and J Cartledge

An assemblage of 38 identifiable animal bones was recovered from block FE (Table 52). The majority of which came from the thick layer of wind-blown sand (255) that infilled the structure. Sheep/goat again dominate the sample, but cattle and pig are present, as are two bones of red deer and one of whale. Gnawing was not found on any of the bones and only one bone has evidence for butchery. The rapid accumulation of wind-blown sand would also enhance preservation. Four bird bones were identified from the sand (255) infilling the kiln/barn: a golden plover, a Manx shearwater, a rook/crow and a shag. A total of 17 fish bones were identified from FE (Table 53) and most of these were herring.

Marine shell – N Sharples

The infill layers produced very few shells because very few samples were taken.

Discussion – N Sharples

The kiln/barn appears to have had a short period of dereliction when it was used to store building stone and this may coincide with the deliberate blocking of the entrance. However, the structure was soon inundated by wind-blown sand that rapidly filled the semi-subterranean structure. During this infilling a small shelter was constructed in the northwest corner. The absence of an obvious floor associated with this structure and the generally low levels of material from all the contexts in this block suggest human activity after the structure was abandoned was minimal and it seems likely that the abandonment of this structure coincides with the abandonment of the settlement.

Activity associated with the use of the kiln/barn (FF) – N Sharples

In the southeast corner of the trench an area of activity was defined by a complex sequence of thin layers rich in charcoal, red ash and shells (Figure 55). The lower part of the sequence can be split between layers adjacent to the east section and those adjacent to the kiln and this corresponds to the underlying construction pits (described as blocks FB and FC).

Adjacent to the east section the sequence begins with

Table 53. Fish and shellfish from FE

a. > 10 mm samples (NISP): b < 10 mm samples (estimated NISP)

	255a	288a	288b	Total
Herring			9	9
Whiting			1	1
Pollack	1			1
Cod	1			1
Hake	1			1
Ling	1			1
Large gadid		1		1
Corkwing Wrasse			1	1
Sea bream	1			1
Total fish	5	1	11	17
Limpets		4		4
Winkle		18		18
Flat periwinkle	1			
Red whelk	1			
Great scallop	1			
Queen scallop	1			1
Iceland cyprine	1			
Mussel	2			2
Total shellfish	7	22		25

Table 54. Pottery from FF

context	weight	sherds	base	body	misc.	platter	Ave. Wght.
660	68	9				3+?6	7.56
659	10	3	2		1		3.33
299	10	5			5		2.00
284	8	3				2+?1	2.67
283	15	4	2		2		3.75
251	2	1			1		2.00
252	79	4	3	1			19.75
Total	192	29	7	1	9	12	6.62

Table 55. Artefacts from FF

context	Bone	Antler	Iron
	Pin	Waste	nail
251	1		1
252		1	
total	1	1	1

a red-brown sand (652), 0.12 m thick, containing many shells. Above this was a sequence of thin layers concentrated in the centre of the section. This began with an orange-yellow sand (651), then a pale brown sand (650), then a dark brown sand with charcoal flecks (298) and then a bright red-orange sand (295).

On the kiln side the sequence begins with a red-brown sand (660), with charcoal flecks. On top of this was a patch of dark brown sand (659) and over this was a charcoal-rich layer (287). Overlying 659 but unrelated to 287 was a patch of orange-brown sand (299).

Covering both these sequences were three more extensive layers. Along the south side of the trench was a thick, red-brown sand (656) that contained lenses of white sand and clusters of marine shells. This was overlain by a red-brown sand (284) and then by a thick brown sand (283), which contained at least two distinct lenses of charcoal.

The areas to the north and east of the kiln/barn were not explored in detail but surface cleaning of the brown sand (251 and 252) did produce some finds.

Sampling – N Sharples

Twelve samples, 81.25 litres of soil, were taken and processed from the FF contexts: 283, 284, 287, 295, 298, 299, 650, 651, 652, 656, 659, 660, and the residue from below 10 mm was sorted from all the samples except 295.

The material from above 10 mm residues was rich consisting of fish bone (an average density of 0.34 pieces per litre), mammal bone (0.31 pieces per litre), pottery (0.15 pieces per litre), marine molluscs (limpets 1.83 individuals per litre, winkles 9.03 individuals per litre) and slag; BOM was also present in isolated contexts. The average densities are the highest for any of the blocks in this trench and comparable to those from the house; this is despite the fact that several samples had categories missing. The distribution of material is scattered with the highest densities coming from different layers. Fish bone and pot were densest in 299, the mammal bone and limpets in 651, winkles in 284 and slag in 650.

The material from below 10 mm residues had high densities of bone, but low densities of fish bones, seed and charcoal. Pot is relatively common, more like the DD rather than the FD assemblage. Three samples, from contexts 298, 650 and 651, had very high densities of slag. Crab, eggshell and coprolite were present and 650 had a high density of coprolite. Two concentrations of seeds were noted in 283 and 287.

Artefacts – J Bond, A Lane, P Macdonald and A Smith

The ceramics from FF are mostly small and undiagnostic sherds (Table 54). However, the presence in 252 of three bases and one large body sherd (average weight 19.8g) suggests that this context was less disturbed than many. The bases include two with organic impressions from 659, one with organic impressions from 283, and a possible very thin base from the same context. The platter sherds make up as much as 41% of the total. They include a hollow rim, one sherd with finger, fingernail, and stab marks with roughened exterior and organic inclusions, another rim of possible platter but very thin (6 mm), a splayed possible platter rim and an angled platter rim.

Three objects were recovered from these deposits (Table 55); a small fragment of a bone pin (Figure 56, 1260), a piece of cut antler tine (Figure 56, 1530) and a fragment of iron nail (1222). They all came from the amorphous brown sand that was found around the structure on the north and east sides.

Carbonised plant remains – S Colledge, R Gale and H Smith

Eight flotation samples were examined from this block (Table 56). All the samples contained barley and oats; in comparison with other samples from the kiln/barn floor,

Table 56. The charred plant remains from FF

sample number	context		volume floated (litres)	volume of charcoal (cm^3)	charcoal density (cm^3/l)	*Hordeum sativum* - grains	*Hordeum sativum* - rachis int frags	*Secale cereale* - grains	*Secale cereale* - rachis frags	*Avena* cf. *sativa* - grains	Cereal indet - grains	Cereals per litre of soil	*Chenopodium* spp.	*Carex* spp. (/*Scirpus* spp.)	Gramineae indet (various spp)	*Linum* sp.	*Plantago* sp.	*Polygonum/Rumex* spp.	Wild seeds per litre of soil	indet/unid specimens	wood charcoal	dung/peat/organic frags
8607	**295**	**FF**	2	2.8	1.4	50	2			13	x	32.50	1			1			1.00			
8608	**298**		1.3	1.4	1.1	28				3	x	24.80	1	1		1			2.40	x		
8609	**299**		7	4.0	0.6	24		11	1	7	x	6.14		1	1	2			0.57		xx	
8612	**651**		5.5	0.6	0.1	6				1	x	1.27		2				1	0.55	x	x	
8613	**652**		11	1.2	0.1	12		1		3	x	1.45				10			0.91		x	x
8696	**656**		5	0.4	0.1	4		3		1	x	1.60							0.00		x	x
8616	**659**		5	1.0		17		4		4	x	5.00							0.00		x	x
8615	**660**		20	10.0	0.5	179		2		11	x	9.60				4	1	2	0.35	x	x	x
	Total		57	21.4		320	2	21	1	43		6.82	2	4	1	18	1	3	0.51			

Table 57. Animal bone NISP from FF

context	Sheep/Goat	Sheep	Cattle	Pig	Cat	Total
251	4		3	2	1	10
252	1	4	8			13
284	2		2	1		5
651	1		2			3
652			3			3
656	1					1
660			2			2
total	9	4	20	3	1	37

they were not rich. Rye grains and flax seeds were present in many contexts, but again not in high numbers. The richest samples were 8607/295 and 8608/298 and these were noted as ash- and charcoal-rich contexts during excavation.

Distinct lenses of charcoal and ash-rich deposits from peat burning occurred in contexts 287 and 283, from which handpicked charcoal samples produced birch and spruce/larch (Table 70). Heather charcoal was recovered from context 656 (sample 8696), which lies between these layers. It has been suggested that this material could represent deliberately redeposited hearth debris, perhaps in an attempt to stabilise the ground. The charcoal analysis, however, was not wholly consistent with these conclusions as spruce/larch was not found in the samples from the kiln/barn floor.

Animal bone – C Ingrem, J Mulville and J Cartledge

An assemblage of 37 identifiable animal bones was recovered from seven of the contexts in block FF (Table 57). Unusually cattle dominate this assemblage but the numbers are too low to place any significance on this observation. Pig, sheep, sheep/goat and cat are the only other species present. The evidence for butchery and gnawing is slight. Two bird bones were identified from context 252: a great black-back gull and a member of the goose species.

A small quantity (n=71) of identified fish bones were recovered from FF. More than half of these were herring, without considering the effects of fractionation, and cod and hake are the next numerous species (Table 58). Again, cod and hake are represented by both cranial and axial

Table 58. Fish bone from FF

a. > 10 mm samples (NISP); b. < 10 mm samples (estimated NISP).

	251a	252a	283a	283b	284a	284b	298b	299a	299b	651	652	652b	656a	656b	659a	659b	660a	660b	Total
Herring				4		24	1		4		3	24		7		24		24	115
Sea trout																		8	8
Salmonid						8													8
Clupeidae											1								1
Saithe														1					1
Pollack																	1		1
Pollachius												24							24
Cod	1	1	3					3			2		1		1		11		23
Hake										1	4						3		8
Ling					1			1											2
Large gadid			2		1								1				1		5
Medium gadid																	1		1
Small gadid																8			8
Total	1	1	5	4	2	32	1	4	4	1	10	48	2	8	1	32	17	32	205

elements, whilst the projected figures for herring suggest that the axial skeleton is represented by anterior abdominal vertebrae as well as posterior abdominal and caudal vertebrae.

Marine shell – N Sharples

Winkles dominate the assemblage from FF providing 82% of the total quantities of shells recovered (Table 59). The bulk of this assemblage was recovered from contexts at the top (284) and bottom (652) of the sequence. The only limpet-dominated assemblage was from a context (651) which seemed to form the base for a sequence of ash deposits. Whelks were the most common other species with only isolated occurrences of other species. Isolated fragments of crab were present in four contexts (284, 299, 651, 660) and there was a concentration of pieces in another context (652).

Discussion – N Sharples

The bright red and orange layers in this block indicate the deposition of peat ash and this, together with the charcoal-rich layers, indicates that the primary source for the FF deposits was hearth material. As these deposits covered an area adjacent to the kiln it may, superficially, seem that they were related to the use of this structure. However, the fire for the kiln is actually inside the barn and ash accumulated in the entrance to the passage and not at the bowl. Only if the drying grain within the bowl accidentally caught fire would it provide a source of charcoal and ash. This does not appear to have happened to the second kiln. These contexts were therefore deliberately deposited, possibly in an attempt to create a hard surface adjacent to the bowl. This could have been simply where people congregated to service and monitor the grain drying in the bowl but it is also possible that the crops were threshed in this area. Threshing to break up the ears of grain is the process that occurs after ears of grain have been dried and it is possible that this took place outside before the grain was taken into the barn for winnowing and storage.

Occupation deposits accumulating on the edge of the mound (FG) – N Sharples

In the area to the west of the kiln/barn, occupation deposits spread down the slope from the building's walls. In the main trench immediately adjacent to the kiln/barn these deposits were only superficially explored but a 2 m wide trench, 4 m long, was opened up to the west (Figure 54) and the archaeological deposits in this trench were completely excavated. This area was particularly badly damaged by rabbits and large areas of the deposits had been destroyed (Figure 78). The trench was extended to the west, by a JCB, to test for the presence or absence of

Table 59. Marine shell from FF

Context	No of samples	Litres	Limpet	Winkle	Flat periwinkle	Dog whelk	Common whelk	Scallop	Mussel	Crab	Crab
											Cancer sp.
283	1	5.5	2	20							
284	1	12.5	42	367	1	4	1	1			+
287	1	6.5	5	14							
295	1	2	2	6							
298	1	1.25	2	23							
299	1	7	3	2					1		+
650	1	3		3							
651	1	5.5	34	24					1		+
652	1	11	18	149	1					+	++
656	1	5	21	55							
659	1	5	1	3							
660	1	20	19	68	1					+	
total			149	734	3	4	1	1	2		

Table 60. Pottery from FG

context	weight	sherds	rim	base	body	misc.	platter	Ave. Wght.
285	13	5	1	1	1	2		2.60
296	25	11				9	1+?1	2.27
661	2	1	1					2.00
663	4	1				1		4.00
672	6	1				1		6.00
674	1	1				1		1.00
675	34	10		1	1	8		3.40
Total	85	30	2	2	2	22	2	2.83

Table 61. Artefacts from FG

context	Antler	Iron			Stone
	Waste	**Pin**	**Nail**	**Rod**	**Flint**
281				1	
661					1
666		1			
671			1		
675	1		2	1	
total	1	1	3	2	1

archaeology (Figure 23). After the removal of 1.15 m of sterile sand a light brown sand layer (672) was reached, containing a small scatter of animal bones. This layer lay below the water table and was submerged before it could be properly recorded. Nevertheless the trench extension confirmed that complex archaeological deposits were not present in this area.

In the main trench the base of the sequence consists of three layers (Figure 54) whose relationship was not established by excavation. Around the west wall of the kiln/barn was a grey sand (674), in the northwest corner was a pink-brown sand (683 probably the same as 668, see below) and covering the rest of the area was a compact brown sand (285). I would guess that 674 represents the fill of the pit containing the kiln/barn, 285 is a surface created at the construction of the building (equivalent to 675 at the base of the FG layers, see below) and 683 is an accumulation of ash derived from cleaning the floor of the structure and dumping the refuse on these slopes. Overlying 674 was a patch of pink sand (673). All of these deposits in the southwest corner of the trench were covered by a layer of white wind-blown sand (286), which may be equivalent to a white sand (297) covering the northeast corner. This was covered by dark brown sand (296) with charcoal flecks and the whole area was then covered with a compact brown sand (281/282 which may be equivalent to 661, see below).

The trench on the west side was designed to define the western edge of the mound, which was not marked by a very distinct break in slope at this point (Figure 78). The deturfing and removal of the underlying wind-blown sand quickly revealed the reason for this. Wind-blown

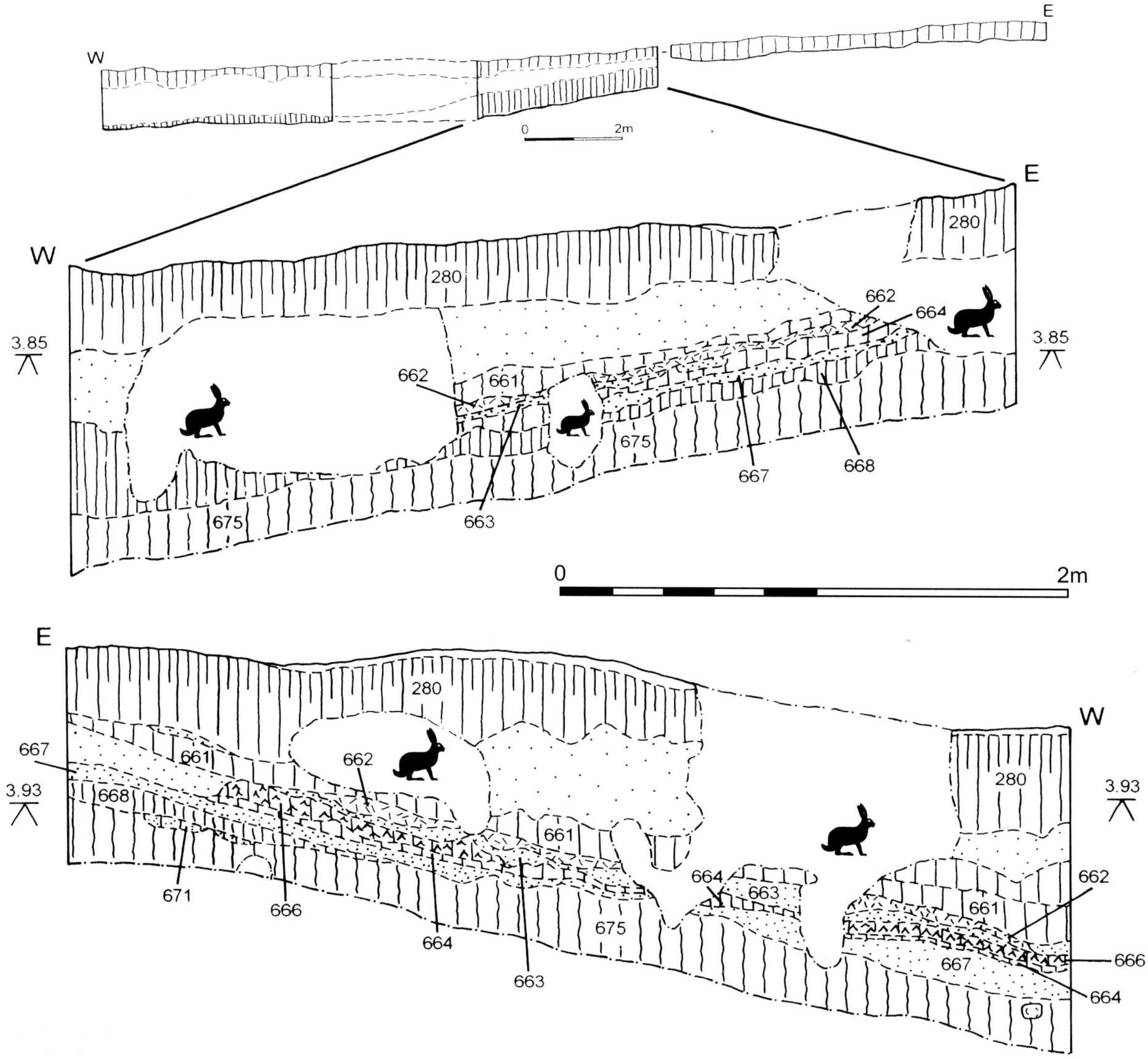

Figure 78. Sections through the occupation layers on the west side of trench F

Figure 79. A view of the north-facing section of the trench to the west of the kiln/barn

sand was accumulating against the edge of the mound and was obscuring the underlying mound topography, which dropped off quite steeply within the limits of the trench. This slope followed the underlying contours of the sterile wind-blown sand, which rose steeply in the trench indicating the prior existence of a mound before the construction of the kiln/barn. Between the two wind-blown sand layers was a series of brown, red-brown and orange-brown sand layers separated by thin layers of yellow sand (Figure 78). The sequence of layers was relatively straightforward but it had been very badly damaged by the massive rabbit burrows that occurred in this area. It will be described from the base to the top.

- A compact dark brown sand (675) with charcoal flecks and a red-brown lens. This layer was up to 0.28 m thick, which is much thicker than any of the overlying layers. A radiocarbon date (OxA-10279) was obtained from a cattle bone in this layer. This produced a date of 863±35 bp, which when calibrated indicates that this occupation layer was deposited within cal AD 1040–1260 (95% probability).
- A pale brown sand with patches of yellow (671). This was restricted to the top of the slope and was thin and discontinuous.
- A compact red-brown sand (668). This was restricted to the top half of the slope and was identified as 683 in the main area of Trench F. It was up to 0.10 m thick.
- A largely yellow sand with pale brown patches (667). This extended from the top to the bottom of the slope and was up to 0.17 m thick at the bottom of the slope.
- A compact dark brown sand (664). This layer extended from the top to the bottom of the slope and was up to 0.08 m thick. It was badly damaged by rabbit burrowing.
- A dark brown sand (666) with a high concentration of marine shells. This only occurred as a restricted layer on the south side of the western trench, where it was 0.08 m thick, but it extended from the top to the bottom of the slope.
- A layer of yellow sand (663). This was a thin layer, only 0.05 m thick, which was restricted to the centre of the western trench but extended across the width of the trench.
- A pale pink sand layer (662). This was a thin layer, up to 0.08 m thick which covered most of the trench.
- A light brown sand layer (661). This covered the centre of the trench and was up to 0.15 m thick.

Unfortunately it is not possible to relate the sequence in this area with the construction of the kiln/barn. It could be suggested that the basal layer (675) was already in existence when the building was constructed or was part of the construction process and that the overlying layers represent activity contemporary with the use of the structure but this is no more than a guess.

Sampling – N Sharples

Seven samples, 130 litres of soil, were taken and processed from FG contexts: 661, 662, 664, 666, 668, 671, 675 and the residues from below 10 mm were sorted for all these samples.

The material from above 10 mm was sparse consisting of occasional occurrences of fish bone (an average density of 0.02 pieces per litre), mammal bone (0.04 pieces per litre), pot (0.02 pieces per litre) and slag. Marine molluscs were the only item present in any quantities (limpets 0.88 individuals per litre, winkles 4.81 individuals per litre). Context 666 was the richest, producing the highest densities of all materials except slag and pottery, which was hardly present at all.

The material from below 10 mm generally contained low densities of material, with only the slag densities medium to high. There were significant concentrations of crab claws in context 666 and to a lesser extent in 661.

Artefacts – J Bond, A Lane, P Macdonald and A Smith

The ceramics in FG are mostly small (2.8g average weight) and undiagnostic sherds (Table 60). They include one 8 mm thick base with a roughened exterior and a very thin base (3 mm) with a roughened exterior. 285 has a very thin (3 mm) rim. 661 has a thin expanded rim. 296 has one definite and one possible platter sherds. The possible platter is an 8 mm thick sherd with a ridged interior. There is also a roughened platter sherd with a perforation. 675 has some unusual miscellaneous sherds – one with a very smoothed exterior, and four thin gritty sherds.

A lump of fired clay (4770; Figure 56) 37 mm by 22 mm by 31 mm was found in 664. This has a very similar fabric to the ceramics and has clearly been squeezed together in someone's hands before firing. Small grooves are present on parts of the surface, which suggest grass impressions similar to those found on the pots. The presence of this lump suggests pottery was being made somewhere in the vicinity of mound 3.

Eight artefacts were found in this block, the largest collection from any block in this trench (Table 61). Most of the objects came from the brown sand (675) at the base of the sequence of occupation layers in the west extension. It contained one cut antler tine (Figure 56, 1972), two iron nails (1974, 1942) and a fragment of iron rod (1958). Another fragment of rod (1679) came from 281 and a nail (1871) from 671. A flint (4768) was found in 661. The most interesting object is an iron dress pin (Figure 56, 1858) from 666.

Carbonised plant remains – S Colledge, R Gale and H Smith

Six flotation samples were examined from this block (Table 62). These contexts had the lowest numbers of cereals per litre of soil from trench F, and amongst the lowest overall from mound 3. All the contexts produced barley and oats but flax was completely absent and rye occurred only infrequently. The richest sample was 8690/668, which

Table 62. The charred plant remains from FG

sample number	context		volume floated (litres)	volume of charcoal (cm^3)	charcoal density (cm^3/l)	*Hordeum sativum* - grains	*Hordeum sativum* - rachis int frags	*Secale cereale* - grains	*Secale cereale* - rachis frags	*Avena* cf. *sativa* - grains	Cereal indet - grains	Cereals per litre of soil	*Buglossoides* sp.	Boraginaceae - charred embryos	*Carex* spp. (/*Scirpus* spp.)	Gramineae indet (various spp)	*Polygonum*/*Rumex* spp.	Wild seeds per litre of soil	indet/unid specimens	wood charcoal	dung/peat/organic frags
8687	**661**	FG	41	3.6	0.1	54				28	x	2.00	1	1				0.05			
8686	**662**		15	0.8	0.1	29				5	x	2.27				1		0.07		x	
8688	**664**		19	1.0	0.1	12	1	1		10	x	1.26						0.00		x	x
8689	**666**		7	0.5	0.1	6				4	x	1.43	1					0.14		x	x
8690	**668**		18	3.0	0.2	96		9		74	x	9.94	2					0.11			
8705	**675**		15	1.4	0.1	23				10	x	2.20			1	1	2	0.27		x	
	Total		115	10.3		220	1	10	0	131		3.15	4	1	1	2	2	0.09			

Table 63. Animal bone NISP from FG

context	Sheep/Goat	Cattle	Pig	Red deer	Total
282	4	1	1	1	7
285		2			2
296	6	6			12
663	1				1
664	4			1	5
666	1				1
668	1				1
672		2			2
675	33	11	2		46
total	50	22	3	2	77
	65%	29%	4%	3%	

had large quantities of barley and oat seed as well as a large quantity of rye grains. The absence of flax links these deposits to the deposits from the kiln/barn floors as does the presence of *Buglossoides* sp. (and possibly other species of Boraginaceae), but the kiln/barn floors also contained a much wider range of wild taxa that were not present in these deposits. It seems likely these layers were derived from cleaning the kiln/barn and that the more exposed location of these contexts led to the destruction (i.e. absence from the archaeobotanical record) of certain more fragile wild seeds.

Charcoal from a flotation sample, 8705, and a hand-picked sample were examined from 675 (Table 70). The former included hazel roundwood measuring about 25 mm in diameter (10 growth rings) and spruce or larch whereas the latter consisted of birch.

Animal bone – C Ingrem, J Mulville and J Cartledge

The animal bone assemblage from FG is the largest from this trench and the third largest from mound 3, contributing 10% of the total assemblage (Table 63). Most of the identifiable bones (46) came from layer 675 and another large group came from layer 296. The assemblage is dominated by sheep/goat and though cattle are well represented pig is rare. Red deer is also present.

Seven bird bones were identified from this block. All

but one came from layer 675, which contained a domestic goose, a domestic fowl, a cormorant, a puffin and two guillemot/razorbill. The remaining bird bone, from a domestic fowl, came from context 668.

A small quantity of fish bone (n=166) was recovered from FG and most of these came from layer 675 (Table 64). The assemblage from 675 was dominated by hake. This predominance of hake is interesting although it could simply represent the disposal of a complete skeleton, which was not considered edible. The majority of remains from the other layers belong to herring, which clearly dominates the assemblage when estimated total NISP is considered (Table 64). The cod and hake samples are of insufficient size to enable conclusions to be drawn regarding body part representation although both cranial and axial elements are present (Table 65). Posterior abdominal and caudal vertebrae dominate the projected figures of body part representation for herring in the <10mm material, with few anterior abdominal vertebrae present and cranial elements absent (Table 65).

Marine shell – N Sharples

Winkles dominated the assemblage from FG providing 84% of the total quantities of shell recorded (Table 66). This was because of two shell-rich layers (664, 666) overwhelmingly dominated by winkles. Two layers (661, 662) produced samples containing only limpets. Crab was present in large quantities in contexts 666, 664 and 661.

Table 64. Fish bone from FG

a. > 10 mm samples (NISP); b. < 10 mm samples (estimated NISP).

	282a	285a	296a	661b	662b	664b	666b	668a	668b	671b	674a	675a	675b	Total
Herring			1	64	12	200	16		64	4			20	381
Large gadid		1												1
Pollack			1								1	4		6
Saithe		1		16		48								65
Cod	1	2						1		2	1	20		27
Hake	1	1										38		40
Ling											2	6		8
Large gadid												6		6
Medium gadid												1		1
Small gadid				16					8					24
Gadid												6		6
Total	2	5	2	96	12	248	16	1	72	6	4	81	20	565

Table 65. The anatomical representation of major fish species from FG

	Herring		Pollack	Saithe		Cod		Hake	Ling
	Above	Below		Above	Below	Above	Below		
Vomer						1		1	1
Premaxilla						2			
Maxilla						3		1	
Dentary	1		1	1		2		2	
Articular								1	
Opercula					8	2			
Otolith					8		2		
Cleithrum								1	
posttemporal						1			
AAV		8				2		5	1
PAV		194	5		16	2		14	4
CV		118			32	7		8	2
Vert.frag		60				3		7	
Total	1	380	6	1	64	25	2	40	8

Table 66. Marine shell from FG

Context	No of samples.	Litres	Limpet	Winkle	Flat periwinkle	Dog whelk	Oyster	Razor	Crab	Crab
										C. maenas
661	1	41	49	0					+	++
662	1	15	32	0						
664	1	19	6	319					+	++
666	1	7	22	254	2	1				++
668	1	18	3	7						
671	1	15	0	2						
675	1	15	2	43			1	1		
total			114	625	2	1	1	1		

Discussion – N Sharples

All of the occupation layers to the west of the house dip from east to west at an angle of approximately 15 to 20 degrees. The levels indicate that the structure revealed in trench F was originally situated on the edge of a sharply defined mound. However, the current edge of the mound is obscured by the accumulation of a thick layer of wind-blown sand, which has flattened out the ground level and makes the present-day mound relatively unimpressive.

The sequence of layers probably represents the unstable nature of the deposits around the kiln/barn. Human activity would have caused the sandy soils to move downslope but some of these layers clearly include material, including carbonised plant remains, dumped by people cleaning out the interior of the kiln/barn. Despite the presence of some small finds and a significant assemblage of animal bones in the primary layers, most of these layers are finds-poor and cannot be compared to the finds-rich midden layers found in other trenches. Deposition was occasional and might have been indirect, through the deliberate or accidental movement of soil. At the same time as these soils were moving downslope, wind-blown sand was being deposited against the settlement mound. These layers could be quite substantial and extensive and they would appear to indicate that the machair was unstable during the thirteenth and fourteenth centuries AD.

Notes

1. This observation is made with reference to the thin section reference collection held by the Ancient Monuments Laboratory at English Heritage, which is managed by Matthew Canti.

6 Test Excavations

Trench E – N Sharples

In 1996 Mike Hamilton undertook a geophysical survey of the mounds and this has been fully described in chapter 2. The survey suggested that the settlement extended well beyond the visible mounds and though this could be corroborated by the presence of surface scatters of pottery in the rabbit burrows and on the cultivated ground, it was felt important to test for the existence of structural remains in these peripheral areas, as the material culture might simply reflect midden dumps. The opportunity was taken to examine a sub-rectangular feature, c. 8 m by 5 m, visible on the gradiometer survey (S15 in Figure 17). The outline of this feature was defined by positive readings, whereas the interior was neutral. The resistivity survey showed this as an area of high resistance. The anomaly was oriented roughly east-west and the patterning suggested the presence of a house with stone walls creating the positive readings.

A trench, 1 m wide and 5 m long, was excavated (Figure 19). This was positioned to cut across the south wall and it was never the intention to do more than confirm the geophysical survey by locating the wall of the house. The excavation was undertaken by Mike Hamilton and took less than a week.

After removal of the turf (220) a layer of white wind-blown sand (221) was removed. This immediately revealed the stones of a wall (Figure 80). Unfortunately the stones were limited to the east side of the trench and it would appear that the trench was positioned over the entrance to the house. The stones suggest the wall was at least 1.10 m thick and in front of the north face were several stones less securely embedded which may be tumble. The thickness of the wall may be misleading as it probably indicates the revetment defining the east side of the entrance passage rather than indicating a solid stone wall footing. The walls in trench D and elsewhere were all revetments for turf walls. The tumble present in the interior of the house in trench E was not present in

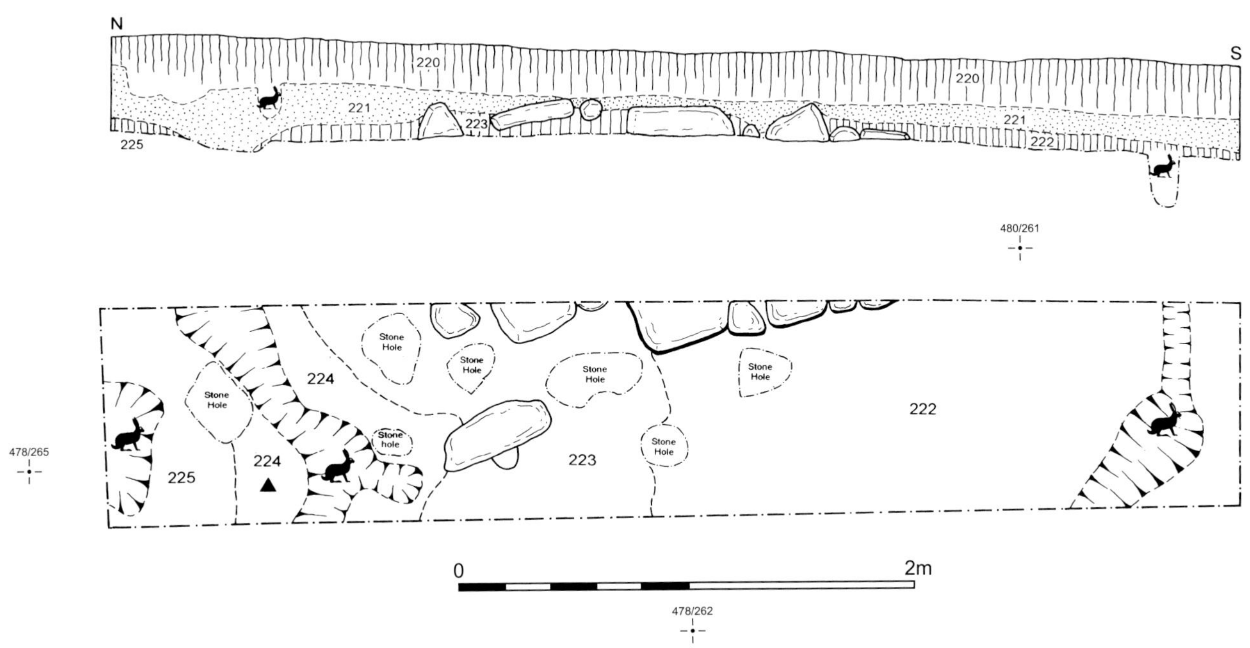

Figure 80. The plan and section of trench E

the house in trench D but it is difficult to understand the significance of these stones, which could also be rough paving, without a more extensive excavation.

Underlying the white sand and surrounding the stones of the wall was a brown sand (222/223/224). Up to 0.20 m of this was removed around the wall to help to define this feature but no underlying layer was observed. At the north end of the trench the brown sand (225) contained a much greater quantity of charcoal flecks that may relate to the position near the centre of the house and therefore possibly close to a hearth. The limited nature of the excavation and the amount of rabbit disturbance in this area again makes a comprehensive interpretation impossible.

Finds – P Macdonald

The only find of note from this trench was a small spherical lump of copper alloy (Figure 56, 1161), which was found in the brown sand 224. This is probably a piece of casting waste and may indicate metalworking in the vicinity.

Trench K – N Sharples

In 1999 another trench was excavated to explore the limits of the settlement and to examine a possible feature defined by the geophysical survey (Figure 23). In the initial plot of the survey a vague linear feature was noted apparently defining the corner of an enclosure in the northeast corner of the area surveyed, some considerable distance beyond the main archaeological prominent areas. This was so vague it was not described in the original report on the survey (Hamilton and Sharples 1996). However, the possibility that it was some form of field boundary was too enticing to ignore and a JCB trench was excavated in 1999. After the removal of just under a metre of sterile wind-blown sand, in a trench roughly 6 m by 2 m, excavation ceased. The trench quickly filled with water as the surface of the machair is only just above the summer water table at this point and so no sections were drawn.

7 Comparative Analysis of Floors and Middens

This chapter will present a summary of the various assemblages recovered from the mound 3 trenches. It will also examine the differences that exist in the composition of material found in the different trenches and in the various contexts and stratigraphic units identified in these trenches. This introduction to the assemblage will provide the basic numerical summaries of the different categories found on mound 3 and ease any comparative analysis of the site with other areas of the Bornais site and other sites, such as Cille Pheadair. It is also hoped that analysis of the different spatial and temporal patterning will aid in the interpretation of these contexts and provide the basis for the more detailed understanding of how the site works, presented in chapter 10.

Pottery – A Lane and J Bond

The mound 3 assemblage is a medium-sized but still useful ceramic collection of some 1472 sherds (Table 67). It is fairly heavily broken up with the average sherd weight being 5.69g. Only a few diameters can be measured accurately due to the variability of the hand-made pottery. No complete profiles are reconstructible and only a few vessel sizes can be reconstructed with any confidence. In spite of these limitations the assemblage can be seen to fit fairly comfortably into the criteria identified in studying The Udal assemblage (Lane 1983) and other Hebridean assemblages of the same period (Lane 1990).

The vessels appear to belong to a fairly limited range of small cups and larger open bowls (Lane 1990, illus. 7.6). Vessels are straight-sided (e.g. Figure 32, 3) or are slightly bow-walled with slightly incurving rims (e.g. Figure 31, 19). All the vessels are fairly open with no narrow constricted necks. Rims are simple with the only sign of elaboration being the appearance of everted rims (e.g. Figure 47, 11) in the later deposits. There is virtually no sign of the decoration of rims, which appears at The Udal (Lane 1990, 123; 1983, 227–8, figs 20–22). Some bases are grass-marked or have the surface cracking which appears to be an analogous process. Bases are flat or sagging with rounded angles (e.g. Figure 47, 15) or sharper angles which can have a slightly footed appearance (e.g. Figure 47, 1; cf. Lane 1990, illus. 7.6 nos 1–3). There is some variation in fabrics with a tendency to thinner and finer material in the later layers though this pottery is so broken up that there cannot be any great certainty about vessel forms or frequency of the type. The few vessel diameters that are measurable vary from

Table 67. A summary of the pottery present in each block

context	weight	Sherds	rim	base	body	misc.	platter	fine	pre-Vik	Ave Wght
DA	42	2			2			1		21.00
DB	3251	417	25	84	42	200	66	35		7.80
DD	3452	729	31	60	82	412	144	49		4.74
DE	750	152	9	18	15	86	24	23		4.93
Topsoil	172	35	2	2	3	21	7	8		4.91
Total	7667	1335	67	164	144	719	241	116		5.74

context	weight	Sherds	rim	base	body	misc.	platter	fine	pre-Vik	Ave Wght.
FB	77	11			6	4	1			7.00
FC	46	12			1	7	4			3.83
FD	141	23		1	6	14	1			6.13
FE	170	32		1	7	24		3	7	5.31
FF	192	29		7	1	9	12			6.62
FG	85	30	2	2	2	22	2			2.83
Total	711	137	2	11	23	80	20	3	7	5.19

150 mm up to 310 mm and indicate the use of fair-sized bowls. However, some much smaller vessels are indicated by thin fine rims and bases, none of which have measurable diameters.

Tables 67 and 68 summarise the diagnostic sherds in the stratigraphic blocks in trench D. The lower deposits in DB contain thick-walled open-bowl forms. Some quite thin rims appear as low as 226 so thinner walled and smaller vessels must have been in use but are too fragmented to reconstruct. There are no fine wares in these layers nor platter and this may be chronologically significant. One sherd of platter appears in 209 though this has an unusual and distinctive squared stabmark which links it to sherds found higher up the sequence in contexts 211 and 204. There are no everted rims in this sequence, bar one doubtful example in 216 and fine ware sherds only

Table 68. The distribution of feature sherds

context	block	rims	inangled	straight	everted	other	Bases	flat	sagging	rounded angle
214	DB	6	2	2			2		? 1	2
210	DB	2		2			10	4		2
209	DB	1	1							
208	DB	1		1			5		3	3
226	DB	3		2			15		15	
216	DB	1		? 1	? 1					
237	DB	2	1			1	3	1	2	1
211	DB	4		3			1	1		
612	DB						36		36	
613	DB						2		2	
247	DB									
227	DB	2	2				5	5		1
232	DB						2	2		1
204	DB	1				1	1			
205	DB	2		1			1		1	
206	DB						1	1		
DB Total		**25**	**7**	**12**	**? 1**	**1**	**84**	**14**	**37**	**10**
615	DD	1			? 1		2		2	
614	DD	5		2	1; ? 2		23	3	7	
604	DD	7	1		1		9	3	2	
605	DD	3		2	1 neck		10	2	3	4
610	DD	1								
243	DD	3	1				1	1		
230	DD	2	2				4		4	
238	DD	1			? 1		4	1	1	1
242	DD	2			2		2			
602	DD	1			1					
611	DD	1		1			1			
609	DD						2		2	
212	DD	4	2	1			2			1
DD Total		**31**	**6**	**6**	**5 & ?4**		**60**	**12**	**21**	**5**
207	DE	0					6		2	1
228	DE	0					1			
231	DE	1	?1				1			
233	DE	0					1			1
234	DE	3		2			5		2	2
235	DE	0					0			
236	DE	1	1				1			1
239	DE	3		1	2		3	1		
240	DE	1			1		0			
DE Total		**9**	**1 ?1**	**3**	**3**		**18**	**1**	**4**	**5**

appear, in numbers, in context 237 and above. It seems likely that these are indicators of chronological change.

The house floors (DD) and related contexts have a similar assemblage to the later contexts in DB, i.e. bowls and cups, though the coarser bowls of DB are less obvious. These open bowls and cups continue in use but everted rims are now common. One probably occurs in 615, a pre-floor pit, but they are definitely present in all three major floor deposits. Sagging and flat bases occur with some signs of an increase in slightly footed flat bases. Grass-marking and cracked basal surfaces occur. A significant feature of the deposits in all three floors is the presence of platter. Fine ware sherds are also a significant feature of the house contexts.

The DE deposits have the same features as the earlier deposits except grass-marking seems to be in decline. Everted rims and open forms are both present. Flat and sagging bases occur and platters are present.

The pottery from trench F is generally small and undiagnostic. There are only two rim sherds, neither of which is diagnostic. The average weight is 5.2g, slightly below the average for the kiln/barn floor layers. There are a few platter sherds but only two vessel rims were recognisable and no profiles, diameters, or vessel forms. None of the bases were very well preserved. Nevertheless they seem to be of the same tradition as the remainder of the mound 3 pottery and are probably of the same date. Context 255 in block FE contains a collection that is clearly from a Late Iron Age context, which is incompatible with the location and must indicate a labelling error during post-excavation.

Artefact distribution – A Clarke, I Dennis, P Macdonald and A Smith

The artefact assemblage from mound 3 is relatively small (Table 69). It consists of 39 pieces of ironwork (excluding demonstrably modern pieces), seven copper alloy objects, eleven bone/antler artefacts, four pieces of antler waste, five stone artefacts and seventeen pieces of flint.

The assemblage was fairly widely dispersed with almost all the stratigraphic blocks producing something. Fifty one objects came from trench D and 22 objects came from trench F. The largest concentration of objects were in the house floors (DD). The stone, flint and bone/

Table 69. The distribution of artefacts

Artefact Group	Artefact Type	DA	DB	DC	DD	DE	E	FB	FC	FD	FE	FF	FG	F	No phase	TOTAL
Vessel	Steatite		0.50		0.50											1
Dress and Ornament	Antler combs		2		2											4
	Pin iron				1								1			2
	Pin bone				2							1				3
	Pin Cu alloy													1		1
	Buckle Cu alloy					1										1
	Buckle/Brooch pin				1				1							2
Tools	Bone clamp														1	1
	Bone handle		2													2
	Bone point				1											1
	Knife							1						1	1	3
	Whetstone		1											1		2
	Spindle whorl					1										1
	Faceted cobble				1											1
Flint			5		8	2							1		1	17
Structural Fittings	Nail/Nail?		1		3		1			2		1	3		2	13
	Holdfast		1												1	2
	Rove		1		2	1									1	5
Miscellaneous	Ring				1											1
	Bar/Bar?		1								1			1		3
	Plate fragment		1		2											3
	Rod/Rod?												2		1	3
	Strip/Strip?				1					1						2
	Sheet (Cu alloy)				1	1									1	3
	Unknown				1											1
Manufacturing debris	Antler tine				1							1	1	1		4
	Bone pin roughout				1											1
	Cu alloy droplet						1									1
TOTAL		0	15.5	0	28.5	6	2	1	1	3	1	3	8	5	9	83

antler artefacts were almost exclusively concentrated in trench D whereas antler waste was most common in trench F. The metalwork assemblage was more widely distributed and it is noticeable that artefacts were more common in trench F; a knife, a possible buckle pin and three pins. The buckle pin (1864) and the knife (1887) come from the fill of the construction pits for the kiln/barn (FC) and the adjacent building (FB). These are otherwise fairly sterile contexts and it seems surprising to find two of the most substantial pieces in these contexts. It is possible that these (and possibly copper alloy dress pin 1739 (Figure 56), though this is not securely stratified) were deliberately deposited during the construction process. Structured deposition may also be an explanation for the copper alloy buckle (1339) in the abandonment deposit (DE) of the house. In contrast the stone and bone/antler artefacts are fragmentary pieces that appear more likely to be accidental losses during domestic activity.

Carbonised plant remains – S Colledge and H Smith

The mean density of charcoal for the site was 0.7cm^3/l and only 39 samples (26.4%) had densities above this value. In comparison with charcoal densities that could be expected as a result of large-scale destructive fires, the overall density for Bornais was relatively low and was more indicative of general scatters of burnt debris. Certain samples, however, had much higher densities than the mean and the contexts from which these were taken may be representative of discrete areas of activity involving the specific use of plant resources, e.g. the preparation of food. The overall preservation of the plant material at Bornais was moderate to poor, as determined by the degree of fragmentation of the remains and the extent to which, for example, the testas of the seeds had survived intact.

There is a significant positive correlation between the charcoal density and the number of cereal items per litre (a correlation coefficient of 0.9751), i.e. samples with higher charcoal densities had greater numbers of cereal items, and *vice versa*. Figure 81 shows the distribution of the Bornais samples in a frequency histogram according to the number of cereal items per litre. The distribution is positively skewed; i.e. there were greater numbers of samples with fewer items. The mean number of cereal items per litre is 18.0 and only 38 samples (25.7%) have numbers above this value. It is interesting to note that of these 38 samples, 26 were from the kiln/barn floors (11 from the upper floor and 15 from the lower floor) and a further two samples were from contexts associated with the kiln/barn. This is consistent with activities associated with the kiln/barn, as would be expected as a result of accidental burning in a corn-drying kiln. Only two of the samples were from contexts within the house floors (i.e.

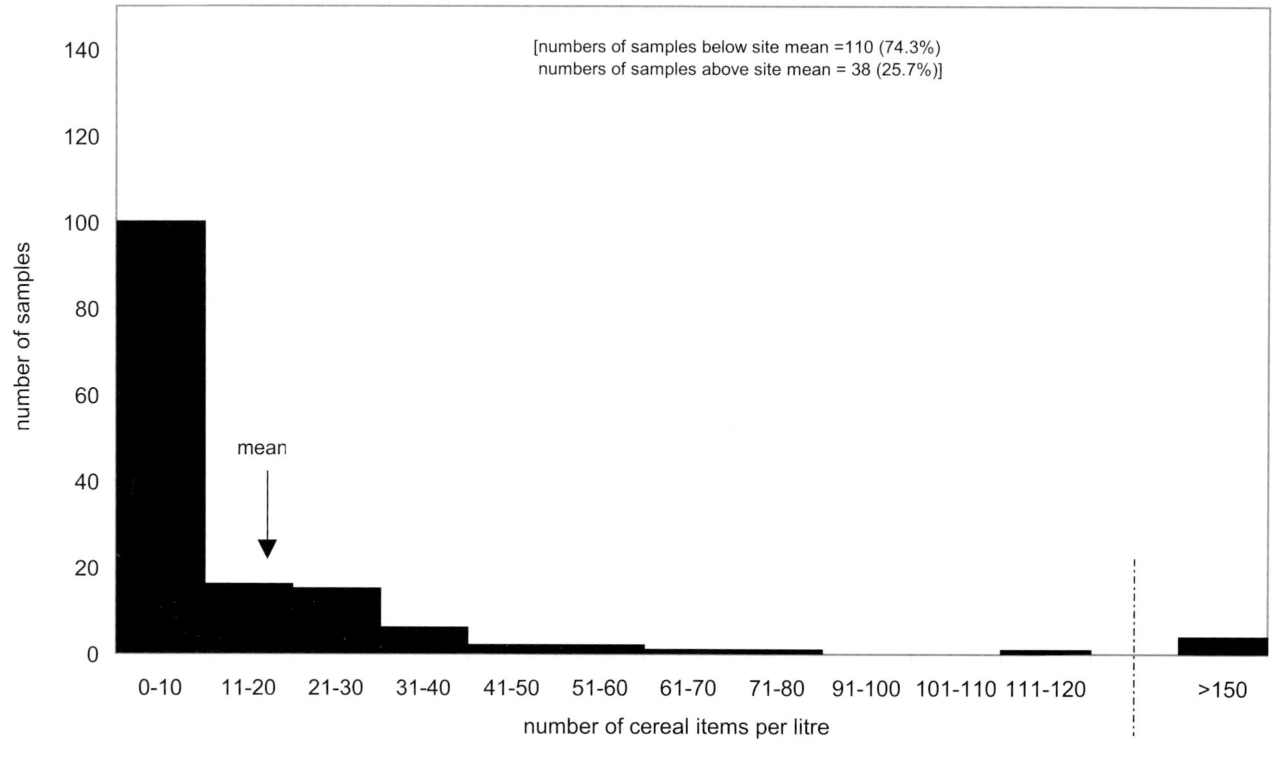

Figure 81. A frequency histogram showing the number of cereal items per litre of soil

the lowest floor level) and three were from hearth fills. The remaining five samples were from kiln/barn occupation contexts (FD) and from an area immediately adjacent to the bowl of the kiln (FF).

The five samples with the greatest numbers of cereal items per litre were the same as those with the highest charcoal densities. Sample 5967/270 had the greatest numbers of items (432.0 per litre) and samples 5994/269, 8685/658, 8708/681 and 5984/278 (199.0, 244.0, 154.4 and 118.0 per litre respectively), also had values much higher than the site mean. These samples were all associated with the use of the kiln/barn and were concentrated around the entrance to the flue. Figure 82 shows the mean number of cereal items per litre for each context group. The extremely high value of 432.0 for sample 5967/270 reduced the clarity of the graph and for this reason it has been omitted. Only four contexts had values above the site mean and all were associated with the use of the kiln/barn.

Ubiquity analysis

An analysis of the ubiquity of the different taxa highlighted the predominance of the cereals. Figure 83 shows the percentage presence in the samples for all the taxa. Only four were present in more than 50% of the samples, three of which were cereals: barley grains (*Hordeum sativum*), rye grains (*Secale cereale*) and oat grains (*Avena sativa*); and one was a weed: *Polygonum/Rumex* spp. Barley and rye rachis were present in more than 10% of the samples as were an additional eight taxa: *Buglossoides* sp., Boraginaceae embryos (most probably the charred embroyos of *Buglossoides* seeds), Caryophyllaceae spp., Chenopodiaceae spp., Cruciferae spp., *Carex* spp., Gramineae spp. and flax (*Linum* sp.). In the majority of samples, the weed taxa were found in extremely low numbers. Flax was present in 73 samples (49%) and in most of these it occurred in low numbers (the mean number of seeds per litre for the 73 samples was 2.8). The presence of flax was restricted almost entirely to the house floors, and four of the six samples with greater numbers of seeds than the site mean were in the lowest floor level: 8077/614, 8024/614, 8031/614 and 8019/614 (values of 107.1, 10.3, 8.9 and 7.0 seeds per litre respectively), all of which occur in the centre of house, to the south of the hearth. The two other samples with high numbers of flax seeds were taken from hearth fills: 5825/609 (8.3 per litre) and 5944/611 (37.5 per litre).

Spatial variation

A majority of the Bornais samples were taken from the house and kiln/barn floors (106 of the 150 samples which produced identifiable plant remains) and the analyses of taxonomic composition, therefore, focused on the relationships between these and associated contexts (e.g. the hearth fills and midden). Figure 84 presents a comparison between the percentage presence of taxa in the samples from the house and kiln/barn floors. The most striking differences in the frequency of occurrence are between barley rachis, rye rachis, *Buglossoides* sp. and Boraginaceae embryos (all of which were more common in

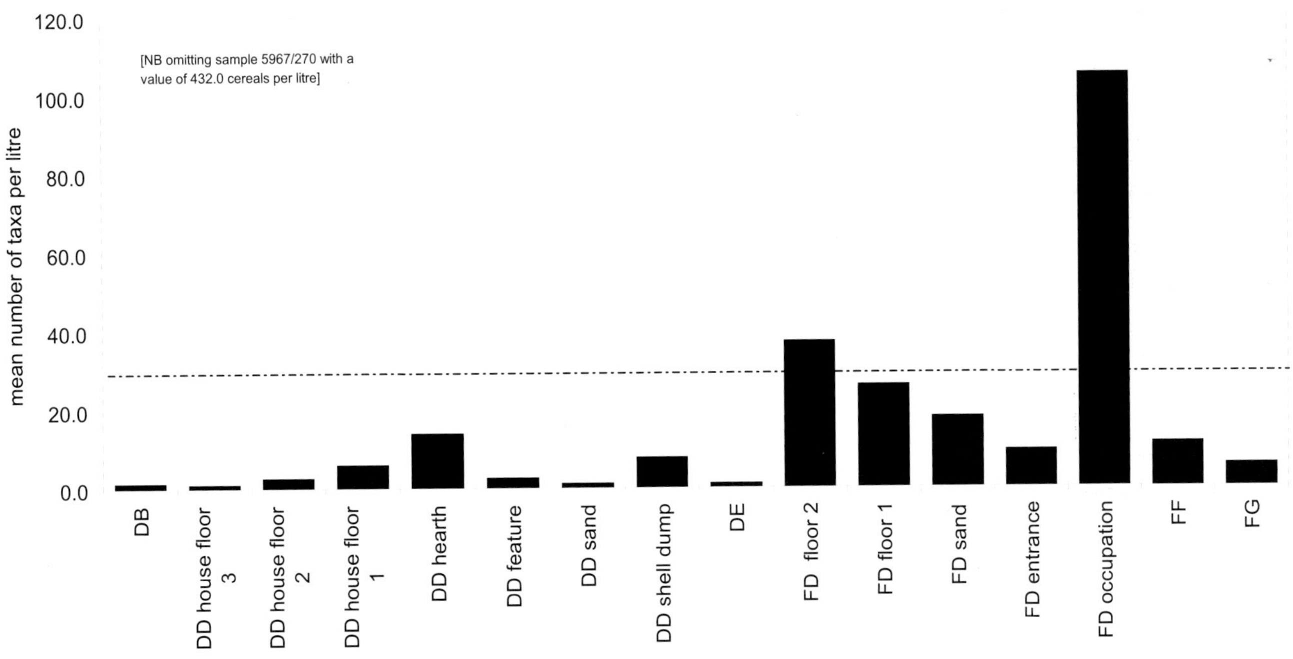

Figure 82. The mean numbers of cereal taxa per litre of soil for each context type

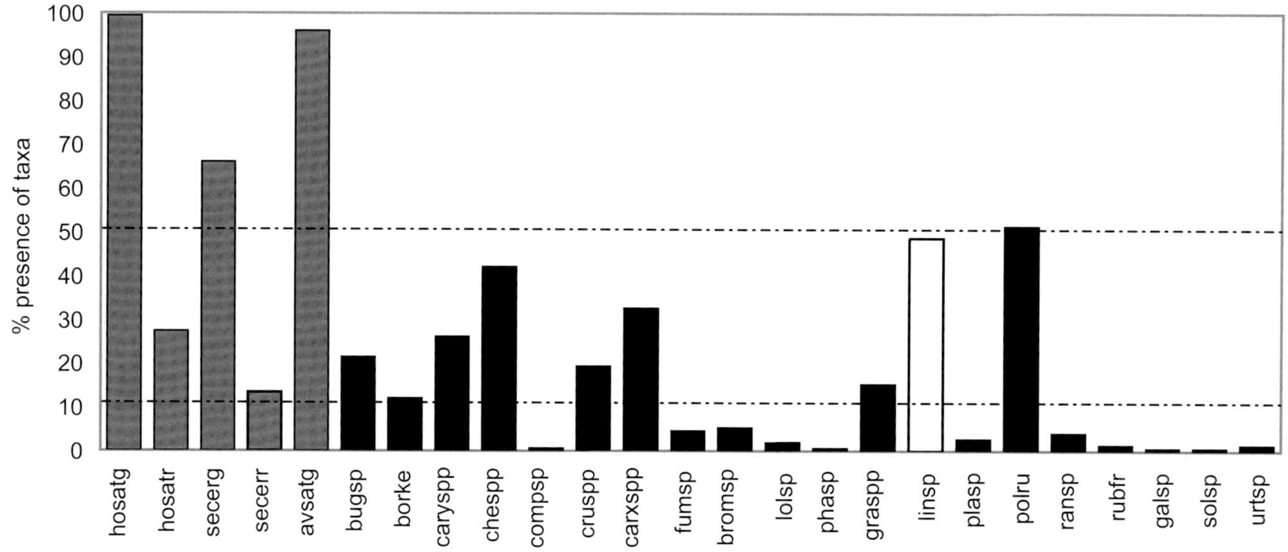

Figure 83. The percentage presence of taxa – all samples all taxa

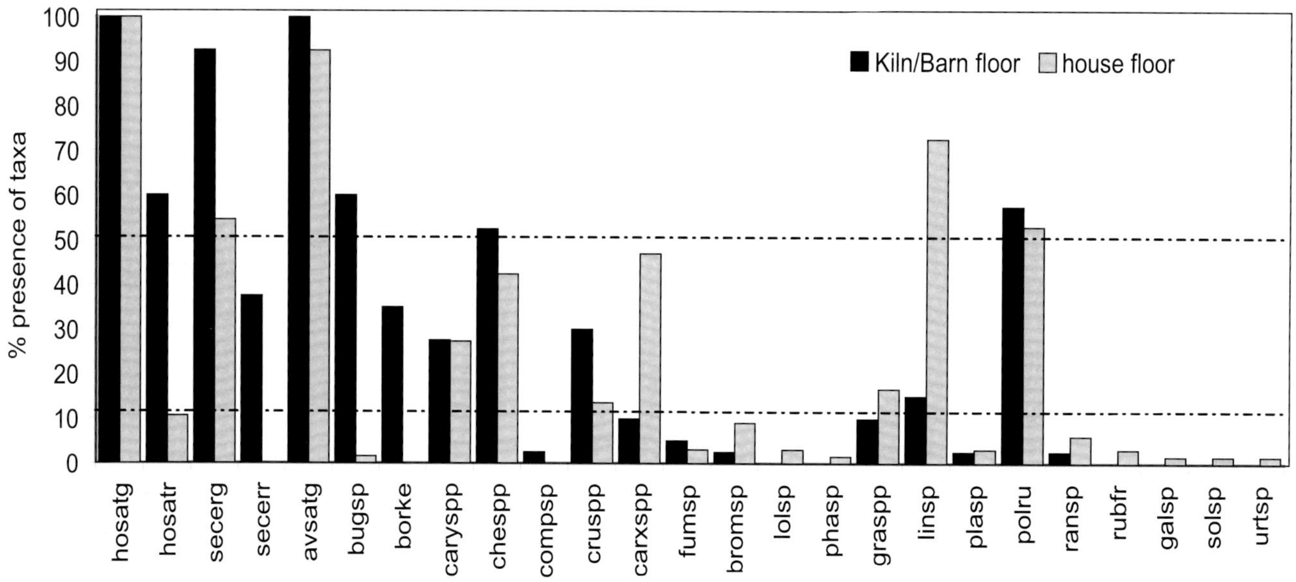

Figure 84. A comparison of the percentage presence of taxa from the house and kiln/barn floors

the kiln/barn floors), and *Carex* spp. and flax (both of which were more common in the house floors). It is perhaps significant that more taxa were identified in the house floors (22) than in the kiln/barn floors (19). This may be an artefact of taphonomic processes rather than a reflection of actual differences in original suites of plants, whereby the higher temperatures of the kiln would have resulted in the 'loss' of the more fragile remains and, consequently, preservation of fewer taxa. This would not, however, account for the more frequent occurrence of the barley and rye rachis internodes in the kiln/barn. It could be expected that this pattern would be reversed if the high temperatures were responsible for lower taxa diversity, given that these chaff items have been found to be less robust once charred than, for example, grains (Boardman and Jones 1990, 9). The distribution of the remains between kiln/barn and house may reflect differences in the use and preparation of the cereals. According to ethnobotanical studies, the earlier stages of crop processing would be expected to produce chaff as a by-product, whereas later stages focus on the removal of smaller materials such as the remaining weed seeds

(Hillman 1981). The association, therefore, of chaff with the kiln/barn is consistent with the parching, threshing and winnowing of the crop in this structure, whereby these activities would result in a by-product including chaff, such as barley rachis. This material might have been thrown on the fire in the kiln flue. The final stages of cleaning the crop include the medium and fine sieving, which would result in the removal of weed seeds. This may account for the greater number of weed taxa in the house contexts.

Compositional variation

Figures 85, 86 and 87 show the relative proportions of crop and weed taxa in the samples from the house (DD) and kiln/barn floors (FD), hearth fills (DD) and slope deposits (FG), though for the purposes of comparison it should be noted that the upper house floor comprises one sample only. In these analyses, it is important to compare taxa that may have similar preservation histories, i.e. those that come into contact with fires with the same frequency and exhibit a similar degree of robustness once charred. Otherwise the relative proportions are more likely to be a reflection of differential preservation rather than of the original composition of plant resources. For this reason, the cereals and weeds have been plotted separately. Figure 86 is, perhaps, slightly misleading as it cannot be assumed that cereals and flax would have been exposed to fires (either deliberately or accidentally) with similar regularity, and it is even less likely that the 'survivability' of grains/seeds would have been the same. It has been shown that seeds with a high oil content (e.g. flax) are highly combustible and, as such, are unlikely to survive in recognisable form once exposed to fires (Wilson 1984, 202). It should, therefore be noted, that flax may be under-represented in Figure 86.

Figure 85 presents the proportions of cereal taxa in the different contexts. Of note in this graph is the fact that the middle and lower house floors have greater proportions of barley grains and lower proportions of oat grains than the kiln/barn floors. On the basis of the relative percentages of these two cereal taxa, the hearth fills are similar in composition to the samples from the house floors and the slope deposits (FG) are similar to those from the kiln/barn floors. The associations of the house floors with the hearth fills and the kiln/barn floors with the slope deposits (FG) are more obvious in Figure 86, in which flax has been included with the cereals. In this graph a distinction is made between contexts with and without flax; in the kiln/barn floors and the FG occupation layers it is clearly absent. Although less obvious, rye grains and rye rachis also occur in larger proportions in the kiln/barn floor and FG samples in comparison to the house floor and hearth samples (with the exception of the middle house floor).

Figure 87 shows the relative proportions of the weed taxa present in >10% of samples. The differences between the two sets of contexts are again apparent in this graph and most noticeably on the basis of the presence of *Buglossoides* sp. and Boraginaceae embryos in the kiln/barn and FG occupation layers. Of note also are the relatively high proportions of *Carex* sp. in the middle and lower house floors.

Based on the weed taxa alone, the compositional variations between the various contexts indicate that the FG occupation layers are most likely to be derived from the kiln/barn whilst the debris from the hearths is likely to have been spread over the house floors. These associations are highlighted by the occurrence of flax only in the hearth fill and house floor samples (with the exception of 11 seeds in the kiln/barn floor samples). The absence of taxa other than Gramineae spp., *Buglossoides* cf. *arvense* sp. and Boraginaceae in the FG occupation layers compared to the kiln/barn floor does not substantiate interpretations for the movement of material from the kiln/barn to the FG occupation layers. This may reflect differential survival, and the better survival of the generally larger items in the FG occupation layers. Alternatively, it may reflect the generation of a by-product at a particular stage of crop processing (such as sieving) and the charring of this separated material, somewhere other than the household fire or kiln flue fire, before then entering these layers.

Statistical analysis

The patterns highlighted in the ubiquity analyses and in the comparisons of relative proportions of taxa were also apparent using multivariate statistical techniques. Correspondence analysis enabled the co-variation relationships between the taxonomic composition of samples from mound 3 and the different context types to be investigated. The programmes used were CANOCO and CANODRAW (ter Braak and Smilauer 2002). Figure 88 presents the results in graphical form (e.g. bi-plots) of correspondence analysis on data sets comprising samples from the house and kiln/barn floors (106), hearth fills (9) and FG occupation layers (5), and crop (5 cereal items + flax = 6) and weed taxa (present in >10% of samples = 8 taxa). In all the plots, the first two principal axes are shown; axis 1 is horizontal and axis 2 is vertical. Figure 88A shows the output plot from the analysis of samples from the house and kiln/barn floors and six crop items (cereals and flax). The two sets of floors are clearly separated on axis 1, with the floors from the house (middle and lower) associated with flax and the kiln/barn floors more closely allied with rye grains and rachis, oat grains and barley rachis. Of note in this plot is the fact that there is also a distinction between the upper and lower kiln/barn floors along axis 2.

The samples from the upper floor appear to be influenced by barley rachis and oat grains, whereas those from the lower floor are allied with rye grains and chaff. In this plot and in others, the sample from the upper house floor is grouped with the kiln/barn floors. Figure

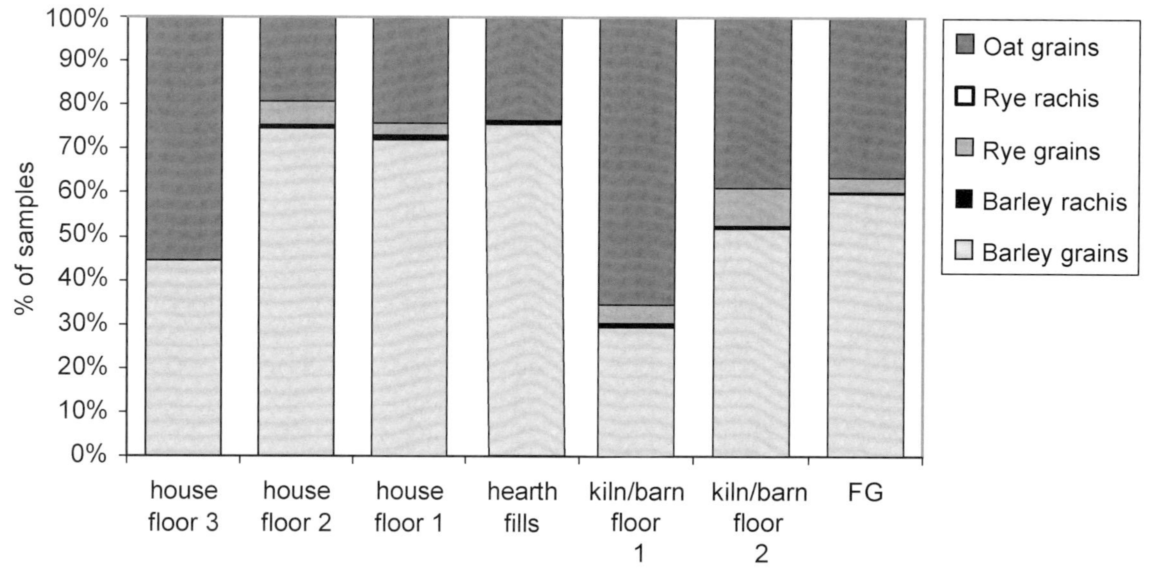

Figure 85. The proportions of cereal taxa in the house and kiln/barn floors, hearth fills and middens

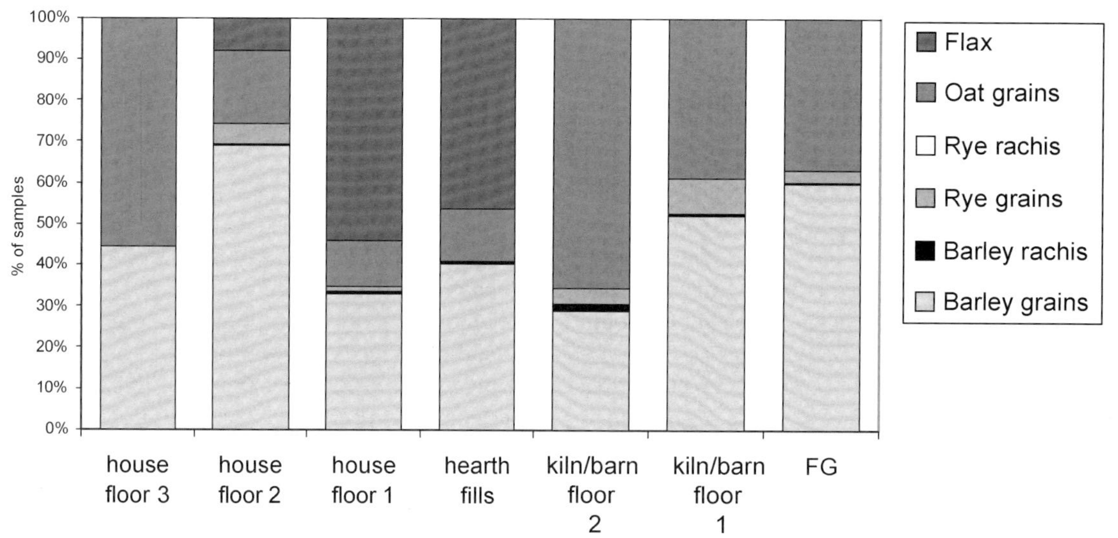

Figure 86. The proportions of cereal taxa and flax in the house and kiln/barn floors, hearth fills and middens

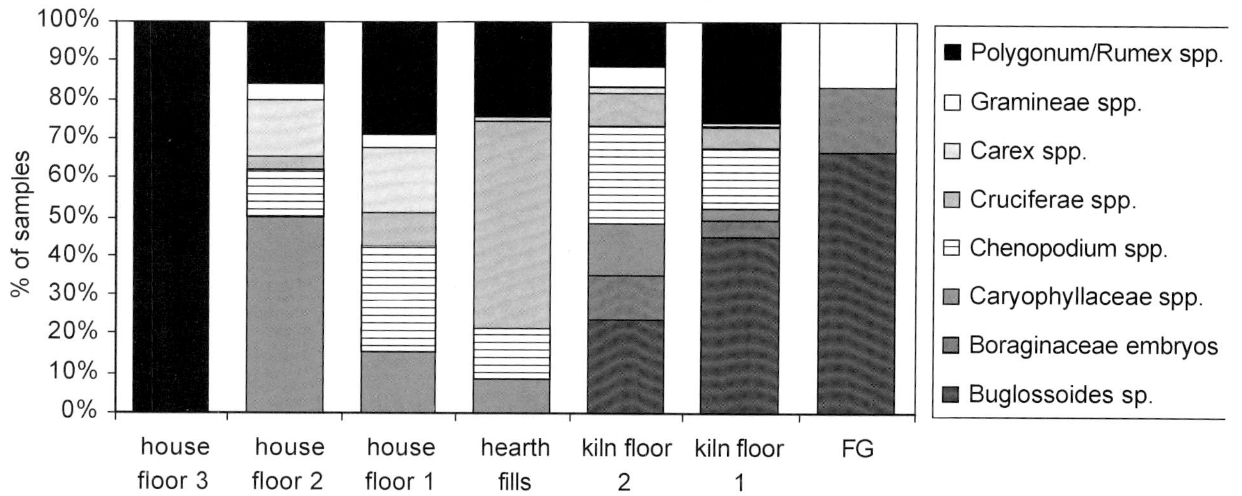

Figure 87. The proportions of weed taxa (present in >10% of samples) in the house and kiln/barn floors, hearth fills and midden

88B presents the results of correspondence analysis on the same sets of samples with the cereal taxa only. Again, the two sets of floors are separated along axis 1. In this plot the middle and lower house floors are associated with barley grains and the kiln/barn floors, as in the previous plot, are influenced by rye grains and rachis, oat grains and barley rachis. There is some separation of the two kiln/barn floors (along both axes), but less clearly than in Figure 88A. Figure 88C shows the results of analysis of the samples from the house and kiln/barn floors with the weed taxa. As with the previous two plots, the two sets of floors are separated along axis 1, the kiln/barn floors are associated with *Buglossoides* sp. and Boraginaceae embryos and the house floors (the upper house floor is not included in this analysis) are influenced by Caryophyllaceae spp., *Carex* spp. and Gramineae spp. These results also highlight the differences between the upper and lower kiln/barn floors, based on taxonomic composition. The lower kiln/barn floor is associated with rye grains and rachis whereas the upper kiln/barn floor is associated with barley rachis and oat grain, as seen in the graphs showing relative proportions of the different cereal taxa (Figures 85 and 86).

Figures 88D and 88E are repeats of Figures 88B and 88C with the addition of samples from the hearth fills and FG occupation layers. The distributions of the samples from the house and kiln/barn floors and the relationships between them are similar to those presented in Figures 88B and 88C. Of note in these plots is the fact that the hearth fill samples appear to be associated with the house floors. It is less clear, however, with which set of floors the FG samples are associated.

The large scale and thorough sampling strategies enabled statistical investigations of the overall composition of the samples, highlighting the differences in the quantity and taxonomic composition of the samples from the house and kiln/barn floors, and the associations of related contexts. This information has enabled an investigation of the use of plant resources in the different areas of the site that can be related to the results of other analyses, such as microdebitage, thin section analysis, sediment analysis, faunal and fish remains. Furthermore, these analyses highlight associations of certain weed taxa with particular crops and contexts, which can help in the investigation of land use and cultivation strategies.

Charcoal – R Gale

As might be anticipated, a rather narrow range of indigenous trees and shrubs was identified (Table 70). Heather was by far the most common woody species, with stem diameters measuring up to 10 mm, although mostly much thinner. The charred seeds and seed capsules of *Calluna vulgaris* were recorded, although fairly sparsely, from floor and hearth contexts in the house (see Tables 12 and 14). It is probable that the charcoal represents the same species, although the inclusion of other northerly members of the Ericaceae, such as *Erica* (heather), *Arctostaphylos*, *Empetrum* and *Vaccinium* cannot be discounted. These sub-shrubs are typical of acid heathland in northern Britain, although on blanket bogs and in mires *Calluna vulgaris* tends to be dominant, sometimes with *Erica tetralix* (Polunin and Walters 1985). In the Scottish islands, heather played an important role in the local economy and most parts of the plant were utilised, e.g. for bedding, thatch, brushes, fodder, animal litter, ropes, dyes and fuel (Fenton 1978a).

Birch was also relatively frequent although mainly in the handpicked samples, which included larger fragments. The charcoal was mostly too fragmented to assess whether the birch wood derived from narrow roundwood or trunk; an incomplete segment of roundwood from context 242 measured about 30 mm in diameter (estimated at 40 mm prior to charring). In northern Britain, birch woodlands are often open in character, either on grassland or with bilberry (*Vaccinium myrtillus*); hazel (*Corylus avellana*) and juniper (*Juniperus communis*) are frequent in the shrub layer (Polunin and Walters 1985). Both hazel and juniper were identified from the charcoal. Dwarf birch (*Betula nana*) might also have grown locally.

Alder (*Alnus glutinosa*) and a member of the Salicaceae (willow or poplar) were sparsely represented and are indicative of wetter soils than those tolerated by birch, hazel or juniper. A single piece of oak (*Quercus* sp.) from the lower floor of the house (context 614) suggests that this taxon may have grown on the island, although perhaps only occurring sparsely and in the more sheltered valleys.

Spruce (*Picea* sp.) and/or larch (*Larix* sp.) was also recorded in the charcoal deposits, almost certainly from pieces of largewood. Both taxa are exotics in Britain and although the wood may represent artefactual remains, it is more likely to have been gathered on the foreshore as driftwood.

The house

The earliest charcoal deposits, obtained from an accumulation of sand (DB), produced narrow ericaceous stems and hazel. The origin of this material is not clear although it could be related to activity associated with the early house (DA).

Firewood was clearly used in the house (DD) but probably as an adjunct to peat fuel. During the early phase of occupation (DD1, context 614) firewood appears to have consisted predominantly of heather, although hazel and oak were also recorded from floor 1 and spruce or larch from the bottom of the hearth (context 611). Fewer samples were available from the middle and upper floors (DD2 and DD3) and, hence, it was not possible to discern evidence of species dominance. The taxa identified from DD2 included birch, heather, hazel and willow/poplar and, from DD3, birch and spruce or larch.

The single hearth was sited opposite the entrance

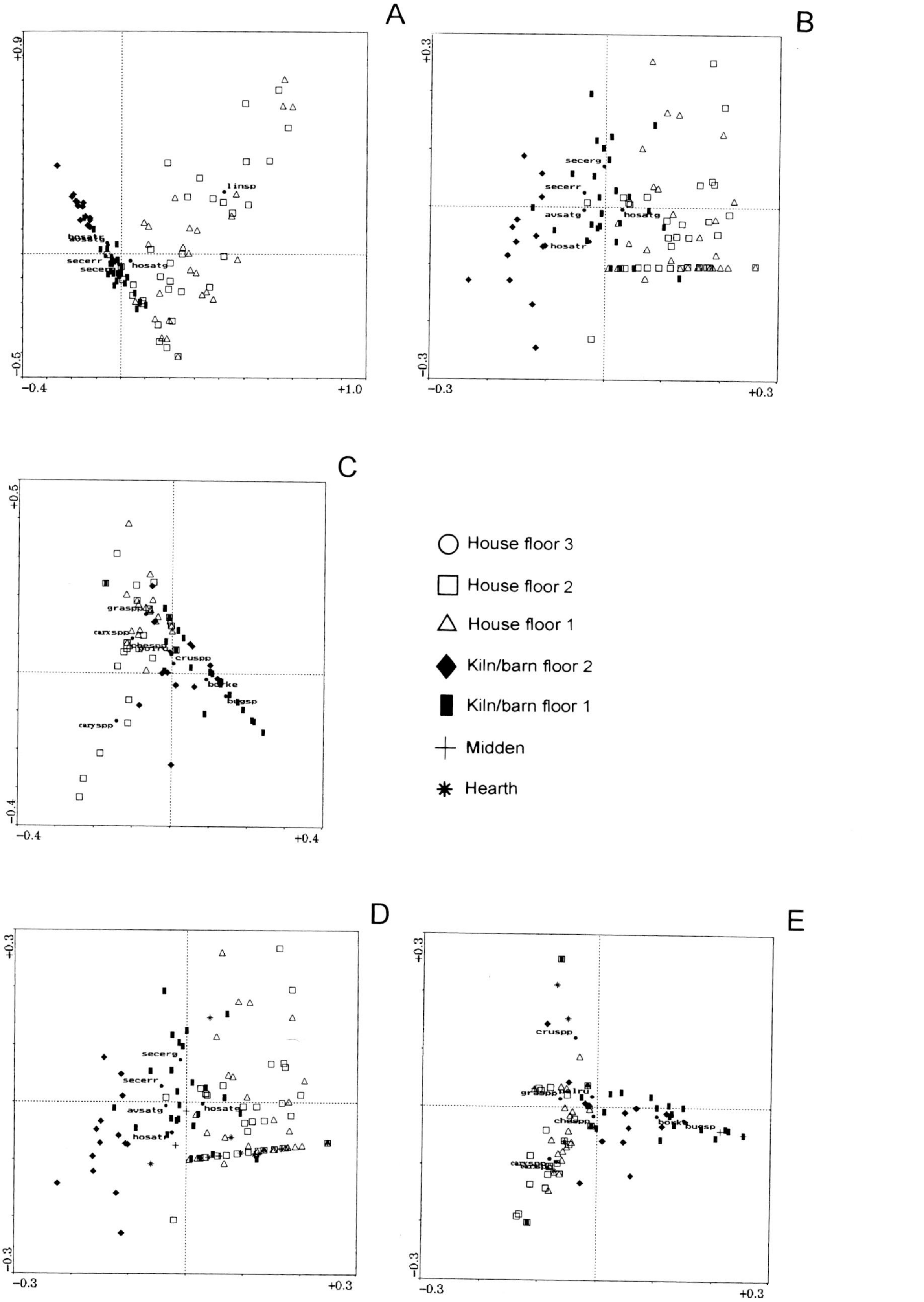

Figure 88. Correspondance analysis. A. cereals and flax from the house and kiln/barn floors; B. cereals from the house and kiln/barn floors; C. the weeds (present in >10% of samples) from the house and kiln/barn floors; D. cereals from the house and kiln/barn floors, hearth fills and midden; E. weeds from the house and kiln/barn floors, hearth fills and midden

Table 70. The charcoal identifications

	Sample	Context	*Alnus*	*Betula*	*Corylus*	Ericaceae	*Quercus*	Salicaceae	*Juniperus*	*Picea/Larix*
DB	5750	227			3					
DB	5818	247				2				
DB	Handpicked	210				2				
DD	Handpicked	249				cf. 1				
DD	5944	611								1
DD/1	8034	614				9	1			
DD/1	8036	614			2					
DD/1	8038	614				1				
DD/1	8042	614				20				
DD/1	8045	614				1				
DD/1	8046	614				10				
DD/1	8048	614				1				
DD/1	8056/8063	614			1	4				
DD/1	8057	614				15				
DD/1	8063	614				15				
DD/1	8069	614				11				
DD/1	8076	614				1				
DD/2	5906	604			1	21				
DD/2	5892	605				2				
DD/2	5913	605						1		
DD/2	5806	610		2						
DD/2	5940	610				6				
DD/2	5945	610		1						
DD/2	8016	610		1						
DD/3	Handpicked	230		1						
DD/3	Handpicked	242		1						
DD/3	5808	242								1
DE	5773	234				1				
FC	Handpicked	290		1						
FD	8713	293							4	
FD/1	8636	276	2	2	1					
FD/1	8651	276		1						
FD/1	8657	276				3				
FE	Handpicked	288		2						
FF	Handpicked	283		4						31
FF	Handpicked	287		6						5
FF	8696	656				3				
FG	8705	675			2					1
FG	Handpicked	675		2						

passage and, throughout the occupation of the house, this served as the main source of heat. With the ready availability of slow-burning peat, it was probably common practice amongst householders to keep hearth fires burning more or less continuously and the ashes (and associated charcoal) might also have been retained in the hearth for relatively long periods to enhance the radiant heat. Inevitably, charcoal spilled from the hearth and/or escaped the broom and became incorporated into the surface of the floor or accumulated in the more inaccessible corners and crevices around the base of the walls (Figures 42 and 44).

The ancient and traditional use of ash as an insecticide has been recorded from numerous countries and recent experiments have confirmed that the application of ashes to floors and stored food products is, indeed, an effective method of controlling pests and parasites (fleas and lice) (Hakbijl 2002). If similar methods were employed in the Bornais house and associated kiln/barn, this may explain the charcoal-rich floor layers.

The kiln/barn

The function of the kiln/barn was probably twofold, i.e. corndrying and winnowing. Charcoal was examined from contexts 290 and 293 and though the origin of this material is unknown the use of juniper and birch wood as fuel is implied. Charcoal deposits were much denser on the lower floor (276) and were concentrated on the west side and in a central line across the long axis of the building (Figure 71). It was evident from the thick layer of peat ash on the main floor deposit (276) that peat formed the major fuel, whereas firewood and dung were less important (see above 115). Charcoal from southern, northern and central parts of context 276 indicated the use of alder, birch, hazel and heather.

Peat ash and charcoal-rich layers (FF) in an area adjacent to the kiln/barn almost certainly originated as hearth waste and was dumped to consolidate a surface. Charcoal from contexts 656, 283 and 287 was identified as heather, birch and spruce and/or larch; and birch, hazel and spruce/larch were also recorded from context 675, from occupation deposits accumulating on the edge of the mound (FG).

Mammalian bone – J Mulville

The distribution of the assemblage is summarised in Table 71, where NISP counts are shown for all species in both the hand-collected and sieved material. MN counts and elements, for the most frequently occurring species in each trench, are shown in Table 72. Domestic species dominate the assemblage: cattle, sheep, pig, horse, cat and dog. There is a smaller quantity of wild species: red deer, otter, seal, whale and one small mammal.

The most abundant species, using NISP, is sheep; they dominate the assemblage making up over half of the whole assemblage. Cattle make up around a third of the assemblage, with pig forming only 7%, and small amounts of dog and cat present. The most abundant wild species is deer at 3% with the other wild species present at around 1%. The minimum number of individuals was calculated (Table 71) and reflects the NISP, with sheep most abundant followed by cattle and pig.

Intra-site comparison

The bone is unevenly distributed throughout the units, with the majority of identified bone coming from two units, DD (21%) the house floors and DB (45%) contexts preceeding the Norse house (Table 71). It is possible to compare the relative abundance of the species between the two principal excavation areas. Table 71 demonstrates that trench D has a wider range of species associated with it; in addition to the main food animals, dog, horse, cat, otter, seal and whale are found. The only material recorded from trench F and not the house is a single small mammal femur. If we compare the proportion of the main food animals, it can be seen that whilst the predominance of sheep is maintained in both areas, sheep and to a lesser extent pigs are more common in trench F, whereas trench D has a higher proportion of cattle (Figure 89). The MNI was calculated for each area and reaffirms the higher numbers of sheep found in both the areas.

The overall body part representation is examined for both trenches separately (Table 72). The relative abundance of the elements (calculated as MNE) is compared with the number of elements expected if the complete skeletons of the minimum number of individuals (MNI) were discarded on site. Figures 90 and 91 compare the data for sheep and cattle for the two trenches. The number of pig bones is too small for such treatment. Overall every part of the sheep and cattle skeleton is present, indicating that entire animals were deposited on the site. The low proportion of most elements recovered suggests that many pieces of bone were destroyed, highly fragmented or disposed of in areas away from the excavation.

For sheep a smaller range of elements was present in trench F than in trench D. There are relatively fewer jaws found in the house and more forelimb bones, perhaps associated with an emphasis on prime meat-bearing bones. Trench F has a higher proportion of metacarpals and tibiae, elements with less meat upon them. Cattle have a similar pattern with a wider range and greater proportion of bones recovered from the larger assemblage associated with the house. Again there is a slightly greater emphasis on the upper limbs, those associated with prime meat, in the house. The sample of pig bone whilst being small does allow us to note that the majority of bone is from the upper prime meat-bearing limbs, with no metapodia and few toes present.

A much higher percentage of whalebone fragments, relative to the number of identified animal bones, was found in trench F (Table 73). This is particularly true of the fill of the quarry (FB) and the floors in the kiln/barn (FD). The units associated with trench F also showed the highest proportion of burnt whalebone.

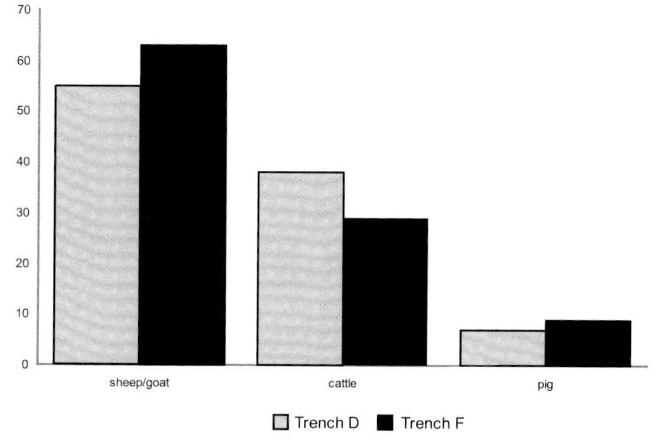

Figure 89. The relative abundance of the principal domestic species in trenches D and F

Table 71. A summary of the animal species (NISP) present in each block

Unit		*Sheep*	Sheep/Goat	Cattle	Pig	Dog	Cat	Horse	Red deer	Seal	Otter	Whale	Small mammal	Total	
	Hand-collected														
DA		*3*	3	1	0	0	0	0	0	0	0	0	0	4	1%
DB		*19*	170	114	18	10	1	2	11	0	1	0	0	327	45%
DD		*29*	80	55	14	2	0	1	1	2	0	1	0	156	21%
DE		*8*	26	21	3	0	0	0	2	0	0	0	0	52	7%
Total House		59	279	191	35	12	1	3	14	2	1	1	0	539	
			52%	*35%*	*6%*	*2%*	*<1%*	*1%*	*3%*	*<1%*	*<1%*	*<1%*	*0%*		
FB		*0*	11	2	1	0	0	0	0	0	0	0	0	14	2%
FC		*0*	2	2	1	0	0	0	0	0	0	0	0	5	1%
FD		*0*	12	4	1	0	0	0	1	0	0	0	1	19	3%
FE		*3*	21	7	7	0	0	0	2	0	0	1	0	38	5%
FF		*4*	13	20	3	0	1	0	0	0	0	0	0	37	5%
FG		*0*	50	22	3	0	0	0	2	0	0	0	0	77	11%
Total Barn/Kiln		7	109	57	16	0	1	0	5	0	0	1	1	190	
			57%	*30%*	*8%*	*0%*	*1%*	*0%*	*3%*	*0%*	*0%*	*1%*	*1%*		
Total		*66*	388	248	51	12	2	3	19	2	1	2	1	729	
			53%	*34%*	*7%*	*2%*	*<1%*	*<1%*	*3%*	*<1%*	*<1%*	*<1%*	*<1%*		
	Sieved		5	1											

sheep/goat percentage includes animals identified as sheep

Table 72. The representation of skeletal elements

		Trench D									Trench F								
		Cattle			Sheep/Goat			Pig			Cattle			Sheep/Goat			Pig		
		MNE	MNI	%	MNE	MNI	%	MNE	MNI	%	MNE	MNI	%	MNE	MNI	%	MNE	MNI	%
Head	Horn	1	7	*14*	3	10	*30*					4	*0*		7	*0*			
	Occipital Condyle		7	*0*	2	10	*20*				0	4	*0*	0	7	*0*			
	Premax	1	7	*14*	1	10	*10*				0	4	*0*	2	7	*29*			
	Zygomatic	3	7	*43*	1	10	*10*				0	4	*0*	1	7	*14*			
	Mandible	7	7	*100*	7	10	*70*	1			2	4	*50*	4	7	*57*	1		
	LM3/Dp4	4	7	*57*	4	10	*40*	1			1	4	*25*	1	7	*14*			
Neck	Atlas	2	7	*29*	2	10	*20*	1			1	4	*25*		7	*0*	1		
	Axis	2	7	*29*	2	10	*20*					4	*0*		7	*0*			
Front Limb	Scapula	3	7	*43*	10	10	*100*				1	4	*25*	1	7	*14*			
	Humerus p.	2	7	*29*	4	10	*40*	1			0	4	*0*	2	7	*29*	1		
	Humerus d.	4	7	*57*	8	10	*80*	3			1	4	*25*	2	7	*29*	1		
	Radius p.	4	7	*57*	8	10	*80*				2	4	*50*	1	7	*14*			
	Radius d	2	7	*29*	4	10	*40*				1	4	*25*	1	7	*14*			
	Ulna	2	7	*29*	6	10	*60*				1	4	*25*		7	*0*			
	Metacarpal p.	3	7	*43*	4	10	*40*				1	4	*25*	4	7	*57*			
	Metacarpal d.	2	7	*29*	3	10	*30*				0	4	*0*	1	7	*14*			
Hind limb	Pelvis	2	7	*29*	4	10	*40*				1	4	*25*	2	7	*29*			
	Femur p.	3	7	*43*	4	10	*40*	1			2	4	*50*	2	7	*29*			
	Femur d.	5	7	*71*	6	10	*60*	2			2	4	*50*	2	7	*29*			
	Patella	1	7	*14*	2	10	*20*				1	4	*25*		7	*0*			
	Tibia p.	3	7	*43*	6	10	*60*	1			4	4	*100*	3	7	*43*			
	Tibia d.	2	7	*29*	7	10	*70*	1			2	4	*50*	7	7	*100*			
	Metatarsal p.	1	7	*14*	2	10	*20*				1	4	*25*	1	7	*14*			
	Metatarsal d.	2	7	*29*	2	10	*20*				1	4	*25*	1	7	*14*			
	Calcaneum	3	7	*43*	3	10	*30*				0	4	*0*	1	7	*14*			
	Astragalus	3	7	*43*	4	10	*40*	1			1	4	*25*	1	7	*14*	1		
	Navicular Cuboid	2	7	*29*	1	10	*10*				1	4	*25*	1	7	*14*			
Feet	Phalanx I	13	56	*23*	19	80	*24*	1			3	24	*13*	12	56	*21*	2		
	Phalanx II	12	56	*21*	8	80	*10*	3			3	24	*13*	6	56	*11*	1		
	Phalanx III	11	56	*20*	5	80	*6*	2			3	24	*13*	3	56	*5*			
mni		7			10			1			4			7			1		

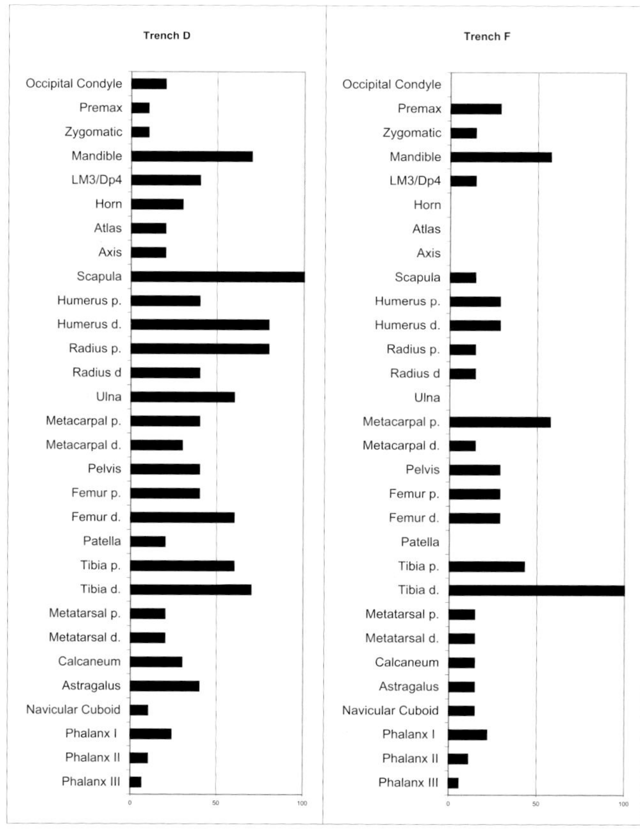

Figure 90. A comparison of the body part abundance of sheep from trenches D and F

Figure 91. A comparison of the body part abundance of cattle from trenches D and F

Bird bones – J Cartledge

Fifty-five bird bones were identified to both domestic and a wide variety of wild species or families (Table 74). The domestic species include domestic fowl and goose. The wild species are represented mainly by seabirds and waders and include gannet, Manx shearwater, shag, cormorant, golden plover, turnstone, curlew, gull species, members of the auk family (puffin and guillemot), teal, rock dove, hedge sparrow, song thrush and skylark, and a rook or carrion crow.

The assemblage was relatively evenly split between the two main trenches with 23 bones recovered from trench D and 29 bones recovered from trench F. It is significant that trench F produced the larger assemblage of bird bones as this contrasts with the distribution of animal bones and fish bones and certainly does not represent either the volume of soil excavated or the density of occupation in these two trenches. The distribution is not otherwise surprising with most of the bones coming from the intensively sampled floor layers in both trenches. The only other blocks to produce substantial quantities of bones were DE and FG, which were consistently rich in faunal remains.

Table 73. The distribution of whale bone fragments

Unit	Fragments	% of ident
DB	1	<1%
DD	10	6%
DE	3	6%
FB	2	14%
FD	10	53%
FE	5	13%
FG	5	6%
Total	36	

Table 74. A summary of the bird species present in each block

Species	DB	DD	DE	E	FB	FC	FD	FE	FF	FG	Total
cf Common/Herring Gull		3	1	2	2						8
cf Domestic Goose										1	1
cf Dunnock (Hedge sparrow)			2								2
cf Great black-back gull	1		1	1		1			1		5
cf Rock dove (skeleton#1)							4				4
cf Skylark		1									1
cf Song thrush		1									1
Cormorant	1						2			1	4
Curlew						1					1
Domestic fowl		2	1				1			2	6
Domestic fowl (bantam)			1								1
Gannet		1	1			1					3
Golden plover		1						1			2
Goose species							3		1		4
Guillemot		1									1
Guillemot/Razorbill		2								2	4
Manx Shearwater								1			1
Puffin							1			1	2
Rook/Crow								1			1
Shag								1			1
Teal			1								1
Turnstone			1								1
Total	2	12	9	3	2	3	11	4	2	7	55

Fish bones – C Ingrem

A total of 3,073 fish bone fragments were identified from mound 3 using the criteria laid out in the methodology (Table 75). Of these, the majority (2,245) were recovered from the <10mm sieved samples and 828 fragments were identified from the >10mm material.

Eighteen species are present: – tope (*Galeorhinus galeus*), herring (*Clupea harengus*), salmon (*Salmo salar*), sea trout (*Salmo trutta*), pike (*Esox lucius*), eel (*Anguilla anguilla*), conger eel (*Conger conger*), whiting (*Merlangius merlangus*), pollack (*Pollachius pollachius*), saithe (*Pollachius virens*), cod (*Gadus morhua*), haddock (*Melanogrammus aeglefinus*), hake (*Merluccius merluccius*), ling (*Molva molva*), scad (*Trachurus trachurus*), corkwing wrasse (*Crenilabrus melops*), ballan wrasse (*Labrus bergylta*), mackerel (*Scomber scombrus*) and flounder (*Platichthys flesus*). In addition, Sparidae (sea bream), Gasterosteidae (stickleback) and Bothidae are represented, the latter by a vertebra belonging to a probable megrim (*Lepidorhombus whiffiagonis*) (Table 75).

Overall, the entire assemblage is dominated by the remains of herring, which comprise over two-thirds of the total NISP (Table 75). However, this is only visible in the sieved samples and although the number of individual species represented in both groups is similar it is clear that the >10mm material is dominated by the remains of large gadids, particularly cod and hake. The other species are present only as trace taxa and make up less than 15% of the total.

Intra-site distribution

Table 76 shows species distribution according to block. The majority (n=2,307) of fish remains are derived from the house floors (DD), with smaller concentrations recovered from the kiln/barn occupation (FD), the occupation layers (FG) and an accumulation layer (DB). As mentioned earlier it is clear that, in all but one block, herring are the dominant species and that the vast majority of their remains are vertebrae from the posterior abdominal and caudal region of the skeleton. With the exception of the house floor layers (DD) and the occupation associated with the kiln/barn (FD), the sample sizes are small and may represent the random re-distribution by wind action of fish bones previously deposited elsewhere. Nevertheless, it is noticeable that a sizeable collection of hake bones was recovered from FG.

A comparison of the occupation deposits suggests that herring might have been decapitated prior to being smoked in the vicinity of the kiln/barn, whereas floor layers in the Norse house with their predominance of vertebrae are more likely to represent consumption waste. Cod, although the second most numerous species, is only present in relatively small numbers but in contrast to the pattern seen for herring, it appears that both heads and bodies of these large fish were present.

Marine shell – N Sharples

The overwhelming majority of the marine shell recovered from Bornais were winkles and limpets (Table 77). Other shellfish present included periwinkle (flat, common and rough), top shell (grey), whelk (common, dog and red), oyster (common), mussel (common and horse), Iceland cyprine, razorshell (dog) and scallop (queen and great), but these never reached quantities greater than 1% of any assemblage. The most common species after winkles and limpets were flat periwinkles and dog whelks, which were found largely on the house floors. Winkles dominated almost all of the samples. The only area where limpets

Table 75. Fish species representation according to retrieval method (NISP)

	Samples		Hand collection	Total	%
	<10mm	>10mm	>10mm		
Tope	1			1	*<1*
Herring	2060	9	2	2071	*67*
Salmon	3			3	*<1*
Sea trout	4	1		5	*<1*
Sea trout?	1			1	*<1*
Argentine?	1			1	*<1*
Salmonid	12			12	*<1*
Pike		1		1	*<1*
Eel	11			11	*<1*
Conger eel	1		2	3	*<1*
Whiting	30			30	*1*
Pollack	8	21	25	54	*2*
Saithe	26	13	7	46	*1*
Pollachius	3			3	*<1*
Cod	15	186	183	384	*12*
Haddock		2		2	*<1*
Hake		60	104	164	*5*
Ling		25	27	52	*2*
Large gadid	7	61	67	135	*4*
Medium gadid	12	9	5	26	*1*
Small gadid	28	1		29	*1*
Gadidae	2		11	13	*<1*
Scad	2			2	*<1*
Sparidae	4	1	1	6	*<1*
Corkwing Wrasse	2			2	*<1*
Ballan wrasse			1	1	*<1*
Labridae	4			4	*<1*
Labridae?	1			1	*<1*
Mackerel	2		1	3	*<1*
Stickleback	1			1	*<1*
Megrim?			1	1	*<1*
Flounder	1	1		2	*<1*
Flatfish	3			3	*<1*
Total	2245	391	437	3073	

Table 76. Fish species representation according to block (NISP)

	DB	DD	DE	FB	FC	FD	FE	FF	FG	Other	Total
Tope		1									1
Herring	20	1724	29	6		196	9	26	57	4	2071
Salmon		3									3
Sea trout		4						1			5
Sea trout?			1								1
Argentine?			1								1
Salmonid		10				1		1			12
Pike						1					1
Eel	2	7	1			1					11
Conger eel		3									3
Whiting	1	27				1	1				30
Pollack	5	30	2	3	1		1	1	6	5	54
Saithe	1	31	1	2		1		1	8	1	46
Pollachius								3			3
Cod	50	231	21	5	4	3	1	23	26	20	384
Haddock		1	1								2
Hake	20	66	11	5	1	2	1	8	40	10	164
Ling	7	27	2	1	1	3	1	2	8		52
Large gadid	25	74	11	3		4	1	5	7	5	135
Medium gadid	1	21	1			1		1	1		26
Small gadid		26						1	2		29
Gadidae		3							6	4	13
Scad		2									2
Sparidae		4				1	1				6
Corkwing Wrasse		1					1				2
Ballan wrasse	1										1
Labridae		4									4
Labridae?		1									1
Mackerel	1	1				1					3
Stickleback		1									1
Megrim?				1							1
Flounder		2									2
Flatfish	1	2									3
Total	135	2307	82	26	7	216	17	73	161	49	3073
%	*4*	*75*	*3*	*1*	*<1*	*7*	*1*	*2*	*5*	*2*	

became a more dominant species was in the early occupation of trench F. Several samples from the construction of an adjacent building (FB) and from early soil accumulation on the western edge of the mound (FG) were exclusively limpet and in the lowest floor of the kiln/barn (FD/1) the two species were almost equivalent. However, this pattern did not last and in the later contexts in this trench winkles are even more dominant than they are in trench D.

Crab – J Light

A spreadsheet of determinations arising from examination of the crab shell samples (Table 78) shows that three taxa have been identified in the samples, based upon the chelae. These are the edible (brown) crab (*Cancer pagurus*), the shore crab (*Carcinus maenas*) and the velvet swimming crab (*Liocarcinus cf. depurator*). These taxa are not distributed randomly through the samples. The floor layers of the house (DD) and contexts west of the kiln/barn (FG) yielded dominantly *Carcinus* fragments and *Cancer* fragments are sparse. In contrast fragments associated with contexts southeast of the kiln/barn (FF) are dominantly *Cancer* chelae. The crab shell fragments, even those of the large species *Cancer pagurus*, are from small animals.

It is not easy to make sense of the samples/contexts where there are very small amounts of shell. By way of background information, small pieces of crab exoskeleton are a consistent component of shell sands from western Scotland, but they never seem to occur at high density (Light pers. obs.). From a database of 50 analysed samples of sublittoral sediment samples from the West Shetland Shelf only two samples contained crab shell representing 0.9% wt as a component, and the majority contained <0.05%, i.e. 4–5 grains from a c. 5g sample (Light 2003). Similar analytical profiles are obtained from shell sands collected from the littoral environment. On this basis concentrations of crab shell, such as occur in the sample 8689/666, are significant and they do represent the waste of an exploited marine resource. This hypothesis is

Table 77. The marine shell distribution by block

	DB	DD	DE	FB	FD	FE	FF	FG
Patella vulgata L., common limpet	162 (26%)	3140 (25%)	170 (33%)	37 (90%)	124 (37%)	4 (16%)	149 (17%)	114 (15%)
Gibbula cineraria (L.), grey top shell		5	1					
Littorina littorea (L.), winkle	446 (73%)	9454 (74%)	339 (66%)	4 (10%)	194 (58%)	18 (72%)	734 (82%)	625 (84%)
Littorina obtusata (L.), flat periwinkle	2	121	6		4	1	3	2
Littorina saxatilis (Olivi), rough periwinkle		10	1					
Nucella lapillus (L.), dog whelk		24	2				4	1
Buccinum undatum (L.), common whelk		3			1		1	
Neptunea antiqua (L.), red whelk						1		
Mytilus edulis L., common mussel	1	15			2	2	1	
Modiolus modiolus (L.), horse mussel							1	
Pecten maximus (L.), great scallop		2	1		1	1		
Aequipecten opercularis (L.), queen scallop		1			2	1	1	
Ostrea edulis (L.), common or flat oyster			1					1
Artica islandica (L.), Iceland cyprine	1					1		
Ensis siliqua (L.), pod razor shell			2					
Ensis spp., razor shell		1	1					1
Total	**612**	**12776**	**524**	**41**	**328**	**28**	**844**	**744**

Table 78. A detailed list of the crab remains

Sample	context	block	identification	comments
5750	227	DB	Crab chela fragment unident.	Too worn to identify
5771	232	DB	Crab chela fragment unident.	
5905	604	DD	Crab chela *Liocarcinus* sp.	
5893	604	DD	Crab chela unident.	Same as 5921/605
5924	604	DD	Chela fragments of *Cancer* sp.	Applies to 2 fragments: Burnt and shell is thicker indicating larger individuals than most in the assemblage
5921	605	DD	Crab chela unident.	Same as 5893/604
8026	614	DD	Crab chela fragment	Burnt, a fourth taxon?
5822	610	DD	Crab chela	A fourth unident. taxon?
8063	614	DD	*Liocarcinus* sp. chela	
5871	603	DD	Chela fragment unident.	
5898	604	DD	Chela fragment *Carcinus maenas*	
5848	601	DD	*Carcinus maenas* chela	Burnt
8073	614	DD	2 crab chelae	Larger *Carcinus maenas,* smaller *Liocarcinus* sp.
8007	610	DD	cf *Carcinus maenas* chela	Burnt
5773	234	DE	Crab chela fragment	*Liocarcinus* sp.
5751	228	DE	2 small frags, one chela	Both worn
5991	269	FD	Smaller fragment is crab chela	Larger fragment is barnacle plate - in capsule
8603	284	FF	Crab chela fragments? *Cancer* sp.	Burnt
8613	652	FF	4 *Cancer* sp. chela frags + 1 other sp. chela	Most burnt.
8607	295	FF	Not crab chela	Other decapod chela/pereipod?
8613	652	FF	Non-appendage carapace fragments and worn *Cancer* sp. chela	
8612	651	FF	*Cancer* sp. fragment, tip of pereipod?	
8609	299	FF	*Cancer* sp. chela fragment	From small individual
8615	660	FF	Worn crab chela, cf *Carcinus maenas*	
8689	666	FG	Assorted frags of mixed spp.including *Cancer*	Minority of fragments burnt, these are *Cancer* sp. Larger complete chelae are *Carcinus maenas* and *Liocarcinus* sp. Examples of all 3 taxa separated
8687	661	FG	Assorted frags incl. cf *Carcinus maenas*	
8687	661	FG	Chela fragments of *Carcinus maenas*	Some burnt
8688	664	FG	Non-appendage carapace fragments	Burnt
8687	661	FG	Non-appendage carapace fragments	All from same taxon
8687	661	FG	Assorted frags incl. cf *Carcinus maenas* chela	
8688	664	FG	cf *Carcinus maenas* chelae + assorted fragments	

reinforced by the fact that, for mound 3, most crab material comes from the house floors (DD) and the slope deposits in trench F (FG). Only one fragment relates to any context representing the use of the kiln (FD). There is slightly more from FF contexts that, although adjacent to the kiln/barn, are believed to be hearth material deposits. These FF samples contain some of the larger chelae. The largest assemblage came from FG contexts and one sample (8689/666) contained some 350 carapace fragments. These contexts have been interpreted as the debris from cleaning the floor of the kiln/barn but the surviving floors have not produced many crab remains.

A comparison of the sorting data – N Sharples

A total of 389 samples or 3732 litres of soil were taken and processed from mound 3 (Table 79). All of these samples were floated and the residues over 10 mm sorted. Fine sorting of the material below 10 mm was restricted to 259 samples (Table 80), and most of these samples were sub-sampled to reduce the amount of residue sorted. Over two-thirds of the samples processed came from trench D and this represents the extensive sampling of the much larger house floors in this trench.

The sampling strategy, and to a large extent the excavation strategy, was concerned with the examination of the floor layers of both the house (60.9% of the samples) and the kiln/barn (25.1% of the samples); otherwise only the activity to the east of the kiln/barn (FF) produced more than ten samples. This makes comparison of the different deposit groups difficult and probably best left to the future, when a more varied selection of deposits have been sampled and analysed. However, it is noticeable that the non-house contexts of blocks DB, FB and FF tended to produce some of the larger densities of unburnt mammal bone and fish bone. This is particularly the case with the material recovered from the fine residue (less than 10 mm) sort (Table 80). In contrast the densities of pottery in these contexts were generally lower than the house floors, in both heavy and fine residues. It is also significant that the samples from the deposits on the slopes to the west of the kiln/barn (FG) have the lowest densities of almost all categories of material indicating that this was not an area where material was routinely deposited.

The large quantities of samples from the house and kiln/barn floors make it possible to compare the quantities of material present in each structure. The materials that have the most significant differences are illustrated in Figure 92 and this indicates that the house floors had many more substantial concentrations of bone, fish bone and pottery. The only categories of material that were better represented in the kiln/barn were slag, coprolite and carbonised plant remains. It is likely that the fish bone, mammal bone and pottery fragments in the house can be related to food preparation and consumption activities. The slag in the kiln/barn can be connected to the fire in the flue and it is likely that higher temperatures were achieved here than in the hearth in the house. The carbonised plant remains clearly relate to the specialised use of the kiln/barn. The coprolite concentrations are more surprising and may indicate either the kiln/barn had relatively open access or that dogs were kept in the building for some of the time.

Geochemical analysis of the different floor layers – P Marshall and H Smith

The analyses have provided information on the chemical and magnetic properties of the floor layers. The most consistent pattern to emerge is the close association of P, N and χ, which is most likely to reflect the make-up of the floors, with peat ash a dominant constituent. As discussed previously, the burning of organic materials concentrates elements such as P and the act of burning enhances χ. In all cases, at or near the location of a hearth, P and χ are elevated. In many cases, the distribution of the ash is not restricted to the site of the hearth itself. In the cases of the house floors, material is spread towards the entrance. In the case of the barn, the entire floor appears to be composed of, or rich in, ash, possibly suggesting deliberate use in the construction of a solid surface.

Enhanced P concentration is found in association with χ and peat ash in the floors at mound 3, as seen for example in the north area of the lower house floor. The same is seen at the site of Cille Pheadair (Brennand, Parker Pearson and Smith 1997), where similar analyses were undertaken on floors in the Norse houses and outbuildings. Here, not only were very high levels of P found (e.g. ranging from 388 – 6468 mg/kg and 3321 – 9196 mg/kg), but in some cases these were not in association with ash deposits or enhanced χ. In house 312 on floor 204 at Cille Pheadair, the highest concentrations of P occurred at the far east end of the building, where thick organic-rich deposits had accumulated, whereas the most enhanced χ occurred in the central area in association with the ash spreads of the elongated central hearth (Brennand, Parker Pearson and Smith 1998; Smith, Marshall and Parker Pearson 2001). At Bornais, the elevated levels of P to the north of the lower house floor are likely to represent organic materials accumulated in the less accessible edges of the floor.

The archaeological floor deposits can be compared with modern samples of known origin, in order to demonstrate the levels of enhancement from background levels and possibly throw light on the formation of these floors and the activities associated with their formation. For example, modern peat ash samples, midden samples (animal dung) and machair field samples, amongst other materials collected, can be compared to the archaeological deposits. Samples of machair have yielded total P values of 391 mg/kg and 408 mg/kg and total N values of 710 mg/kg and 615 mg/kg. In the case of P, this is much lower than the levels occurring on the archaeological

Table 79. A summary of the data derived from the above 10 mm sieving

(only blocks and categories with several samples are presented).

	Samples	Litres	Fish bone		Bone		Pottery		Slag	Limpet		Winkle	
DB	8	175	36	0.21	51	0.29	16	0.09	2	156	0.89	411	2.35
DD/3	86	767	75	0.1	80	0.1	87	0.11		455	0.59	991	1.29
DD/2	74	744	154	0.21	194	0.26	131	0.18		667	0.9	2031	2.73
DD/1	69	688.5	352	0.51	271	0.39	178	0.26		1487	2.16	4426	6.43
DD	28	149.5	9	0.06	27	0.18	11	0.07		46	0.31	218	1.46
DE	6	87	5	0.06	16	0.18	8	0.09		170	1.95	339	3.9
Total	271	2611											

	Samples	Litres	Fish bone		Bone		Pottery		Slag	Limpet		Winkle	
FD/2	32	209.1	9	0.04	28	0.13	2	0.01	0	19	0.09	56	0.27
FD/1	54	636.1	5	0.01	55	0.09	2	0	102	111	0.17	128	0.2
FD	12	54.95	1	0.1					10	1	0.13	13	2.69
FE	1	9.5			1	0.11				4	0.42	18	1.89
FF	12	81.25	28	0.34	25	0.31	12	0.15	22	149	1.83	734	9.03
FG	7	130	3	0.02	5	0.04	2	0.02	11	114	0.88	625	4.81
Total	118	1121											

Table 80. A summary of the data derived from the below 10 mm sieving

The data is expressed as the average density per litre of soil.
(only blocks and categories with several samples are presented).

Block	Samples	Litres	Bone	Burnt bone	Fish bone	Seed	Charcoal	B.O.M.	Pot	Slag
DB	3	48	67.87	16.92	158.37	0.3	34.48	222.24	0.73	15.17
DD	18	104	4.71	36.49	68.03	32.01	62.33	121.97	11.46	4.38
DD/1	64	629.5	4.71	16.7	191.68	3.41	98.38	153.55	10.94	6.39
DD/2	73	740.5	8.47	13.42	85.72	0.66	44.26	70.38	4.96	21.35
DD/3	5	42.5	4.92	6.37	46.92	0.5	12.04	28.76	1.75	3.77
DE	5	77	5.46	5.34	217.31	0.21	8.45	114.13	1.4	22.29
Total	168	1641.5								

Block	Samples	Litres	Bone	Burnt bone	Fish bone	Seed	Charcoal	B.O.M.	Pot	Slag
FB	2	6	27.1	6.8	23	2.5	11	49.5	1.3	5.1
FD	17	89.45	6.53	14.34	9.27	8.09	14.29	288.52	0.33	278.66
FD/1	31	350.7	12.56	7.46	18.92	1.02	6.43	63.08	0.4	305.24
FD/2	22	148.1	7.46	13.53	21.54	1.08	8.49	320.98	4.03	530.73
FE	1	9.5	5.26	2	6.32	1.68	3.68	7.37	0.21	6.32
FF	11	82	30.1	13.5	24.3	7.22	22.08	234.8	5.1	613.1
FG	7	130	7.76	0.92	12.57	1.82	12	54.34	1.13	78.86
Total	91	815.75								

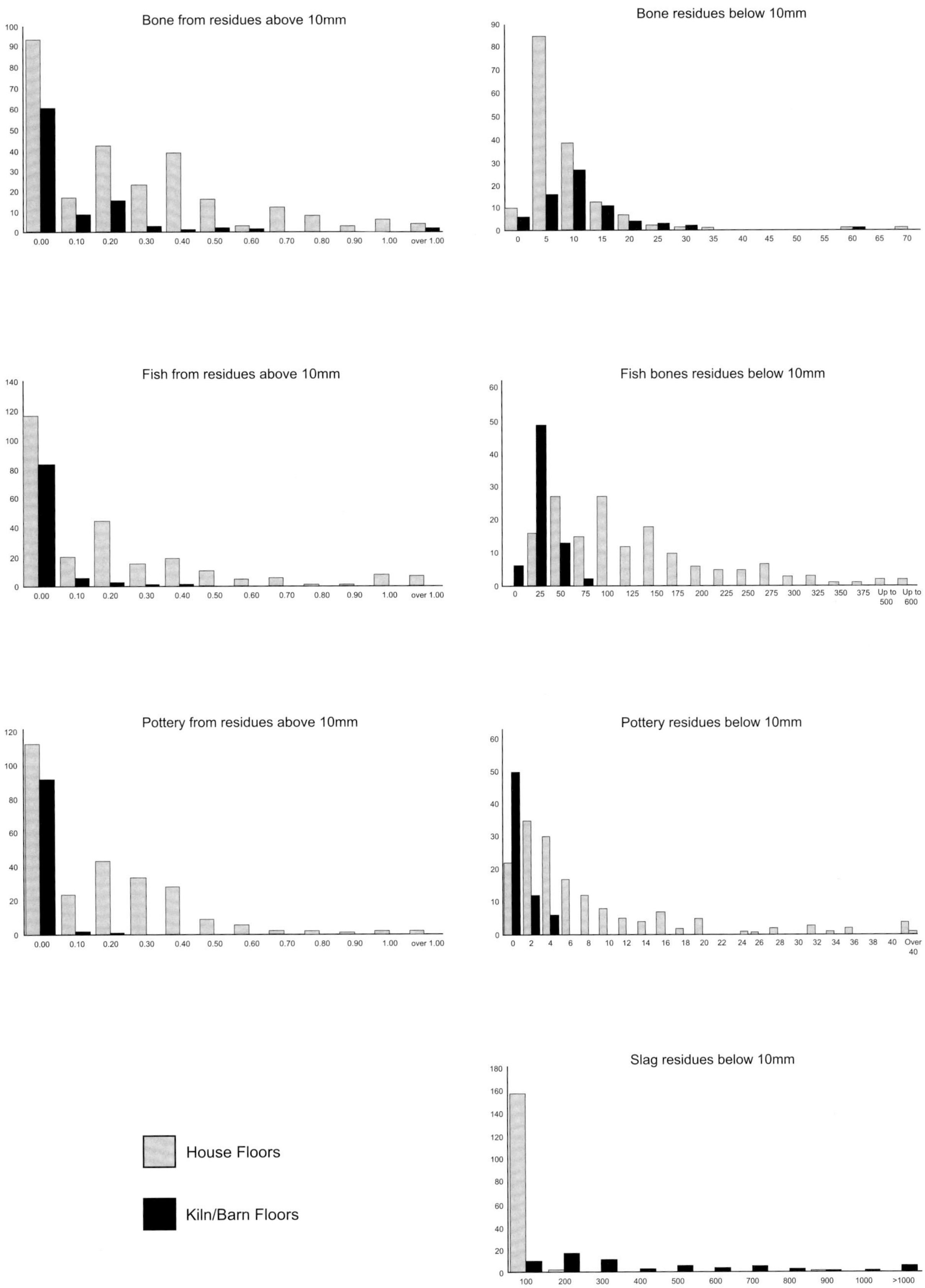

Figure 92. Graphs of the residue distribution from mammal bone, slag, pot and fish bone from the kiln/barn and house floors. There were negligible amounts of slag in the above 10 mm residue. The X-axis is the density per litre of soil; the Y-axis the number of samples

floors, although there is little variation in the N values.

In contrast, modern ash and midden samples display elevated values. Modern ash samples have yielded total P values of 1713 mg/kg, 5613 mg/kg and 4318 mg/kg and total N 8077 mg/kg, 567 mg/kg and 5324 mg/kg for respective samples) whilst P and N values for modern midden samples, as to be expected, are very high (e.g. total P 8155 mg/kg and 4838 mg/kg; total N 12189 mg/kg and 16324 mg/kg). These data merely indicate where elevated levels are found in modern materials and deposits and have provided some clues as to the formation of the floors, especially when considered in conjunction with the other lines of evidence (e.g. thin section analysis).

Discussion – N Sharples

The analysis of the material from the two main trenches has revealed considerable differences not just between the occupation of the two buildings but also, though in a much more limited fashion, with the areas surrounding the buildings. The principal differences between the kiln/barn and the house are:

1. The house floors have a sizeable pottery assemblage whereas the kiln/barn floor assemblage is practically negligible.
2. Finds from the house were largely broken tools abandoned or accidentally lost. Kiln/barn finds were less common and included antler waste from artefact production activities and some complete objects that appear to have been deliberately placed in specific contexts.
3. The animal bones from the house indicate a slight preference for cattle as opposed to sheep/goat and pig and there are more prime meat bones than waste.
4. There is a broader range of species in the house but whalebone, which may indicate artefact production, is more common in trench F. Trench F also has a larger collection of bird bones.
5. Fish bones are much more common in the house and indicate consumption of herring and cod heads around the hearth. The bones from the kiln/barn in contrast indicate the processing and possibly smoking of herring in the building.
6. Crop remains are present in very large numbers, particularly in the kiln/barn, and this probably indicates parching and winnowing in this structure whereas those from the house indicate fine cleaning prior to use.
7. The kiln/barn also has higher densities of slag, which possibly indicates the relatively high temperatures of the fire in the kiln flue.
8. The kiln/barn has higher densities of coprolite, which suggests it was either used for a kennel or was a building relatively accessible to dogs.

The principal observation from the deposits outside these buildings concerns the source of the deposits on the western slopes of trench F (FG). The slope deposits are remarkably impoverished in terms of the material present. It has been suggested that these layers may represent material from sweeping the kiln/barn floors. This interpretation is supported by the crop species present in both deposits. However, the slope deposits lack the distinctive weed assemblage that was found on the floor and they also contain large quantities of crab, which were not present on the floor. There are clearly additional factors to consider.

8 The Chronology

Radiocarbon dating – P Marshall

Introduction

Eleven radiocarbon determinations have been obtained on samples, three bone and eight charcoal, from Bornais Mound 3. The samples were processed by the Oxford Radiocarbon Accelerator Unit between 2000 and 2001. The samples were prepared and measured using the methods outlined in Hedges, Bronk Ramsey and Housley (1989) and Bronk Ramsey and Hedges (1997). The pre-treatment method used for the bone samples was a collagen extraction (Hedges and Law 1989; Hedges *et al* 1989) followed by gelatinisation and separation by filtration (Bronk Ramsey, Pettitt, Hedges, Hodgins and Owen 2000). The laboratory maintains a continual programme of quality assurance procedures, in addition to participation in international comparisons (Rozanski, Stichler, Gonfiantini, Scott, Beukens, Kromer and van der Plicht 1992; Scott, Harkness and Cook 1988). These tests indicate no significant offsets and demonstrate the validity of the precision quoted. The results, given in Table 81, are conventional radiocarbon ages (Stuiver and Polach 1977), and are quoted in accordance with the international standard known as the Trondheim convention (Stuiver and Kra 1986). The radiocarbon determinations have been calibrated with data from Stuiver *et al* (1998), using OxCal (v3.5) (Bronk Ramsey 1995; 1998). The date ranges have been calculated according to the maximum intercept method (Stuiver and Reimer 1986), and are cited in Table 81 at two sigma (95% confidence). They are quoted in the form recommended by Mook (1986), with the end points rounded outwards to 10 years. The probability distributions are derived from the usual probability method (Dehling and van der Plicht 1993; van der Plicht 1993). Those ranges printed in italics in the text are derived from mathematical modelling of archaeological problems.

Analysis and interpretation

The calibrated dates given in Table 81 are accurate estimates of the dates of the samples; however, in archaeological terms they are not exactly what we want to know. Of much greater interest and potential importance are the dates of the archaeological events represented by those samples. Absolute dating information, in the form of radiocarbon measurements on the animal bone and carbonised plant material, can be combined with the relative information provided by stratigraphic relationships between samples to provide estimates of the dates of this activity.

These *posterior density estimates* are not absolute;

Table 81. Radiocarbon results

Laboratory Number	Sample ref. Number	Material	Radiocarbon Age (BP)	$\delta^{13}C$ (‰)	Calibrated date range (95% confidence)	Posterior density estimate (95% probability)
OxA-10273	BO99/5854/214	bone, sheep	1065±35	-21	cal AD 890–1030	*cal AD 970–1040 (93%) or cal AD 1140–1160 (2%)*
OxA-10274	BO99/5089/215	bone, cattle	1004±32	-21.4	cal AD 980–1160	*cal AD 900–920 (3%) or cal AD 960–1030 (92%)*
OxA-10275	BO99/5906/604	carbonised seed, Hordeum sp.	880±32	-22.5	cal AD 1030–1250	
OxA-10276	BO99/5964/269	carbonised seed, Avena sp.	537±34	-25.8	cal AD 1320–1440	*cal AD 1320–1350 (12%) or cal AD 1380–1440 (83%)*
OxA-10277	BO99/5971/269	carbonised seed, Avena sp.	521±32	-25.9	cal AD 1320–1450	*cal AD 1330–1350 (7%) or cal AD 1390–1450 (88%)*
OxA-10278	BO99/8629/276	carbonised seed, Avena sp.	563±33	-25.8	cal AD 1300–1440	*cal AD 1300–1420*
OxA-10279	BO99/8707/675	bone, cattle	863±35	-22.5	cal AD 1040–1260	*cal AD 1070–1090 (1%) or cal AD 1120–1280 (94%)*
OxA-10291	BO99/5909/604	carbonised seed, Avena sp.	580±70	-22.9	cal AD 1310–1450	*cal AD 1310–1450*
OxA-10292	BO99/8045/614	carbonised seed, Avena sp.	590±50	-24.8	cal AD 1290–1440	*cal AD 1290–1410*
OxA-10304	BO99/8077/614	carbonised seed, Avena sp.	660±50	-26	cal AD 1270–1410	*cal AD 1270–1400*
OxA-10305	BO99/8633/276	carbonised seed, Avena sp.	705±50	-24.2	cal AD 1220–1400	*cal AD 1220–1400*

they are interpretative estimates, that can and will change as further data becomes available and as other people choose to model the existing results from different perspectives.

The methodology used to combine these different sorts of information is a form of Markov Chain Monte Carlo sampling, and has been applied using the program OxCal v3.5 (http://units.ox.ac.uk/departments/rlaha/), which uses a mixture of the Metropolis-Hastings algorithm and Gibbs sampler (Gilks, Richardson and Spiegelhalther 1996; Gefland and Smith 1990). Details about the algorithms used by OxCal can be accessed from the on-line manual or in Bronk Ramsey (1995; 1998). The specific algorithms used in the models described below can be derived from the structures in Figures 93, 94 and 95, or from the chronological query language files, which are contained in the project archive.

In the analyses undertaken we have chosen to impose a uniform prior distribution on the spread of dates, while assuming that the dated samples represent independent events and a random sample of a relatively constant level of human activity, see Bronk Ramsey (2000) for further details of its implementation. Such an approach has been used because when radiocarbon dates are constrained by relative dating information it has been shown that there is a danger that the posterior density distributions may be spread evenly across a plateau in the calibration curve, irrespective of the actual age of the material dated (Steier and Rom 2000). This is due to the fact that the statistical weight of a group of measurements naturally favours longer overall spans.

The house samples

The six samples from trench D comprise: a cattle bone (OxA-10274) and a sheep bone (OxA-10273), from the brown sand below the walls of the house, and two carbonised seeds from successive house floors: OxA-10292 and OxA-10304, both *Avena* sp. from the first floor, and OxA-10275 and OxA-10291, *Hordeum* sp. and *Avena* sp. from the second floor.

The two determinations from the first floor are not

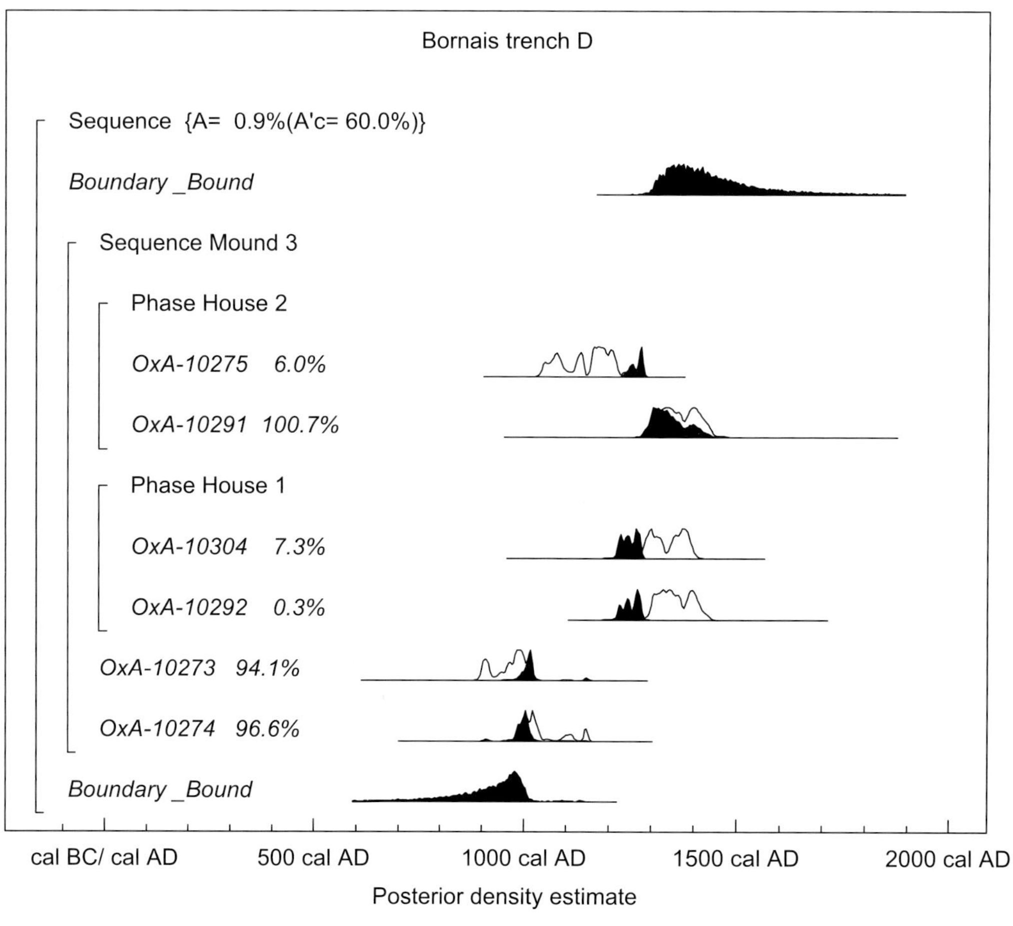

Figure 93. Probability distributions of dates from Bornais mound 3 trench D: each distribution represents the relative probability that an event occurs at a particular time. For each of the radiocarbon dates two distributions have been plotted, one in outline, which is the result of simple radiocarbon calibration, and a solid one, which is based on the chronological model used. The large square brackets down the left hand side along with the OxCal keywords define the model exactly

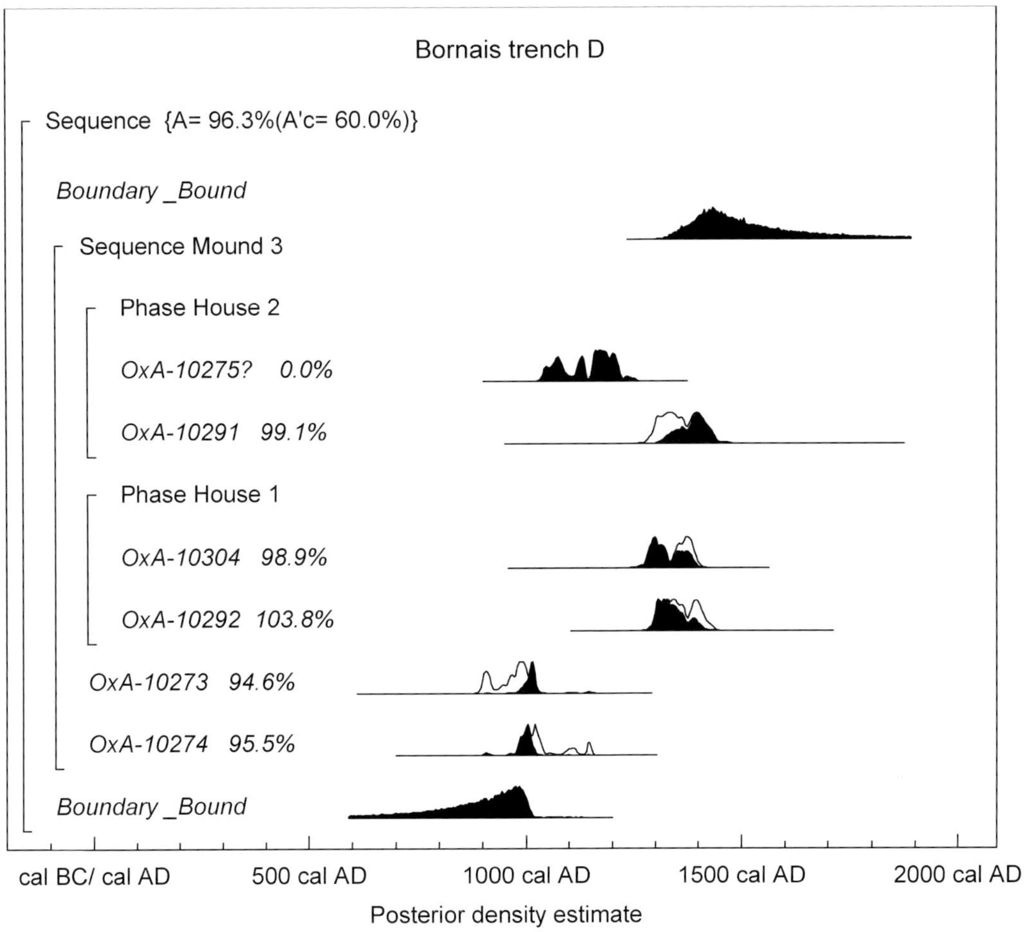

Figure 94. Probability distributions of dates from Bornais mound 3 trench D: each distribution represents the relative probability that an event occurs at a particular time. For each of the radiocarbon dates two distributions have been plotted, one in outline, which is the result of simple radiocarbon calibration, and a solid one, which is based on the chronological model used. The large square brackets down the left hand side along with the OxCal keywords define the model exactly

statistically different (T'=1.0; n=1; T'(5%)=3.8; Ward and Wilson 1978) which may mean that the material is of the same actual age. However, it is possible that if the floor material accumulated over a relatively short period of time it could produce such results. The two determinations from the second floor are statistically different (T'=14.8; n=1; T'(5%)=3.8; Ward and Wilson 1978) suggesting that the material represents two distinct episodes of activity.

The model (Figure 93) shows very poor agreement between the radiocarbon and stratigraphic evidence (A=0.9%). It is thus probable that one or more of the samples is either intrusive or residual. If OxA-10275 is excluded from the model (Figure 94) the index of agreement increases to A=96.3%. The three remaining determinations from the house floors (OxA-10291–2 and OxA-10304) are not statistically different (T'=1.3; n=2; T'(5%)=6.0; Ward and Wilson 1978) which may mean that the floor material accumulated over a relatively short period of time. Given that the initial construction of 'floor layers' in houses is a complex process, it is likely that OxA-10275 represents residual material from previous activity on the site, incorporated into the floor.

Mathematical analysis provides estimates for the length of time over which the house was in use of between *0–60 years (at 68% probability) and 0–110 years (at 95% probability)*. The small number of dates available is, however, likely to mean that the estimate tends to suggest that activity continues for longer than it really did. The start of the occupation associated with the use of the house is *cal AD 1210–1370* (68% probability) and the end of activity associated with the second floor of the house is cal *AD 1320–1470* (68% probability).

The kiln/barn samples

The five samples from trench F comprised a cattle bone (OxA-10279) from an occupation layer to the west of the kiln/barn, together with two carbonised seeds (*Avena* sp.) from the lowest floor of the kiln/barn (OxA-10278 and OxA-10305) and the upper floor of the kiln/barn (OxA-10276 and OxA-10277).

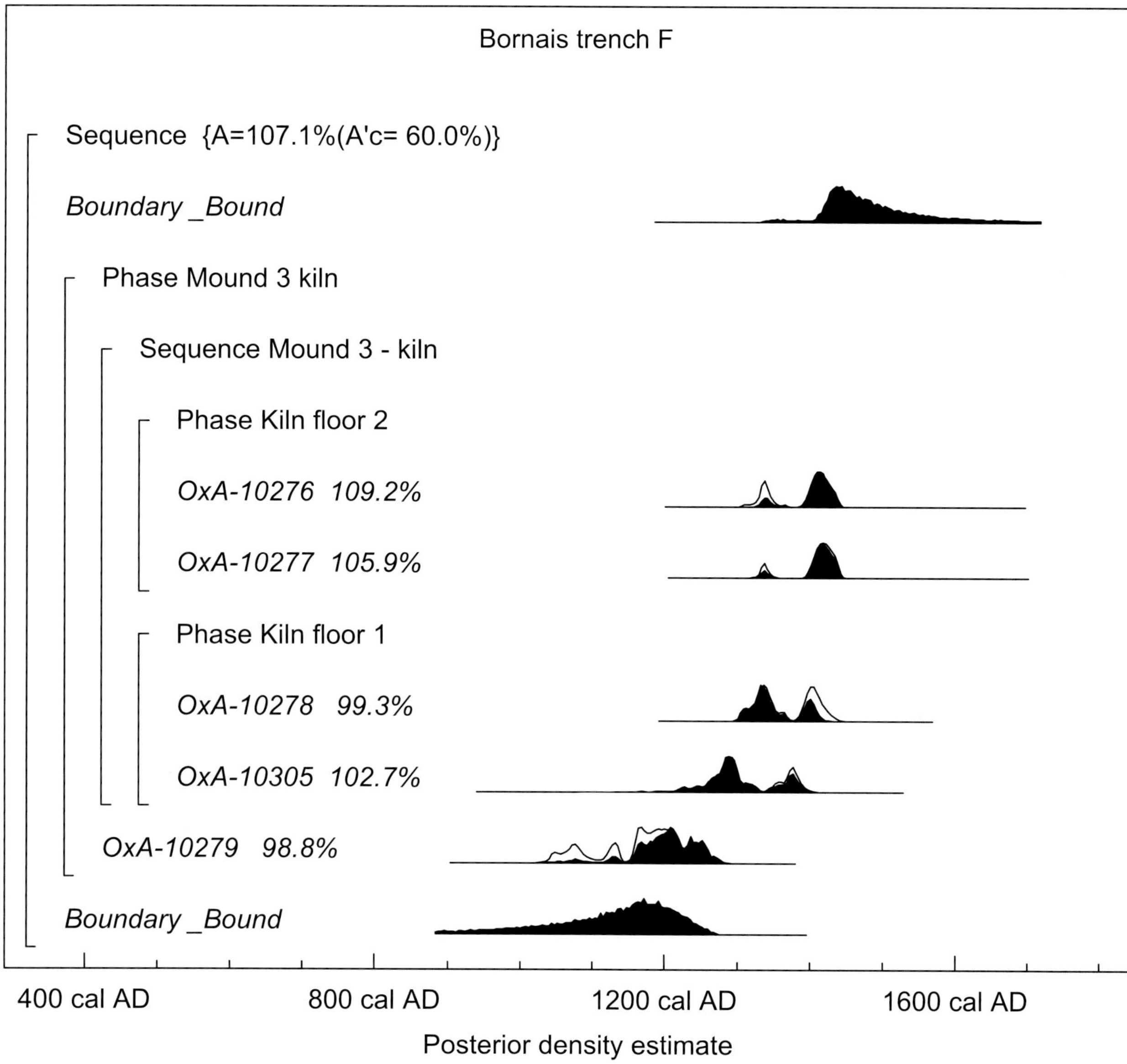

Figure 95. Probability distributions of dates from Bornais mound 3 trench F: each distribution represents the relative probability that an event occurs at a particular time. For each of the radiocarbon dates two distributions have been plotted, one in outline, which is the result of simple radiocarbon calibration, and a solid one, which is based on the chronological model used. The large square brackets down the left hand side along with the OxCal keywords define the model exactly

The two determinations from floor 2 are not statistically different (T'=0.1; n=1; T'(5%)=3.8; Ward and Wilson 1978) which may mean that the material is of the same age. However, it is possible that if the floor material accumulated over a relatively short period of time it could produce such results. The two determinations from floor 1 are statistically different (T'=5.7; n=1; T'(5%)=3.8; Ward and Wilson 1978), and thus probably represent two separate periods of activity.

The model (Figure 95) shows good agreement between the stratigraphic and radiocarbon evidence (A=107.1%), and provides estimates for the length of time over which the kiln/barn was in use of between *80–170 years (at 68% probability) and 30–200 years (at 95% probability).* The small number of dates available from the kiln/barn is, however, likely to mean that the estimate tends to suggest that activity continued for longer than it really did. The start of activity associated with the use of the kiln/barn is *cal AD 1240–1390* (68% probability). The end of the activity associated with the use of the kiln/barn is *cal AD 1400–1480* (68% probability).

9 Resource Exploitation

In the introduction to this volume the landscape of South Uist was conveniently divided into a series of zones that run roughly north-south up the length of the island. Thus as an individual moves from the west coast they emerge from the sea onto a spectacular sandy beach, and then traverse a wide machair plain on which the settlement at Bornais is located. As they move further east they come to the area of rock and loch that is the current location for settlement on the island. This landscape becomes increasingly boggy as they progress inland and upward towards the mountains that dominate the eastern half of the island. These different landscapes are ecologically very distinctive with contrasting vegetation and they provide a suitable framework for analysing the resources exploited by the inhabitants of the settlement at Bornais.

The Sea. 1. Fish – C Ingrem

The considerable number of fish remains recovered from mound 3 is evidence that fish provided a significant contribution to the diet. The fact that all of the species were either marine or spend part of their life in the sea indicates that the majority of fishing was marine in nature. The large number of herring vertebrae leaves little doubt that this species was being specifically targeted whilst their relative abundance, particularly in comparison to large gadid species, suggests that herring were the fish most often consumed. This pattern is unlikely to result purely from differential disposal related to fish size since gadid remains dominate both midden and domestic contexts at sites in the Northern Isles (see below).

In addition to herring, it appears that the inhabitants were also eating cod and hake on a regular basis, with the occasional consumption of pollack, saithe, haddock and ling. It is probable that the more palatable trace taxa such as salmonids, eels, mackerel, sea bream, wrasse and flatfish were eaten occasionally. However, the small and very small gadids recovered from the <10mm material may well represent gut contents of larger fish.

Fish ecology and fishing techniques

The majority of the herring remains fell into the small size category with a few belonging to the medium and very small size categories. However, during recording it was noted that those classified as medium belonged to the lower end of the range. The majority were similar in size to a reference specimen known to have been 235mm in length. According to Wheeler (1968), this indicates that the majority were over three years old and as such classified as adult. Adult herring eat crustacea and small fish such as sand eels, gobies, whiting, herring and flatfish. This could account for the presence of very small (<150mm) gadids in the sieved samples. Adult herring generally frequent deep waters, greater than 200m, although during spawning many move inshore. Spring and summer spawning grounds exist both in the Minch and in deeper water at the edge of the continental shelf to the west of the Hebrides (Harden Jones 1968). It is therefore probable that a locally abundant supply of herring was available during the Norse period. If as Harden Jones (1968) suggests, the young of fish spawned in the Minch remained in the vicinity until adult, then herring caught here would be expected to include a considerable proportion of young fish. In contrast, the larvae of fish spawned on the edge of the continental shelf to the west of Bornais are carried north by the Atlantic current (Harden Jones 1968). A catch of herring from this location would therefore be expected to consist entirely of adults, as is the case for the herring remains from Bornais.

Although herring can be caught on lines, the quantities recovered from Bornais suggest that the late Norse inhabitants were probably catching them at night using the more common method of drift nets. These were probably cast from open boats made of wood. The size of the mesh is crucial in determining the location of herring fishing. It is possible that mesh size was designed to catch only adult herring, whilst allowing the young herring to escape through the net. However, it seems unlikely that the occupants at Bornais would have deliberately avoided catching a valuable food source, unless cultural taboos dictated or plentiful economic resources allowed. This suggests that the virtual absence of young herring in the samples reflects their absence at the catch site, thereby favouring summer fishing at the edge of the continental shelf to the west of the Hebrides. An offshore, night-time activity of this nature would have involved considerable risk, time and capital investment. Consequently, fishing would probably have involved elements of mystique and camaraderie usually associated with terrestrial hunting.

The majority of cod remains were derived from adult fish between 600–1200mm in length. Adult cod feed on fish such as herring, sand eels, haddock and codling, supporting the suggestion that the small and very small trace taxa could represent gut contents. In general, only small, young cod are found inshore (Wheeler 1969) suggesting again, that many of the fish from mound 3 were caught in deeper offshore waters.

Hake is also a relatively deep-water fish but migrates into shallow water in summer. It is unlikely that deep-water fishing was practised during the winter months owing to the frequency of stormy weather, which suggests that hake were probably caught in shallower water during the summer months. Of course, it is possible that large hake were found inshore all year prior to over-fishing (Wheeler 1976).

Ling are also generally found in deep water (Wheeler 1969). The small number of bones recovered suggests that they were incidental catches, and as with the other large gadids, were probably caught offshore with the use of small boats and baited lines. A variety of bait would have been used which could have included mackerel, haddock and eel, and which could account for the presence of such species in the assemblage. As with herring fishing, offshore fishing for large gadid fish would have involved high risk and required greater technology and investment in equipment than inshore fishing. Of course, it is possible that these large gadoids were caught during herring fishing trips, whilst waiting for the appearance of a shoal, or accidentally in the nets.

Although adult pollack and saithe also inhabit offshore waters they are known to move inshore during the summer months when they would have been available from the shore. Whiting remains belonged to fish less than 150mm to 300mm in size, indicating that they were aged between 1–3 years. These immature fish are also found close inshore where they occur in shoals (Wheeler 1969). The species present as trace taxa inhabit a variety of habitats; seasonal migrations of many of the species such as tope, scad and the flatfish also involve a movement from inshore waters in the summer to deeper water in the winter. Therefore, the dangers associated with offshore fishing during the winter months combined with migration habits of some species suggests that both offshore and inshore fishing were practised during the summer. The small gadids and trace taxa such as sea bream, wrasse, flounder and conger eel were probably caught from the shore using baited lines or poke nets, possibly from craig seats or small boats. The relatively small number of inshore fish recovered from mound 3 suggests that this was practised on a small-scale, domestic level involving low risk, low technology and little investment.

Other species such as eel, flounder and the salmonids can or do inhabit both estuarine and freshwater habitats at some stages in their lifecycle. The small size of the eel remains suggests that these fish were either caught inshore, possibly in the intertidal zone, or represent the prey of larger fish. The salmonids, being such good eating fish, were probably deliberate catches. They are known to inhabit the sea during the summer but it is equally possible that the freshwater lochs were exploited. If salmonids and flounder were caught in fresh water this is also likely to have involved the use of nets, baited lines and possibly traps.

The Sea. 2. Mammals – J Mulville

Two species of sea mammal were present in the bone assemblage, seal and whale. All the seal bone was found in the house floors (DD). Only two pieces of cetacea were complete enough to record. One was a fragment of a medium-sized cetacean rib, from house floor 3; the other was the vertebra of a large cetacean, from sand infilling the kiln/barn (FE). The latter had been butchered with a chopper, the lateral processes removed and the bone scorched. Other, non-recordable, fragments of cetacean bone were recovered, including a rib distal end and many small pieces of often burnt bone.

Nearly half the recovered fragments of cetacean bone were recorded as burnt to some degree. The high oil content of cetacean bone makes it a useful fuel (Mulville 2002). In the Faeroes fresh cetacean bone was used as an alternative to peat at the turn of the century and burnt whalebone was found at the Norse settlement at Freswick, Caithness (Morris, Batey and Rackham 1995). McGovern's (1992) review of Norse Icelandic sites noted that bones of all species were burnt with some degree of selection in favour of sea mammals. The large whale vertebra from mound 3 was probably scorched during heating of the bone to extract the oil from the cancellous tissue (Greenfield pers. comm.).

Pinnipeds (seals) and cetacea can both be actively hunted at sea although the evidence we have to date suggests that seals were preferentially exploited on land. The two seal bones and a single tooth from mound 3 were not identified to species, but the presence of a juvenile tibia suggests the capture of a seal pup in the first few weeks of life. This is likely to be a grey seal, as the young are born on land and are incapable of swimming for the first three weeks (Corbett and Harris 1991), making them easy targets for hunters. From this we can demonstrate the seasonal exploitation of the grey seal during the autumn breeding season. The uninhabited islands off the Outer Hebrides are important breeding grounds for the Atlantic seal today. Records show that seal culling for skins and other products occurred in the historic period.

Seals are a valuable source of meat, blood, blubber, skins and sinew. There is ethnographic evidence from many Inuit groups of the almost total use of the seal carcass (Grigson and Mellars 1987). The blubber is especially important and can be used as both food and fuel. Fenton (1978a) notes that in Orkney and Shetland a good-sized seal could yield over 20 litres of oil.

The whalebone present on the site may be derived from stranded animals; at present zooarchaeological evidence neither confirms nor denies the possibility of active whale procurement (Mulville 2002). The Norse sites of Bornais and Cille Pheadair demonstrate a greater range of cetacean species and a larger proportion of whalebone compared to the Iron Age (Mulville 2002). This rise in cetacean utilisation may reflect an increase in the active procurement of whales and dolphins by hunting and/or driving ashore.

The Shore. 1. Shellfish – N Sharples

The dominant position of winkles in the shellfish assemblage from mound 3 is not surprising as currently winkles are regarded as a desirable edible resource, which can still be purchased as a seafood today. Limpets, however, are not and the ethnographic record in the Northern Isles (Fenton 1978a) suggests they were never an important food resource. Human consumption of limpets appears to occur in times of famine or if people have a seasonally restricted access to other foodstuffs. This does not seem to be an adequate explanation for the Bornais assemblage or for assemblages from many other sites in the Atlantic fringe, which generally produce massive quantities of limpets widely scattered through the occupation layers. An alternative to human consumption is that they were used for fishing bait or as animal feed. The most likely animal to benefit from a shellfish supplement is the pig and these were present at Bornais, though not in great numbers. It is possible that a pig could consume a limpet without it being shelled but it is unlikely that the shell would emerge whole and there is no evidence for gnawed shells.

The fish bait interpretation has much to recommend it. Line fishing from the shore and from boats would benefit from the use of a ground bait regularly distributed around the fishing station and mashed-up shellfish is an acceptable ground bait. However, again it seems pointless to bring shellfish to the site to be shelled only then to return to the shore to fish. It would also not require the careful shelling of the limpet. The easiest way to create a ground bait would be to pound the shellfish with a rock, creating a mush, which would include the shell. It seems likely, therefore, that both winkles and limpets were eaten by humans and having consumed limpets I can testify that they are not unpleasant eating.

All of the main species would have been obtained from the intertidal zone of a rocky shore. The beach at Bornais, which currently lies a third of a kilometre to the west of the site, is a sandy beach which is not a suitable environment for these species. The nearest rocky coastline is the point of Ardvule, 2.5 km from the site. This is not a great distance away but it is still surprising that the inhabitants of Bornais chose to collect so many shellfish and bring them back to the settlement. It would have been far more effective to shell the animals close to the shoreline and then bring the meat back to the site. The shell makes up about 66% of the weight of a limpet (Evans and Spencer 1977, 215). The possible explanations for this include:

- The desire to have fresh shellfish available at the settlement.
- That the shells were a desirable resource.

The desire for fresh shellfish might be a sensible interpretation if the meat deteriorated quickly after shelling but the absence of water-retaining tanks at the settlement undermines this idea unless shellfish can be kept alive in simply a damp environment or the inhabitants had water retaining bags. Shells have been a desirable resource to add to midden material as their presence can encourage water retention in the very freely draining soils of the machair. Furthermore, the shells need not have served a practical function. The accumulation of midden around the machair settlements might have had a symbolic element. The conspicuous display of midden material could have been a metaphor for the fertility of the settlement and a sign of the wealth of the inhabitants. Shellfish would have provided an easily accessible resource that would bulk up the size of the settlement midden.

Measurements

Measurements were taken for four samples from Bornais (Figure 96) and, for comparison, three samples from Dun Vulan (Parker Pearson and Sharples 1999). The length and height of complete, well-preserved shells were taken and a sample of 100 shells was regarded as a minimum. The Bornais samples comprised the shells from three house floors and one from a sample taken specifically to recover shells, from shell midden 247, which lay below the house floor. Unfortunately none of the other layers produced samples with enough complete limpets to justify measurements. The floor samples are slightly different from the midden sample as they represent a dispersed spread of individuals whereas the midden sample represents a concentrated mass. This may indicate the midden sample was the result of a single incident of collection, whereas the floor samples were not.

Analysis of the Bornais floor samples indicates a steady decline in the mean size of the limpet from a length of 38.8 mm and height of 13.9 in floor 1, to a length of 37.1 mm and a height of 12.91 mm in floor 3 (Table 82). The ratio of length/breadth does not change significantly and suggests there was no shift in the location of the resource exploitation area with respect to a high/low water mark (Evans 1973). The midden sample, which underlies the floors, has, compared to the floor samples, a low mean length (37.2 mm) but the height is average to high (13.6) and produces a length to height ratio that is lower than the floor samples. This suggests that these shells were located nearer the high-water mark and, though small, they generally would have contained more meat than the shells on the house floor. Initially the midden indicates the exploitation of a prime resource high up on the shore and therefore reasonably accessible. The floor layers suggest that this resource was no longer accessible and

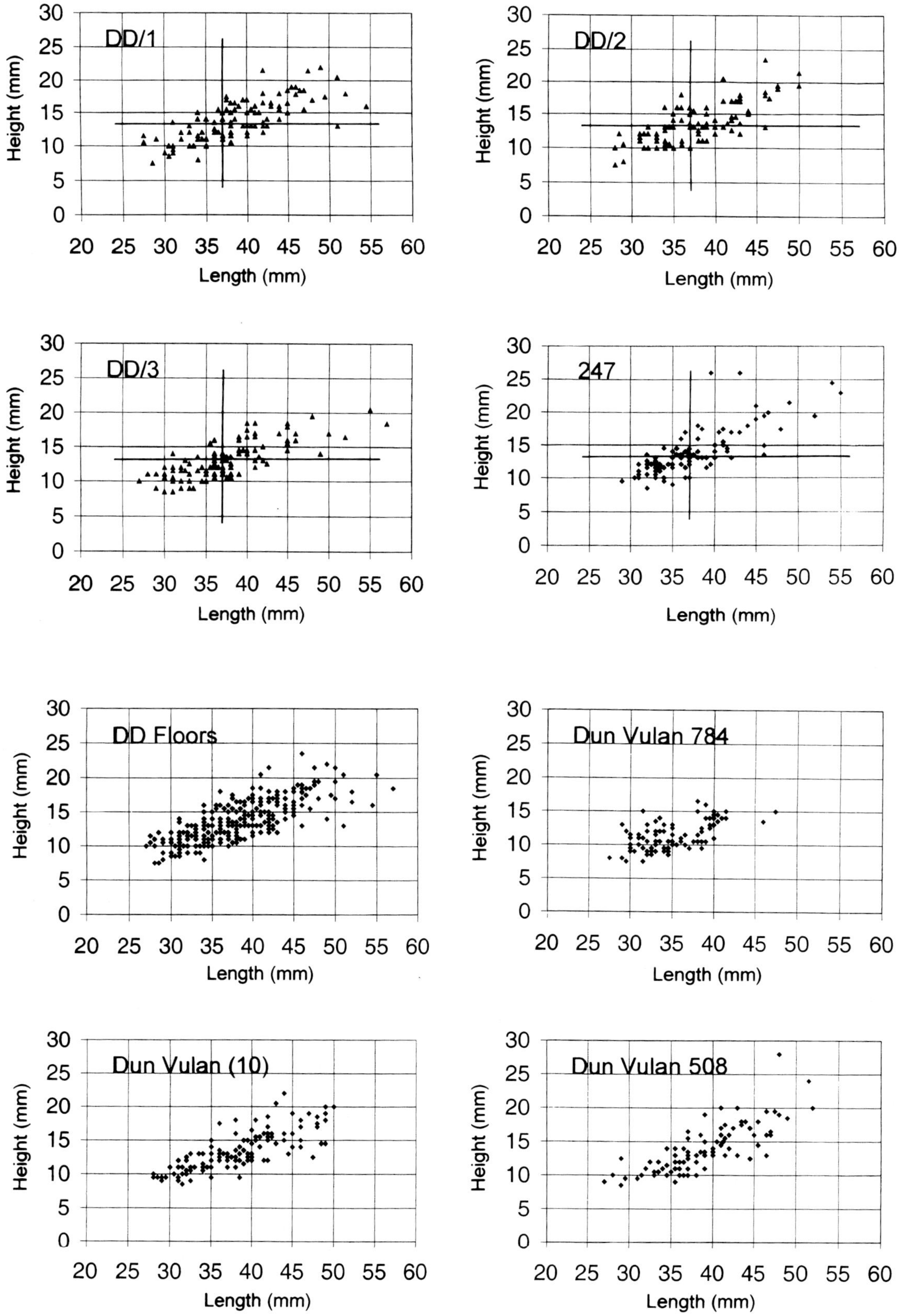

Figure 96. The size distribution of the limpets from the house floors DD/1, DD/2 and DD/3, the midden layer 247, a cumulative diagram of all the house floors compared to the samples from Dun Vulan layers 784, 10 and 508. The crosses on the upper diagrams indicate the average length and height of limpets from all the house floors

Table 82. The average dimensions of limpets (mm) in samples from Bornais and Dun Vulan

Site	Context	mean length	mean height	mean length/ height ratio
Bornais	DD 1	38.8	13.9	2.84
Bornais	DD 2	38	13.7	2.82
Bornais	DD 3	37.1	12.9	2.91
Bornais	DD all	37.9	13.5	2.86
Bornais	Midden 247	37.2	13.6	2.8
Dun Vulan	10	38.1	13.3	2.92
Dun Vulan	508	38.7	13.8	2.88
Dun Vulan	784	34.8	11.2	3.16

that the inhabitants had to exploit a resource lower down the shore line and that gradually the shells available from this resource zone became smaller and smaller. These patterns may indicate the overexploitation of a restricted resource zone that was routinely harvested by the inhabitants of this house.

The Dun Vulan samples were all from dense concentrations of shells and so are likely to represent specific collection events rather than piecemeal accumulation. Two of the samples are similar to the samples from Bornais: 508 which comes from a dump of shells associated with the broch revetment and dating to around 0 BC/AD and 10, an occupation layer associated with the post-Medieval activity in front of the broch entrance. However, one of the samples was quite different; 784 was an occupation deposit at the base of the platform sequence which was only slightly exposed by the excavations. The limpets from this layer had a lower mean length (34.8 mm) and height (11.2 mm) than all the other contexts and it is clear from Figure 96 that this is because the larger shells are missing, as these are not particularly small shells. The limpets present also had a much higher mean ratio of length to height, which indicates they were from closer to the low-water mark. These limpets were a particularly poor resource. They suggest either that the available resource was grossly over-exploited or that the person who collected these individuals only had access to the most over-exploited areas of the shore.

It is hoped that a comparable sample of natural shellfish can be obtained from the Ardvule peninsula and in future it will be possible to estimate which portion of the tidal environment the different limpets are coming from and whether the samples we have are smaller than the ecological optimum. It would certainly seem likely that the continuous collection that occurred during the Iron Age and Norse periods would reduce the optimum size of the animals available.

Coastal exploitation

If we accept the conclusion that both the limpets and winkles were being brought to the site to be eaten by the inhabitants then we have to consider why these molluscs had such a significant position in the diet of the inhabitants. The calorie contribution of the molluscs to the inhabitants might have been quite small in a diet which would seem to have been based on cereals, which grew well in the South Uist environment, fish which are found in large numbers in the surrounding seas, and large mammals (cattle and sheep) though these appear to be kept for secondary products such as milk and wool, and are only consumed later. It is possible that protein was in short supply in the late winter and early spring and that shellfish provided a valuable seasonal supplement but I would like to suggest that the importance of the shellfish was more related to the nature of social relationships within the community and between the communities that occupied the west coast of South Uist.

Routine exploitation of the adjacent coastline would have been an important task for the residents of Bornais and all the settlements of South Uist. The coast was a source for many important resources, as well as shellfish. These include:

- Seaweed, which was used as a foodstuff for people and animals, a fertiliser, a fuel and a source for dyes.
- Driftwood, which was used for fuel and building work.
- Seals and stranded cetaceans, which provided oil, meat, bone and skins.
- Birds and eggs collected in large quantities from cliff colonies but also available on most shores.
- Fish, which would have traditionally have been caught from the shore – it is unlikely that the increasing importance of offshore fishing from boats would totally replace shore fishing.
- Stone, the shore being the best place to collect and quarry stone for both house building and tool making.

Some of these resources would have been harvested when required (i.e. stone), some are seasonal resources (i.e. birds), some occur in relation to events such as storms (i.e. seaweed) and some would have been chance discoveries, which could not be predicted (i.e. driftwood, strandings). The latter in particular would have required routine monitoring of the coastline, particularly after storms. Shellfish are one of the resources which would have been constantly available with each visit and it may be that the collection of shellfish was one way of justifying a routine trip to the coast which otherwise did not result in any worthwhile discoveries. This may explain why only limpets and winkles were harvested, as these are easily accessible whereas bivalves, such as mussels or oysters, lie underwater for most of the time and razorshells can only be dug out at low tide.

Access to the coast, and its resources, is likely to have been carefully controlled by the different communities who occupied South Uist. These resources are unlikely to have been free to all and this was certainly not the case in the recent past when the Receiver of Wrecks kept a tight control over material, including timber, washed ashore (Angus 2001, 171–185). Coastal resources are currently not regarded as particularly important to the communities of South Uist but this was not the case in the past when the commercial exploitation of seaweed, kelp, was of considerable significance (Symonds 1999a). In the nineteenth century access to kelp was controlled by the land owner but this was not necessarily the case in the Norse period. A less hierarchical model for ownership may be that currently in use to allocate peat, which is still the principal fuel for many islanders. The peat comes from cuttings in the open moorland of the island. Each cutting belongs to an individual and he/she has the exclusive rights to the peat in a prescribed area. The open moorland is partitioned between the different townships of the island and the allocation of a peat cutting is controlled by the township grazing committee. Every newcomer to the island has to apply to the grazing committee for a cutting. Access to a cutting is only guaranteed by the continued use of the cutting and if the cutting is not used then it can be reallocated to someone else. In her examination of the practice of fowling on St Kilda, Harman (1997, 209) outlines a variety of sharing mechanisms which were used to allocate birds harvested on the islands.

I would envisage a similar carefully controlled series of rights existed in the past in relation to the shoreline. Individual farms or families would have had rights to certain areas, which had been negotiated through the community. More importantly these rights would only have been maintained by continuous practice. Shellfish collection might well have been the most demonstrable way of establishing these rights of access to the shore and the dumping of large quantities of shells around the settlement was a visual statement of this right.

Another important aspect of the routine collection of shellfish would have been the creation of a relationship between the task, the time it was carried out and the particular group within the community who undertook this task. Shellfish collection might have been a female task and the routine nature of the task may be one of the features that established this relationship. However, it should be noted that kelp collection in recent times was a male task, though this may be because this was a commercial activity that was part of the cash economy. Birding and egg collection also seem to be male roles though again this could be misleading as the records are dominated by evidence for the spectacular collection of birds from the massive sea cliff colonies. This is a dangerous activity, which cannot be compared to the routine collecting of the eggs of ground-nesting birds. It also seems likely that children would have played a role in the collection of shellfish as the assemblage is restricted to the easily obtainable species and collection would not require much physical strength.

The Shore. 2. Crab – J Light

There are three possible reasons for the presence of crab in the samples from mound 3: consumption of food, use as bait and the gut contents of fish. They could have been harvested as food and, given the small size of the crabs at Bornais, this is most likely to have been for a composite dish. In countries of continental Europe during the present day *Carcinus maenas* and *Liocarcinus* spp. are regularly eaten. In Spain, for example, the latter species is something of a delicacy. The small crabs are eaten as entities, but also are included in fish stocks.

Other depositional pathways also need to be considered. Small crabs are used as bait for fishing but if they had been collected for that purpose, I would expect preparation or processing for those purposes to be carried out on the shore and not within dwellings. I have watched local fishermen at the water's edge, in the tropics, dismember small shore crabs, place the limbs in a concave stone to serve as a mortar and use another stone to grind them up with sand to make a paste which they use as a bait for fishing.

Another important consideration is the fact that small crabs make a contribution to the diet of fish and other marine predators, which might have been exploited by the inhabitants of the site. A relevant observation from background information supplied with the mound 1 samples is that the most productive layer (305) was both crab- and fish-rich. The crab shell fragments could, therefore, represent the residue of gut contents discarded in the middens.

There are a number of puzzles regarding crab shell in middens in comparison to its relatively low abundance in natural littoral and sublittoral sediments. Although I have no numerical evidence other than my data from shell sand analysis, it is intriguing that crab shell is so minor in otherwise shelly sediments, compared with the occurrence of live animals in marine habitats. This is especially marked when one considers the question of ecdysis: one decapod crustacean individual potentially produces several moults during its lifetime. Set against this, however, is the fact that resorption of calcium carbonate occurs just prior to ecdysis, so this may reduce preservation potential of the moulted carapace.

Another enigma is the fact that the Bornais material has not yielded crab shell from considerably larger animals, notably *Cancer pagurus*. Large specimens can be found at extreme low water in the present day and I would have thought this resource would have been available to the Bornais settlement. Similarly, lobsters hole up in crevices, which dry out, albeit briefly, when low on the shore but lobster shell is seldom reported from archaeological sites. Were the smaller crabs all that the occupants could find, or does this observation re-inforce a hypothesis for the crab shell as a secondary waste product?

To refine interpretation it would be useful to collect and analyse some samples of the local shell sand from various horizons in relation to the shoreline in order to elucidate the relative abundance of crab shell in the sediments. Without these comparative data I cannot rule out the wind-blown sand as contributing at least some crab shell to the settlement deposits, especially those contexts not associated with house occupation, associated activity or midden accumulation.

In the absence of quantitative data from local Bornais sediments, the concentrations of crab shell in the samples are nevertheless higher than would be expected to occur in natural sediment deposits. In any event, all the material is reported from archaeological contexts. As such the crab remains have been introduced to the settlement by its inhabitants. Various agents of introduction have been considered:

- collection of crabs as a contribution to the diet of the inhabitants,
- collection for fishing bait,
- a secondary waste product derived from discarded gut contents arising from exploitation of fish or other marine resources by the settlement's inhabitants.

The small size of the chelae from all three species identified in the samples and the absence of large chelae of the edible crab (*Cancer pagurus)* tend, on balance, to strengthen the case for the latter two options.

The Shore. 3. Wood – R Gale

An important source of wood and fuel on this deforested island was provided by driftwood and, as recorded from other sites on the Western Isles, timber was washed up in dimensions large enough to supply structural components (Taylor 1999; Church 2002). Although evidence of marine borers was not observed in the charcoal from mound 3, there is no doubt that the fragmented pieces from wide trunks, branches or planks of spruce or larch derived from driftwood. Neither taxon is native to Britain and the most likely sources in this context would be northern Europe and North America. As indicated by archaeological records, the collection and use of driftwood on the west coast of Britain was not restricted to Scotland but occurred as far south as the Scilly Islands (Gale 1996; Keepax and Morgan 1978).

Liminal resources. Birds – N Sharples and J Cartledge

The bird bones found at the site are not so easily categorised in this analysis of resource areas as by their nature they move between areas depending on whether they are nesting or feeding, and the season of the year can also make a significant difference to where they are located in the landscape or if they are located in the landscape. As is the case with most bird bone assemblages from northern Scotland, the Bornais assemblage is a disparate assemblage that includes many different species but with no numerical domination by any species. The species range across a number of habitats (Table 83) but are dominated by seabirds that are commonly found on the coast, and birds found on open moorland and agricultural landscapes. The presence of these birds should occasion no surprise as these environments characterise the South Uist landscape and the birds are common on the island today (Cunningham 1991). The more unusual birds are those that are commonly found in woodland or that nest in shrubs and hedgerows; even these species, however, are present on the island today.

The Machair. 1. Plants – S Colledge and H Smith

The carbonised plant assemblage has provided evidence for the use of plant resources both in the immediate vicinity of the Bornais settlement and beyond. This includes which plants were collected and from where in the landscape, and which areas of land were under cultivation. The island divides broadly into three zones: the machair, the blackland and the upland. The areas used for cultivation in the recent past were mainly the machair and the blackland, each with different advantages and disadvantages in relation to cultivation. The machair can also be sub-divided into 'high' and 'low' machair, the former nearer the shore is less organic, rich and dry. The upland zone supported heath, grassland and bog and a range of useful plants and shrubs with food or material value.

The crops and weed seeds found at Bornais are similar to those found at the other Norse period site on South Uist (i.e. Cille Pheadair) and mostly show continuity from earlier periods. Barley is the dominant cereal, although oats and rye occur in larger quantities than on earlier sites (i.e. Dun Vulan; Smith in Parker Pearson and Sharples

Table 83. Bird species by habitat

Species	Total		Nesting habitat	Feeding habitat
Guillemot	1	Charadriiformes	Cliff	Offshore
Guillemot/Razorbill	4	Charadriiformes	Cliff	Offshore
Gannet	3	Pelecaniformes	Cliff	Offshore
Rock dove (skeleton#1)	4	Columbiformes	Cliff	Rocky coast, farmland and grassland
Common/Herring Gull	8	Charadriiformes	Cliff, ground	Wide ranging but common on shoreline
Great black-backed gull	5	Charadriiformes	Cliff, stack	Beaches and coastal waters
Cormorant	4	Pelecaniformes	Cliff, trees	Coastal and inland waters
Shag	1	Pelecaniformes	Cliff, caves	Coastal waters
Manx shearwater	1	Procellariiformes	Burrows	Offshore
Puffin	2	Charadriiformes	Burrows	Offshore
Curlew	1	Charadriiformes	Ground	Damp moorland, meadows, shores and estuaries
Goose species	4	Anseriformes	Ground	Grassland and farmland
Skylark	1	Alaudidae	Ground	Farmland, grassland and moorland
Golden plover	2	Charadriiformes	Ground	Farmland, grassland and moorland
Teal	1	Anseriformes	Ground nr water	Freshwater lochs, moorland pools and muddy coasts
Turnstone	1	Charadriiformes	Ground nr water	Rocky coast
Dunnock (Hedge sparrow)	2	Passeriformes	Bushes	Widespread particularly heaths and moors
Song thrush	1	Passeriformes	Bushes, trees	Woodland and farmland with bushes/trees
Rook/Crow	1	Passeriformes	Trees, bushes	Farmland and settlements
Domestic fowl	6			
Domestic fowl (bantam)	1			
Domestic goose	1			
Total	55			

1999). Flax is present at both Norse sites, Bornais and Cille Pheadair, and represents a new introduction. Wheat was not recovered from samples at Bornais, although it occurs in low numbers at Cille Pheadair. At Bornais, the wild taxa are dominated by weeds of arable and waste ground. The most common species are *Polygonum/Rumex* spp., *Carex* spp., *Chenopodium* spp., Gramineae spp. and *Buglossoides* cf *arvense*. These weeds indicate damp and free-draining ground, of both acidic and alkaline soils.

The different growth requirements of the crop species together with the habitat preferences of the wild taxa can provide some indication of which areas might have been cultivated. The blackland and blackland/machair transition are generally better suited to higher productive barley cultivation than the higher areas of machair, because the sandy machair is easily exhausted and destabilised without periods of fallow, whilst the blackland can tolerate continual cropping if regularly fertilised (Smith 1994). The machair can be easily ploughed, but in the recent past has been treated more as an 'outfield' because of susceptibility to erosion and/or exhaustion. In some areas the machair can be prone to seasonal flooding, as seen around the Bornais settlement nowadays during the winter months. Common oat is considered to be better suited to the heavier, loamy ground of the blackland and peatlands rather than the machair land (Smith 1994) whereas bristle oat, a traditional crop of the Hebrides, is well suited to the different soil types – machair, blackland and cultivated peatlands (especially when treated with lime). Rye is well suited to the drier areas of the machair, where the oat and barley will not grow successfully. Flax favours well-drained but fertile ground – as found in some areas of the fertilised machair.

The majority of weed seeds recovered from Bornais could represent a range of ground conditions and together with the dominance of barley, this indicates continuity with earlier Iron Age practices in South Uist (Smith and Mulville 2004). However, some changes in the arable cultivation are apparent. In the Norse period at Bornais and Cille Pheadair, rye and flax are introduced and barley and oats occur in greater densities than previously, probably indicating intensified cultivation. The flax and rye have known preferences for dry and sandy ground, such as the machair. Gromwell, which is found in large numbers in some samples at Bornais, is also associated with lighter sandy soils and would support the use of the higher areas of machair for cultivation at Bornais. Corn spurrey, *Spergularia arvensis*, another indicator of light sandy soils, is found on the floors of buildings at Cille Pheadair in the Norse period. Neither of these occurs in the Iron Age and, together with the presence of rye and flax on the Norse settlements, indicates the likely use of machair for cultivation of these crops, especially the higher areas near the coast which have less organic material..

Oats and barley, suited to the less sandy and dry areas, might also have been grown on the damper ground, found where blackland merges with machair or in the well manured 'infields' created immediately adjacent to the settlement. The blackland/machair transition is the preferred ground for cultivation in recent times and although prone to seasonal flooding (as with areas of the machair) the ground can tolerate more continual cropping. Many of the weeds found at Bornais and at Cille Pheadair (as for the earlier periods) indicate damp ground, which could support the use of these areas, or alternatively the lower-lying areas of the machair.

The heavier, loamy machair ground is well suited to cultivation, although winter and spring flooding in the lower-lying areas might have limited access for part of the year. Rye and flax are not well suited to heavy (poorly drained) ground. It is likely, therefore, that the plant evidence is indicating the use of, or expansion onto, the drier parts of the machair, for cultivation of the new crops and/or expansion in the cultivation of oats and barley. It is also likely that the damper areas of ground continued to be used.

In Orkney, at the site of Pool, cultivation is also thought to have spread on to poorer sandy areas in the Norse period (Bond 1998), although here it is associated with bristle oat rather than rye and flax.

The occurrence of flax and gromwell in very different and separate deposits at Bornais is interesting owing to the suitability of both to the machair. In terms of cultivation and processing, this evidence indicates that gromwell and flax are not linked, unless the gromwell was carefully removed as a weed from the flax and disposed of elsewhere. More likely is the cultivation of flax in ground free of gromwell and the importation of gromwell to the kiln/barn as a plant or as a weed of a cereal crop. The association of rye (grains and rachis) and oat with the kiln/barn and FG occupation soils, where gromwell occurs, suggests an expansion in the areas under cultivation – to dry areas of machair where rye would flourish, and where bristle oat would also grow well.

The Machair. 2. Mammals – J Mulville

The use of the machair as an area to graze and fold stock can be explored through the faunal remains. The small sample of metrical data will be examined in future volumes and due to the small number of adults no data is available for sexing the animals.

Fusion data for the three food species are presented in Table 84. Many sheep die young, with one third of the bones coming from animals dying in their first year. After this the mortality rate increases slowly, with only small numbers of animals dying in their second and third years and just under one half of the population going on to maturity.

One fifth of the cattle bones come from animals that die during their first year. There is a large increase in slaughter in the second year with over twice as many animals dying, leaving only half the population alive after 2 years. After this time the mortality increases slightly, with about a third of cattle surviving beyond their fourth year.

Figures 97 and 98 compare the information available from dentition; a total of 20 records for cattle and 18 records for sheep were used, including loose dP4s and M3 for both species. This method allows a more detailed analysis of the animals' first year to be made and is different to the information produced by fusion. Dental ageing provides evidence that cattle have a higher initial mortality rate, with 25% of the population dead by the end of the first month. The mortality rate reduces after this with a further 5% dying in the next five months and over half of the population was dead by the end of the first year.

This early mortality is not demonstrated in sheep. No very young individuals were recorded, although just over 20% die in the first year. Twice as many cattle as sheep are dead by stage D (1–2 years). However a continuing high rate of slaughter for sheep in their second to third year means that, like cattle, by stage E (3–4 years) only about one fifth of the population is still alive, and thereafter the two species follow a similar management regime.

The dentition results indicate a much higher rate of slaughter in the first year for cattle and a lower rate for sheep than the fusion evidence provides (Table 84, Figure 97). This may be a function of the poorer preservation of juvenile bone, which for cattle is compensated for by recovery of the relatively large dP4s. It is harder to explain why dentition indicates that fewer sheep are dying young, unless the heads of these younger animals are not being returned to the site or they are suffering from a greater degree of taphonomic destruction than the longbones.

The neonatal individuals present in the assemblage indicate that cattle calved near the settlement whilst the lack of neonatal sheep suggests that lambing took place away from the settlement. Another alternative is that the smaller and more fragile neonatal sheep bones have been preferentially destroyed by the scavenging activities of dogs and pigs. The low numbers of the scavenging species and the low proportion of gnawed bone suggest this is not the case and, although slightly more robust, the presence of many neonatal cattle bones indicates good preservation and recovery at the site. Thus we can say that sheep, which lamb in the early spring, were kept away from the settlement at this time. There is no evidence for any walls or fencing on the machair and wherever land was cultivated and crops were grown, flocks of sheep would quickly have become a nuisance. The large number of sheep dying later in their first year could demonstrate a cull of animals in autumn when grazing becomes poor, or over winter, to compensate for the lower or non-existent

Table 84. Bone fusion data for the major domestic species

Sheep/Goat

	Element	Fused	Unfused	Neonate	% unfused
	Humerus d.	9	0	1	
	Radius p.	8	0	2	
	Scapula	5	1	1	
	Pelvis	1	4	1	
Subtotal < 1 year		23	5	5	30%
	Tibia d.	8	3	0	
	Metacarpal d.	2	0	2	
	Metatarsal d.	0	1	1	
	Metapodial d.	3	4	0	
Subtotal < 2 yrs		13	8	3	46%
	Calcaneum	5	2	0	
	Femur p.	0	1	1	
	Radius d.	2	1	1	
	Ulna p.	0	2	1	
	Humerus p.	0	4	0	
	Tibia p.	3	3	2	
	Femur d.	0	0	3	
Subtotal < 3.5 yrs		10	13	8	68%

Neonates	Total	% Neonates
16	88	18%

Cattle

	Element	Fused	Unfused	Neonate	% unfused
	Scapula	3	0	0	
	Pelvis	1	1	0	
Subtotal < 1 year		4	1	0	20%
	Humerus d.	1	1	1	
	Radius p.	2	1	0	
Subtotal < 2 year		3	2	1	50%
	Tibia d.	4	1	0	
	Metacarpal d.	1	2	0	
	Metatarsal d.	3	1	0	
	Metapodial d.	1	3	2	
	Calcaneum	1	4	1	
Subtotal < 3 year		10	11	3	58%
	Femur p.	1	1	1	
	Femur d.	1	2	2	
	Ulna p.	0	1	0	
	Radius d.	1	2	0	
	Tibia p.	1	0	0	
	Humerus p.	1	1	1	
Subtotal <4 year		5	7	4	69%

Neonates	Total	% Neonates
8	51	16%

Pig

	Element	Fused	Unfused	Neonate	% unfused
	Humerus d.	1	1	0	
	Radius p.	0	0	0	
	Scapula	0	0	0	
	Pelvis	0	1	0	
Subtotal < 1 year		1	2	0	67%
	Metacarpal d.	0	2	0	
	Metatarsal d.	0	1	1	
	Tibia d.	0	2	0	
Subtotal < 2 yrs		0	5	1	100%
	Calcaneum	0	1	0	
Subtotal < 3 yrs		0	1	0	100%
	Femur p.	0	2	1	
	Femur d.	0	0	1	
	Ulna p.	0	0	0	
	Radius d.	0	0	0	
	Humerus p.	0	1	1	
	Tibia p.	0	1	0	
Subtotal < 4 yrs		0	4	3	100%

Neonates	Total	% Neonates
4	17	24%

Based on shaft fusion evidence

Loose epiphyses not included in this calculation

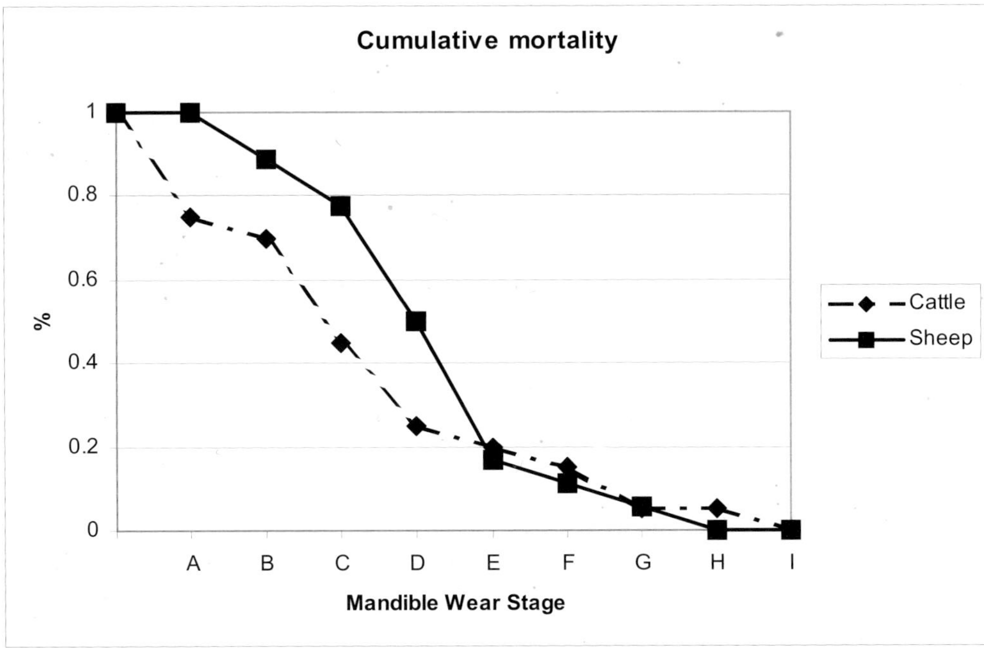

Figure 97. A cumulative mortality curve for cattle and sheep based on mandible wear stages

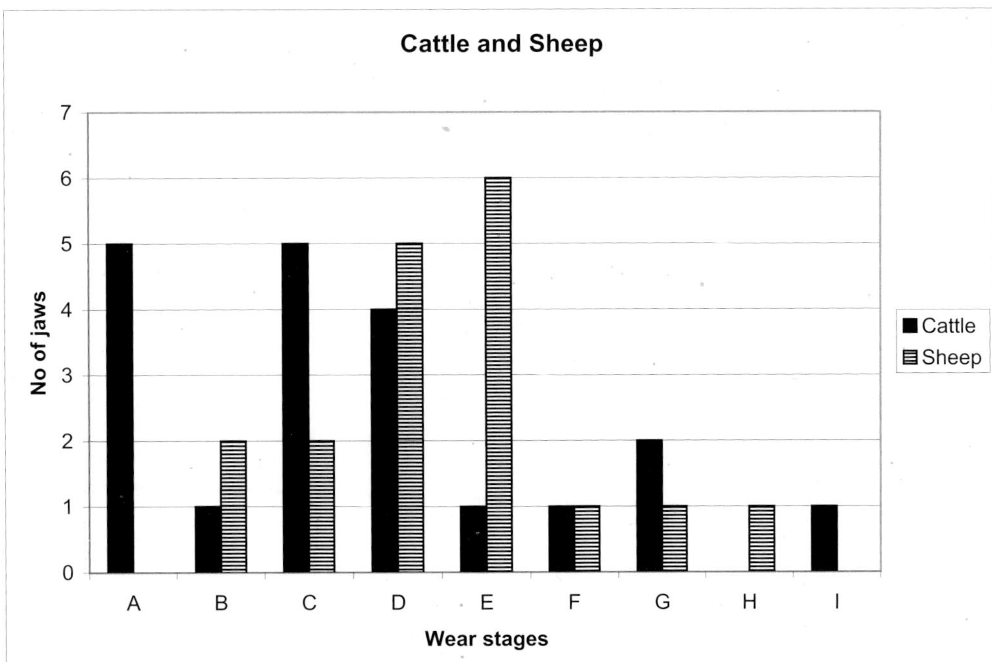

Figure 98. Mandible wear stages for cattle and sheep

milk yields from the cattle. Although there is no animal bone evidence that live sheep were ever brought to the settlement, autumn-culled animals could have been brought down from the hills after the cultivated land had been cleared. At this point the excess animals would have been slaughtered before the winter and the remainder of the herd would have been kept on the fields over winter to feed on the stubble and manure the land.

On the other hand the bone evidence does demonstrate that cattle were kept close to the settlement. This probably occurred to help with calving and to initiate and establish milking before the slaughter of excess calves, and the possible movement of the animals away from the settlement and the surrounding cultivated land. Horses were also breeding at the site since neonatal bones and deciduous teeth are present; like cattle, these larger animals might have required closer husbanding during breeding and again this demonstrates the ability of the Norse to keep the larger stock away from cultivated land. The management of the few pigs is problematic as it has been suggested that rooting pigs would have destroyed the plant cover and exposed the light unconsolidated soils to the strong winds characteristic of the Hebrides (Serjeantson 1990). We have no evidence for animal housing at the sites, and whilst it is likely that the animals were kept on pannage, the quantities available are likely to have been small. Further detailed analysis of pig dental hypoplasia (Dobney and Ervynk 2000) and stable isotope analysis is planned to elucidate the diet and management of this species.

The machair was a controlled, cultivated environment and whilst domestic stock could have been managed to preserve crops, the red deer would have posed a threat. Deer tend to live up in the hills in spring and summer, returning to lower ground for the autumn and winter, although lack of fodder could have brought them down at other times of year when crops were still in the fields. We do not know how deer were discouraged from feeding on crops and it is possible that the proximity of the fields to human settlement and the few dogs present played a role in this.

The remains of dogs were found only in trench D, mostly in DB, but also in the house floors (DD). All of the dog bone present is fused, suggesting older individuals. A few cat bones were recovered, from a DB layer around the main house and an FF layer outside the kiln/barn.

The Moorland. 1. Plants – H Smith and S Colledge

The evidence for wild edible plants, for example the pips of berries, indicates the collection of fruits such as bramble (*Rubus* cf *fruticosus*). The presence of heather indicates collection from the heathland areas, which lie to the east of the site, beyond the blackland and undulating, intermittently rocky ground. The moor would have been a source of many useful resources – including sedges and grasses, the seeds of which could represent materials deliberately collected from this higher and more distant ground although these are plants which could also be found on land nearer to the site. Peat would also have been derived from the moorland area. Fragments of possible peat were present in the majority of samples, from most contexts, at Bornais. Peat ash found on the site in hearth areas and floor layers (supported by thin section analysis and sediment analysis) verifies the collection of peat as fuel, although it might also have been collected for use in building (i.e. roofing material). Heather can be used for thatching as well as for fuel, bedding, ropes and brushes and the tips of the plant can be used to produce a yellow dye (Beveridge 1911; Smith 1994). Heather was also used as fuel, and was the preferred fuel for starting small fires when the kiln was in operation (Smith 1994).

Other questions related to the use of the land to the east of the site must also be addressed, such as the collection of hay and the use of sheilings, changes that might have occured in the Norse period. The damper and lower lying areas of blackland/machair are where hay is mown in the present day and these would have been near to the settlement. Areas of grazing suitable as sheilings include those in the central areas in the island, where the blackland merges into the peatland, and in the hills. Several of the present day place names in these central areas include the Gaelic word meaning sheiling, Geàrraidh (eg Gearraidh Bhailteas, Stadhlaigearraidh and Groigearraidh on South Uist) which is a word of Norse origin. The inter-relationship between the use of these areas of land for grazing, cultivation of cereals and the growth of hay is likely to have been very dynamic depending on the number of people and cattle and the need for food, fodder and manure. The type and proportion of cultivated crops would have driven the agricultural cycle with decisions being linked to season. In turn this would have influenced which animals were moved away from the settlement, cereal fields and hayfields.

The Moorland. 2. Trees – R Gale

In addition to member/s of the heather family, the range of indigenous woody species identified from the charcoal included hazel, birch, alder, oak, willow/poplar and juniper. Hazel and birch were comparatively frequent and might have flourished in sheltered valleys; the wood structure of both taxa was indicative of moderate growth and did not suggest that either had been subjected to particularly harsh or stressed conditions. The scant evidence of the remaining species named may correlate either with their low distribution in the local woodland or a total absence in the arboreal flora of the island. If the latter, it would seem that these species were imported from neighbouring islands or the mainland either as timber or artefacts.

Pollen records from Loch a'Phuinnd show that prior to about 7000 BC, juniper and birch formed the dominant woodland on South Uist but, after this date, juniper dramatically gave way to hazel and heather (Fossitt 1996). Larger communities of juniper, however, appear to have survived on the Faeroe Islands until the Viking settlers arrived when it was virtually eradicated through over-exploitation (Larson 1991) – the extensive use of the wood at Toftanes was verified by finds of barrel staves, wickerwork and rope. Following the juniper decline, Fossitt's (1996) pollen diagram also demonstrates that, roughly three to four thousand years ago, there was a transition from a woodland dominated environment (which supported predominantly hazel and birch but also Scots pine, oak, wych elm, alder and willow) to moorland.

The Moorland. 3. Mammals – J Mulville

The only wild terrestrial mammals found at Bornais are red deer. The majority of their remains were found in DB and DE with a few other fragments scattered throughout the other units. The normal habitat for red deer is woodland but the Scottish herds have become adapted to living in open moorland. These animals were hunted in the late spring (mid-May to June), as demonstrated by the presence of the limb bones of a newly born fawn, but as yet there is no other evidence for seasonality available from bones or antler. Once hunted and slaughtered, at least some entire animals were returned to the settlement; there are teeth, skull and toe bones present as well as meat-bearing bones. The ageing evidence demonstrates that mainly adults were procured, no doubt for their larger carcass size, although one sub-adult is present. The presence of a neonate is interesting, although, as only one individual is present, it may merely represent the chance find of a fawn or the offspring of a slaughtered doe. Antler was an important resource for the production of tools (see chapter 10) and could have been collected from hunted animals or more likely as shed antler. Antlers are shed in late February or March but whilst shed antlers can be collected any time of year, red deer use shed antler as a source of calcium (Sharples 2000a, 113) so a swift collection would gather the largest quantities.

The moorland also provides upland grazing for cattle and sheep. By excluding animals from the settlement in mid-summer the grass could have been rested and the risk of stock trampling the ripening crops avoided. Historic accounts suggest that cattle were kept on high pasture between June and August, with the herders living in sheilings. The seasonality evidence from Bornais suggests that sheep remained away from the settlement for most of the year, with cattle moving up into the moorland after they had finished calving in late May and June (see above p. 167). About six to eight weeks seems to have been the customary length of time spent at the shielings. At the summer grazing cattle were milked, and cheese and butter were produced as the only practicable way of first storing and then carrying home the milk. There are large numbers of sheilings in upland areas of South Uist, and it is likely that that summer transhumance to sheilings also occurred in the Norse period.

Discussion – N Sharples

The inhabitants of the settlement clearly exploited a wide range of environments and seem to have diversified into the exploitation of resources that were previously under-utilised in the Iron Age, and an important feature of the site was the discovery of a large fish bone assemblage. This assemblage was surprisingly dominated by herring, a species which, though known to be of considerable importance in the developing urban economies of England, Ireland and Continental Europe, has not been previously recorded in any quantity from northern Scotland (see chapter 11). The consistent size of the fish found suggests that the fishing grounds lay to the west on the edge of the continental shelf and it was probably fished in the summer months. The large size of the cod found at the site supports the view that deep-sea fishing was practised by the inhabitants of the settlement. The cod (as well as ling) would normally be caught by line fishing, but the most efficient way of catching herring is by drift netting at night. This is a more communal activity and the potentially large numbers of fish caught might have been an important commodity traded south to the towns of the Irish Sea.

Other sea resources are rather rare but it is possible that seabirds, such as gannet and guillemot, were caught using lures pulled behind a boat (O'Connor pers. comm.). The number of seals and whales represented by the bone assemblage from mound 3 is minimal but this may not be representative of the Bornais assemblage as analysis of the mound 1 assemblage has identified a much larger collection of whalebone. A detailed analysis of the cetacean finds from South Uist (Mulville 2002) has suggested that Norse exploitation of whales might, for the first time, have included hunting certain species at sea but it is still likely that exploitation was dominated by the casual discovery of strandings on the west-facing coastline of South Uist.

A detailed analysis of the shellfish from mound 3 has argued that the exploitation of the shoreline was important for a number of key resources including building stone and timber. It is likely that this exploitation was tightly controlled and deeply embedded within the routine practice of the settlement. Regular visits would have been required to guarantee the discovery of isolated and unusual strandings such as a whale or a good piece of timber. Access to pressurised resources such as edible seaweed and shellfish might have been restricted to prescribed areas. Nevertheless the absence of evidence for the exploitation of certain species, such as large crabs and lobsters that are only available at low-water mark, indicates that this resource area was not fully exploited.

The machair plain that surrounds the settlement at Bornais is undoubtedly the principal resource area for the settlement. It was not only the area for growing crops and grazing animals, but also provided a range of resources including birds (such as curlew, plovers, dunnock and skylark) and bird eggs (which have yet to be examined), as well as wild plants and turves, which were the principal structural material for the buildings occupied (see chapter 11). It is clear from an analysis of the densities of carbonised plant remains present in the samples from mound 3 that cereal cultivation was becoming increasingly important to the inhabitants of the west coast of South Uist. The dominant cultivated species remained barley, but oat (introduced in its cultivated form in the Late Iron Age) had become a very important crop and rye was also becoming increasingly important. Flax could have been deliberately introduced by the Norse settlers but Late Iron

Age flax is known from the Northern Isles (Holden in Sharples 1999). The variety of species present suggests that there was a much more extensive area of the landscape under cultivation than in the Iron Age and it is possible that particular species were being planted in areas that were most suited to their cultivation. Flax and rye, for instance, are more suited to the drier areas of the machair. Barley and oats in contrast require damper ground and would have been more suited to the margins of the machair and the blacklands or possibly to well-maintained and manured infields surrounding the settlement. Excavations at mound 2A clearly indicate that this settlement mound was created on top of a thick ploughsoil.

Unfortunately the exploitation of the machair has apparently never involved the creation of field boundaries, which makes analysis of the landscape difficult. It does, however, suggest the domestic animals had to be controlled either by constant human supervision or by movement away from the settlement area. Seasonal movement is certainly a feature of the historical exploitation of this and other highland landscapes and it would certainly be appropriate on South Uist. Extensive areas of summer grazing are available in the centre of the island and on the east coast. These landscapes were generally not permanently settled but do contain large numbers of sheilings that were occupied in the summer. Some of these sheiling sites are substantial settlements with numerous small structures, sometimes built into prominent mounds. This is likely to indicate long-term seasonal occupation dating to at least the Viking period and perhaps back into prehistory.

This upland landscape also provided other resources. The most important was probably peat, which was an essential source of fuel in a landscape that was then largely treeless. Heather is the most dominant plant in the upland areas and this again would have been harvested as it could be extensively used for rope making, thatching and as bedding for animals and people. It is possible that small stands of trees survived in some of the more isolated valleys and these would have been a very important source of wood for tools. Fruits and berries were also an important seasonal resource. Finally wild animals and birds would have been found in this area and red deer in particular was an important resource because they provided antler, which was essential for the production of tools (this will be discussed in detail in a future volume).

10 Site Activities

Chapter 7 explored the differences between the principal structures and some of the other more productive areas. In this chapter these differences will be explored in greater depth and the assemblages present will be analysed in order to identify the different activities that were undertaken on mound 3 and how these activities were organised across the mound. This analysis begins with an examination of the artefactual material, looking at evidence for manufacturing activity, the use of vessels, the importance of personal adornment and the presence of tools and structural fittings. There is also a discussion of the significance of the slag found on the mound. The artefactual material hints at the complexity of activity present but the quantities are small and the more important information comes from the analysis of the animal bones (fish, bird and mammal) and plant remains. These provide clear evidence for an agricultural community closely involved with managing and processing animals and crops into foodstuffs.

Artefact classes – A Clarke, P Macdonald and A Smith

Manufacturing evidence

The manufacturing evidence from mound 3 is restricted to evidence for the making of antler and bone tools, a drop of copper alloy from trench E and a piece of fired clay from FG. The antler tine tips form a distinct group of discards; that is, pieces of raw material discarded because they are of no use or have had any usable material stripped from them. The twisted tine (1972, Figure 56) is an example of an unusable piece – straight strips of antler are required for most purposes. Tine 1429 (Figure 33) is also too curved and thin to provide a useful thickness of solid material and has been discarded, after some exploratory cuts at the base to test the thickness of the solid layer. The smaller tine tips (1373 and 1530; Figure 56) are examples of tines that have had strips of solid material pared off the surface before discarding the remainder. The softening and wear of the tine point itself is rarely diagnostic of human use, and occurs during the deer's lifetime when the antlers are used for displays known as thrashing and wiping. Thrashing is when the stag thrashes bushes and vegetation with his antlers, and wiping is when the stag scrapes his antlers along the ground. Sets of trophy antlers can usually be observed to have wear on the tips of the tines.

The tine tip discards are indicative of comb-making – the pared strips of material removed from the tines are suitable for the manufacture of side plates for composite combs, and there are no other artefacts from the site which could have been manufactured from this type of material. However, there is an absence of other indications of comb-making on mound 3, such as small offcuts from tooth plate trimming or cylinders of antler beam characteristic of tooth plate manufacture. It may be possible that material components for combs were being made or roughed out here and taken elsewhere for assembly (mound 2A appears to be the principal focus for comb manufacture).

The pin roughout (1361) is a piece of cattle-sized long bone, which has been roughly cut with a knife and pared down into a pin shape. It might have been discarded because of the amount of cancellous tissue visible at the head end. The pin is of the large size characteristic of Norse pins.

The piece of clay (Figure 56, 4770) is an interesting item. It has a very similar if not identical fabric to the clay used for potting and when wet has been squeezed together to form a lump which has then been fired. It suggests the production of potting clay in the vicinity of mound 3 though there was no comparable evidence from either of the two structures excavated.

Vessels

The vessels present at Bornais could potentially have been made from ceramic, stone, bone, metal and wood and from Bornais there is evidence for all but wooden vessels. On mound 3 the evidence is limited to ceramic vessels, though the presence of at least one steatite bowl is indicated by a small fragment (1509/1513; Figure 33). The surviving interior surface is smooth with a shiny finish, the exterior is much rougher. The fragment is too small to estimate the original size or shape of the bowl.

The ceramic assemblage was heavily fragmented and it is inappropriate to carry out an extended discussion of these pieces prior to the analysis of the much larger and more complete assemblages from mound 2. Nevertheless it is clear that the assemblage is dominated by relatively crudely made vessels with thick walls often encrusted with charred residues. These are clearly cooking pots. Finer vessels, often with everted rims in the later phases, are more likely to be for serving food, and some may even be drinking vessels, but these vessels are so heavily fragmented that no profiles have been recovered. The flat dishes, known as platters, are a very distinctive feature of the Norse ceramic assemblages from the Hebrides (Lane 1990). They resemble the bakeplates of the Northern Isles and Norway (Weber in Crawford and Ballin Smith 1999) and they are likely to indicate a local response to a cultural requirement for a particular type of foodstuff (flat bread) where a stone suitable for this use was not available.

The ceramic assemblage is heavily concentrated in the house (DD) and the absence of any quantity of ceramics in the kiln/barn probably indicates that this structure was not regularly used for the cooking or consumption of food.

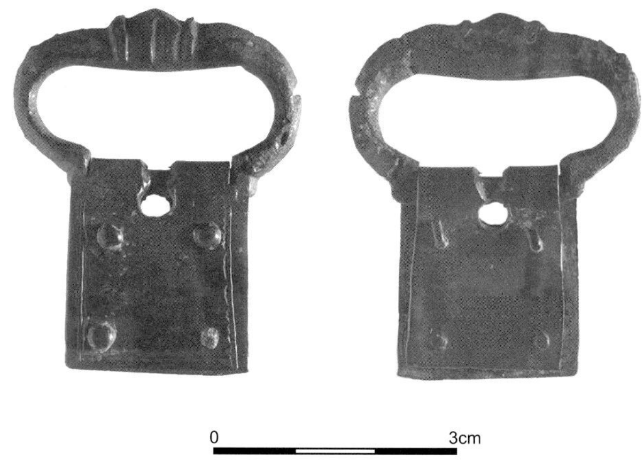

Figure 100. The copper alloy buckle, 1339

Dress and ornament

A range of objects was found which can be associated with the dress and adornment of the human body. These included the fragmentary remains of four combs, six pins (iron, copper alloy and bone/antler), a copper alloy buckle and possibly an iron pin from either a buckle or a brooch.

There are two side plate (1438, 1467, Figure 99) and two tooth plate (1061, 1579) fragments made from antler: all are from the same type of single-sided, tapering comb. The side plates have a trapezoidal section, with decoration formed by parallel incised lines, divided into panels by longitudinal incised lines. This type of comb is known from York (MacGregor 1985, 90), Whithorn (Nicholson in Hill 1997, 482) and Dublin. They are known as a type F3 comb in Ireland (Dunlevy 1988, 366) and are dated from the tenth to the twelfth centuries. The side plate fragments do not come from the same comb but all the pieces are from closely similar combs, indicating that they all probably emanated from the same workshop or maker.

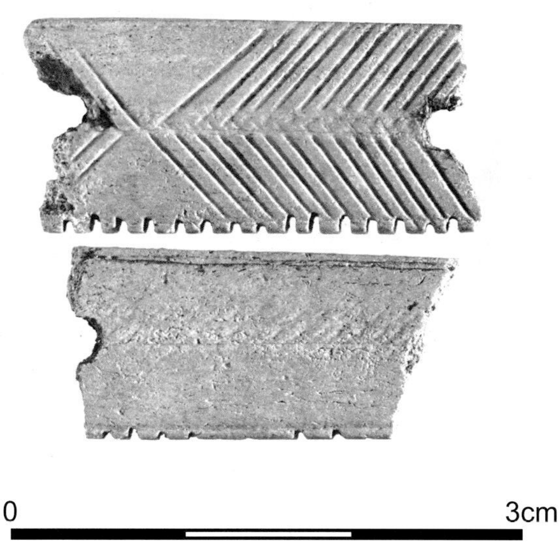

Figure 99. Two fragments of comb side plate: 1438 top, 1467, bottom

Three, not particularly diagnostic bone pin fragments (1315, 1380, 1260) could come from either Late Iron Age or Norse pins. The fairly large size of the pig fibula fragment (1380) is more characteristic of Norse period pins, which generally tend to be much larger than Late Iron Age pins.

The buckle (1339) has an oval-shaped frame with a folded rectangular plate (Figure 100). The plate has a border of opposed punched triangular motifs which can be paralleled on several buckles from Medieval London (i.e. Egan and Pritchard 1991, 112–115, nos 502, 514, 520, 533 and 535), which range in date from the second quarter of the thirteenth century to the second half of the fourteenth century. A similar date for the example from Bornais is not an unreasonable suggestion. 1864 is either an iron loop-headed spike or possibly the pin from a buckle or a pennanular brooch.

The club-headed pin (1739, Figure 101) is a classic example of a Hiberno-Norse dress pin recorded in large numbers from Dublin (O'Rahilly 1973; 1998) and Waterford (Scully 1997). The only substantial Scottish assemblage comes from Whithorn where 45 examples were recovered (Nicholson and Hill in Hill 1997, 364–368) but other isolated examples have been found in the Western Isles (Close-Brooks 1995, illus. 10). O'Rahilly (1998, 31–32) claims that well-made, highly decorated examples of the club-headed type were common in the twelfth century contexts at Dublin and Nicholson and Hill (in Hill 1997, 366) date this type to the late twelfth to early thirteenth century at Whithorn. Unfortunately the unstratified location of the pin makes it impossible to use this dating evidence. A possible iron dress pin (1858, Figure 101) was recovered from the western extension to the kiln/barn trench (FG). The crook-shaped head of this pin is paralleled by a mid-twelfth to early thirteenth century copper alloy, so-called zoomorphic-headed pin from Waterford, Co. Waterford (Scully 1997, 442, fig. 15: 1.28) and by a copper alloy example from Bornais

Figure 101. A copper alloy dress pin, 1739, and an iron pin, 1858

Figure 102. A fragment of bone clamp, 1221

Figure 103. An iron knife, 1887

Figure 104. A rectangular sectioned whetstone, 1434

mound 1. However, there are no close parallels for the artefact in iron and consequently its identification as a dress pin is not certain. The number of known iron dress pins is small but this is probably an under-representation of iron dress pins as a result of preferential rates of survival and recognition.

Tools

A wide range of tools were found made from bone, stone and iron. These consist of one clamp, a bone point, two bone handles, three iron knife fragments, two whetstones, a spindle whorl and a faceted cobble tool.

The clamp (1221, Figure 102) is quite an interesting find – these clamps are common finds on urban Scandinavian Viking and Medieval sites, and are alleged to have been used in comb-making although there is no *prima facie* evidence for this – they could equally be used in fine woodworking or even leather working, for holding small objects while working or while adhesives cure. MacGregor (1985, 62, 172) explains the principles and the arguments for their use. The other bone tools are not particularly diagnostic. The fine point or small awl (1578) is of a type found commonly on sites in the Western and Northern Isles in the Iron Age and Norse periods. The hollowed long bone and fragment of a similar object (1066 and 1065) are possibly from handles. The surface of the more complete one is slightly polished, perhaps from handling but there are no other signs of wear or use.

Iron knives are difficult artefacts to typologically classify and date, even when recovered complete, because of the inevitable changes to their original form caused by sharpening and wear and close dating of the examples from mound 3 is not possible. The most complete piece (1887, Figure 103) is an example of Ottaway's Group A2 (Ottaway 1992, 562–564), similar in form to both an Anglo-Scandinavian example from Coppergate, York (Ottaway 1992, 561, fig. 227, no. 2773) and a late thirteenth century example from London (Cowgill, de Neergaard and Griffiths 1987, 82, no. 28, fig. 55).

Both whetstones are small – just a tip survives of 1324 – and they have quadrilateral cross-sections formed from the use of all four sides of the stone. A high gloss is present on some faces of these whetstones and the steatite whetstone (1434, Figure 104) also has striations running the length of two of the worked faces. The use of steatite, which was most certainly imported from Shetland or from further afield in Scandinavia, and the use of quadrilateral-sectioned whetstones are particular features of the Norse period. The spindle whorl fragment (1346) is made of steatite and is a truncated cone shape. This form of spindle whorl is a Norse type and they are common at the Brough of Birsay though larger in size than the whorl from Bornais (Curle 1982, illus. 43). The faceted cobble (1525) is small in size and appears to have been used infrequently, leaving just light wear traces.

Structural fittings

The iron assemblage was dominated by pieces that can be classified as structural fittings. These comprise six definitely identified nails, two probable nails, five strips which are possible nail stems, two holdfasts and five roves.

Where identifiable the nails are all of a flat-headed or roughly flat-headed form. Flat-headed nails are a common type; for example they formed the vast majority of the nails recovered from the Coppergate excavations, York (Ottaway 1992, 607). None of the nails were complete (their surviving lengths vary from 17.5 mm to (estimated) 68 mm) and their poor preservation and small number prevent any sophisticated statistical analysis. Where complete the shapes of the nail heads range from sub-rectangular to rectangular in shape. The stems are all rectangular in cross-section and their thicknesses vary from 5 mm (1413) to 8 mm (1479). Where identifiable, two of the nail stems are set centrally on the heads (1479 and 1413) and two are off-centre (1836 and 1974). Flat-headed nails were used mainly in furniture, such as boxes and chests, but also served as architectural fittings (Ottaway 1992, 613). It is possible that several of the nails were originally used with roves to form holdfasts.

Holdfasts, or clench bolts, are fittings consisting of a nail and a perforated plate (rove) which are used to join two timbers. The nail is hammered through the timbers, the rove is then placed over the protruding end of the nail, the surplus length of which is cut off before it is hammered over. This arrangement prevents the nail from pulling back through the wood. Both of the mound 3 holdfasts have rectangular-sectioned stems, and although their overall lengths are 29 mm (1325) and c.35 mm (1436), the distance between their inner faces and heads are 16 mm and c. 19 mm respectively. Although diamond-shaped roves were recovered during the excavation of the other mounds at Bornais, both the five individual roves and those on the two holdfasts from mound 3 are flat and rectangular in shape. The stems of both holdfasts are set at an oblique angle to their heads and roves, rather than being set at a right angle to them, indicating the way in which they were used to join timbers (cf. Ottaway 1992, 617, fig. 257).

Holdfasts are known from a variety of Romano-British (Manning 1985, 132–134), Early Medieval (e.g. Ottaway 1992, 617–618) and Medieval (e.g. Goodall 1993, 146–147, fig. 108; Scully 1997, 474, fig. 15: 14.11; Clark 1997, 159) sites. Although commonly associated with shipbuilding, holdfasts are also known from a range of timber objects and features such as doors, partitions, hatches and carts (Ottaway 1992, 618; Lyne 1996, 149; Clark 1997, 159). It is uncertain whether the Bornais holdfasts represent evidence for shipbuilding at the site, the reuse of wood from ships, either as fuel or as timber, or the use of holdfasts as non-maritime fittings.

Miscellaneous iron

Thirteen miscellaneous fragments of iron were recovered. Most of these can be classified, following Ottaway (1992), into:

- bars, defined as having a maximum width to maximum thickness ratio of less than 4:1 and being markedly wider and thicker than strips (Ottaway 1992, 493);
- plates, defined as usually having a thickness of 6mm or less and a maximum width to maximum thickness ratio greater than 4:1 (Ottaway 1992, 501);
- strips, defined as having a maximum width to maximum thickness ratio of less than 4:1 (Ottaway 1992, 493).

These miscellaneous fragments could justifiably be identified as scrap, that is the broken pieces of other objects, which would be suitable for recycling. However, the even distribution of these pieces across the various context groups suggests that they were casually lost or discarded rather than collected together for recycling. This suggestion is supported by the lack of smelting or smithing slags on mound 3.

Slag and related materials – T Young

The slags from mound 3 are characterised by their occurrence in very small pieces. The assemblage includes only three pieces of slag over 10g (11, 15 and 18g) and the remainder of the collection includes only slag fragments below 3g. This is in stark contrast to the large slag blocks on mound 1 and mound 2A (Young 2002). There are two logical interpretations for this lack of large pieces. One possibility is that they were removed and deposited elsewhere; the other that they were not produced by the activities taking place in the mound 3 structures. The complete lack of large blocks, or even of small pieces likely to have been derived from the sort of slag sheets recorded on mound 1, strongly suggests that they were not being produced in the mound 3 hearths.

A high proportion (approximately 15% in the samples examined) of the fine slags from mound 3 are magnetic, and can be easily separated from the pickings by magnet. These magnetic slags are typically brownish in colour and are dominated by small spiky sintered fragments, but also include blebs and spheroids suggestive of a more freely flowing material. The spheroids are particularly interesting because of their resemblance to spheroidal hammerscale (Figure 105). They differ from spheroidal

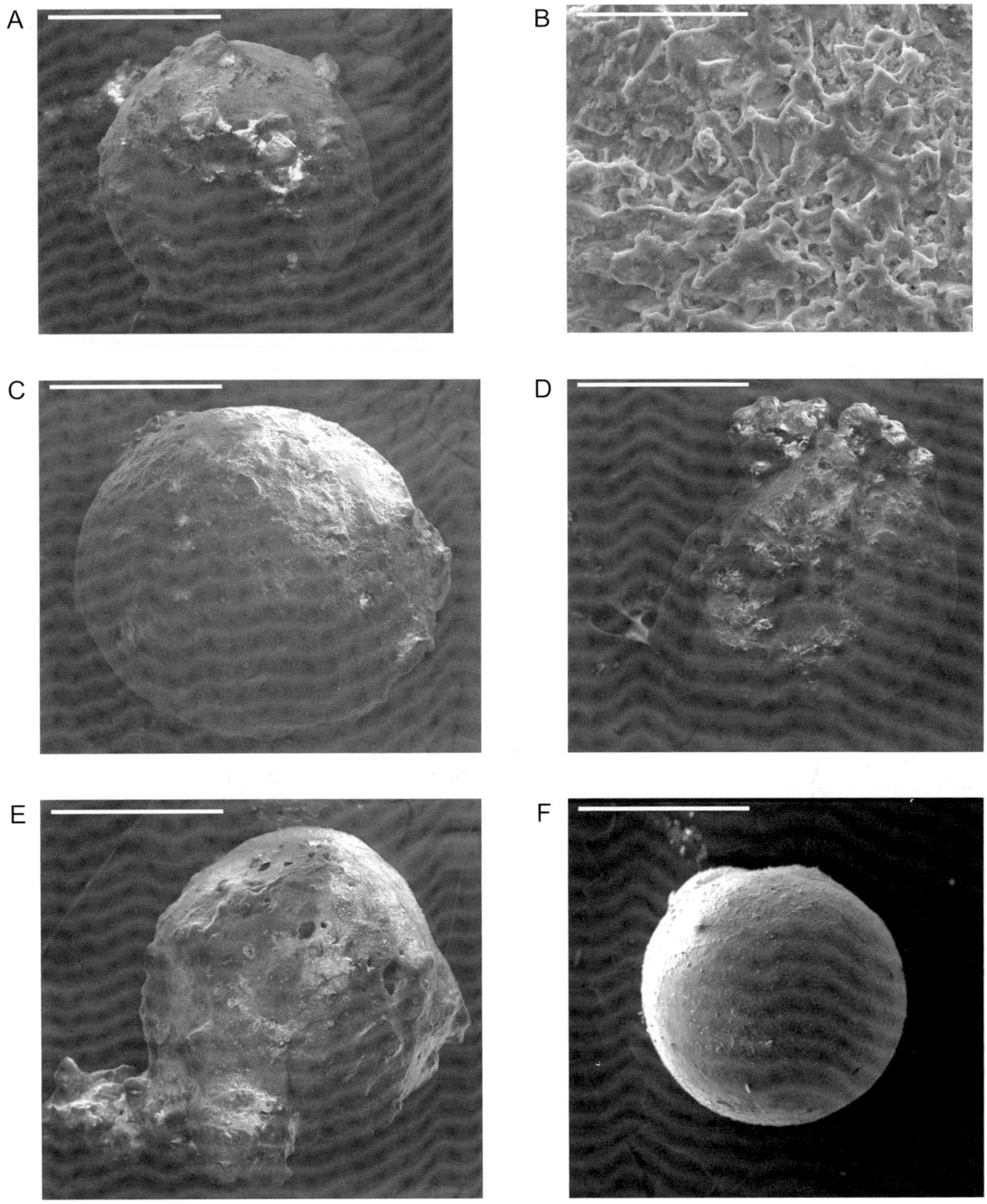

Figure 105. Spheroidal slag particles from sieved residues. A-E from mound 3 context 276 (lower kiln/barn floor) sample 8662. Scale bars 1 mm except B which is 100 µm. A. Non-magnetic spheroid. C–E. Magnetic spheroids and sub-spherical particles. B. Surface detail of magnetic spheroid. F. Spheroidal hammerscale for comparison from Late Roman blacksmithing deposits (Caerwent *basilica)*

hammerscale in being less perfectly spherical and in having a more irregular surface when seen under the scanning electron microscope (Figure 105). At the scale of observation when being picked from the sieve residues under a binocular microscope the two particle types would not easily be separable.

The non-magnetic fraction is dominated by pale grey to creamy yellow fragments of sintered sand and glassy slag. These textures also dominate the coarser fraction of the slag. They are typically porous and friable. Their low density means that few of the slag pieces of this type in the >10mm fraction weigh more than 2g. A few of the glassy slag fragments are darker, sometimes almost black, but typically still bearing pale quartzo-feldspathic grains.

The only pieces greater than 10mm are all of a dark glass, presumably of a more iron-rich composition and more free-flowing.

The distribution of the slag in the floor of the kiln/barn suggests that this was derived from the fire lit in the kiln flue. The distributions on the house floors, though much less clear, appear also to be controlled by the position of the hearth. This patterning together with the detailed analytical study of the large slags from mound 1 (Young 2002 and to be published in a future volume) suggest that the Bornais slags can confidently be assigned a non-metallurgical origin.

Fish – C Ingrem

An important feature of the fish bone assemblage is a notable under-representation of herring elements derived from the skull. This is probably partly a consequence of taphonomic processes causing destruction of the less robust cranial bones. However, their virtual absence in such a well-preserved and intensively sampled assemblage suggests that cultural factors are involved. It would not be surprising if the heads of herring were removed prior to cooking and consumption, and disposed of outside of the house, whilst evidence from the kiln/barn and barn suggests that decapitation might have preceded smoking. The absence of cut marks on the bones does not preclude this scenario, as decapitation does not necessarily require the use of a knife or blade (Jones 1995). It follows that herring are likely to have been cooked and served with the rest of the vertebral column remaining in the body of the fish, a method of preparation still used today. If this were the case then the evidence for gnawing seen on some of the bones might have been inflicted by human chewing.

The pattern for cod contrasts with that seen for herring. The under-representation of the more fragile skull bones and the cleithrum is likely to be the result, at least in part, of differential preservation. However, the over-representation of other, more robust cranial elements such as the premaxilla when compared to vertebrae cannot be explained by differential preservation alone. Vertebrae are generally considered the most robust and most likely fish elements to survive; therefore their relative under-representation on a site with such good preservation is likely to result from cultural practices. Cranial elements are often over-represented at midden sites where they have been interpreted as processing waste (Barrett 1997). Here, they are from a house floor, an unlikely location to dump waste. Cod heads contain a considerable amount of meat and it was suggested that they were being consumed at Beachview Birsay (Rackham 1996). It is therefore possible that fish heads were being cooked and eaten, leaving the fillets to be processed and stored for later consumption. Although abdominal vertebrae, are consistently better represented than caudal vertebrae the presence of the latter suggests that some fish were consumed whole.

Hake are too few in number to draw conclusions regarding body part representation but the pattern appears comparable to cod and suggests that a similar consumption and processing strategy might have been used for other large gadids.

Fish processing and the implications for trade

There is little evidence to suggest that fish were being processed on a large scale although it seems that some herrings might have been decapitated and smoked in the kiln/barn. In general, body part representation suggests that herring were being consumed at the site and the heads discarded elsewhere. The body part representation of cod suggests that some fish might have been processed for storage and later consumption but this does not appear to have been done on a large scale. As the herring heads appear to have been disposed of elsewhere it is quite possible that a midden exists in the vicinity where the heads and other waste were dumped. The large size of the majority of cod-family fish makes it likely that they would have been served as filleted portions and the majority of their bones also disposed of outside the house. However, the relatively small number of gadid bones recovered and the evidence for consumption of cod heads suggest that these fish were not plentiful, at least not in comparison to herring.

As the site is domestic in nature the fish remains are likely to represent the remains of cooking and consumption rather than processing waste. It is possible that surplus fish were being caught and processed elsewhere. The ethnohistoric evidence suggests that the large-scale processing of cod-family fish took place either partly at sea and/or at processing stations close to the shore (Martin 1995). Therefore, processing waste such as heads and vertebrae would be disposed of in middens located away from domestic sites.

Bone modification and disposal

There is no reason to assume that the majority of the fish from the floor layers were deposited by any agent other than human activity. They are all derived from a domestic context and only a small proportion display evidence of gnawing, which might well have been inflicted by humans. The presence of a few cut marks on some bones attests to the use of a sharp blade, probably during decapitation and processing. In particular, the consistency in the location of cut marks on cod supracleithra suggests that some fish were decapitated in the traditional manner, through the appendicular region. Few bones display evidence of burning, which is not surprising given the short cooking time required for fish. It does, however, indicate that fish remains were not generally thrown on the fire.

Birds – J Cartledge

All of the bird species can be eaten and most of the bones present on site probably come from birds that were eaten. Several bones come from skeletons that had not reached maturity and a cormorant radius from context 675 has been cut with a knife. It would appear, therefore, that not only were domestic species being kept but that a range of wild species was hunted. Bird hunting has long been a recognised occupation of the islanders. Many of the wild birds are species for which there is a history of consumption in the Hebrides including gannets, puffins, guillemots and gulls (Beatty 1992). In the last century, the gannet was a major food source for many remote Scottish communities, and special licences are still issued to the men of Ness in Lewis to harvest young 'gugas' from Sula Sgeir (Thom 1986).

Animals – J Mulville

There are differences in tapophonomy and deposition in the house floor layers, occupation deposits and the kiln/barn that reflect different activities across mound 3. Very little bone was burnt, only 2% overall, the highest proportions were found in the small samples from the deposits beside the kiln (FF) (10%) and the occupation layers (FG) associated with the barn (8%, Table 85). Overall 16% of bones were gnawed by canids, probably dogs. The highest levels of gnawing were found in the pre-house sand blow (FA), the accumulation layer under the house floor (DB) and the floor itself (DD).

Butchery was found on 5% of bones with the highest levels in deposits representing the use of the kiln/barn (FD) and later infilling (FE) of the barn. Butchered bone was also found in layers associated with the use of the house (DD). The bone evidence suggests that deposits around the house (DB) contain secondary butchery waste, with prime meat-bearing bones appearing here in slightly higher numbers than elsewhere (Table 72). However the presence of the full range of bones from cattle and sheep, and to a lesser extent pig, suggests that for these animals on-site slaughter was occurring and all part of the animals were being fully utilised. The relative lack of butchery marks on some of the pig bone could relate to the small sample size.

We have evidence of activity at Bornais in: the spring and early summer owing to the presence of bones of newborn sheep, calves and horses; later in the summer when herring were being fished; and again in autumn, when seal pups were hunted. Future work on the seasonality of slaughter in adult animals will examine when older animals were killed, consumed and deposited at Bornais.

The movement, distribution and disposal of plant materials – S Colledge and H Smith

The analysis of the plant remains has shown clear associations of certain crops and wild taxa with particular buildings and deposits: flax only occurs in the house, where barley also occurs in large quantities, whereas oat and rye are associated with the kiln/barn. Many of the

Table 85. The percentage of gnawed, burnt and butchered bones from each block

		Gnawing	Burnt	Butchery
DA		0	0	0
DB	Accumulation	20	1	7
DD	House floors	19	2	5
DE	Post house deposits	8	3	5
	Average House	12	2	4
FA	Pre-kiln/barn sand blow	23	0	0
FB	Adjacent structure/house	0	0	0
FC	Kiln/barn construction	0	0	0
FD	Kiln/barn occupation	5	0	10
FE	Kiln/barn infill	0	3	3
FF	Kiln/barn associated activity	6	6	13
FG	Occupation layers	12	9	3
	Average Kiln/barn	7	3	4
Average for all units		16	2	5

weed taxa are found both in the samples from the house and the kiln/barn floor, for example knotgrasses/docks (*Polygonum/Rumex* spp.). Some taxa, however, show strong associations with particular contexts – for example gromwell (*Buglossoides* sp.) and probably other species of Boraginaceae (represented by the charred embryos) with the kiln/barn deposits whilst sedge (*Carex* sp.) is associated with the house floors.

These trends clearly illustrate a difference in the storage and/or use of plants on the settlement. The occurrence of large numbers of cereal grains and the association of rye and barley chaff with the kiln/barn structure implies that crop processing took place in this building. This is consistent with the activities expected to have taken place in a barn with a drying oven, for example parching, threshing and separation of the chaff from the grain. The occurrence of weed seeds in the kiln/barn floor is also consistent with crop processing activities, as these could have fallen from or been deliberately removed from the crop during the different processes required to clean the grain.

Accounts of traditional agricultural activities and cereal processing in the Outer Hebrides can be found in historical documents (Martin 1716; Walker 1764) and ethnographic studies (Smith 1994). The use of corn drying kilns (Gaelic *ath* or *asoul*) in North and South Uist in the late eighteenth century is noted in some accounts (Buchanan 1793; Walker 1764). The small circular kilns described in these accounts are the same as those described in use on South Uist in ethnographic accounts for the early twentieth century (MacDonald 1993; Smith 1994). The kiln bowl and flue were usually constructed within a solid rectangular block located at one end of the barn (usually the north end). The kiln bowl was c. 1m in diameter across the top and tapered down to c. 0.6 m in diameter across the flat bottom, with a final depth of c. 1m. The flue consisted of a long tunnel constructed of large flat stones which led from the base of the kiln bowl to an opening in the side of the block (Smith 1994). These kilns have obvious structural similarities in form and dimension to the kiln found at Bornais, particularly the first phase where the kiln bowl is more circular.

The kiln was prepared for use by constructing a platform of twigs or sticks over the kiln bowl, in the shape of a shallow cone (placed edge to middle). This was covered in a thin layer of straw to prevent the corn falling through, but not too thick to prevent the heat from passing through. The fire, usually fuelled with peat, was lit in the mouth of the kiln flue. The parching operation would require careful attention, both to avoid sparks from the fire (very risky in a building with a thatch roof and storing dry crops) and also to turn the corn frequently, moving it away from hot spots (Smith 1994). The process would often take place at night, with story-telling accompanying the activities.

The kiln was most often used to parch the barley. Whole ears of barley (or threshed grain) were laid on a platform and parched until they were crisp to touch. Once the ears were parched, they were thrown onto the floor of the barn and then threshed using a flail. The winnowing of the corn would take place either inside or out (depending on the weather), using a board or canvas. It was usual for the waste material either to blow away or to be fed to the animals, but some of the waste material would be thrown onto the fire (Smith 1994). In this way, and through accidents during the parching process, material might have been charred.

On a smaller scale, grain crops may have been pot-dried over the fire (Fenton 1978), which would quickly harden and crisp the grain ready for grinding. Alternatively, hot stones could be rolled over the grain in a container (of straw, or cloth etc), as noted for St Kilda (Fenton 1978). A process likely to generate charred remains that could persist in the archaeological record, is 'graddaning'. Here a sheaf of hand-pulled cereals was held over the fire to burn off the chaff and dry the grain ready for immediate threshing and grinding (Stewart 1980) – a quick but potentially wasteful method. Hillman (1981) refers to the sheaf burning of milk ripe or fully ripened crops, noting that such activities could generate charred ears, culm nodes and weed seeds.

Crop processing is linked to the kiln/barn structure through the occurrence of large numbers of cereal grains and rye and barley chaff, but it is not possible to suggest exactly which crop processing activities were taking place. This material is likely to have been carbonised on the fire in the flue and then raked out of the fire across the floor. The sandy matrix of the barn floor at Bornais made the surface yielding and allowed the charred remains to become impressed into the floor. This floor might not have been sufficiently hard to thresh the grain inside the building. In the early twentieth century South Uist kiln/barns, the barn floors were laid with clay and gravel to make a hard surface suitable for threshing, but these buildings are located on the gneiss bedrock of the blacklands, which is uneven and required levelling (Smith 1994 and forthcoming).

Barley is the most commonly occurring cereal in the house, and the low quantities of chaff suggest that it was brought in as cleaned or partially cleaned crop. The occurrence of many weed seeds, including goosefoots (*Chenopodium* spp.), Cruciferae spp. and Caryophyllaceae spp. and the dominance of sedge (*Carex* sp.) in the house samples may reflect the final stages of cleaning of the crop (e.g. fine sieving) and the deposition of waste onto the household fire, and at a later stage the spreading of ash and the charred remains from the hearth across the floor. Alternatively, the high proportion of *Carex* spp. seeds may reflect the use and subsequent disposal of sedges as flooring or bedding etc. The occurrence of flax in the house confirms that it was stored, processed and/or cooked here, whereby caches of seeds were either accidentally or deliberately exposed to the fire. This might have been the result of preparation for food, or the extraction of oils, or even the result of seed falling from plants drying above the fire (Dickson and Dickson 2000), although the large numbers of seeds would suggest the latter is less likely.

It is possible that there was some movement of materials between the house and the kiln/barn. Unlike the house fire, which is likely to have been in constant use, the fire in the kiln/barn is more likely to have been lit intermittently, on an 'as and when needed' basis. A simple and effective means of doing this would have been to carry embers, a lighted stick or other material from the household fire to the barn. This might explain why, although flax is mostly found in the house floor deposits, 11 seeds of flax occur in the barn. The lighting of a fire might also involve the use of crop remains as kindling and if this was a frequent event it could explain the enhanced quantities of carbonised plant remains from the floor of the kiln/barn.

Firewood – R Gale

The analysis of floor deposits suggests that peat supplied the main source of fuel, especially in the corn-drying kiln. Wood, dung, cereal processing waste and probably other types of dried herbaceous material were also used but perhaps in a more supplementary way, as kindling or to boost the temperature. There was some evidence to suggest that heather, rather than other woody taxa, was more frequently used in the house than in the kiln/barn, especially in the primary floor. This may be related to function or to the secondary use (recycling) of heather from other purposes, e.g. the renewal of bedding or thatch. Traditionally, heathland in Britain has been seasonally burnt off to encourage the new growth of heather for stock grazing (Edlin 1949) but, in sparsely wooded areas, a more productive use for these valuable resources would have been to crop and store the heather for fuel.

Discussion – N Sharples

The analysis of the material from the two principal trenches on mound 3 has provided a considerable amount of useful information about the nature of activities in this area of the settlement at Bornais. It must be emphasised, however, that this picture is limited by the restricted nature of the work discussed here. Mound 3 is a part of a much larger settlement which includes several farms that are certainly contemporary with the structures discussed. Work on mound 2 indicates that a large and prestigious farmhouse was present and this was probably the centre of the settlement from the pre-Viking period through the Norse settlement and up to the end of the settlement in the fourteenth/fifteenth century. Mound 2A in contrast was an area of arable, which was only occupied after mound 2. A sequence of buildings is present and these seem quite small and insubstantial in the final phases. Associated with these structures is important evidence for manufacturing activity, which includes large quantities of comb-making debris.

The excavations indicate that a range of different activities was undertaken on different parts of the site and to a certain extent this explains some of the characteristics of the material found on mound 3. The artefact assemblage, for instance, is relatively impoverished compared to the other trenches. Very few complete objects were recovered and the range of decorative artefacts such as combs, pins and buckles is restricted and probably indicates the low status of the inhabitants of this building in comparison to the other structures. Tools are similarly uncommon discoveries and these appear to be nails, roves or holdfasts with only a few broken artefacts.

It is important to emphasise that the excavation of mound 3 was strictly limited, with most of the material coming from two structures that date to the final occupation of the mounds. Excavation of the deposits outside the buildings was very limited and did not include any of the substantial midden deposits where most of the messy external processing is likely to have taken place. This may explain the relatively small numbers of mammal bones as the initial dismemberment of the carcass is likely to have taken place outside buildings and the waste would have been disposed of in the principal external middens. Nevertheless, despite these limitations, it is possible to identify differences in the activities undertaken in the kiln/barn and the house that suggest they had distinctive roles in the processing of material from farming and hunting activities.

Analysis of both the fish and the crop remains suggests that the kiln/barn was involved in the primary processing of foodstuffs. The fish bone evidence is more tenuous but Ingrem notes the presence of herring heads in the kiln/barn and this contrasts with the absence of heads in the house. Herring was therefore present in the kiln/barn before they had been fully processed for consumption, which is what seems to be going on in the house. The presence of the corn-drying kiln may indicate that herring were smoked in this building and this is certainly a process which could have been used to preserve the fish. However, the quantities of fish bones present on the floor of the kiln/barn were limited and this suggests that the basic processing of herring occurred outside and again that the waste was disposed of onto the middens or was fed to animals.

The large gadids (such as cod) were processed in a quite different manner. The presence of skull bones on the house floors (DD) suggests fish heads were consumed in the house and this may indicate the low status of the inhabitants. However, it is possible that large cod were filleted prior to consumption and if this were the case then the main body parts would have been disposed of elsewhere. The consumption of cod fillets in the house would not leave any obvious archaeological trace.

The evidence for crop processing likewise indicates the kiln/barn had a primary role in processing material. This primary role is not surprising given the presence of a kiln/barn that architectural parallels indicate was associated with drying cereals. However, drying occurred outside the building and the presence of large quantities of carbonised plant remains on the kiln/barn floors suggests the building had other important roles in the processing of crops. The presence of a winnowing hole opposite the entrance to the building indicates that this was related to the separation of the chaff from the grains and this interpretation is supported by large quantities of rye and barley chaff on these floors. The waste was presumably used to fuel the fire for the kiln and was then redistributed over the floor. Threshing must have occurred between drying and winnowing but it seems unlikely that this took place in the kiln/barn as this is a relatively confined space. It could have occurred just to the east of the kiln/barn (FF) where there was an area of redeposited ash, which would have provided a hard surface. The material from the house floors (DD) lacks concentrations of chaff and many of the weed seeds present in the kiln/barn, suggesting that the crop was cleaned before it entered the house.

One of the principal problems we have in understanding the final phase of crop processing is the absence of any evidence for grinding the grain into flour. No querns have been found on any of the mounds at Bornais, or at Cille Pheadair, and this strongly suggests that the cereals were taken from the settlement to a mill where the grain was ground into flour and then returned to the settlement to be made into bread. Unfortunately our knowledge of the mills of South Uist is very limited. In contrast to many areas of the Western and Northern Isles of Scotland small horizontal (Norse) mills are not a common feature of the landscape. This may be partly explained by the geography of South Uist. The machair plain where most of the settlements are located is not characterised by the presence of many fast-flowing streams that can be easily channelled for mills (an exception is at Howmore where there was an important Late Medieval mill). The streams are mainly found in the upland central and eastern parts of the island, which is some distance from the main settlement area. It is possible, therefore, that a centralised system of larger mills, rather than a dispersed system using small horizontal mills, was established; alternatively querns were used but carefully disposed of away from the settlement.

Evidence for activity other than that associated with agriculture and food consumption is rare from this mound. The pottery assemblage represents the domestic activities one would expect in a house, cooking and food consumption, and it is perhaps most interesting to note the lack of this material from the kiln/barn. The artefact assemblage was poor and contributes very little to our understanding of the range of activities undertaken. Many of the complete pieces are deliberately placed items in foundation or abandonment layers (a practice also noted at Cille Pheadair, M. Parker Pearson pers. comm.) and do not therefore reflect activity undertaken on the site. A few fragments of waste from bone working suggests this was an activity undertaken in a domestic context though specialist areas (mound 2A) are also known on the site. One large piece of fired potting clay also hints at the possible production of ceramics in the vicinity of the structures examined.

11 Discussion

The wider context – N Sharples

Three Viking/Norse settlements have now been excavated on South Uist: two as part of the SEARCH project described in the introduction, Bornais and Cille Pheadair (Brennand, Parker Pearson and Smith 1998; Parker Pearson, Brennand and Smith 1996) and a third, Drimore (MacLaren 1974), which was excavated prior to construction of the Rocket Range. The only other excavated sites on the Outer Hebrides are The Udal on North Uist (Crawford 1974; 1981; 1986; Selkirk 1996), which has been extensively excavated but not published, and Barvas on the Isle of Lewis (T. Cowie pers. comm.), which was only test pitted and again is still unpublished. Norse material was also recovered during the excavation of the Beaker settlement at Rosinish, Benbecula (Shepherd and Tuckwell 1977) and the Late Iron Age settlement of Bostadh on Lewis (Neighbour and Burgess 1996). For further contemporary settlements one has to turn to northern Scotland or the Isle of Man.

Unfortunately we know very little about the sequence at Drimore (MacLaren 1974), as the excavations were impeded by the presence of a high water table, which restricted excavation below the floor. The area excavated was also tightly defined around the edge of the identified house even though it was clear that the structural evidence continued to the east. The building exposed was 14 m long and 5 m wide, roughly oval in shape with a rounded west end and a straight east end, and with a single north-facing entrance located towards the west end. There was a central ash floor area, 8 m long and 1.5 m wide, partially paved at the east end. There is some evidence that this is a composite house that includes stretches of masonry that belonged to earlier and possibly later buildings (see Graham-Campbell and Batey 1998, 175–177 for a reinterpretation). Nevertheless, it was observed that the material found on the floor was concentrated in the area around the east end of the hearth. The only diagnostic artefact was an early Viking period comb (Graham-Campbell and Batey 1998, 177) and, though a few pieces of pottery may indicate later occupation somewhere nearby, it is clear that the remains exposed were several hundred years earlier than the structures from mound 3.

The most important excavation of a Norse settlement in the Western Isles occurred at The Udal on North Uist and, though we are still awaiting the final publication of this site, sufficient is known from the interim reports (Crawford 1974; 1981; 1986; Selkirk 1996) to indicate that this is a key site for understanding the Viking settlement of the island and the later Medieval occupation of the islands. The excavator believes The Udal North was occupied continuously from the fourth or fifth centuries AD through to the end of the seventeenth century when it was abandoned, probably as a result of a series of massive sand blows (Selkirk 1996, 84). The evidence for the earliest Viking occupation consists of one complete house, fragments of at least two more houses, an outbuilding, small enclosures and a large enclosure, both of turf and stone. The excavator interpreted the large enclosure as a fort. There was extensive evidence for plough cultivation in the area between the two clusters of buildings (Selkirk 1996). These early Viking houses were succeeded by a single house, which has a distinctive bicameral form. The building is oriented NE-SW and has a pair of entrances which lead into the principal living area at the north end of the building. In the south wall of this room is a passage, which leads into a small subsidiary room. The construction of this building was dated to the period AD 1200–1250 and it is directly comparable to House 500 at Cille Pheadair (Brennand, Parker Pearson and Smith 1998). The building was succeeded by a dispersed settlement of five buildings. There appears to be one dominant structure, which Crawford interprets as a tacksman's house, and three to four houses, which belonged to 'servants' (Selkirk 1996, 85). These structures are likely to be at least partly contemporary with the structures from Bornais mound 3 and it is therefore unfortunate that no detailed plans have been published. They are described as 'double stone walled buildings, double walled to keep out the wind, but hip-gabled at the ends, with roofs of the traditional thatch' (Selkirk 1996, 84), which suggests they are somewhat different to the buildings discussed below. Detailed analysis of the extensive material recovered from The Udal has still to be undertaken but reports on the bones and the pottery are available and have been consulted by specialists working on the Bornais material.

The Norse settlement at Cille Pheadair dates from c. AD 1050 to c. AD 1350 (Parker Pearson pers. comm.). The site was founded on wind-blown sand, though a Pictish burial was discovered only 70 m to the south and Iron Age or later settlements were apparently destroyed by the sea in the areas immediately to the south and north of the site (Brennand, Parker Pearson and Smith 1998). Nevertheless the settlement was clearly established some time after the Viking colonisation of the island and abandoned slightly before the end of the settlement on Bornais mound 3. The mound at Cille Pheadair was estimated to be 50 m north-south and the settlement appears never to have had more than one substantial building at any time during its occupation.

A striking feature of Cille Pheadair (and Bornais) is the sequence of house construction. Houses were built, occupied for a short period, abandoned and then rebuilt. The rebuilt house was carefully positioned to overlap but not completely cover the previous house and, where possible, the later house incorporated part of the structure of the original house. At Cille Pheadair the first house was a small timber structure, oriented north-south, which extended out of the area excavated. This was succeeded by stone revetted houses; the second of these, House 500, was 14 m long and 5 m wide, and again oriented north-south. The internal space of this house was divided in two: a large room dominated by a central long hearth and with access to the outside through a door facing east, and a small room accessible only through a passage at the north end of the first room. This house was eventually replaced by a smaller building, 8.2 m long and up to 4 m wide, oriented east-west. The internal area was undivided and dominated by a large central hearth. The entrance was located on the north side and was towards the east end of the house. The final house was a small building, 6.90 m long and 3.15 m wide, oriented north-south. This was again undivided and dominated by a large central hearth. There was a double entrance in the middle of the north half of the house. Both the later smaller houses were associated with separate ancillary structures and it seems likely that in some sense these represent the extra space that was an integral part of the earlier house. This arrangement of small house and ancillary building is similar to the pattern in mound 3 and the houses are remarkably similar in size. Spatial analysis of the material inside these houses (Smith, Marshall and Parker Pearson 2001) indicates a consistent focus for activity around the end of the long hearth that is furthest from the door to the house and this is similar to the pattern noted at Drimore.

The architectural development noted at Cille Pheadair suggests the architectural characteristics of the house on mound 3 at Bornais gradually evolved from larger Viking structures, such as Drimore and the houses on mound 2, during the twelfth and thirteenth century AD. The final house at Cille Pheadair has a very similar external appearance to the mound 3 house but the internal organisation of space is significantly different. The Cille Pheadair house retains a long hearth similar to those in the earlier houses, with activity focused at the end of the hearth away from the entrance. In the mound 3 house the hearth has become much smaller and the focus of activity has become the area just inside the entrance.

Bornais – N Sharples

The extensive nature of the settlement at Bornais has been discussed in chapter 2 and excavation has established that this is a very long-lived settlement, which spans the period from the Middle Iron Age through the Viking settlement to the fifteenth century AD. A detailed discussion of the overall significance of the settlement is inappropriate in the current publication, and instead this discussion will focus on the wider ramifications of the information from mound 3. It must, however, always be borne in mind that mound 3 is only a component part of the larger settlement. Our understanding of the mound 3 sequence is also strictly limited. The original test trench revealed a long sequence of structural activity similar to that present at Cille Pheadair and the other Bornais

Figure 106. A view of the house in trench D during excavation in 1999 from the southwest

Figure 107. A conjectural reconstruction of the house in trench D

mounds but excavation was limited to the examination of a single house (Figure 106) and one of the ancillary structures associated with the occupation of this house.

The house

A conjectural reconstruction of the building excavated on mound 3 is presented in Figure 107. This depicts the building as a turf and timber structure. Turf is a Norse building material of considerable importance in the North Atlantic (Owen forthcoming) and well documented in Scotland in the recent past (Walker, MacGregor and Stark 1996). The thickness of the turf wall at Bornais is indicated by the entrance passage, which extends 1.7 m from the internal wall. Further indirect evidence for the width of the walls comes from comparison with the final house at Cille Pheadair, which was surrounded by a drainage gully (Brennand, Parker Pearson and Smith 1998). The existence of an internal timber structure is suggested by the insubstantial nature of the low wall that defines the interior of the mound 3 house. There was no observable collapse from this wall and it maintained a consistent height of about 0.25 m, which suggests that it never stood any higher and that its prime purpose was to support a timber superstructure.

Comparable standing structures largely composed of turf and timber have been well studied by Ágústsson (1982). He divided the turf and timber houses of Iceland into two principal types: Ridge Beam Houses and Rafter Houses. In the Rafter Houses the principal supports are timber posts along the sides of the house. These timbers support a wall plate into which a tie beam and the roof rafters are jointed. A distinctive feature of the houses illustrated by Ágústsson is the presence of stone pads and stone walls below the timber supports. These features are comparable to the low walls found in trench D. The principal internal features of the Bornais reconstruction are the stone revetment walls, a timber wall plate into which the wall posts have been jointed, a wall plate at roof level into which the roof rafters are set and tie beams linking the rafters. The timber wall plate running along the stone revetment wall is a feature that is not strictly necessary (and it is not visible in the Ágústsson examples). It has been added because the revetment walls were made from small stones and seem a bit fragile to support a major structural timber. The rafters of the roof support laths and the roof is first covered by thin turves, before being thatched. The thatch is held in place by ropes weighted with stones. This reconstruction is based on examples of recent thatching described by Walker, McGregor and Stark (1996).

In the illustration a considerable amount of timber has been used to line the interior and this may be misleading particularly as on South Uist timber would have been a scarce resource that had to be imported. It would be possible to drastically reduce the amount of timber used. The wall planking is not structural and could be removed either to reveal the interior of the turf walls or to be replaced by wattle or textiles. It would also be possible to replace the thatched roof with turf, but the importance of cereal cultivation (see above) suggests that straw would have been available for thatch. Reeds are also fairly plentiful in the shallow lochs that dominate the west side of South Uist.

The most important feature of the occupation of the house is the location of the hearth in the centre of the northern half of the interior, opposite the east-facing entrance (Figure 108). This hearth was a kerbed rectangular box filled with ashes and contrasts with the earlier hearths found on mound 2 and throughout the sequence at Cille Pheadair, which are long and do not have a kerb. This clearly represents a marked change in the organisation of activity inside the house and creates a feature found in later houses up to the early twentieth century.

The earliest occupation, floor 1, has some very distinctive patterns of refuse deposition/accumulation (Figure 109). The principal concentrations of material are found to the north of the hearth, on the east side, between the hearth and the entrance, and in the area to the south of the entrance. The concentration to the north of the hearth has large quantities of pottery, including platters and several bases, as well as limpets and winkles. There are reasonable quantities of mammal bone but low quantities of fish bone. Burnt organic material and slag have high densities but charcoal, burnt bone and carbonised plant remains have low densities. The northern corners of the building are areas with consistently low densities of material. The area of high densities on the east side of the house is slightly different to the area north of the hearth. Immediately east of the hearth, samples are rich in bone, shellfish, charcoal, burnt organic material and, to a lesser extent, burnt bone, cereals and fish bone but they only have low densities of pot. Magnetic susceptibility readings are also high in this area. These concentrations decline towards the doorway. As one moves south along the east wall there is a gap before the next concentration of material. This is characterised by high densities of bones, charcoal, winkles and limpets with most of the other categories well represented. These concentrations all tail off to the south except for slag, which has high densities at the very southern limits of the floor on the east side.

The areas on the west and south sides of the hearth are quite different, with much lower densities of material. The whole of the west side of the house is characterised by low levels of magnetic susceptibility, phosphorus and nitrogen and finds of pottery. The densities of charcoal, flax, barley and big fish bones are high close to the hearth and there were also moderate levels of bone, shellfish, slag and burnt organic material across the area. The area to the south of the hearth has low densities of almost every category except fish bones and large fragments of mammal bones. An important feature of the central part of the house is the presence of samples with very high densities of flax and barley. These samples coincide with high magnetic susceptibility readings but most finds categories have low or moderate densities in this area, though small fragments of unburnt bone are concentrated in the area immediately to the east of this concentration, indicating a possible bone-working area. The concentration of crop remains coincides with the ash-filled feature cut from later layers and it is possible that this later intrusion of hearth fills has inadvertently been excavated as part of this layer. There was no floor layer noted along the south end of the building and, though it is impossible to be certain, it may be that this

Figure 108. A view of the house during excavation with the half sectioned hearth in the foreground, from the north

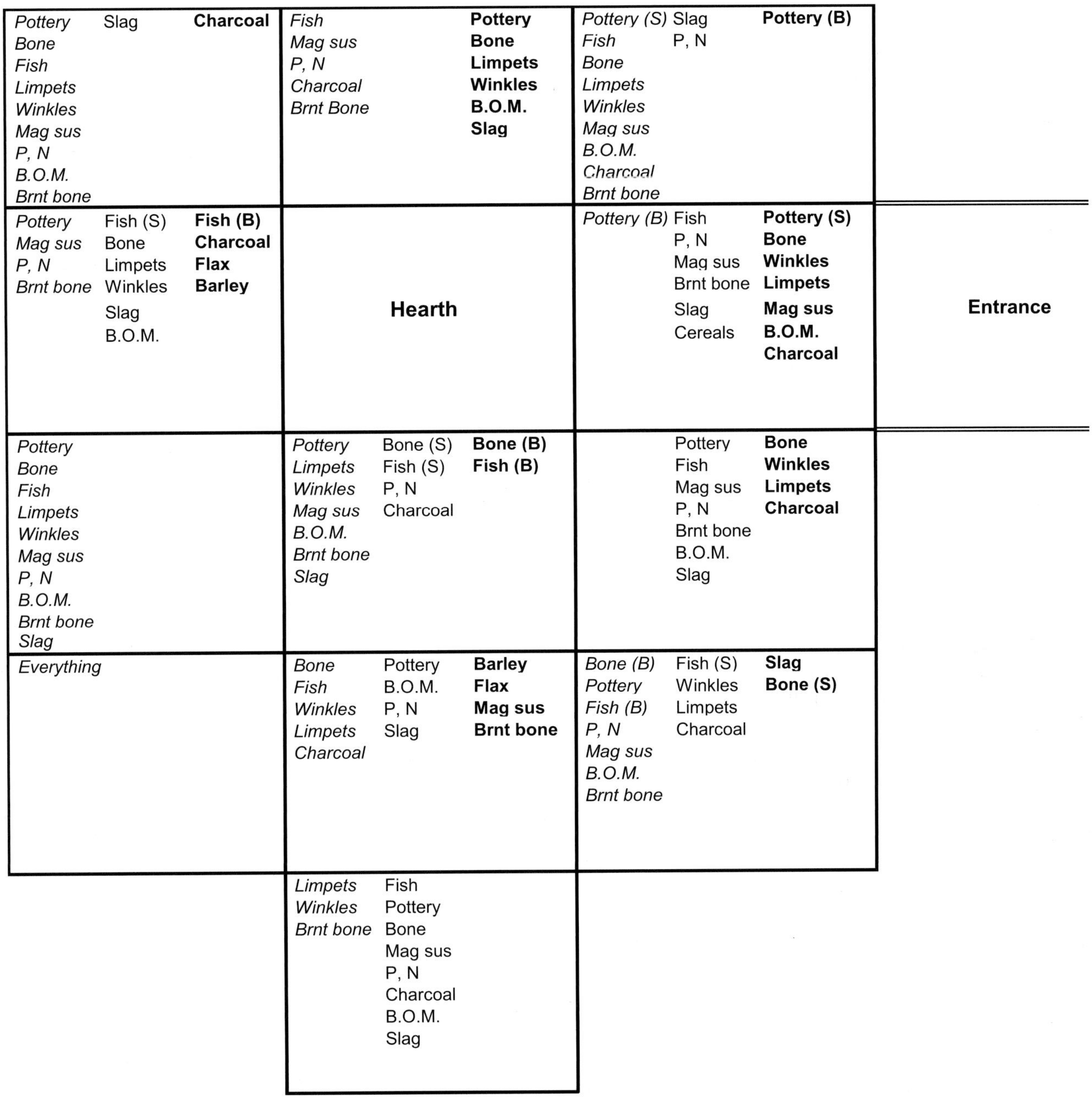

Figure 109. House floor 1: A summary of the distributions presented in chapter 4. Below average quantities are listed in italics, above average quantities are in bold

indicates the position of beds. It is possible that the occupants had quite well-built timber beds in the fourteenth century and that these would have restricted the accumulation of a floor layer.

The high densities of material from around the hearth suggest that this was the focus for activity within the house. The most likely source for most of the material present in the floor appears to be from the consumption of food and the cooking of food, but other activities, such as bone tool-making, might also have created debris. The generally high densities of material and, in particular, charcoal, burnt organic material and, to a lesser extent, slag on the east side of the hearth, may indicate that this was where meals were cooked. Food consumption could have taken place all around the hearth but, if this was the case, then it would appear that the occupants were consuming different foodstuffs. The principal location was to the north of the hearth where bone and shellfish were associated with pottery, which may indicate the status of the position. The position to the west of the hearth had few animal bones but quite large quantities of fish bones and flax and barley. The fish bones might

Mag sus *P, N* *Slag* Pottery (S) Bone (S) Winkles Brnt bone **Pottery (B)** **Bone (B)** **Fish** **Limpets** **Charcoal** **B.O.M.**	*Pottery* *Fish* *Limpets* *Winkles* *Charcoal* *B.O.M.* *Slag* Bone Mag sus Cereals Brnt bone **N, P**	*Slag* Bone (S) Limpets Winkles P, N Mag sus Charcoal B.O.M. **Pottery** **Bone (B)** **Fish** **Cereals** **Brnt bone**	
Mag sus *Slag* P, N Bone (B) **Flax** **Barley** **Pottery** **Bone (B)** **Fish** **Limpets** **Winkles** **Charcoal** **B.O.M.** **Brnt bone**	**Hearth**	*Slag* *Limpets* P, N Mag sus Fish (S) Winkles Cereals Brnt bone **Pottery** **Bone** **Fish (B)** **Charcoal** **B.O.M.**	**Entrance**
P, N *Charcoal* *B.O.M.* *Slag* Mag sus Pottery Fish Limpets **Bone (B)** **Barley** **Winkles** **Brnt bone**	*Pottery* *Bone (B)* *Fish (S)* *Limpets* *Winkles* *B.O.M.* *Brnt bone* *Slag* Bone (S) Fish (B) **Mag sus** **P, N** **Charcoal** **Cereals** **Weeds**	*Pottery* *Mag sus* Bone Winkles Limpets P Cereals Brnt bone B.O.M. **Fish** **N** **Charcoal**	
	Charcoal *Slag* Bone Brnt bone P, N Mag sus **Pottery** **Fish** **Winkles** **Limpets** **B.O.M.** **Barley**		
Winkles *Limpets* *Mag sus* Pottery Bone Fish (S) **Charcoal** **B.O.M.** **Brnt bone** **Slag** *Fish (b)*	*Bone* *Fish* *Winkles* *Brnt bone* Pottery Limpets Barley B.O.M. **Slag** **Weeds** **Charcoal**		

Figure 110. House floor 2: A summary of the distributions presented in chapter 4. Below average quantities are listed in italics, above average quantities are in bold

represent food processing rather than consumption. The position to the south of the hearth was restricted to bones of fish and mammals. A simplistic gendered interpretation of this pattern would be that the male head of the household was seated at the north side of the hearth with his wife on his left-hand side preparing the meals, a dependent adult (female?) was located on the right-hand side and a younger (male) member of the household sat opposite him.

The understanding of floor 2 is impeded by the removal of an unsampled strip across the centre of the house and the rabbit disturbance in the southeast corner. The pattern, however, is clearly different to that visible in floor 1 (Figure 110). The distribution around the hearth can be analysed in detail and the samples from the south provide an interesting contrast with these results.

In the north half of the house the principal concentrations of high density samples occur to the west of the hearth and to a lesser extent to the east of the hearth. The northwest corner of the house has some of the highest densities of material found on this floor. The only category of material to have lower than average results was slag and this is surprisingly absent from the area around the hearth. The levels of magnetic susceptibility and, marginally, of phosphorus and nitrogen are also quite low. Fish bone and limpets are particularly high in this corner. These high densities continue down the west side of the house where bone, fish bone, charcoal, burnt bone and burnt organic material have particularly high densities. Barley is also well represented in this area and one of the samples produced an unusually high concentration of flax. The magnetic susceptibility, phosphorus and nitrogen remain quite low. Numbers gradually decline to the south and charcoal and burnt organic material are particularly low whereas winkles and small fragments of burnt and unburnt bones remain high.

The principal concentration on the east side of the building is in the northeast corner. Most categories of material in this area have high densities. As one moves down the east side of the house the range of samples with high densities of material begins to drop. Between the entrance and the hearth, charcoal, burnt organic material, pottery, bone and big fish bones have above average densities. Limpets and to a lesser extent winkles have below average densities. South of the entrance densities are lower, though not low, with the exception of one sample next to the house wall, which produced high densities of fish bone, charcoal and burnt organic material.

The areas to the north and south of the hearth have low densities of most material and this is particularly true of the area to the south of the hearth where there is quite a large area with some of the lowest densities from this floor. The only categories to have average, or above average, densities from this area are charcoal and carbonised plant remains. This area produced some of the highest densities of flax from this floor. The area of low density to the north of the hearth is much more restricted but provides a significant gap between the high densities in the two corners. The only sample to have a high density, of small bone fragments, was located adjacent to the hearth and may indicate bone working at this location.

The south end of the structure has high densities of many categories of material. In the centre of the house the pottery and fish bone, winkles and limpets have particularly high densities and phosphorus, nitrogen and to a lesser extent magnetic susceptibility are enhanced. These densities tend to decline towards the wall except for cereals and wild seeds, which increase. In the southwest corner there are some very high densities of charcoal, burnt bone, slag and burnt organic material and this is the only area of the floor with high densities of slag. Small fish bones are also present in reasonable quantities but pot and bone are only average and shellfish have quite low densities.

An important feature of the second floor layer is its marked contrast with the primary floor. The west side of the house appears to have been the focus for food preparation whereas the area to the north of the hearth shows very little evidence of deposition. The northeast corner is also very rich in most materials and levels remain reasonably high along the east side. The area to the south of the hearth has generally very low densities and this is comparable to the pattern of floor 1. Many of the samples with high densities come from the edge of the floor against the walls and it is possible this indicates the systematic cleaning of this floor, particularly around the hearth and in the centre of the building. The south end of the floor has surprisingly high densities of material and it is possible that this represents the deliberate redeposition of material from around the hearth to create a floor in this area.

A narrative interpretation of the transformation of the patterns between floor 1 and 2 can be suggested. If we can accept the very simplistic gendered interpretation for floor 1, then the striking absence of material on the north side of the hearth in floor 2 may represent the death of the male head of the household. The two females located on either side of the hearth continue to occupy the house and the shift in emphasis from the east to the west may indicate the growing importance of the younger female as the original female head of the household grows old. The absence of any evidence of food consumption to the south of the hearth indicates the departure of the dependent male.

The kiln/barn

The survey and the excavation of mound 3 suggest that three ancillary structures existed to the south of the excavated house. It was only possible to excavate one of these structures. This proved to be a very distinctive building, probably a barn with an attached corn-drying kiln. The principal features of the building are illustrated in the reconstruction drawing (Figure 111). The roofed

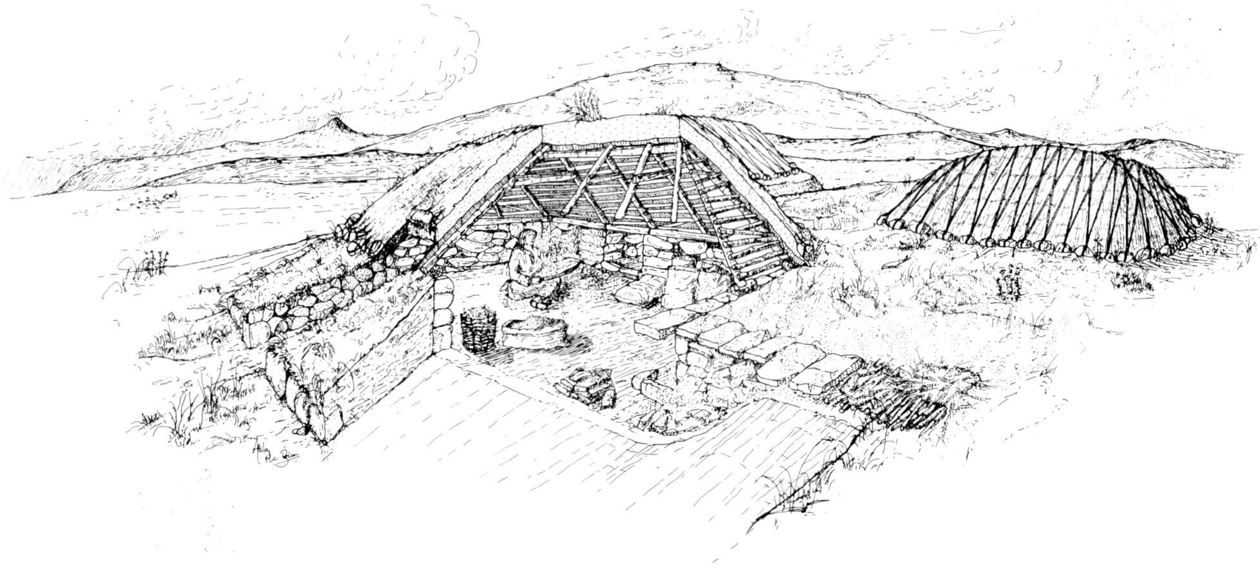

Figure 111. A conjectural reconstruction of the kiln/barn in trench F

part of the building is roughly rectangular, 3.8 m by 4.6 m, with the kiln extending below the south wall and lying well outside the roofed area. The entrance faced west and opposite it there was a winnowing hole. This structure was partially subterranean with the eaves resting on the ground surface on the east side, and on a low wall on the west side. Two phases of kiln can be recognised; though the first phase is relatively unexplored it appears to be a circular bowl with a relatively short passage. The second phase has a long passage and quite a small L-shaped bowl.

These structural phases may correspond to the two floors found inside the roofed part of the structure. Soil micromorphology clearly indicates that the lower floor was created during the use of the barn and comprised material dropped during the occupation of the building and by the raking out and dispersal of ash produced by a fire positioned in the entrance to the kiln. Unlike the house floors the kiln/barn floors produced negligible quantities of artefacts, pottery and mammal or fish bones. Instead they produced large quantities of carbonised plant remains and other debris from the kiln fire. This debris was concentrated along the west wall between the flue and the entrance. The small quantities of bone, pot and shellfish were, in contrast, scattered across the interior and suggest that activity inside the building included some food consumption. The fish bone assemblage was interesting as it included herring heads and there is a possibility that these indicate processing and smoking of herring inside this building. The lower floor also produced relatively large quantities of coprolite and this suggests that the structure was used as a kennel or that it was accessible to dogs. If we are correct in assuming that grain was stored as well as processed in the building then it seems very unlikely that the structure was open. A more plausible interpretation is that dogs were kept in the structure to provide security from theft and control of vermin. The material from the upper floor is much more reduced and patterns were less obviously focused, suggesting the building was less frequently used.

Late Norse and Medieval corn drying-kilns are found at Jarlshof, Shetland (Hamilton 1956, 192, fig. 86) and in a slightly earlier context at Beachview, Birsay, Orkney (Morris 1996, illus. 86, 87). Both of these kilns exhibit features that are characteristic of kilns in the Northern Isles but are quite different to the example exposed at Bornais. They are situated inside the corner of a substantial building and are circular. It is assumed that they had dome-shaped corbelled roofs similar to the late nineteenth and early twentieth century examples (Fenton 1978, 375–387) still surviving on the islands. The nineteenth and twentieth century corn-drying kilns on South Uist and Barra are similar to the Bornais kiln but very different from the Orcadian examples. Several of these have now been excavated (Branigan and Foster 1995, fig. 48; Symonds 1997; H. Smith pers. comm.) and Smith (1994) has examined their use in recent times. These kilns are characteristically placed in one half of a rectangular building and are surrounded by a built-up platform. The flue entered the kiln at ground level from the edge of the platform and access to the bowl was from the surface of the platform. The principal difference between the recent structures and the structure found at Bornais is that access to the bowl of the Bornais structure was from outside the building.

Plants – H Smith

The analysis of the Bornais plant material enabled an investigation to be made that was two-fold. First, it provided information relating to the activities away from the site, focusing on the collection and cultivation of plants in the landscape surrounding the site. Second, it enabled a detailed study of the activities related to plant use around the settlement itself, following the movement and distribution and final disposal of the materials in and outside the different buildings. The present limitations to interpretations of the assemblage are in the preservation of the material and the level of identification that is possible. Statistical analysis of the Bornais assemblage has highlighted associations of weed taxa and crops.

Plant remains have been recovered from other Norse settlement sites in the Western Isles, namely Barvas (Dickson 1981), The Udal (unavailable) and Cille Pheadair (Ballantyne 1999; Hastie 1998; Smith and Boardman forthcoming). Hulled six-rowed barley was the dominant cereal crop at both Bornais and Cille Pheadair, as it was in the Iron Age. However, it occurs in much higher densities in the Norse period. Alongside this, there is an increase in oat (*Avena sativa*) and rye (*Secale cereale*) (Smith and Mulville 2004). The expansion in oat cultivation in the Norse period at Bornais mirrors a trend seen at other sites in Scotland for this period (Dickson and Dickson 2000). Rye is present at both Bornais and Cille Pheadair, and represents the first recorded occurrence of this cereal as a deliberately cultivated crop on the Uists (there is one possible rye grain from the Iron Age settlement at Dun Vulan; Smith in Parker Pearson and Sharples 1999). Similarly, rye is first recorded in the Northern Isles at the Norse site of Westness, on Rousay, Orkney (Dickson and Dickson 2000). Rye is tolerant of poor and especially dry soils, and is well suited to cultivation on the drier areas of the machair. This would have enabled an expansion onto ground less suitable for the cultivation of barley.

Flax (*Linum* sp.) appears for the first time in the Western Isles in the Norse period, where it is recorded at both Bornais and Cille Pheadair in large numbers and at Barvas, Lewis (Dickson 1981). In the Northern Isles, flax seeds were found at the pre-Norse sites of Howe, Orkney (Dickson in Ballin Smith 1994, 132) and Scalloway, Shetland (Holden and Boardman in Sharples 1998, 99) but it only occurs on a regular basis on Norse sites (Dickson and Dickson 2000, Bond and Hunter 1987) and this is likely to be when it was first cultivated as a crop (Dickson and Dickson 2000). Flax is a valuable crop providing fibres and seeds rich in oil (Dickson and Dickson 2000). The preparation of flax fibres for weaving is complex and it should not be assumed that the presence of flax seeds represents the cultivation of the crop primarily for fibres (Bond and Hunter 1987). Even the presence of implements associated with the processing of flax fibres is not unequivocal evidence, because these could also be used for combing and spinning wool (Dickson and Dickson 2000). Flax is a valuable oil plant (Linseed contains 35–40% oil). There are various methods for the extraction of the oil, including pressing and boiling, and these may often result in the clumping together of the sticky, oily seeds (as found at a Norse site in Limerick; Dickson 2000). It has been suggested that seeds found around hearths represent domestic use, whereas seeds dropped from stems hung up to dry after the retting process, are likely to be more widely distributed (Dickson and Dickson 2000). The seeds found at Bornais do not show signs of being pressed and were concentrated on the house floor, near the hearth.

Flax is not tolerant of frost or heavy rain, nor of overly heavy or light soils. High rainfall aside, flax is well suited to cultivation in the Hebrides, where the machair provides the free-draining soil conditions it demands, although fertility would have to be maintained and competition from weeds minimised (Bond and Hunter 1987; Dickson 2000). Records of planting and harvesting dates for Shetland (sown early May, pulled mid August) indicate that flax has a relatively short growing season (Dickson and Dickson 2000). On the Hebrides, rye and oats were sown at the beginning of April and barley in the latter half of May, with reaping beginning about the 15th of August (Walker 1764). If the planting of flax was equally late on the Hebrides, it would mean that crop sowing was spread over a long period in the spring and early summer.

The increase in cereal cultivation, the increasing importance of oat and rye, and the appearance of flax is demonstrated at both Bornais and Cille Pheadair. Interestingly, at Bornais these changes in cultivation are associated with the first direct evidence of a structure involved with crop-processing – a barn with an in-built kiln. This would support suggestions of intensification in arable cultivation, as indicated by the increased quantity of barley and oat remains found at this site. The preferences of rye and flax for free-draining soils, together with weed seeds such as gromwell (*Buglossoides* sp.), with preferences for lighter sandy soils, could signify an expansion in arable production onto areas of sandy machair (perhaps used as an outfield). At Pool in Orkney, a similar expansion onto poorer sandy areas is also seen in the Norse period (Bond 1998) although this is in association with bristle oat rather than flax and rye. The weed floras at Bornais also contain many common arable weeds such as goosefoots (*Chenopodium* sp.), knotgrasses (Polygonaceae), dock (*Rumex*), buttercups (*Ranunculus*), and members of the pink family (Caryophyllacea), that generally reflect damp ground. These might have grown alongside the arable crops or have been brought to the site when grasses and sedges were collected. Grass and sedge seeds are common at Bornais, as they are at Cille Pheadair and earlier sites. Heather and crowberry indicate collection from heathland areas. Peat was collected from the heathland areas for fuel and this may explain the presence of some wild plants on the site (for example grasses, sedges, buttercups etc).

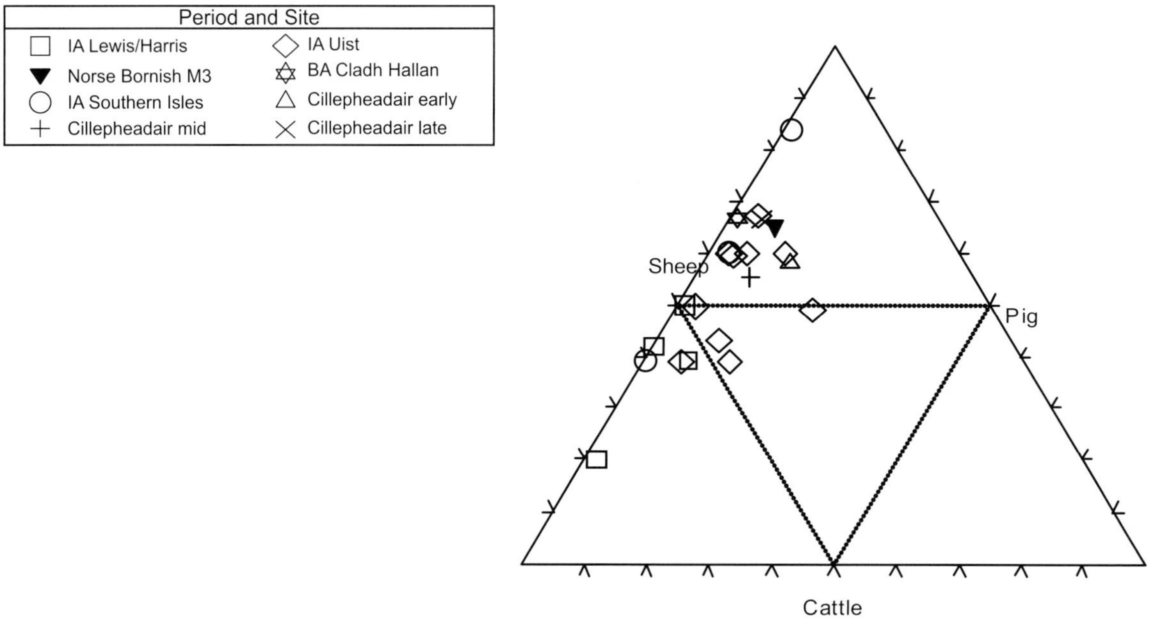

Figure 112. A comparison of the principal species found on settlements in the Western Isles

Table 86. A comparison of the principal animal species present at relevant Uist settlements (NISP)

	Sheep	Cattle	Pig
Bornais Late Iron Age	49	45	6
Udal (IXc-X)	70	27	3
Udal (VII-IX)	66	31	3
Mound 3 Trench D	55	38	1
Mound 3 Trench F	63	29	1
Cille Pheadair	56	34	10

Animals – J Mulville

The small assemblage of bones from mound 3 demonstrates a reliance on farming and fishing, supplemented to some extent by the occasional use of wild resources. Farming was more focused on meat production than in the earlier Iron Age, with a lesser emphasis on milk production. This may be a reflection of an improved ability to over-winter animals. There is little evidence for the use of wild animals, land or marine, as a food source – although there is a small amount of red deer and cetacean bone present.

Bone assemblages have been recovered from Bostadh (Thoms pers. comm.), The Udal (Serjeantson 1984), Rosinish (Serjeantson n.d.) and Cille Pheadair (Lloyd 1999; Ward 1999; Kaplan 1999) (Table 86). There is an increase in the range of domestic species in the Norse period, with goat (*Capra hircus*) appearing at Cille Pheadair. Figure 112 shows the relative abundance of domestic species at a number of other Hebridean sites.

Compared to the Late Iron Age at Bornais mound 1, the significance of sheep increased in the Norse assemblages with a corresponding decrease in the amount of cattle. Bornais and Cille Pheadair both have similar quantities of domestic species; sheep make up over one half of the identified assemblage with cattle accounting for about one third. There is also intrasite variation: on mound 3 there are more sheep recovered from the kiln/barn compared to the house. Pigs are always present in smaller proportions and their abundance varies between the sites. All South Uist Norse sites have a smaller proportion of pig than is found at the Middle Iron Age settlements. The situation on North Uist, at The Udal, is slightly different with an assemblage containing a higher proportion of sheep in both the Viking (IXc-X) and Medieval (VII-IX) phases than found on the South Uist sites.

Although there are similarities between the Iron Age and Norse sites on South Uist in terms of the relative abundance of species there are differences in the age of slaughter for cattle, but not for sheep. In prehistory the majority of the cattle died very young, whilst at the Norse sites they tended to live longer (Figure 113). This difference in age affects the contribution sheep and cattle made to the diet. An adult cow would have provided about 400 kg of meat, about 13 times that of an adult sheep at 30 kg (Vigne 1992); on the other hand, a neonatal calf would have only produced a similar amount to an adult sheep. Thus, in the Iron Age, the diet was probably made up of similar amounts of young beef and mutton, whilst in the Norse period beef would have made a greater contribution, owing to the larger carcass size of adult cattle, even though the numbers of sheep increased.

The high number of cattle neonates has been linked to milk production in prehistory (Mulville, Bond and Craig forthcoming) and the changes visible in the Norse period suggest a shift in the focus of animal production, from milk to meat at Bornais and Cille Pheadair. It is possible that a decline in neonatal mortality was due to other factors such as an improvement in husbandry methods. Calf deaths have been linked to poor fodder provision (McCormick 1998), particularly over winter, but the prehistoric neonatal mortality patterns demonstrate the death of animals only a few weeks old, before any concerns regarding winter fodder would have arisen (Mulville, Bond and Craig forthcoming).

The Norse data demonstrate a peak in slaughter of animals of between 8 and 30 months. If the cattle were born in May/June, the earliest that they could have been slaughtered would be in midwinter – in their first year, a time when animals have lost much of the weight gained from the summer grazing. It is more likely that these animals were killed during the summer/autumn of their second or third years, after regaining any weight lost over the winter. Although an autumnal slaughter of these older animals is probable, at present it is impossible to provide a more detailed estimate on the timing of death.

This change in focus away from the Iron Age strategy of high infant mortality is not a universal Norse phenomenon (Figure 113). At The Udal neonatal mortality remained high. On the Northern Isles there was an increase in calf neonatal mortality in the Norse period, which has been linked to an intensification of dairy production (Bond 2004; Serjeantson and Bond forthcoming).

Sheep show a similar picture of mortality through time (Figure 114); they were most valued for their meat although their wool would have also been utilised. There are differences of emphasis between the Norse sites; animals died earlier at The Udal, and at Bornais where most animals were killed between 1 and 3 years, whereas at Cille Pheadair there were two peaks of slaughter at 1 and 4–6 years. Thus Bornais had a slightly higher rate of mortality in the first couple of years and a lower rate later in life than that seen at Cille Pheadair. The increase in sheep age at Bornais and Cille Pheadair, relative to the Iron Age and The Udal, suggests that more yearlings were being overwintered and that a fleece was being taken off them before they were slaughtered for meat. This provides more evidence of a change in animal management towards retaining larger flocks, and indeed cattle herds, over the winter.

The increase in the quantities of overwintered stock on South Uist demonstrates a distinct change in animal husbandry compared to prehistory. This might have occurred because the Scandinavian Norse preferred meat to milk and were capable of overwintering more stock. As noted above, there is some evidence of changes in land management, with intensified cultivation of oats and barley and an expansion in the area of land worked, and it is possible that this could have increased fodder provision.

Pigs died young at Bornais. Their primary use as meat animals resulted in few animals surviving beyond one year. Pigs mature early and can breed at a young age, removing the need for a large stock of adults. There is little change in their exploitation over time, and no

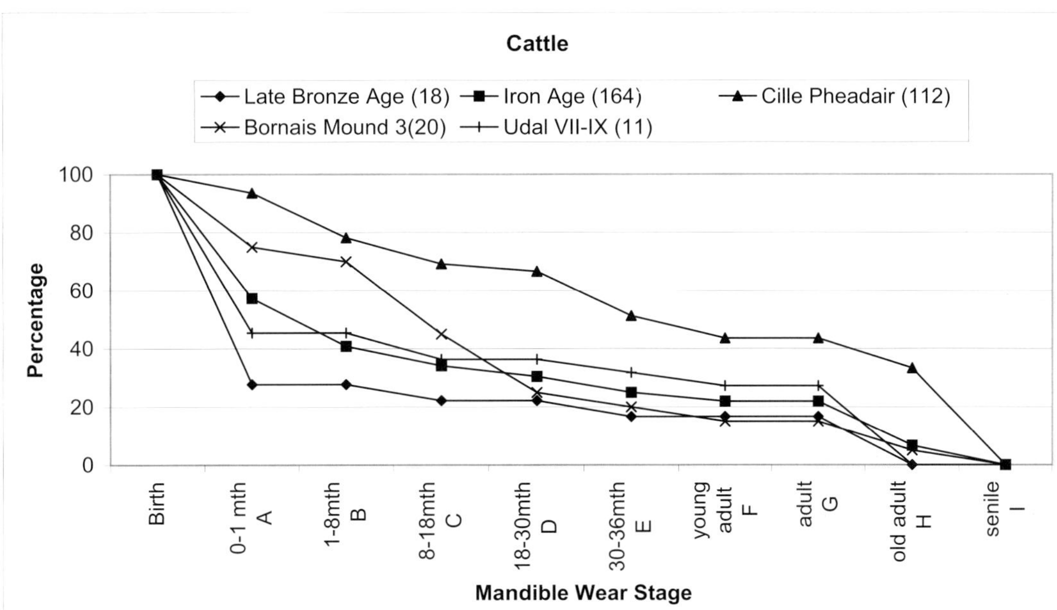

Figure 113. A comparison of the mandible wear stages of cattle from several sites in the Western Isles

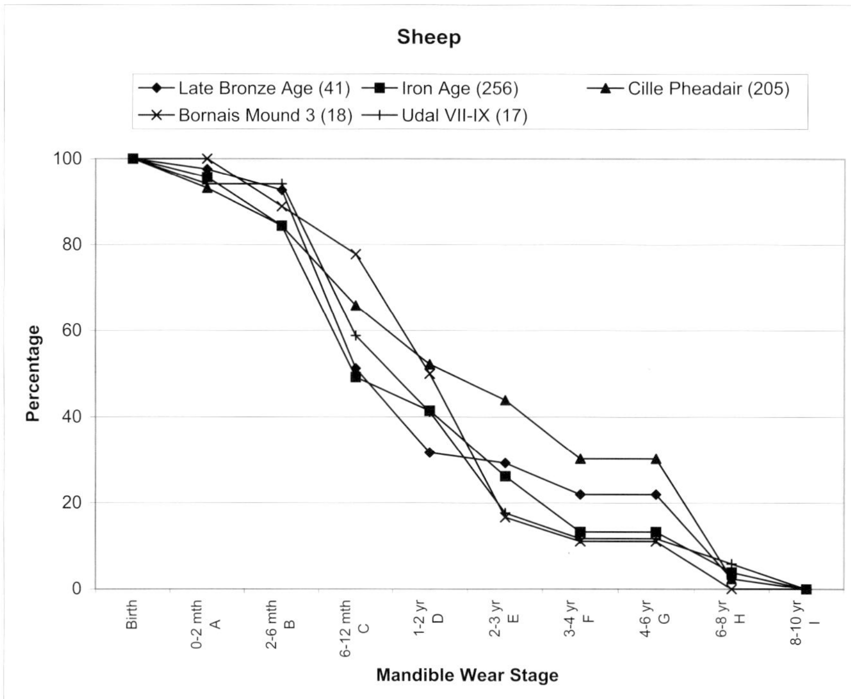

Figure 114. A comparison of the mandible wear stages of sheep from several sites in the Western Isles

evidence of wild boar consumption. Horse is present on a greater proportion of Norse than Iron Age sites, and the presence of very young horses at The Udal and Bornais indicates a breeding population. The first evidence of possible horse consumption on the islands is found at Norse Cille Pheadair, where two bones bear knife marks. Butchery is also recorded at Udal North, although the period to which the remains belong is uncertain. The butchered horse at Cille Pheadair post-dates Pope Gregory III's 732 edict forbidding the consumption of horseflesh, but it is found in the same phase as two pendant crosses.

The 'exotics' recovered from Iron Age Dun Vulan (Mulville in Parker Pearson and Sharples 1999, 265) – badger and pine marten – do not appear in Norse contexts. Red deer, roe deer, hare, otter and seal are still present but in small numbers. The use of cetacea continued with an increase in the range of species represented (Mulville 2002). The proportion of red deer at Bornais mound 3 and Cille Pheadair is low at around 3%, but the other settlement mounds at Bornais have a higher proportion of deer. At The Udal there are fewer deer and the majority of the remains are of antler. Antler is present at Bornais and Cille Pheadair but it does not dominate the assemblages. Bone fusion evidence suggests that a breeding population of red deer was still present on the islands, and neonates are found at Bornais.

Fish – C Ingrem

Although only a small assemblage, the fish remains from The Udal (Serjeantson 1984) show considerable similarities with those from Bornais, with regard to species representation. Herring was common throughout its occupation, and particularly so during the Norse and Medieval phases. In contrast to Bornais, large cod-family fish dominated the assemblage. However, this may reflect differences in sampling strategy as not all the deposits at The Udal were sieved through a fine mesh. At both sites, cod and hake were the most numerous of the large gadoid fish, indicating exploitation of offshore waters and a considerable investment in resources and technology in order to meet fish requirements. Serjeantson (1984) suggests that herring were caught inshore, using poke nets or lines. This implies that the herring from The Udal were caught to the east of the Hebrides. This contrasts with the situation at Bornais where it appears more likely that herring were caught in offshore waters at the edge of the continental shelf. Inshore fishing is evident at both The Udal and Bornais from the presence of whiting, and exploitation of the freshwater lochs is possibly signified by the presence of trout.

At Rosinish, Benbecula (Serjeantson, n.d.), another small assemblage of Norse fish remains was recovered. As with the remains from The Udal, the assemblage is dominated by large gadoids, principally cod, although single fragments of hake and herring were recovered. Again this may be a consequence of the sampling strategy. More recently, the predominant species in an assemblage of fish bones from a Norse midden at Bostadh, Lewis was also found to be herring and the elements recovered belong to specimens of approximately 350 mm in total length (Cerón-Carrasco pers. comm.).

In the Northern Isles, several Norse sites have been excavated which have produced large fish bone assemblages. These have all been dominated by gadoid fish of which high proportions were large or very large. At Freswick Links (Jones 1995) herring was present but only in relatively small numbers and none of the other sites have produced herring in sufficient quantity to merit more than a cursory mention. Many of these sites are middens, which, by their nature, are unlikely to produce the same pattern as a house floor. However, the evidence suggests that the Norse inhabitants of these more northerly islands were targeting large cod-family fish rather than herring to meet their fish requirements.

This difference may be linked with differences in economic practice and the local abundance of different species. There is evidence from several sites, such as Robert's Haven (Barrett 1997) and St. Boniface (Cerón-Carrasco 1998), to indicate that cod-family fish were being processed for storage and later consumption. Barrett (1997) suggests that the Northern Isles might have been involved in the trade of dried fish; if so, this would have provided a stimulus for offshore cod fishing. In contrast, there is no evidence from Bornais to suggest that large cod-family fish were being processed for trade. Ethnohistoric accounts from the Northern Isles (Fenton 1978a) suggest that herring fishing was an offshore activity carried out later in the season than cod fishing. During the winter months, stormy seas would have greatly increased the risk to small open boats and it unlikely that offshore fishing was carried out during the winter from either location. However, Martin (1995) mentions that, in 1906 in the Western Isles, herring were caught in early summer and spring and summer spawning grounds are known to exist nearby. Therefore the unusually large number of herring recovered from Bornais probably reflects their local availability during warmer months of the year when the seas were calm enough to allow boats to venture offshore. The presence of hake at three Norse sites in the Western Isles indicates that these fish were also locally available at this time.

A number of Iron Age sites have now been explored in the southern isles and these provide a good indication of the nature of pre-Norse fishing in the islands. A significant amount of fish bone was recovered from an Iron Age site on Pabbay, and small amounts from Sandray and Mingulay, all small islands to the south of Barra (Ingrem in Branigan and Foster 2000). The assemblages were dominated by young saithe and other inshore species such as red sea bream *(Pagellus bogaraveo)* and ballan wrasse. A similar picture is seen at Iron Age sites on North Uist such as Sollas (Finlay 1991), Hornish Point and Baleshare (Cerón-Carrasco 1994). The most important site is Dun Vulan where a significant quantity of fish remains were recovered using the same sampling procedure as that used at Bornais (Cerón-Carrasco 1999). This was a Middle Iron Age broch and Late Iron Age settlement, only 1.8 km from Bornais, which is located on the shore of a sheltered anchorage on the Ardvule peninsula (Figure 3). The fish remains were dominated by gadoid species, in particular young saithe, but large gadoids such as cod and hake were also present and there was no evidence for herring. As with the fish remains from mound 3, a wide range of other species were also recovered. Cerón-Carrasco (1999) suggests that this reflects exploitation of the immediate environment.

The apparent deliberate targeting of young saithe during the Iron Age suggests that inshore fishing, perhaps with the aid of small boats or from craig seats, was the chief means of obtaining fish during this period. The absence of herring at Dun Vulan, which lies in close proximity to Bornais, suggests that these were only available offshore and either that the necessary technology was not available or that these earlier communities were not prepared to risk the perils of deep water. The difference in the species exploited at the two sites suggests that fishing became more intensive in the Norse period with a focus on offshore fishing for herring and large cod-family fish.

At most sites in the Northern Isles (such as Buckquoy [Wheeler 1976], Brough of Birsay [Sellar 1982] and St Boniface [Cerón-Carrasco 1998]) where both Iron Age and Norse deposits have been recovered, fish remains are more abundant in the Norse deposits. As with the evidence from species representation, this suggests that fishing became more intensive over time and that fish played a greater role in the diet. At present, the only other site in the Outer Hebrides for which comparative data is available is Rosinish (Serjeantson n.d.). This also suggests that fish were more important in the diet during the Viking period.

The fish remains from Bornais mound 3 suggest that the Norse inhabitants were practising a unique fishing strategy based on adult herring. This reliance on herring to meet fish requirements is not seen at any of the Iron Age or other Norse sites from either the Western or Northern Isles although a similar picture is hinted at by other Hebridean material, suggesting that it might have been common practice in the Western Isles during the Norse period. The Bornais herring are assumed to have been caught in offshore waters at the edge of the continental shelf, to the west of the Hebrides. Offshore fishing in general requires a considerable investment of time and capital; in addition it involves high risks. Herring fishing is generally carried out at night using drift nets, hence it is likely to have possessed a certain mystique and invoked a sense of camaraderie amongst the participants. Large cod-family fish required a different method of capture involving baited lines but it is possible that they were caught whilst waiting for the appearance of a shoal of herring.

After capture, it appears that herring and the large cod-family fish received different treatment. Herring were probably beheaded prior to cooking and consumption, the heads being disposed of elsewhere either for animal food or manure. In contrast, both whole cod and cod heads were being consumed. The body was probably wind-dried for storage and later consumption when resources were scarce.

Artefacts – A Clarke, P Macdonald, A Smith

The small size of the artefact assemblage from mound 3 makes generalization impossible and detailed comparison with other Norse and Medieval assemblages will only be worthwhile after the publication of the assemblages from the other mounds. Provisional analysis of the large assemblage from mound 2 indicates a rich diversity of most artefact types associated with the large buildings found on this mound.

The bone and stone assemblages produced objects quite typical of Norse settlements in the Northern Isles (Hunter 1986; Morris 1989; 1996; Morris, Batey and Rackham 1995). The iron assemblage is more substantial and broadly comparable with ironwork assemblages recovered from a range of urban and rural Early Medieval and Medieval settlement sites such as Coppergate, York (Ottaway 1992), Late Viking Age and Medieval Waterford, Co. Waterford (Scully 1997), the Early Medieval manor at Goltho, Lincolnshire (Goodall 1987), Hen Domen, Montgomery (Goodall and Goodall 2000; Higham and Rouillard 2000) and Norwich, Norfolk (Margeson 1993).

The only evidence for craft activity or production of artefacts on mound 3 is restricted to the presence of antler off-cuts and a partially produced bone pin. Metal-working is conspicuously absent. The principal focus for craft activity at Bornais appears to have been mound 2A where substantial quantities of antler waste indicate the manufacture of composite combs.

Pottery – A Lane

The Bornais mound 3 assemblage is a small but interesting pottery group, important because it is stratified and fairly well dated. In particular the house floor material provides the first published Hebridean assemblage dated to the fourteenth and fifteenth century. However, because much of the pottery is from floors it is heavily trampled and only a few diameters and profiles can be reconstructed.

The earliest material comes from the pre-house accumulation (DB). The lowest layers here are radiocarbon dated to the later tenth and earlier eleventh century. These have sherds from thick-walled open-mouthed bowls with sagging and flat bases. The lowest layers have no platter sherds, which appear part-way up the sequence. There are no everted rims in the pre-house layers though a finely made everted rim comes from a pit sealed by the first floor of the house (DD). Open-mouthed bowls and everted rims occur in the first floor as well as significant numbers of platter sherds. This assemblage is radiocarbon dated to the late thirteenth to late fourteenth century AD and the presence of similar vessel types in floor 2 can be dated to the fourteenth to fifteenth century AD. The pottery from the kiln area is even more fragmentary and provides little useful information though the rarity of platter in these contexts may be of significance. The absence of decoration in both groups is striking.

The mound 3 assemblage can be compared against the interim statements about The Udal Norse period pottery and unpublished information on pottery from other sites. The absence of platter in the lower layers at Bornais confirms the suggestion by Iain Crawford that these pottery discs are a feature of the later Norse period rather than the initial Viking period (Crawford and Switsur 1977, 131). Analysis of The Udal pottery showed platter sherds (<1%) and everted rims in Crawford's primary Viking level X at The Udal (Lane 1983, 131, 170, 182, 243–250), although platter was a much more significant feature (12%) of his later Norse level IXc (Lane 1983, 187). There were also a significant number of decorated sherds in The Udal Viking/Norse assemblage. This included slashed rims, 'wavy rims' and a few incised and stabbed body sherds (Lane 1983, 250, figs. 20–22). The total absence of these features from Bornais and from Cille Pheadair (Parker Pearson pers. comm.) raises a question about the reliability of The Udal data, which is still unpublished. Either the tradition of decorated ceramics started earlier on North Uist or some of the Viking pottery there is Late Medieval in date. The Bornais evidence, suggesting that platters were still being used in the fourteenth century AD, also undermines the use of platter to identify specifically Viking Age settlement (Sharples and Parker Pearson 1999, 43) since this very distinctive pottery was in use from the tenth or eleventh century to the fourteenth or even fifteenth century if the calibrated radiocarbon dates are to be accepted.

The origin, date range and function of the Hebridean platters remain a matter of considerable importance. Crawford suggested that these thin ceramic discs may be baking plates (Crawford and Switsur 1977, 131). Their size, thin profile and frequent evidence for heat exposure on their lower surfaces make this an attractive proposition. Indeed no alternative function has been suggested.

The only close parallels are the ceramic 'plates' from the fifth to eighth century Anglo-Saxon settlement of Mucking, in Essex (Hamerow 1993, 5–7). Here pottery discs 180–210 mm in diameter and 10–20 mm in thickness are reported with deep finger impressions on the surface and 'heavy grasstempering' (Hamerow 1993, 40, 54–55, e.g. fig. 103, 38.3). Hamerow was unable to find close parallels for these 'plates' and cited The Udal evidence as a chronologically distant parallel (Hamerow 1993, 55). She also suggested that these pottery discs were baking plates, noting sandstone griddles at Vallhagar on Gotland from a Migration period settlement (size 250–300 mm and 10–20 mm thick; Stenberger 1955, 843).

Affinities have been suggested for the Hebridean platters with the steatite bakestones known from sites in Orkney, Shetland and Norway. Steatite bakestones are 300–600 mm in diameter and 5–25 mm thick with grooving tooled into the surfaces (Weber in Crawford and Ballin Smith 1999, 135). These were in use at the Biggings, Shetland, by 1100–1200 and continued in use as late as the seventeenth century (Weber in Crawford and Ballin Smith 1999, 137). They are known from other late Norse sites in Orkney and Shetland. At Oslo they first appear c. 1100 though associated baking implements are known earlier and certainly by the mid-eleventh century (Weber in Crawford and Ballin Smith 1999, 138). These Norwegian and Northern Isles' steatite discs have been firmly associated with the baking of flatbrod – a thin unleavened crisp bread which was a staple food from as early as the Viking period.

The relationship between these bakestones and the sandstone griddles of Vallhagar and similar flagstone roundels from the Northern Isles is uncertain (Weber in Crawford and Ballin Smith 1999, 139). The Mucking evidence suggests that ceramic griddles might have been in use in parts of northern Europe before the Viking Age but have probably not been recognised as such. The Hebridean platters do seem likely to have had a similar function to the Norwegian bakestones and imply an important change in diet and cooking behaviour on the Hebridean sites. Just as Ballin Smith has raised the issue of whether steatite bakestones began in the early Viking Age (Crawford and Ballin Smith 1999, 127) so how early platters start in the Hebrides is an important social and cultural question.

Clearly the closer definition of an early Viking assemblage, which may be recognisable on mound 2 at Bornais, the terminal dates for platter on other sites, and an initial date for the decorated rims and shoulder sherds seen at The Udal, are all necessary if we are to extract the maximum cultural and chronological information from the Hebridean Viking and Norse pottery sequence.

The end of settlement on the machair – N Sharples

Recent fieldwork on South Uist suggests that the occupation of the machair was a relatively constant feature of settlement since the Bronze Age (Sharples, Parker Pearson and Symonds 2004). Initially this occupation appears to have been transitory and unstable but by the beginning of the Iron Age there seems to be a system of long-lived settlements spaced relatively evenly along the machair, and Bornais is one of these settlements. This settlement pattern appears to have been radically reorganised in the Medieval period. Field survey of the machair (Parker Pearson 1996) has demonstrated that the number of settlements post-dating the mid-fifteenth century is minimal. The excavation of Bornais suggests that this settlement was abandoned in the early fifteenth century and excavation at Cille Pheadair suggests that this settlement was abandoned only slightly earlier in the fourteenth century. The new settlements dating to the fifteenth, sixteenth and seventeenth centuries were located on the rock and loch landscapes that lie immediately to the east of the machair plain. Most of the excavations in this area have been concentrated on the eighteenth and nineteenth settlement at Airigh Mhuillin (Symonds 2000) but test excavations at Beinn na mhic Aongheis (Marshall, Mulville and Parker Pearson 1996) have produced pottery of fifteenth to seventeenth century date and indicate the likely location of the descendants of the inhabitants of Bornais. The distribution of these Late Medieval settlements is depicted on the 1805 Bald map and the settlements appear as nucleated clusters quite different to the contemporary dispersed townships.

The settlement disruption appears to have been a major event and can be contrasted with the long period of settlement continuity, which withstood the Viking colonisation of the islands and other major socio-cultural changes. Unfortunately it is difficult to provide a specific interpretation of this event and historical evidence is very poor for the region. It would be convenient to associate this abandonment with the political changes that mark the incorporation of the Hebrides into the Kingdom of Scotland, and a mass exodus of the Norse inhabitants is possible (B. Crawford pers. comm.), but the chronology does not actually fit. The islands were transferred in the middle of the thirteenth century AD some time before the abandonment of the machair in the fourteenth to fifteenth centuries AD. An archaeological interpretation of this disruption is hampered by the lack of excavation of the Late Medieval settlements of the fifteenth and sixteenth centuries. Furthermore, it is unlikely that these settlements will ever provide the high-quality evidence that exists in the machair settlements. Not only is the stratigraphy in the blacklands much compressed but also bone, a very important material for the interpretation of both economy and society, is not preserved in these acidic landscapes.

In his discussion of the abandonment of The Udal that, exceptionally, was abandoned several centuries later than the South Uist sites, Crawford (Selkirk 1996) suggested that this was due to a period of machair instability that was recorded in the earliest Harris estate papers. Machair instability can be caused by particular weather conditions such as a sustained drought followed by high winds and it is possible that similar adverse environmental changes in the fourteenth and fifteenth centuries could have provided a major incentive for movement onto the stable blacklands. These natural conditions could have been exacerbated by the intensification of agriculture noted in the discussion of the crop remains. The cultivation and destabilisation of areas of the machair, which had hitherto been left undisturbed, would have been potentially disastrous. The evidence from mound 3 could partially support a period of increased instability. It is clear that the kiln/barn was completely filled with wind-blown sand soon after it was abandoned. The absence of sand inside the house may be because the turf and timber structure was systematically dismantled and therefore provided nothing to trap the drifting sand. A possible anthropogenic reason for increased instability may have been the expansion of cereal cultivation that followed the uptake of new crop species such as flax and rye. These could be planted on the drier areas of the machair, which are precisely the areas most susceptible to erosion. However, this interpretation cannot stand on its own as the sequence at many of the other sites excavated includes substantial sand blow events which occurred in earlier periods, and yet these did not result in the abandonment of the settlement of the machair plain.

In a previous discussion of this issue (Sharples and Parker Pearson 1999) it was suggested that the abandonment of the machair may be explained by a combination of the economic and political changes that took place after the transfer of the islands to Scotland. The desire to live on the blacklands might have been an expression of the increasing importance of cattle and the upland grazings in the centre of the island. The trade in cattle was an important feature of the later economy of the west coast of Scotland and it is possible that South Uist was involved in this trade. Sheep would also have been located on the upland grazings but current understanding suggests that these would not have provided a commercial wool crop and the bone assemblage suggests that they were important as a source of meat. Since this suggestion was made, the detailed analysis of the animal bone has provided some interesting evidence. There appears to have been a shift from an emphasis on milk production to an emphasis on the consumption of meat, which could be a by-product of a trade in cattle. If this were the case then it will be important to document the increasing importance of meat during the Norse period on mounds 2 and 2A. The significance of herring fishing is also relevant to this argument. If the large quantities of herring bones present in the mound 3 house are a by-product of herring fishing for trade with the towns in Ireland, then it is quite possible that this relationship declined in the fourteenth and fifteenth centuries AD. Political changes meant the Western Isles became increasingly connected to Scotland, whereas Ireland, and Dublin in particular, developed closer connections with England.

This explanation for the settlement shift from the machair to the blacklands assumed that this movement was a matter of choice and that the dislocation of settlement was not part of a wider dislocation of people. There is some evidence to support this assumption. The most important is the continuity in architecture and settlement organisation indicated by the structures exposed on mound 3. The short house and corn-drying kiln are very similar in size and form to structures constructed at the beginning of the twentieth century on South Uist (Smith 1996) though these are mostly constructed in stone. The excavations of mound 3 at Bornais and at Cille Pheadair (Brennand, Parker Pearson and Smith 1998) indicate that house shape and use evolved gradually during the five centuries that followed the Viking colonisation of the islands. The initial longhouse plan sub-divided into a main room and a subsidiary, smaller room by the twelfth century. The hearth is a central feature of the larger room and is long and rectangular, with a concentration of finds indicating cooking and other activities at the end furthest from the door. The principal change in this format, represented by House 500 at Cille Pheadair, is the loss of the small room. This became a separate ancillary structure used for a variety of functions, including cereal processing. The next change was a transformation of the internal arrangements. The long hearths disappeared in the fourteenth century to be replaced by small hearths. These were located close to the entrance indicating a significant change in the focus of activity inside the house. Cille Pheadair was abandoned prior to this final stage of development but Bornais was abandoned after this transformation. It is important to note that, in none of the buildings excavated, has there been any evidence for a substantial internal byre nor have any external free-standing byres been observed. It seems likely that cattle were overwintered in the open, which would be perfectly feasible given the island's relatively mild climate. Many of the eighteenth and nineteenth century houses at Airigh Mhuillin were split into a byre and a living area; these large houses are quite different to the Norse and more recent houses on the island, and it is important to establish why this is the case.

Another feature of the relationship between the machair and the blackland settlement is indicated by the construction of the small structure inside the kiln/barn. Similar structures were also present in the final house at Cille Pheadair, and on Bornais mounds 2 and 2A. The only final house, so far excavated, without such a structure is that on mound 3. The most likely interpretation of these structures is that they were seasonal shelters constructed after the abandonment of the settlement. If we are correct in assuming that the settlement was deliberately abandoned because of a conscious decision to resettle on the adjacent blacklands then it seems likely that the inhabitants of the new settlements would have had direct ancestral links with the occupants of the machair settlements. The construction of shelters in the abandoned houses might therefore have been a deliberate attempt to maintain links with the old settlement. These structures could have had a functional significance, providing shelter for people watching animals grazing on the machair or during ploughing, sowing, weeding and harvesting of the crops planted on the machair. This would explain the evidence for intermittent floors in a structure excavated on mound 2. However, some structures, such as that in the corn-drying kiln in mound 3, have no evidence for occupation and other structures are too small to have been useful shelters. It is possible that these corner structures had a more than practical significance as a place for shelter; perhaps their very construction was sufficient to establish a focus for remembrance and meditation on the relationship between the ancestors who occupied the machair and the displaced people now living on the blacklands.

Conclusion – N Sharples

The discovery and excavation of the settlement of Bornais has, together with the excavations at Cille Pheadair, transformed our understanding of the Norse settlement of the Western Isles. Prior to these excavations the settlements of the region were difficult to understand and it was impossible to relate the region to the much better documented areas of Orkney, Shetland and the Isle of Man. The machair survey indicates that Norse settlements were plentiful and provides important information about the distribution of these settlements on the island of South Uist (Parker Pearson 1996; Sharples and Parker Pearson 1999; Sharples, Parker Pearson and Symonds 2004). The excavation of Bornais has revealed a settlement that was in existence for a long period prior to the Viking colonisation of the Western Isles. Provisional interpretation suggests that it was taken over by a Viking who established himself in a large and typically Norse house on mound 2. The settlement subsequently expanded during the eleventh and twelfth centuries before it was abandoned in the fifteenth century, when the occupants of the machair moved inland to the less archaeologically sensitive areas of the blacklands. The expanded settlement consisted of five principal foci, which appear to be discrete settlement units and the excavation of one of these foci on mound 3 is the subject of this report. Partial excavation of the mound concentrated on a house surrounded by ancillary buildings, one of which, a kiln/barn, was excavated. The excavation produced important evidence for the agricultural economy of the occupants, and detailed analysis of the house floors has provided a considerable amount of information on the organisation of domestic living space.

Appendix 1: Context List and Concordance Summary

Context	Mound	Block	Context type	Same as	Fill of	Filled by	Small finds
201	3	D	Turf and topsoil				
202	3	D	White sand				
203	3	D	Enclosure wall				
204	3	DB	Brown sand	205, 206			1066, 1065, 1226
205	3	DB	Brown sand	204, 206			4745
206	3	DB	Brown sand	204, 205			
207	3	DE	Brown sand	235, 228, 233, 234, 239			4765, 4766
208	3	DB	Brown sand				
209	3	DB	Yellow sand				
210	3	DB	Brown sand				1061, 1225
211	3	DB	Brown sand				1227, 4729a-d
212	3	DD	Floor layer; DD/2 and DD/3				1223, 4702
213	3	DC	Wall				
214	3	DB	Dark grey sand				
215	3	DB	Yellow sand				
216	3	DB	Light grey sand	607			
217	3	DA	House wall				
218	3	DA	Floor layer				
219			Cancelled				
220	3	E	Topsoil				
221	3	E	Yellow sand				
222	3	E	Brown sand				1162
223	3	E	Brown sand				/1162
224	3	E	Brown sand				1161
225	3	E	House floor				
226	3	DB	Orange sand	606			
227	3	DB	Brown sand	232			
228	3	DE	Brown sand	235, 207, 233, 234, 239			1310
229	3	DE	White sand				
230	3	DD	Floor layer DD/3	238, 602, 601, 242, 245, 248			1315, 1323
231	3	DE	Brown sand	236, 233, 234, 239			
232	3	DB	Brown sand	227			1325, 1326
233	3	DE	Brown sand	235, 228, 207, 234, 239, 236, 231			
234	3	DE	Brown sand	235, 228, 207, 233, 239, 236, 231			1346, 1339
235	3	DE	Brown sand	228, 207, 233, 234, 239			
236	3	DE	Brown sand	231, 233, 234, 239			
237	3	DB	Brown sand				1513

238	3	DD	Floor layer DD/3	230, 602, 601, 242, 245, 248			1578, 4695
239	3	DE	Brown sand	235, 228, 207, 233, 234, 236, 231			
240	3	DE	Brown sand				1535
241	3	DE	Rabbit disturbance				
242	3	DD	Floor layer DD/3	238, 230, 602, 601, 245, 248			
243	3	DD	Yellow sand				1361, 1525
244	3	DD	Floor layer DD/2	604, 605, 610			
245	3	DD	Floor layer DD/3	248, 238, 230, 602, 601, 242			1380, 1582
246	3	DD	Hearth layer	603			
247	3	DB	Orange sand				
248	3	DD	Shell layer	245, 238, 230, 602, 601, 242			
249	3	DD	Floor layer DD/3	608			1584
250	3	F	Grey sand				1324, 1373
251	3	E	Red brown compact sand				1260, 1222
252	3	E	Mid brown sand				1530
253	3	E	Cancelled				
254	3	FE	Yellow sand				
255	3	FE	Yellow sand				1492
256	3	FE	Brown sand				
257	3	FE	Dark grey sand				
258	3	FE	Brown sand				
259	3	FC	Wall	266, 261, 267			
260	3	FE	White loose sand	265			
261	3	FC	Wall	266, 259, 267			
262	3	FE	Wall	263			
263	3	FE	Wall	262			
264	3	FE	Wall				
265	3	FE	White sand	260			
266	3	FC	Wall	261, 259, 267			
267	3	E	Cancelled	266, 261, 259			
268	3	FE	Mid brown sand				
269	3	FD	Floor layer	278			
270	3	FD	Floor layer				
271	3	FD	Floor layer				
272	3	FD	Light brown sand	274			
273	3	FD	Mid brown compact sand				
274	3	FD	White sand	272			
275	3	FD	Brown compact sand				1836

276	3	FD	Floor layer				1875, 1853
277	3	FD	Burnt layer	658			
278	3	FD	Floor layer	269			
279	3	F	Turf line				
280	3	F	Top soil				1678, 1665
281	3	FG	Dark brown sand	282			1679
282	3	FG	Compact brown sand	281			
283	3	FF	Charcoal layer				
284	3	FF	Red orange compact sand				
285	3	FG	Brown orange compact sand				
286	3	FG	White sand	297			
287	3	FF	Charcoal feature				
288	3	FE	Brown sand	289			
289	3	FE	White sand	288			
290	3	FC	Brown sand		686		1864
291	3	FC	Pale brown compact sand				
292	3	FD	Dark brown loose sand				
293	3	FD	Dark brown loose sand				
294	3	FC	Dark brown sand				
295	3	FF	Red orange clay				
296	3	FG	Dark brown sand				
297	3	FG	Clean white sand	286			
298	3	FF	Dark brown loose sand				
299	3	FF	Pink orange brown clay				
600	3	D	Grey white sand				1555
601	3	DD	Floor layer DD/3	238, 230, 602, 242, 245, 248			1583
602	3	DD	Floor layer DD/3	238, 230, 601, 242, 245, 248			1580
603	3	DD	Hearth layer	246			
604	3	DD	Floor layer DD/2	244, 605, 610			1428, 1562
605	3	DD	Floor layer DD/2	610, 604, 244			1429, 1509, 1413, 1554
606	3	DB	Orange sand	226			
607	3	DB	Light grey sand	216			1438, 1434
608	3	DD	Floor layer	249			1579
609	3	DD	Hearth layer				
610	3	DD	Floor layer DD/2	605, 604, 244			
611	3	DD	Hearth layer				
612	3	DB	Brown sand				
613	3	DB	Brown sand				

614	3	DD	Floor layer DD/1				1467, 1479, 1481, 1581, 2685, 4694, 4696, 4703, 4767, 4769
615	3	DD	Pit fill				
616	3	DD	Pit fill				
617	3	DD	Pit fill				
650	3	FF	Pale brown sand				
651	3	FF	Orange pink sand				
652	3	FF	Compact red sand				
653	3	FD	Pale brown sand				
654	3	FD	Dark brown sand				
655	3	FC	Grey sand				
656	3	FF	Red brown sand				
657	3	FD	Charcoal				
658	3	FD	Burnt layer	277			
659	3	FF	Dark brown compact sand				
660	3	FF	Red brown ash				
661	3	FG	Light brown sand				4768
662	3	FG	Pink ash				
663	3	FG	White sand				
664	3	FG	Dark brown compact sand				
665	3	FB	Brown sand		684		1887
666	3	FG	Dark brown clay deposit				1858
667	3	FG	Disturbed white sand				
668	3	FG	Red sand	683			
669	3	FB	Red brown compact sand		684		
670	3	FB	Dark brown compact sand		684		
671	3	FG	Pale brown sand				1871
672	3	FG	Brown sand				
673	3	FG	Pink clay deposit				
674	3	FG	Grey loose sand				
675	3	FG	Dark brown compact sand				1972, 1942, 1974, 1958
676	3	FD	Orange clay deposit				
677	3	FD	Compact clay deposit				
678	3	FD	Charcoal feature				
679	3	FB	Red loose sand		684		
680	3	FA	Pale grey sand	685, 688, 682, 689			
681	3	FD	Burnt layer				
682	3	FA	Pale brown sand	685, 680, 688, 689			

683	3	FG	Red layer	668			
684	3	FB	Building cut			670, 669, 679, 665	
685	3	FA	White sand	680, 688, 682, 689			
686	3	FC	Kiln/barn cut			290	
687	3	FD	Floor layer				
688	3	FA	Pale grey sand	685, 680, 682, 689			
689	3	FA	Pale grey sand	685, 680, 688, 682			
690	3	FC	Dark brown sand				
691	3	DD	Yellow clayey sand				
692	3	FC	East arc of walling of early kiln	693			
693	3	FC	West arc of walling of early kiln	692			
694	3	FD	West wall of kiln				
695	3	FD	East wall of kiln				

Appendix 2: Artefact Catalogue – A Clarke, I Dennis, P Macdonald and A Smith

The catalogue entries follow the format as below:
Find no Context Block Sample no Coordinates
Object type and material
Written description. Condition assumed to be good unless otherwise indicated.
Measurements are in millimetres.

WORKED BONE & ANTLER: CATALOGUE

PERSONAL OBJECTS

Combs

1438 607 DB 446.1E 284.5N
Side plate fragment from single-sided comb. Antler.
Tapering side plate fragment, trapezoidal-shaped section, with 2 parallel longitudinal incised lines at mid-rib level, one lightly incised, one more heavily incised, and a third longitudinal line along the lower edge. Diagonal incised lines present in two groups on upper and lower halves of side plate form a chevron pattern. Irregularities in spacing indicate that these are individually hand-cut rather than using a double-bladed saw or similar tool. The side plate has broken across rivet holes at each end, both rivet holes showing iron staining indicating iron rivets were used. Nicks from cutting of teeth are present along lower edge, confined within the lower incised line.
W 27mm H 13-12.6mm Tooth spacing 6 per 10mm

1467 614 DD
Side plate fragment from single-sided comb. Antler.
Tapering side plate fragment, trapezoidal-shaped section, with 2 longitudinal incised lines along the upper and lower edges and the mid-rib point. There are faint incised diagonal lines across the upper half only. One edge has broken across a rivet hole with iron staining, indicating iron rivets were used. Nicks from cutting of teeth are limited to the area within the lower incised line. Condition fairly good but slightly abraded.
W 23mm H 11.3-10.7mm Tooth spacing 6 per 10mm

1061 210 DB 440E 287.5N
Tooth plate from single-sided comb and 1 loose tooth. Antler.
Tooth plate with sloping upper edge and rivet hole with iron staining on one side. Width is complete and tooth plate is unbroken. Five teeth are missing, and the remaining 5 are slightly ridged but not heavily worn. There is a roughly cut perforation in the centre of the solid part. It is possible that this relates to a repair of the comb, although no iron staining is present, so a bone or antler peg might have been used. The degree of splaying visible on the hole indicates cutting with a blade rather than drilling, and is clearly secondary to the manufacture of the comb. It is equally possible that the hole was cut after the parent comb was broken up, once the tooth plate was loose.
W 19mm H 11.5-9.75mm Tooth length (max) 15.5mm Tooth spacing 5 per 10mm

1579 608 DD 5928
Tooth plate from single-sided comb. Antler?
Comb tooth plate, all teeth missing, rivet hole on one side. Upper edge appears to be sloping. Width appears complete. Burnt? – dark grey-brown colour.
W 13mm H 12-8.5mm Tooth spacing 5 per 10mm

Pins

1315 230 DD 445.63E 282.09N
Pin head and shank fragment. Probably cattle-sized long bone.
Pin, roughly shaped four-sided head with some cancellous tissue still present, but high gloss polish overall indicating extensive use. Marks from knife cutting and faceting still visible on shank.
L 44mm Head 5 by 5.5mm

1380 245 DD 444.92E 288.26N
Pin/point shank and point frag. Pig fibula?
Pin or point fragment, with flattened cross section and some slight surface glossing but no great polish or wear. Fairly fine point.
L 73mm max Dia 7 by 8.5mm

1260 251 FF
Pin shank fragment. Material cannot be distiguished.
Very small fragment of pin shank, with some remnants of gloss polish although surface abraded.
L 11mm Dia 5 by 5.3mm

TOOLS

Clamp

1221 Unstratified
Clamp fragment. Whale bone.
One end of one half of a whale bone clamp, broken across the iron pivot hole, which is heavily stained with iron. The pivot hole has been cut roughly with a large blade.
L 52mm W min 10.5mm max 21mm Th max 8.5mm

Point

1578 238 DD 5733
Fine point fragment. Probably sheep-sized long bone.
Fine point fragment, tapering from flattened shaft area to very fine point, with some slight glossing and striations visible on flat surface.
L 35mm MW 4.7mm Th 2mm

Handles?
1066 204 DB
Hollowed sheep metapodial.
Sheep metapodial with both ends cut and smoothed. Surface slightly polished but no other indications of working marks or use. A segment has broken off one end, which would be a similar shape to find 1065, but it is not the same piece.
L 79mm Dia 10 by 13mm

1065 204 DB
Fragment of hollowed sheep metapodial.
Fragment of cut long bone, with smoothed cut end and high gloss polish. May be from similar object to find 1066, but does not fit.
L 28mm Dia 8mm

MANUFACTURING EVIDENCE

Antler Working Waste
1429 605 DD 443.46E 287.67N
Discard. Antler tine.
Antler tine, roughly chopped at beam end and surface removed on one side, possibly to test thickness of solid material. End smoothed, probably during deer's lifetime. Probably discarded as too thin and curved to provide useful raw material.
L 165 mm Dia max 18 by 20mm

1530 252 FF
Discard. Antler tine tip.
Antler tine tip, has been pared down on two sides and there are indications that strips of solid material had been removed from the entire tine before the tine tip was cut off and discarded. Base cut straight across. Entire tip is smooth, probably from wear during deer's lifetime.
L 45mm max Dia 13 by 14mm

1972 675 FG 431.71E 260.1N
Discard. Antler tine.
Antler tine, only signs of working are sawing marks on beam end. Technique of cutting and snapping used. Tip worn smooth during deer's lifetime. Tine is fairly thin and twisted, so probably discarded as no useful solid material could be got from it.
L 89mm Dia at beam end 22 by 19mm

1373 250 F 443.95E 266.16N
Discard. Antler tine tip.
Antler tine tip, from tine which has had strip of solid material removed before tine tip broken off and discarded. Abraded and polished, possibly from post-depositional sand/wind erosion, also some root damage on surface.
L 48mm MDia 14 by 8mm

Pin roughout
1361 243 DD 444.75E 281.45N
Pin roughout, cattle-sized long bone.
Length of cattle-sized long bone with numerous cut marks and small chatter marks from knife whittling. Interior of long bone visible at one end, and possibly discarded because of the extent of cancellous tissue at that end.
L 100mm MDia 10 by 8mm

COARSE STONE

Tools
1324 250 F 439.55E 265.60N
Whetstone. Red fine-grained micaceous sandstone.
Fragment, tip surviving. Four faces worn to quadrilateral cross-section. All faces are worn very smooth and three have a glossy finish.
ML -; MW 11mm; MTh 10mm

1434 607 DB 446.64E 284.28N
Whetstone. Steatite.
Four faces worn to a quadrilateral cross-section. Two faces are worn smooth to a concave profile and glossy finish. The other two opposite faces are rougher with visible longtitudinal striations. Square-ended.
ML 52mm; MW 15mm; MTh 13mm

1525 243 DD
Faceted cobble. Oval cobble of ?amphibolite.
Single, small, pecked facets on either end. Two patches of pecking on one side.
ML 80mm; MW 35mm; MTh 27mm

1346 234 DE 442.2E 286.54N
Spindle whorl. Steatite.
Fragment, half surviving. Ground to shape. Perforation has been bored from both faces and forms an hour-glass cross-section. Truncated cone shape.
Dia 23mm; MTh 13mm; dia hole 6mm

Vessels
1509 605 DD
1513 237 DB
Bowl fragment. Steatite.
Two small fragments conjoin to form a small piece of a probable bowl. The interior is worn very smooth and the exterior is slightly rougher.
ML -; MW -; MTh 18mm

METAL

Buckle
1339 234 DE 442.85E 288.06N
Oval-shaped buckle with folded rectangular plate, copper alloy. The oval-shaped frame has a narrowed, off-set bar and a decorative, ornate outer edge. This decorative moulding consists of a notched lip set between two narrow ribs. The folded plate is recessed for the frame and contains a slot terminating in a circular perforation which accommodated the missing pin. The plate was secured to a leather strap by four copper alloy rivets; mineralised traces of the leather survive between the two faces of the plate. Three sides of the front face of the plate are decorated with a double incised line flanked on their outer edges by punched, opposed shallow triangular motifs. This skeumorphic decoration deliberately imitates the forms of stitching associated with leatherwork.
L of frame 22mm, W of frame 34mm, Th of frame 4mm, L of plate 25mm, MW of plate 21.5mm.

Pins
1739 us F 441.39E 268.56N
Dress pin, copper alloy
A well-preserved Hiberno-Norse club-headed dress pin. The upper surface of head is decorated with radiating lines, underside undecorated. A pronounced collar separates the head and shank. The slightly crooked, octagonal-sectioned, shank expands slightly in the middle before tapering to a fine point. All 8 faces of the shank are decorated with alternate lines of punched triangles and punched chevrons.
L 102mm, head W 7.8mm, shank MW 4mm

1858 666 FG 432.2E 268.43N
Dress pin, iron.
Possible pin with tapering circular-sectioned stem which is turned over at its thickest end to form an elongated, crook-shaped rectangular-sectioned loop. The tip is missing.
L 87mm, stem MDia 4mm.

1223 212 DD
Dress pin ?, iron.
Probably rectangular-sectioned (dimensions 3mm x 4mm) tapering strip fragment, broken at both ends. Possibly, but not certainly, part of a pin.
L 76mm.

1580 602 DD 5863
Pin or strip, Copper alloy.
Thin strip fragment, plano-convex in section, tapering to a rounded point at one end and broken at the other. The strip is bent twice along its length. Possibly part of a binding or the pin from a brooch.
Surviving L 29mm, MW 2mm, Th 1mm.

1864 290 FC 444E 265N
Pin or loop-headed spike, iron.
A rectangular-sectioned pin or spike tapering to a blunt point at one end and formed into a loop at the other. This object could be a small loop-headed spike or the pin from an iron buckle or penannular brooch.
L 63mm, internal dia of loop 7-8mm.

Knives
1887 665 FB 443.1E 264.9N
Knife, iron.
The back of the blade is slightly angled at approximately halfway along the blade's length. The cutting edge is relatively straight although the 20mm nearest the tip is slightly concave, presumably because of preferential sharpening. The rect-angular-sectioned tang, which tapers from the blade towards its missing tip, is set midway between the back of the blade and the cutting edge.
L 91mm.

1660 Unstratified
Blade, iron.
Fragment of a narrow and slightly tapered blade. The back of the blade is largely straight, although it begins to convexly curves downwards towards the narrowest end of the fragment. The cutting edge is relatively straight. Possibly from a knife or shears.
L 63mm, back of blade Th 3.5mm.

1678 280 F 442.24E 263.3N
Tang, iron.
Rectangular-sectioned tang which widens, through a gently curved shoulder, into the end of a lost blade. Possibly from a knife.
L 105mm.

Structural fittings
1479 614 DD 444.97E 284.72N
Nail, iron
Corroded nail fragment with a rectangular-sectioned stem and an incomplete head of uncertain form.
L 27mm.

1836 275 FD
Nail, iron.
Incomplete flat-headed nail with a distorted rectangular-sectioned stem.
Surviving L 25mm.

1875 276 FD 8622
Nail, iron.
Distorted and incomplete flat-headed nail with a rectangular-sectioned stem.
Surviving L 34mm.

1942 675 FG
Nail, iron.
Incomplete probable flat-headed nail with a rectangular-sectioned stem.
Surviving L 17.5mm.

1974 675 FG
Nail, iron.
Nail with a flat, rectangular-shaped head and an off-centre rectangular-sectioned stem. The lower half of the stem is missing.
Surviving L 22mm.

1413 605 DD 444.54E 286.00N
Nail, iron.
Flat-headed nail, broken into three pieces.
L (estimated) 68mm.

1428 604 DD 442.10E 287.11N
Nail ? iron.
Rectangular-sectioned, tapering bar fragment. Probably the stem of a nail.
L 32.5mm.

1871 671 FG
Nail? iron.
Probable sub-rectangular shaped nail head. Heavily corroded. Dimensions 20mm x 21mm.

1227 211 DB
Strip (possible nail stem), iron.
Rectangular-sectioned, tapering strip. Deformed into a slight S-shape and broken at both ends. Possibly a nail stem.
L 84mm.

1222 251 FF
Strip (possible nail stem), iron.
Rectangular-sectioned strip, broken at both ends. Possibly a nail stem.
L 22mm.

1162 222/3 E
Strip (possible nail stem), iron.
Rectangular-sectioned tapering strip, broken at both ends. Possible nail stem.
L 38mm.

1837 Unstratified
Strip (possible nail stem), iron.
Rectangular-sectioned tapering strip, broken at both ends. Possible nail stem.
L 33mm.

1713 Unstratified
Strip (possible nail stem), iron.
Rectangular-sectioned strip, broken at both ends. Possible nail stem.
L 25mm.

Holdfasts
1325 232 DB 441.98E 289.71N
Holdfast, iron.
Rectangular-sectioned stem, the head is incomplete and of uncertain form while the other end has been hammered over a rectangular-shaped rove (dimensions 27mm x 23mm).
L 29mm.

1436 Unstratified
Holdfast, iron.
Distorted rectangular-sectioned stem, the head is incomplete but apparently sub-rectangular in shape while the other end has been hammered over a rectangular-shaped rove (dimensions 31.5mm x 22mm).
L c.35mm.

1226 204 DB
Rove, iron.
Roughly rectangular with a sub-rectangular hole in the centre.
Dimensions 28mm x 18mm.

1310 228 DE 445.4N 281.86N
Rove, iron.
Rectangular-shaped rove with a central, circular perforation (dia c.5mm).
Dimensions 21mm x 20mm.

1323 230 DD 445.13E 282.21N
Rove, iron.
Rectangular with a central, circular hole (dia 6-7mm).
Dimensions 35mm x 21mm.

1481 614 DD 442.76E 286.53N
Rove, iron.
Rectangular with a central, circular hole (dia 6-7mm).
Dimensions 35mm x 21mm.

1662 Unstratified
Rove, iron.
Rectangular with a central, circular hole (dia 5-6mm).
Dimensions 23mm x 21mm.

Miscellaneous
1581 614 DD 8076
Ring, iron.
Small ring, broken and slightly distorted, circular in cross-section (dia 1-2mm).
External dia 11-12mm.

1326 232 DB
Bar, iron.
Rectangular-sectioned, tapering bar fragment.
L 23mm, dimensions of cross-section at thickest end 9mm x 6mm, dimensions of cross-section at thinnest end 5mm x 5mm.

1492 255 FE
Bar, iron.
Slightly distorted, rectangular-sectioned, tapering bar fragment. Apparently cut at a 45 degree angle across its thickest end.
Surviving L 59mm, dimensions of cross-section at thickest end 13mm x 11mm, dimensions of cross-section at thinnest end 11mm x 9mm.

1665 280 F 442.19E 263.01N
Bar, iron.
Rectangular-sectioned tapering bar fragment, curved and broken at its narrowest end. Possibly a part of a tool such as a chisel, punch or wedge.
L 66mm, MW 10mm, MTh 8mm.

1225 210 DB
Plate fragment, iron.
Irregular-shaped fragment perforated by a rectangular-headed nail or rivet.
49mm x 31mm, Th 6mm.

1582 245 DD 5828
Plate fragment, iron.
Irregular-shaped plate fragment.
23mm x 12mm, Th 2-3mm.

1584 249 DD 5840
Plate fragment, iron.
Irregular-shaped plate fragment.
23mm x 18mm x 1mm.

1713 Unstratified
Rod, iron.
Circular-sectioned rod fragment, slightly distorted and broken at both ends.
L 47mm, Th 6-8mm.

1679 281 FG 437.21E 263.50N
Rod, iron.
Circular-sectioned rod fragment.
L 31mm, MDia 5mm.

1958 675 FG
Rod, iron.
Narrow, circular-sectioned rod fragment. Possibly from a pin or needle.
L 25mm, Dia 3mm.

1353 240 DE
Sheet fragment, copper alloy.
Irregular-shaped sheet fragment, broken into 15 sub-rectangular pieces.
The largest fragment is 16mm x 8mm x 1mm in dimensions.

4703 614 DD 8036
Sheet fragment, copper alloy.
Irregular-shaped sheet fragment.
L 17mm, W 10–11mm, Th 1mm

2684 us
Sheet, copper alloy
A large irregular piece of copper alloy sheet. The upper edge appears to be original but the other three sides have been roughly cut. The bottom edge is bent almost perpendicular prior to cutting. Two rectangular holes have been punched through the sheet parallel to the upper edge. The sheet has been cut between the two punch marks to create two small rectangular sections of sheet. Similar rectangular sections appear to have been cut from the sheet in the adjacent area.
L 83mm, W 34.2mm, Th 1mm.

1853 276 FD 440.27e 269.27n
Strip, iron.
Narrow strip fragment, broken at both ends and slightly curved towards one end. Possibly part of a binding.
L 40mm, W 8-9mm, Th 2-2.5mm.

1583 601 DD 5855
Strip, iron.
Strip fragment, possibly twisted through a right-angle halfway along its length.
surviving L 20mm, W 4mm, Th 1.5mm.

2685 614 DD 8045
Unknown, iron.
Amorphous fragment.
Dimensions 30mm x 27mm x 21mm.

1161 224 E
Casting waste, copper alloy.
Small, sub-spherical casting. Probably casting waste.
Dimensions 12mm x 8.5mm x 7mm.

FLINT

1554	605	DD	5916	Retouched flake – notched concave
1555	600	US		Flake
1562	604	DD	5911	Flake
4694	614	DD	8039	Flake broken at both ends
4695	238	DD	5777	Flake (possible retouch)
4696	614	DD	8072	Flake
4702	212	DD	5534	Block reduced
4729a	211	DB		Chip
4729b	211	DB		Flake
4729c	211	DB		Awl/Borer
Flake bifacially worked to create point at the end. Signs of heavy use.				
4729d	211	DB		Microlith
Blade, back blunted by retouch to create a microlithic form				
4745	205	DB		Flake weathered
4765	207	DE		Block reduced
4766	207	DE		Flake
4767	614	DD	8060	Chip
4768	661	FG	8687	Microchip
4769	614	DD	8072	Flake

Appendix 3: Catalogue of Illustrated Pottery – A Lane

Figure 31. Block DB

1 2 conjoined platter rims, 6-9mm thick, grey upper, blackened lower, inangled rim. (204)

2 1 platter sherd, 9mm thick, orange lower, grey upper, fingered, stabbed rectangular hole. (204)

3 1 rim, 6-8 mm thick, blackened exterior, grey/buff interior, upright with slightly outturned exterior lip. (204)

4 1 base sherd, buff exterior, grey interior, 8-13mm thick, 31cm diameter, rounded basal angle, sagging base, slight grass-marking. (208)

5 2 conjoined base sherds, black exterior, grey interior, 10-12 mm thick, rounded basal angle, slightly sagging, angled slab construction, 16cm diameter. (208)

6 1 rim, 6-10mm thick, round rim top, grey-buff exterior, grey interior (208)

7 1 platter sherd, 8-10mm thick, buff, lightly sooted upper and base, fingered upper. (211)

8 2 conjoined rims, fabric E, 3-4mm thick, round rim top, straight sided. (211)

9 1 rim, 7-8mm thick, grey, white residue, rounded rimtop possibly wavy though too small for certainty. (211)

10 1 platter sherd, 7-8mm thick, grey upper, blackened base, stabbed rectangular hole. (211)

11 1 platter rim, 8-11mm, pinched rim, grey fingered upper, blackened cracked base. (211)

12 1 rim, 5-7 mm thick, round rim top, slightly inturned. (227)

13 1 platter sherd, 8-9mm thick, buff, tapering pointed pierced hole. (232)

14 1 rim, 10-12mm thick, blackened, rounded rim top, irregular straight/slightly out-turned, angled slab construction. (237)

15 1 fabric E rim, 5-6mm thick, irregular rim top, folded construction join, slightly inturned form. (237)

16 1 platter rim, 8-9mm thick, inward angled rim, fingered upper. (237)

17 1 platter rim, 6-14mm thick, inward angled rim, slightly upturned, blackened and sooted on inside and out. (237)

18 1 platter rim, 5-9mm thick, flat rim, fingered upper. (237)

19 2 conjoined rims, 5-6mm thick, straight or slightly inturned. (226)

20 14 base sherds, 1 body and 2 misc, grey/buff, 8-17mm thick, convex walls, sagging base, slight foot, sharp angle, grass-marked, diameter 15cm. Open bowl. (612)

21 22 base sherds, blackened, 10mm thick, sagging base, cracked exterior, c. 20cm diameter. (612)

Figure 32: Block DB

1 1 platter sherd, 8-11mm thick, grey upper, orange base, angular stabbed hole, roughened exterior. (209)

2 1 rim, 8-9mm thick, blackened exterior, grey wiped interior, flat with slight exterior lip. (209)

3 2 conjoined rims, 7-8mm thick, blackened exterior, grey interior, slightly rounded rim top, slab construction marks, possible diameter of 20cm. Open convex bowl. (210)

4 1 body sherd broken just above basal angle, 12-18mm thick, angled slab join. Probable open bowl. (210)

5 2 conjoined rims, 9mm thick, sooted exteriors, grey interior, rounded irregular rim top. (214)

6 2 conjoined rims, 9mm thick, grey-buff, flat top, straight-sided. (214)

7 1 basal angle, 12-15mm thick, sooted exterior, grey interior, rounded basal angle broken before base. Probable sagging base open bowl. (214)

Figure 47. Block DD

1 2 conjoined bases, 8-9mm thick, blackened surfaces, slightly sagging base, cracked exterior surface, irregularly footed. Same vessel as rim 2. Probable convex bowl. (230)

2 1 rim, 6-7mm thick, blackened surfaces, rim flat and rounded, incurved rim, same vessel as 1. (230)

3 1 rim, 5mm thick, flattened rim top. (238)

4 1 rim, fabric E, 6-8mm thick, orange/buff exterior, short sharply everted rim. (242)

5 1 base, fabric E, 5mm thick, blackened exterior and interior, slightly sagging, rounded basal angle, convex form. (238)

6 1 rim (as above 5), fabric E, 6-8mm thick, orange/buff exterior, short sharply everted rim, fingered marks on neck, organically wiped on exterior, blackening along interior rim edge. (242)

7 1 rim, 6-7mm thick, blackened lower exterior, abraded short everted rim, rounded body. (602)

8 1 base, 5-8mm thick, flat footed base, grass-marked, curved wall. (604)

9 1 rim, 7mm thick, rounded rimtop. (604) 5918.

10 1 rim, 4-6mm thick, flat rimtop. (604) 5937.

11 1 rim, ? fabric A, 4-6mm thick, round rimtop, sharply everted form, round-bodied vessel, blackened exterior, blackened inner rim. (604)

12 1 rim, 5-6mm thick, grey-buff, flattened rimtop, possibly convex. (604)

13 1 platter rim, blackened surfaces, 8-10mm thick, outward angled flat rim, cracked lower, fingered upper. (604)
14 1 base, 10-12mm thick, blackened buff exterior, heavily carbonised interior, rounded basal angle. (605)
15 3 conjoined base sherds, fabric C or E, 5-7mm thick, shiny black exterior, grey wiped and sooted interior, sagging base, linear construction marks at base wall join. (605)
16 1 fabric E bodysherd, 4-6 mm thick, buff exterior, blackened interior, organically wiped surface, probably neck sherd broken from everted rim. (605)
17 1 rim, 3mm, flattened. (604) 5922.
18 1 base, 6mm wall 5mm base, blackened inside and out, footed flat base. (614)
19 1 fabric E rim, 5mm thick, buff-grey, probably broken from everted rim. (614)
20 1 rim, 4-6mm thick, rounded rim top, possibly/probably from everted rim. (614) 8020.
21 1 platter sherd, lightly blackened upper and lower, 11mm thick, fingered upper with one stabbed hole. (614) 8070.

22 1 fabric C rim, 5-6mm body, rim 9mm thick, blackened surfaces, short stubby everted rim on round-bodied vessel. (614) 8054.
23 1 rim, 7mm thick, blackened exterior, flattened rimtop. (614) 8034.
24 1 rim, 6mm thick, rounded top. (614) 8062.
25 1 rim, 6-11mm thick, blackened exterior and interior, rounded rim top, open bowl form. (212)
26 1 base, 9-11mm thick, black exterior, buff interior, linear ridge on outside indicating slab construction of basal angle. (212)
27 1 rim, fabric A/E, 8-10mm thick, grey clayey appearance, irregular flat inangled and lipped rim top, open bowl form. (212)
28 1 rim, blackened surfaces, 7mm thick, irregular flat/inangled rim top, slightly inturned. (243)
29 1 base, 12mm thick, blackened exterior, footed basal angle, slab construction join, grass-marked and cracked exterior. (243)
30 1 platter sherd, 6-8mm thick, fingered upper, finely stabbed hole. (243)
31 1 platter sherd, 9mm thick, blackened lower, finely stabbed hole. (243)
32 2 conjoined platter rims, 10-15mm thick, lightly blackened rim and upper, fingered and nail-marked uppers, cracked lowers, inward angled bevelled rim edges. (243)
33 1 rim (+ bodysherd), 10mm thick, rounded rim top, straight sided. (611)
34 1 fabric ?E rim, fine fabric, 4mm thick, orange/grey, slightly curved rimtop, possibly broken from an everted rim vessel. (615) 8082.

Figure 53. Block DE

1 1 base, 7-9mm thick, blackened exterior and interior, sagging base, irregular foot, grass-marked. (207)
2 1 rim, 5-6mm thick, flat rim top with inner lip. (231)
3 2 conjoined rims, 6mm thick, blackened, flat rim top, upright. (234)
4 1 base, 8-10mm thick, blackened exterior, footed slightly rounded base. (234)
5 1 base, 9-10mm thick, blackened exterior, footed basal angle. (234)
6 1 rim, 7-8mm thick, blackened exterior and interior, rounded rim top, slightly inturned profile. (236)
7 1 rim, fabric E, 5-6mm thick, finely smoothed interiors and wiped exteriors, impressed tooling marks at rim/neck junction, short sharply everted rim, round-bodied vessel. (239)
8 1 rim, fabric E, 5-6mm thick, finely smoothed interiors and wiped exteriors, impressed tooling marks at rim/neck junction, short sharply everted rim, round-bodied vessel. Similar to 7 but shorter rim. (239)
9 1 rim, fabric E, 6-7mm thick, irregular rim top – round/flat rolled internally – straight sided vessel. (239)
10 1 base, 9mm thick, blackened exterior, footed base, curving wall. (239)
11 1 rim, fabric E, 5mm thick, wiped blackened exterior, wiped interior, finely finished, short sharply everted rim, formed by folding rim, round rimtop. (240)
12 1 base, 7-13mm thick, blackened exterior grey interior, slab construction, footed base. (201)
13 1 platter rim, 8-10mm thick, grey fingered upper, buff cracked lightly blackened lower. (201)
14 1 base, fabric A/C, 4-6mm thick, black, flat bottomed, rounded basal angle. (233)
15 1 platter rim, 9-11mm thick, grey/buff fingered upper, blackened surfaces especially on lower surface and rim edge, in-angled flat rim. (600)

Bibliography

Ágústsson, H. 1982 Den indre opbygning of det islanske tørvehus. In Myhre, B., Stokulund, B. and Gjærder, P (eds) *Vestnordisk byggeskikk gjennom to tusen år*. Stavanger: AmS-skrifter 7, 173–185.

Allen, S.J. 1989 *Chemical Analysis of Ecological Materials*. Oxford: Basil Blackwell.

Ambrosiani, K. 1981 *Viking Age Combs, Comb Making and Comb Makers in the Light of Finds from Birka and Ribe*. Stockholm: Stockholm Studies in Archaeology 2.

Andersen, P.S. 1991 Norse settlement in the Hebrides: what happened to the natives and what happened to the Norse immigrants. In Wood, I. and Lund, N. (eds*) People and Places in Northern Europe, 500–1600*. Woodbridge: Boydell, 131–147

Angus, S. 1997 *The Outer Hebrides: The shaping of the islands*. Cambridge: The White Horse Press.

Angus, S. 2001 *The Outer Hebrides: Moor and machair*. Cambridge: The White Horse Press.

Armit, I. 1994 Archaeological field survey of the Bhaltos (Valtos) peninsula, Lewis. *Proceedings of the Society of Antiquaries of Scotland* 124, 67–93.

Armit, I. 1996 *The Archaeology of Skye and the Western Isles*. Edinburgh: Edinburgh University Press.

Armit, I. and Braby, A. 1997 Ceann nan Clachan. *Discovery and Excavation in Scotland* 1997, 84.

Badcock, A. and Symonds, J. 2001 Ormiclate Castle. *Discovery and Excavation in Scotland* 2000 (NS) 1, 99.

Bald, W. 1805 *Plan of the Island of South Uist, the Property of Ranald George McDonald Esq. of Clanranald*. Surveyed by William Bald, Assistant to Mr Ainslie, 1805. SRO RHP 38151.

Ballantyne, R. 1999 Norse period use of plant resources in the Outer Hebrides, and an evaluation of charred plant macroremains as indicators of space use. University of Sheffield: Unpublished MSc dissertation.

Ballin Smith, B. 1994 *Howe: Four millennia of Orkney prehistory, excavations 1978–1982* . Edinburgh: Society of Antiquaries of Scotland (Monograph 9).

Ballin Smith, B. 2002 Solving the problems of brochs. *Scottish Archaeological Journal* 23.1, 82–87.

Barnes, M. 1993 Norse in the British Isles. In Faulkes, A. and Perkins, R. (eds*) Viking Revaluations,Viking Society Centenary Symposium 10–15 May 1992*. London: Viking Society for Northern Research, 65–84.

Barrett, J.H. 1997 Fish trade in Norse Orkney and Caithness: a zooarchaeological approach. *Antiquity* 71, 616–638.

Barrett, J.H., Nicholson, R.A. and Cerón-Carrasco, R. 1999 Archaeo-ichthyolgical evidence for long-term socioeconomic trends in northern Scotland: 3500 BC to AD 1500. *Journal of Archaeological Science* 26, 353–388.

Batey, C. 1987 *Freswick Links, Caithness: A reappppraisal of the Late Norse site in its context*. Oxford: British Archaeological Report Int. Ser. 179.

Batey, C.E., Jesch, J. and Morris, C.D. 1993 (eds) *The Viking Age in Caithness, Orkney and the North Atlantic*. Edinburgh: Edinburgh University Press.

Beatty, J. 1992 *Sula: The seabird-hunters of Lewis*. London: Michael Joseph.

Bell, M. 1990 *Brean Down: Excavations 1983–1987*. London: English Heritage (Archaeological report No 15).

Beveridge, E. 1911 *North Uist: Its archaeology and topography*. Edinburgh: William Brown.

Bigelow, G. F. 1985 Sandwick, Unst and Late Norse Shetland economy. In Smith, B. (ed.) *Shetland Archaeology*. Lerwick: The Shetland Times Ltd, 95–127.

Boardman, S. and Jones, G. 1990 Experiments on the effects of charring on cereal plant components. *Journal of Archaeological Science* 17, 1–11.

Boessneck, J.A. 1969 Osteological differences between sheep (*Ovis aries* Linne) and goat (*Capra hircus* Linne). In Brothwell, D.R. and Higgs, E.S. (eds) *Science in Archaeology*. London: Thames and Hudson, 331–358.

Boivin, N.L. 2000 Life rhythms and floor sequences: excavating time in rural Rajasthan and Neolithic Catalhoyuk. *World Archaeology* 31, 367–388.

Bond, J.M. 1998 Beyond the fringe? Recognising change and adaptation in Pictish and Norse Orkney. In Mills, C.M. and Coles, G. (eds) *Life on the Edge: Human settlement and marginality*. Oxford: Oxbow Books, 81–90.

Bond, J.M. 2004 Bringing in the sheaves: farming intensification in the post-broch Iron Age. In Housley, R.A. and Coles, G. (eds) *Atlantic Connections and Adaptation: Economics, environments and subsistence in the North Atlantic*. Oxford: Oxbow Books (Symposia for the Association of Environmental Archaeology 21).

Bond, J.M. and Hunter, J.R. 1987 Flax-growing in Orkney from the Norse period to the 18th century. *Proceedings of the Society of Antiquaries of Scotland* 117, 175–181.

Boyd, J.M. and Boyd, I.L. 1990 *The Hebrides*. London: Collins.

Brain, C.K. 1981 *The Hunters or the Hunted? An introduction to African cave taphonomy*. Chicago and London: University of Chicago Press.

Branigan, K. and Foster, P. 1995 *Barra: Archaeological research on Ben Tangaval*. Sheffield: Sheffield Academic Press.

Branigan, K. and Foster, P. 2000 *From Barra to Berneray: Archaeological survey and excavation in the southern isles of the Outer Hebrides*. Sheffield: Sheffield Academic Press.

Brayshay, B.A. and Edwards, K.J. 1996 Late glacial and Holocene vegetational history of South Uist and Barra. In Gilbertson, D., Kent, M. and Gratton, J. (eds) *The Outer Hebrides: The last 14,000 years*. Sheffield: Sheffield Academic Press, 13–26.

Brennand, M., Parker Pearson, M. and Smith, H. 1997 The Viking settlement at Kilphedir (Cille Pheadair), South Uist: Excavations in 1997. Unpublished Dept of Archaeology and Prehistory report, University of Sheffield.

Brennand, M., Parker Pearson, M. and Smith, H. 1998 The Norse settlement and Pictish cairn at Kilphedir, South Uist: Excavations in 1998. Unpublished Dept of Archaeology and Prehistory report, University of Sheffield.

Bronk Ramsey, C. 1995 Radiocarbon calibration and analysis of stratigraphy. *Radiocarbon* 36, 425–430.

Bronk Ramsey, C. 1998 Probability and dating. *Radiocarbon* 40, 461–474.

Bronk Ramsey, C. 2000 Comment on 'The use of Bayesian statistics for 14C dates of chronological ordered samples: a critical analysis'. *Radiocarbon* 42, 199–202.

Bronk Ramsey, C. and Hedges, R.E.M. 1997 Hybrid ion sources: radiocarbon measurements from microgram to milligram. *Nuclear Instruments and Methods in Physics Research B* 123, 539–545.

Bronk Ramsey, C., Pettitt, P.B., Hedges, R.E.M., Hodgins, G.W.L., and Owen, D.C. 2000 Radiocarbon dates from the Oxford AMS system, Archaeometry datelist 29. *Archaeometry* 42, 243–254.

Bullock, P., Fedoroff, N., Jongerius, A., Stoops, G., Tursina, T. and Babel, U. 1985 *Handbook for Thin Section Description.* Wolverhampton: Waine Research Publications.

Buteux, S. 1997 *Settlement at Skaill, Deerness, Orkney. Excavations by Peter Gelling of the prehistoric, Pictish, Viking and later periods, 1963–1981.* Oxford: British Archaeological Report Brit. Ser. 260.

Caird, J. B. 1989 Early 19th century estate plans. In Macleod, F. (ed.) *Togail Tir Marking Time: The map of the Western Isles*. Stornoway: Acair Ltd and An Lanntair Gallery, 49–79.

Campbell, E. 1991 Excavations of a wheelhouse and other structures at Sollas, North Uist, by R.J.C. Atkinson in 1956. *Proceedings of the Society of Antiquaries of Scotland* 121, 117–173.

Canti, M. 1999 The production and preservation of faecal spherulites: animals, environment and taphonomy. *Journal of Archaeological Science* 26, 251–258.

Cerón-Carrasco, R. 1994 The investigation of fish remains from an Orkney farm mound. In Van Neer, W. (ed). *Fish Exploitation in the Past, Proceedings of the 7th meeting of the ICAZ Fish Remains Working Group*. Tervuren: Annales du Musée Royale de l'Afrique Centrale, Sciences Zoologiques n° 274, 207–210.

Cerón-Carrasco, R. 1998 Fishing: evidence for seasonality and processing of fish for preservation in the Northern Isles of Scotland during the Iron Age and Norse times. *Environmental Archaeology* 3, 73–80.

Cerón-Carrasco, R. 1999 The fish bones. *In* Parker Pearson, M. and Sharples N.M. 1999, 234–274.

Church, M. 2002 Carbonised plant macrofossils and charcoal. In Harding, D.W. and Dixon, T.N. (eds) *Dun Bharabhat, Cnip: An Iron Age settlement in west Lewis*. Edinburgh: Department of Archaeology, 121–130.

Clapham, A., Tutin, T. and Moore, D. 1989 *Flora of the British Isles (3rd edition).* Cambridge: Cambridge University Press.

Clark, A.J. 1990 *Seeing Beneath the Soil*. London: Batsford.

Clark, J. 1997 Medieval ironwork. In Driscoll, S.T. and Yeoman, P.A. *Excavations within Edinburgh Castle in 1988–91*. Edinburgh: Society of Antiquaries of Scotland (Monograph 12), 154–162.

Clarke, D.V. and Sharples, N.M. 1985 Settlements and subsistence in the third millennium BC. In Renfrew, C. (ed.) *The Prehistory of Orkney*. Edinburgh: Edinburgh University Press, 54–82.

Close-Brooks, J. 1995 Excavation of a cairn at Cnip, Uig, Isle of Lewis. *Proceedings of the Society of Antiquaries of Scotland* 125, 253–277.

Coles, J.M. 1960 Scottish Late Bronze Age metalwork: typology, distributions and chronology. *Proceedings of the Society of Antiquaries of Scotland* (1959–60) 93, 16–134.

Collins, J.S.H. 1999 Fossils explained 25: crab claws. *Geology Today* May-June, 114–117.

Corbett, G.B. and Harris, S. 1991 (eds) *The Handbook of British Mammals*. Oxford: Blackwell Science, 3rd edition.

Courty, M.-A., Goldberg, P. and Macphail, R. 1989 *Soils and Micromorphology in Archaeology*. Cambridge: Cambridge University Press.

Cowgill, J., de Neergaard, M. and Griffiths, N. 1987 *Knives and Scabbards*. London: Her Majesty's Stationery Office.

Cowie, T.G., Bruce, M. and Kerr, N. 1993 Appendix: the discovery of a child burial of probable Viking-Age date on Kneep Headland, Lewis 1991: interim report. In Batey, C.E., Jesch, J. and Morris, C.D. (eds) *The Viking Age in Caithness, Orkney and the North Atlantic*. Edinburgh: Edinburgh University Press, 165–172.

Crawford, B.E. 1985 The Biggins, Papa Stour – a multi-disciplinary investigation. In Smith, B. (ed.) *Shetland Archaeology*. Lerwick: The Shetland Times Ltd, 128–158.

Crawford, B.E. 1987 *Scandinavian Scotland*. Leicester: Leicester University Press.

Crawford, B.E. and Ballin Smith, B. 1999 *The Biggings, Papa Stour, Shetland. The history and excavation of a royal Norwegian farm*. Edinburgh: Society of Antiquaries of Scotland (Monograph 15).

Crawford, I.A. 1974 Norseman and Gael. *Scottish Archaeological Forum* 6, 1–15.

Crawford, I.A. 1981 War or peace – Viking colonization in the Northern and Western Isles of Scotland reviewed. In Bekker-Nielsen, H., Foote, P. and Olsen, O. (eds) *Proceedings of the Eighth Viking Congress, Aarhus, 24–31 August 1977*. Odense: Odense University Press, 259–269.

Crawford, I.A. 1986 *The West Highlands and Islands. A view of 50 centuries: the Udal (North Uist) evidence.* Cambridge: Great Auk Press.

Crawford, I.A. and Switsur, V.R. 1977 Sand-scaping and C14: the Udal, North Uist. *Antiquity* 51, 124–136.

Crowther, J. 1997 Soil phosphate surveys: critical approaches to sampling analysis and interpretation, *Archaeological Prospection* 4, 93–102.

Cummings, V. and Sharples, N. 1999 *The Excavation of a Chambered Cairn at Leaval, South Uist* (Cardiff Studies in Archaeology Specialist Report no 17). Cardiff: School of History and Archaeology.

Cunningham, P. 1991 *Birds of the Outer Hebrides*. Edinburgh: Mercat Press.

Curle, A.O. 1939 A Viking settlement at Freswick Caithness. Reports on excavation carried out in 1937 and 1938. *Proceedings of the Society of Antiquaries of Scotland* 73 (1938–9), 71–110.

Curle, C.L. 1982 *Pictish and Norse Finds from the Brough of*

Birsay 1934–74. Edinburgh: Society of Antiquaries of Scotland (Monograph 1).

Davis, S.J.M. 1992 *Rapid Method for Recording Information about Mammal Bones from Archaeological Sites*. London: Ancient Monuments Laboratory.

Dehling, H. and van der Plicht, J. 1993 Statistical problems in calibrating radiocarbon dates. *Radiocarbon* 35, 239–244.

Dickson, C.A. 1981 The macroscopic plant remains, in Barvas Machair, Lewis. Unpublished report, Department of Botany, University of Glasgow.

Dickson, C.A. and Dickson, J.H. 2000 *Plants and People in Ancient Scotland*. Stroud: Tempus.

Dobney, K. and Ervynck, A. 2000 Interpreting developmental stress in archaeological pigs: the chronology of linear enamel hypoplasia. *Journal of Archaeological Science* 27, 597–607.

Dockrill, S.J. 1984 A resistivity survey at Tofts Ness, Sanday, Orkney. *Proceedings of the Society of Antiquaries of Scotland* 114, 586–588.

Dockrill, S.J. 1986 Resistivity survey of two settlement sites at Tofts Ness, Sanday, Orkney. *Proceedings of the Society of Antiquaries of Scotland* 116, 561–565.

Dodgshon, R.A. 1998 *From Chiefs to Landlords: Social and economic change in the western Highlands and Islands, c. 1493–1820*. Edinburgh: Edinburgh University Press.

Driesch, A. von den 1976 *A Guide to the Measurement of Animal Bones from Archaeological Sites*. Philadephia: W.B. Saunders Company (Peabody Museum Bulletin 1).

Driesch, A. von den and Boessneck, J. 1974 Kritische Anmerkungen zur Widerristhohenberechnung aus Längenmassen vor- und frühgeschichtlicher Tierknochen. *Säugetierkundliche Mitteilungen* 22, 325–48.

Dunlevy, M. 1988 A classification of early Irish combs. *Proceedings of the Royal Irish Academy* 88C, 11, 341–422.

Dunwell, A.J., Cowie, T.G., Bruce, M.F., Neighbour, T. and Rees, A.R. 1995 A Viking Age cemetery at Cnip, Uig, Isle of Lewis. *Proceedings of the Society of Antiquaries of Scotland* 125, 719–752.

Edlin, H.L. 1949 *Woodland Crafts in Britain*. London: Batsford.

Egan, G. and Pritchard, F. 1991 *Dress Accessories c.1150 – c.1450*. London: HMSO.

Einarsson, B.F. 1995 *The Settlement of Iceland: a critical approach. Granstaðir and the ecological heritage*. Reykjavik: Hið islenska bókmmentafélag.

Entwistle, J.A. and Abrahams, P.W. 1997 Multi-element analysis of soils and sediments from Scottish historical sites. The potential of inductively-coupled plasma-mass spectrometry for rapid site investigation. *Journal of Archaeological Science* 24, 407–416.

Entwistle, J.A., Abrahams, P.W. and Dodgshon, R.A.D. 1998 Multi-element analysis of soils and sediments from Scottish historical sites. Interpreting land-use history through the physical and geochemical analysis of soil. *Journal of Archaeological Science* 25, 53–68.

Entwistle, J.A., Abrahams, P.W. and Dodgshon, R.A.D. 2000 The geoarchaeological significance and spatial variability of a range of physical and chemical soil properties from a former habitation site, Isle of Skye. *Journal of Archaeological Science* 26, 287–303

Entwistle, J.A., Dodgshon, R.A.D. and Abrahams, P.W. 2000 An investigation of former land-use activity through the physical and chemical analysis of soil from the Isle of Lewis, Outer Hebrides. *Archaeological Prospection* 7, 171–188.

Evans, J.G.E. 1973 *What to do with shellfish on archaeological sites*. Unpublished manuscript.

Evans, J.G.E. and Spencer, P. 1977 The mollusca and environment, Bukquoy, Orkney. In Ritchie, A. (ed.) Excavations of Pictish and Viking-age farmsteads at Buckquoy, Orkney. *Proceedings of the Society of Antiquaries of Scotland* 108, 215–219.

Evans, R.T. and Tylecote, R.F. 1967 Some vitrified products of non-metallurgical significance. *Bulletin of the Historical Metallurgy Group* 8, 22–23.

Fairhurst, H. 1971 The wheelhouse site A'Cheardach Bheag on Drimore machair, South Uist. *Glasgow Archaeological Journal* 2, 72–106.

Fenton, A. 1978a *The Northern Isles: Orkney and Shetland*. Edinburgh: John Donald.

Fenton, A. 1978b *The Island Blackhouse*. Edinburgh: Historic Scotland.

Finlay, J. 1991 Animal bone. In Campbell, E. (ed.) Excavation of a wheelhouse and other Iron Age structures at Sollas, North Uist by R.J.C. Atkinson in 1957. *Proceedings of the Society of Antiquaries of Scotland* 121, 147–148.

Fleming, A. forthcoming. The blacklands survey: Cill Donnain and Gearraidh Bhailteas townships. In Smith, H. and Parker Pearson, M (eds*) From The Machair to the Mountains: Archaeological survey and excavations on South Uist*. Sheffield: Sheffield Academic Press.

Fleming, A. and Woolf, A. 1992 Cille Donnain: a Late Norse church in South Uist. *Proceedings of the Society of Antiquaries of Scotland* 122, 329–50.

Folk, R.L. and Hoops, G.K. 1982 An early Iron-Age layer of glass made from plats at Tel Yin'am, Israel. *Journal of Field Archaeology* 9, 455–466.

Fossitt, J.A. 1996 Late Quaternary vegetation history of the Western Isles of Scotland. *New Phytologist* 132, 171–196.

Gale, R. 1996 The pieces of charcoal. In P. Ashbee, Halangy Down, St. Mary's, Isles of Scilly. *Cornish Archaeology* 35, 127–129.

Gale, R. and Cutler, D. 2000 *Plants in Archaeology*. Otley/Kew: Westbury and Royal Botanic Gardens.

Gale, S.J. and Hoare, P.G. 1991 *Quaternary Sediments*. London: Belhaven Press.

Gelfand, A.E. and Smith, A.F.M. 1990 Sampling approaches to calculating marginal densities. *Journal of the American Statistical Association* 85, 398–409.

Getty, R. 1975 *Sisson and Grossman's The Anatomy of Domestic Animals*. 5th edition. Philadelphia: W.B. Saunders Company.

Gilbertson, D., Kent, M. and Gratton, J. 1996 *The Outer Hebrides: The last 14,000 years*. Sheffield: Sheffield Academic Press.

Gilbertson, D.D., Schwenninger, J-L., Kemp, R.A. and Rhodes, E.J. 1999 Sand-drift and soil formation along an exposed north Atlantic coastline: 14000 years of diverse geomorphological, climatic and human impacts. *Journal of Archaeological Science* 26, 439–469.

Gilks, W.R., Richardson, S. and Spiegelhalther, D.J. 1996 *Markov Chain Monte Carlo in practice*. London: Chapman and Hall.

Goodall, I.H. 1987 Objects of iron. In Beresford, G. (ed.) *Goltho: the develoment of an early medieval manor c.850–1150*. London: English Heritage (Archaeological Report 4), 177–187.

Goodall, I.H. 1993 Structural ironwork. In Margeson, S. (ed.) *Norwich Households. Medieval and post-medieval finds from Norwich Survey excavations 1971–78.* Norwich: The Norwich Survey and Norfolk Museums Service (East Anglian Archaeology Report No. 58), 143–148.

Goodall, I.H. and Goodall, A. 2000 Metalwork from the motte excavations at Hen Domen 1988–1992. In Higham, R. and Barker, P. *Hen Domen, Montgomery. A timber castle on the English-Welsh border.* Exeter: University of Exeter Press, 94–98.

Graham-Campbell, J.A. 1976 The Viking Age silver and gold hoards of Scandinavian character from Scotland. *Proceedings of the Society of Antiquaries of Scotland* 107, 104–135.

Graham-Campbell, J.A. 1980 *Viking Artefacts: a select catalogue.* London: British Museum.

Graham-Campbell, J.A. 1995 *The Viking-Age Gold and Silver of Scotland (AD850–1100).* Edinburgh: National Museums of Scotland.

Graham-Campbell, J.A. and Batey, C.E. 1998 *Vikings in Scotland: An archaeological survey.* Edinburgh: Edinburgh University Press.

Grant, A. 1982 The use of tooth wear as a guide to the age of domestic ungulates. In Wilson, R, Grigson, C. and Payne, S. (eds) *Ageing and Sexing Animal Bones from Archaeological Sites.* Oxford: British Archaeological Report Brit. Ser. 109, 91–108.

Grieg, S.J. 1940 *Viking Antiquities in Scotland.* Oslo: Scientific Research Fund.

Grigson, C. and Mellars, P.A. 1987 The mammalian remains from the middens. In Mellars, P. (ed.) *Excavations on Oronsay: Prehistoric human ecology of a small island.* Edinburgh: Edinburgh University Press, 243–289.

Hakbijl, T. 2002 The traditional, historical and prehistoric use of ashes as an insecticide, with an experimental study on the insecticidal efficacy of washed ash. *Environmental Archaeology* 7, 13–22.

Halstead, P. 1985 A study of the mandibular teeth from Romano-British contexts at Maxey. In Pryor, F. and French, C.A.I. (eds) *The Fenland Project number 1: Archaeology and environment of the lower Welland valley.* Norwich: East Anglian Archaeology Report No. 27, 219–223.

Hamerow, H. 1993 *Excavations at Mucking. Volume 2: the Anglo-Saxon settlement.* London: English Heritage.

Hamilton, J.R.C. 1956 *Excavations at Jarlshof, Shetland.* Edinburgh: HMSO.

Hamilton, M. and Sharples, N.M. 1996 *A Geophysical Survey at Bornish, South Uist, Outer Hebrides, 1996* (Cardiff Studies in Archaeology Specialist Report no 2). Cardiff: School of History and Archaeology.

Hamilton, M. and Sharples, N.M. forthcoming Early Bronze Age settlements at Machair Mheadhanach and Cill Donnain, South Uist. In Parker Pearson, M. and Smith, H. (eds) *From the Machair to the Mountains: Archaeological survey and excavations on South Uist.* Sheffield: Sheffield Academic Press.

Hansson, A-M 1997 *On plant food in the Scandinavian Peninsula in Early Medieval Times.* Stockholm: Archaeological Research Laboratory, Stockholm University.

Harden Jones, F.R. 1968 *Fish Migration.* London: Edward Arnold Ltd.

Harman, M. 1997 *An Isle called Hirte: A history and culture of St Kilda to 1930.* Waternish: Maclean Press.

Hastie, M. 1998 Look to the seeds. An archaeobotanical study. A Viking longhouse and two outhouses, Kilphedir, South Uist. University of Sheffield: Unpublished MSc dissertation.

Hedges, R.E.M. and Law, I. 1989 The radiocarbon dating of bone. *Applied Geochemistry* 4, 249–54

Hedges, R.E.M., Bronk Ramsey, C. and Housley, R.A. 1989 The Oxford Accelerator Mass Spectrometry facility: technical developments in routine dating. *Archaeometry* 31, 99–113.

Henley, C. 2001 Loch a'Choire. *Discovery and Excavation in Scotland 2000* (NS) 1, 99.

Henshall, A.S. 1972 *The Chambered Tombs of Scotland, volume 2.* Edinburgh: Edinburgh University Press.

Higham, R. and Rouillard, M. 2000 Metalwork and other material from the Bailey excavations at Hen Domen, 1960–1990. In Higham, R. and Barker, P. *Hen Domen, Montgomery. A timber castle on the English-Welsh border.* Exeter: University of Exeter Press, 98–110.

Hill, P. 1997 *Whithorn and St Ninian: The excavation of a monastic town, 1984–91.* Stroud: Sutton Publishing and the Whithorn Trust.

Hillman, G. 1981 Reconstructing crop husbandry practices. In Mercer, R. (ed.) *Farming Practices in British Prehistory.* Edinburgh: Edinburgh University Press, 123–162.

Hunter, J.R. 1986 *Rescue Excavations on the Brough of Birsay 1974–82.* Edinburgh: Society of Antiquaries of Scotland (Monograph 4).

Hunter, J.R., Bond, J.M. and Smith, A.N. 1993 Some aspects of Early Viking settlement in Orkney. In Batey, C.E., Jesch, J. and Morris, C.D. (eds) *The Viking Age in Caithness, Orkney and the North Atlantic.* Edinburgh: Edinburgh University Press, 272–284.

Jones, A.K.G. 1995 The fish material. In Morris, C.D., Batey C.E, and Rackham D.J. (eds) *Freswick Links, Caithness: Excavation and survey of a Norse settlement.* Inverness: Historic Scotland, 154–191.

Jones, M.K. 1988 The arable field: a botanical battleground. In Jones M.K. (ed.) *Archaeology and the Flora of the British Isles.* Oxford: Oxford University Committee for Archaeology (Monograph 14), 86–92.

Judicial Rental (1798) of Clanranald Estates Taken 2nd October to 23rd October, 1798 SRO GD 128/49/3/1. Cited in Caird, J.B. Early 19th Century Estate Plans. In Macleod, F. (ed.) *Togail Tir Marking Time: The Map of The Western Isles.* Stornoway: Acair Ltd and An Lanntair Gallery, 69.

Kaland, S.H.H. 1993 The settlement of Westness, Rousay. In Batey, C.E., Jesch, J. and Morris, C.D. (eds) *The Viking Age in Caithness, Orkney and the North Atlantic.* Edinburgh: Edinburgh University Press, 308–317.

Kaplan, C. 1999 The animal bones: an evaluation of the faunal remains from Norse period Kilphedir. University of Sheffield: Unpublished MSc dissertation.

Keepax, C.A. and Morgan, G. 1978 Charcoal. In S.A. Butcher, Excavations at Nornour, Isles of Scilly, 1969–73: the pre-Roman settlement. *Cornish Archaeology* 17, 98.

Keevil, G.D. 1996 *In Harvey's House and in God's House: excavations at Eynsham Abbey 1991–3.* Oxford: Oxford Archaeological Unit (Thames Valley Landscapes Monograph No.6).

Kenward, H.E., Hall, A.R. and Jones, A.K.G. 1980 A tested set of techniques for the extraction of plant and animal microfossils from waterlogged deposits. *Science in Archaeology* 22, 3–15.

Kratochvil, Z. 1969 Species criteria on the distal section of the tibia in *Ovis ammon f. aries* L. and *Capra aegagrus f. hircus* L. *Acta Veterinaria (Brno)* 38, 483–490.

Lane, A. 1983 Dark-age and Viking-age pottery in the Hebrides, with special reference to the Udal. University College, London: Unpublished PhD thesis.

Lane, A. 1990 Hebridean pottery: problems of definition, chronology, presence and absence. In Armit, I. (ed.) *Beyond the Brochs*. Edinburgh: Edinburgh University Press, 108–130.

Larson, A.-C. 1991 Norseman's use of juniper in the Viking Age Faeroe Islands. *Acta Archaeologica* 61, 54–59.

Lepiksaar, J. 1981 *Osteologia: I. Pisces*. Goteborg: Unpublished manuscript.

Lethbridge, T.C. 1952 Excavations at Kilphedir, South Uist, and the problem of the brochs and wheelhouses. *Proceedings of the Prehistoric Society* 18, 176–193.

Levine, M. 1982 The use of crown height measurements and eruption wear sequence to age horse teeth. In Wilson, B., Grigson, C. and Payne, S. (eds) *Ageing and Sexing Animal Bones from Archaeological Sites*. Oxford: British Archaeological Report Brit. Ser. 109, 223–250.

Light, J.M. 2003 The West Shetland Shelf: A recent storm-dominated, biogenic carbonate system. Department of Geology, Royal Holloway University of London: PhD Thesis.

Lister, A.M. 1996. The morphological distinction between bones and teeth of fallow deer *(Dama dama)* and red deer *(Cervus elaphus)*. *International Journal of Osteoarchaeology* 6, 119–143.

Lloyd, R. 1999 The animal bones: an evaluation of the faunal remains from Norse period Kilphedir. University of Sheffield: Unpublished MSc dissertation.

Lyne, M. 1996 Roman ships' fittings from Richborough. *Journal of Roman Military Equipment Studies* 7, 147–149.

MacDonald, D.A. 1993 Corn-drying kilns in Uist. In Cheape, H. (ed.) *Tools and Traditions: studies in European ethnology presented to Alexander Fenton*. Edinburgh: National Museums of Scotland.

MacGregor, A. 1985 *Bone, Antler, Ivory and Horn*. London: Crook Helm.

MacKie, E.W. 1965 The origin and development of the broch and wheelhouse building cultures of the Scottish Iron Age. *Proceedings of the Prehistoric Society* 30, 93–146.

MacLaren, A. 1974 A Norse house on Drimore machair, South Uist. *Glasgow Archaeological Journal* 3, 9–18.

Maclean, G.M. 1989 Locheynort, South Uist: appraisal of Uist documentary sources c. 1600–1980. Unpublished report, Comman Eachdraidh Uibhist a Deas.

Manning, W.H. 1985 *Catalogue of the Romano-British Iron Tools, Fittings and Weapons in the British Museum*. London: British Museum Publications Limited.

Margeson, S. 1993 *Norwich Households: the medieval and post-medieval finds from Norwich Survey excavations 1971–1978*. Norwich: Norfolk Museums Service (East Anglian Archaeology Report No. 58).

Marshall, P. and Parker Pearson, M. 1997 The Iron Age dun in Upper Loch Bornish: Excavations in 1997. Unpublished Dept. of Archaeology and Prehistory report, University of Sheffield.

Marshall, P. and Smith, H. 1999 The chemical and magnetic analysis of soils. *In* Parker Pearson, M. and Sharples, N. (eds) 1999, 205–209.

Marshall, P., Mulville, J.A. and Parker Pearson, M. 1996 Beinn na Mhic Aongheis 'Hill of the son of Angus': Excavation of Bornish Site 89, South Uist 1996. Unpublished Dept. of Archaeology and Prehistory report, University of Sheffield.

Marshall, P., Mulville, J.A., Parker Pearson, M. and Ingrem, C. 1999 The Late Bronze Age and Early Iron Age community at Cladh Hallan, South Uist: Excavations in 1999. Unpublished Dept. of Archaeology and Prehistory report, University of Sheffield.

Martin, A. 1995 *Fishing and Whaling*. Edinburgh: National Museums of Scotland.

Martin, M. 1716 *A Description of the Western Isles of Scotland*. Bell: London.

Matthews, W., French, C.A.I., Lawrence, T., Cutler, D.F. and Jones, M.K. 1996 Multiple surfaces: the micromorphology. In Hodder, I. (ed.) *On the Surface: Catalhoyuk 1993–95*. Cambridge: The McDonald Institute, 301–342.

Matthews, W., French, C.A.I., Lawrence, T., Cutler, D.F. and Jones, M.K. 1997 Microstratigraphic traces of site formation processes and human activities. *World Archaeology* 29, 281–303.

McCormick, F. 1998 Calf slaughter as a response to marginality. In Coles, G. and Mills, C. (eds) *Life on the Edge: Human settlement and marginality*. Oxford: Oxbow Books, 49–51.

McCullagh, R.P.J. and Tipping, R. 1998 *The Lairg Project 1988–96*. Edinburgh: STAR.

McDonnell, J.G. 2001 Pyrotechnology. In Brothwell, D.R. and Pollard, A.M. (eds) *Handbook of Archaeological Sciences*. Chichester: John Wiley and Sons, 493–505.

McGovern, T. 1992 Bones, buildings and boundaries: palaeo-economic approaches to Norse Greenland. In Morris, C.D. and Rackham D.J. (eds), 1992, 193–230.

McGovern, T.H., Buckland, P.C., Savory, D., Sveinbjarnardottir, G., Andreasen, C. and Skidmore, P. 1983 A study of faunal and floral remains from two Norse farms in the western settlement, Greenland. *Arctic Anthropology* 20, 93–111.

Metcalfe, D. and Heath, K.M. 1990 Microrefuse and site structure: the hearths and floors of the Heartbreak Hotel. *American Antiquity* 55, 781–796.

Middleton, W.D. and Price, T.D. 1996 Identification of activity areas by multi-element characterization of sediments from modern and archaeological house floors using Inductively Coupled Plasma-atomic Emission Spectroscopy. *Journal of Archaeological Science* 23, 673–687.

Mook, W.G. 1986 Business Meeting: recommendations/resolutions adopted by the twelfth international radiocarbon conference. *Radiocarbon* 28, 799.

Morales, A. and Rosenlund, K. 1979 *Fish Bone Measurements: An attempt to standardize the measuring of fish bones from archaeological sites*. Copenhagen: Steenstrupia.

Moreland, J. 1992 Excations at Kirkidale, South Locheynort. Unpublished SEARCH interim report, University of Sheffield.

Morris, C.D. 1989 *The Birsay Bay Project Vol. 1: Coastal sites beside the Brough Road, Birsay, Orkney, excavations 1976–1982*. Durham: University of Durham.

Morris, C.D. 1993 A Norse horizontal mill in Orkney. *Review of Scottish Culture* 8, 20–28.

Morris, C.D. 1996 *The Birsay Bay Project Vol. 2: Sites in Birsay village and on the Brough of Birsay*. Durham: University of Durham.

Morris, C.D. and Rackham, D.J. 1992 *Norse and Later Settlement and Subsistence in the North Atlantic*. Denbigh: Archetype Publications.

Morris, C.D., Batey, C.E. and Rackham, D.J. 1995 *Freswick Links, Caithness: Excavation and survey of a Norse settlement.* Stroud: Alan Sutton Publishing.

Mulville, J. 2002 The role of Cetacea in prehistoric and historic Atlantic Scotland. *International Journal of Osteoarchaeology* 12, 34–48.

Mulville, J. and Parker Pearson, M. 1997 A Late Bronze Age/Early Iron Age roundhouse at Cladh Hallan, South Uist: Excavations in 1997. Unpublished Dept. of Archaeology and Prehistory report, University of Sheffield.

Mulville, J., Bond, J. and Craig, O. forthcoming The White Stuff: Milking in the North Atlantic. In Mulville, J. and Outram, A. (ed.) *The zooarchaeology of fats, oils, milk and dairying.* Oxford: Oxbow Books.

Murphy, C.P. 1986 *Thin Section Preparation of Soils and Sediments.* Berkhamsted: AB Academic Publishers.

Neighbour, T. and Burgess, C. 1996 Traigh Bostadh. *Discovery and Excavation in Scotland* 1996, 113–114.

O'Connor, T.P. 1988 *Bones from the General Accident Site, Tanner Row.* London: Council for British Archaeology (Archaeology of York 15/2).

O'Rahilly, C. 1973 A catalogue and classification of bronze stick pins from the excavations in Dublin 1962–1972. University College, Dublin: Unpublished MA dissertation.

O'Rahilly, C. 1998 A classification of bronze stick-pins from the Dublin excavations 1962–72. In Manning, C. (ed.) *Dublin and Beyond the Pale: Studies in honour of Patrick Healy.* Bray: Wordwell, 23–33.

Ottaway, P. 1992 *Anglo-Scandinavian Ironwork from 16–22 Coppergate.* York: Council for British Archaeology (Archaeology of York 17/6).

Owen, N., Kent, M. and Dale, P. 1996 The machair vegetation of the Outer Hebrides: A review. *In* Gilbertson, D., Kent, M. and Gratton, J. (eds) 1996, 123–132.

Owen, O. 1993 Tuquoy, Westray, Orkney: A challenge for the future? *In* Batey, C.E., Jesch, J. and Morris, C.D. (eds) 1993, 318–339.

Owen, O. forthcoming The Vikings in Scotland: What sort of houses did Viking colonists build?

Pankhurst, R. and Mullin, J. 1991 *Flora of the Outer Hebrides.* London: Natural History Museum Publications.

Parker Pearson, M. 1995 Cille Donnain, South Uist: excavations of a Late Norse church site in the Western Isles. Unpublished Dept. of Archaeology and Prehistory report, University of Sheffield.

Parker Pearson, M. 1996 South Uist machair: archaeological survey and management project: Part II, 1993–1996. Unpublished Dept. of Archaeology and Prehistory report, University of Sheffield.

Parker Pearson, M. and Richards, C. 1994 Architecture and order: spatial representation and archaeology. In Parker Pearson, M. and Richards, C. (eds) *Architecture and Order: approaches to social space.* London: Routledge, 38–72.

Parker Pearson, M. and Roper, T. 1994 Cladh Hallan, South Uist, Outer Hebrides: Late Bronze Age/Earliest Iron Age house and Late Bronze Age midden. Unpublished Dept. of Archaeology and Prehistory report, University of Sheffield.

Parker Pearson, M. and Sharples, N.M. 1999 *Between Land and Sea: Excavations at Dun Vulan, South Uist.* Sheffield: Sheffield Academic Press.

Parker Pearson, M. and Smith, H. forthcoming *Cille Pheadair: A Norse-period farmstead on South Uist.* Oxbow: Oxbow Books.

Parker Pearson, M. and Webster, J. 1994 Bornais Mound 2 Viking Age settlement: 1994 excavations interim report. Unpublished Dept of Archaeology and Prehistory report, University of Sheffield.

Parker Pearson, M., Brennand, M. and Smith, H. 1996 Sithean Biorach (Fairy Point), Cille Pheadair, South Uist: A Viking Age and Late Norse settlement. Unpublished Dept. of Archaeology and Prehistory report, University of Sheffield.

Parker Pearson, M., Marshall, P., Mulville, J., Smith, H. and Ingrem, C. 2000 Cladh Hallan: Excavation of a Late Bronze Age to Early Iron Age settlement. Unpublished Dept. of Archaeology and Prehistory report, University of Sheffield.

Payne, S. 1969 A metrical distinction between sheep and goat metacarpals. In Ucko, P.J. and Dimbleby, G.W. (eds) *The Domestication and Exploitation of Plants and Animals.* London: Duckworth, 295–305.

Payne, S. 1973 Kill off patterns in sheep and goats: the mandibles from Asvan Kale. *Anatolian Studies* 23, 281–303.

Payne, S. 1985 Morphological distinctions between the mandibular teeth of young sheep, Ovis, and goats, Capra. *Journal of Archaeological Science* 12, 139–147.

Payne, S. and Bull, G. 1988 Components of variation in measurements of pig bones and teeth and the use of measurements to distinguish wild from domestic pig remains. *Archaeozoologia* 2, 27–65.

Polunin, O. and Walters, M. 1985 *A Guide to the Vegetation of Britain and Europe.* Oxford: Oxford University Press

Rackham, D.J. 1996 Beachview Birsay: the biological assemblage. In Morris, C.D. 1996 *The Birsay Bay Project Volume* 2. Durham: University of Durham.

Ritchie, A. 1974 Pict and Norseman in northern Scotland. *Scottish Archaeological Forum* 6, 23–36.

Ritchie, W. 1979 Machair development and chronology in the Uists and adjacent islands. *Proceedings of the Royal Society of Edinburgh* 77B, 107–122.

Ritchie, W. 1985 Inter-tidal and sub-tidal organic deposits and sea level changes in the Uists, Outer Hebrides. *Scottish Journal of Geology* 21, 161–176.

Rojo, A. 1986 Estimating live length and weight of cod. *North American Archaeologist* 7.4, 329–351.

Roussell, A. 1934 *Norse Building Customs in the Scottish Isles.* London: Williams and Northgate.

Rozanski, K., Stichler, W., Gonfiantini, R., Scott, E.M., Beukens, R.P., Kromer, B., and van der Plicht, J. 1992 The IAEA 14C intercomparison exercise 1990. *Radiocarbon* 34, 506–19.

Schiegl, S., Goldberg, P., Bar-Yosef, O. and Weiner, S. 1996 Ash deposits in Hayonim and Kebara Caves, Israel: macroscopic, microscopic and mineralogical observations, and their archaeological implications. *Journal of Archaeological Science* 23, 763–781.

Schiffer, M.B. 1987 *Formation Processes of the Archaeological Record.* Albuquerque: University of New Mexico Press.

Schmid, E. 1972 *Atlas for the Identification of Animal Bones.* Amsterdam: Elsevier.

Scott, E.M., Harkness, D.D., and Cook, G.T. 1998 Interlaboratory comparisons: lessons learned. *Radiocarbon* 40, 331–40.

Scully, O.M.B. 1997 Metal artefacts. In Hurley, M.F. and Scully, O.M.B. (eds) *Late Viking Age and Medieval Waterford. Excavations 1986–1992.* Dublin: Waterford Corporation, 438–489.

Selkirk, A. 1996 The Udal. *Current Archaeology* 147, 84–94.

Sellar, T.J. 1982 Bone material. In Curle, C.L. *Pictish and Norse Finds from the Brough of Birsay 1934–74*. Edinburgh: Society of Antiquaries of Scotland (Monograph 1), 132–138.

Serjeantson, D. 1984 The mammal, bird and fish remains from the Udal, North Uist. Unpublished interim report.

Serjeantson, D. 1990 The introduction of mammals to the Outer Hebrides and the role of boats in stock management. *Anthropozoologica* 13, 7–18.

Serjeantson, D. 1991 'Rid Grasse of Bones': a taphonomic study of the bones from midden deposits at the Neolithic and Bronze Age site of Runneymede, Surrey. *International Journal of Osteoarchaeology* 1, 73–89.

Serjeantson, D. no date The mammal, bird and fish remains from Rosinish. Unpublished interim report.

Serjeantson, D. and Bond, J. M. forthcoming Cattle and sheep husbandry at Pool: evidence from toothwear analyses. In Hunter, J.R., Bond, J.M. and Smith, A.N. (eds) *Archaeological Investigations on Sanday, Orkney; Volume I, Pool*. Edinburgh: Society of Antiquaries of Scotland.

Sharples, N.M. 1996 *The Iron Age and Norse Settlement at Bornish, South Uist: An interim report on the 1996 excavations* (Cardiff Studies in Archaeology Specialist Report No. 1). Cardiff: School of History and Archaeology. http://www.cf.ac.uk/uwcc/hisar/archaeology/reports/hebrides96/

Sharples, N.M. 1997 *The Iron Age and Norse Settlement at Bornish, South Uist: An interim report on the 1997 excavations* (Cardiff Studies in Archaeology Specialist Report No. 4). Cardiff: School of History and Archaeology. http://www.cf.ac.uk/uwcc/hisar/archaeology/reports/hebrides97/

Sharples, N.M. 1998a *Excavations at Sligeanach, Cill Donnain, South Uist 1998* (Cardiff Studies in Archaeology Specialist Report No. 12). Cardiff: School of History and Archaeology.

Sharples, N.M. 1998b *Scalloway: A broch, Late Iron Age settlement and Medieval cemetery in Shetland*. Oxford: Oxbow Books.

Sharples, N.M. 1999 *The Iron Age and Norse Settlement at Bornish, South Uist. An interim report on the 1999 excavations* (Cardiff Studies in Archaeology Specialist Report No. 16). Cardiff: School of History and Archaeology. http://www.cf.ac.uk/uwcc/hisar/archaeology/reports/hebrides99/

Sharples, N.M. 2000a Antler and Orcadian rituals: an ambiguous role for red deer in the Neolithic. In Ritchie, A. (ed.) *Neolithic Orkney in its European Context*. Cambridge: MacDonald Institute for Archaeological Research, 107–116.

Sharples, N.M. 2000b *The Iron Age and Norse Settlement at Bornish, South Uist. An interim report on the 2000 excavations* (Cardiff Studies in Archaeology Specialist Report No. 18). Cardiff: School of History and Archaeology. http://www.cf.ac.uk/uwcc/hisar/archaeology/reports/hebrides00/

Sharples, N.M. 2003 *The Iron Age and Norse Settlement at Bornish, South Uist. An interim report on the 2003 excavations* (Cardiff Studies in Archaeology Specialist Report No. 26). Cardiff: School of History and Archaeology.

Sharples, N.M. forthcoming. Life histories and the buildings of the Atlantic Iron Age. *In Tall Stories, Proceedings of the Shetland Brochs Conference 2000.*

Sharples, N.M. and Parker Pearson, M. 1999 Norse settlement on the Outer Hebrides. *Norwegian Archaeological Review* 32.1, 41–62.

Sharples, N.M., Parker Pearson, M. and Symonds, J. 2004 The archaeological landscape of South Uist. In Housley, R.A. and Coles, G. (eds) *Atlantic Connections and Adaptation: Economics, environments and subsistence in the north Atlantic*. Oxford: Oxbow Books (Symposia for the Association of Environmental Archaeology 21).

Sharples, N.M., Webster, J and Parker Pearson, M. 1995 The Viking Age settlement at Bornish, South Uist: interim report of the 1995 excavations. Unpublished Dept. of Archaeology and Prehistory report, University of Sheffield.

Shaw, F.J. 1980 *The Northern and Western Isles of Scotland: Their economy and society in the seventeenth century*. Edinburgh: John Donald.

Shepherd, I. and Tuckwell, A. 1977 Traces of Beaker period cultivation at Rosinish, Benbecula. *Proceedings of the Society of Antiquaries of Scotland* 108, 108–113.

Small, A. 1966 Underhoull, Unst, Shetland. *Proceedings of the Society of Antiquaries of Scotland* 98, 225–248.

Smith, H. 1994 Middening in the Outer Hebrides: an ethnoarchaeological investigation. University of Sheffield: Unpublished PhD thesis.

Smith, H. 1996 An environmental and geoarchaeological investigation of recently abandoned farm buildings on the Outer Hebrides. In Gilbertson, D.D., Kent, M. and Gratton, J. (eds) *The Outer Hebrides: The last fourteen thousand years*. Sheffield: Sheffield Academic Press, 195–206.

Smith, H. and Boardman, S. forthcoming. Plant use and land management in the Norse period on the Outer Hebrides: the plant remains from Kilpheder, South Uist. In Parker Pearson, M. and Smith, H. (eds) forthcoming.

Smith, H. and Mulville, J. 2004 Resource management in the Outer Hebrides: An assessment of the faunal and floral evidence from archaeological investigations. In Housley, R.A. and Coles, G. (eds) *Atlantic Connections and Adaptation: Economics, environments and subsistence in the north Atlantic*. Oxford: Oxbow Books (Symposia for the Association of Environmental Archaeology 21).

Smith, H., Marshall, P. and Parker Pearson, M. 2001 Reconstructing house activity areas. In Albarella, U. (ed.) *Environmental Archaeology: meaning and purpose*. London: Kluwer Academic Publishers, 249–270.

Stace, C. 1997 *New Flora of the British Isles* 2nd edition. Cambridge: Cambridge University Press.

Steier, P. and Rom, W. 2000 The use of Bayesian statistics for 14C dates of chronologically ordered samples: a critical analysis. *Radiocarbon* 42, 183–98.

Stenberger, M. 1955 *Valhagar: A migration period settlement on Gotland, Sweden*. Copenhagen.

Stewart, K. 1980 *Crofts and Crofting*. Edinburgh: James Thin.

Stratford, N. 1997 *The Lewis Chessmen and the Enigma of the Hoard*. London: British Museum Press.

Stuiver, M. and Kra, R.S. 1986 Editorial comment. *Radiocarbon* 28(2B), ii.

Stuiver, M. and Polach, H. J. 1977 Discussion: reporting of 14C data. *Radiocarbon* 19, 355–63.

Stuiver, M. and Reimer, P.J. 1986 A computer program for radiocarbon age calculation. *Radiocarbon* 28, 1022–30.

Stuiver, M. and Reimer, P.J, 1993 Extended 14C data base and revised CALIB 3.0 14C age calibration program. *Radiocarbon* 35, 215–30.

Stuiver, M., Reimer, P.J., Bard, E., Beck, J.W., Burr, G.S., Hughen, K.A., Kromer, B., McCormac, F.G., van der Plicht, J. and Spurk, M. 1998 INTCAL98 radiocarbon age calibration, 24,000–0 cal BP. *Radiocarbon* 40, 1041–84.

Sveinbjarnardottir, G. 1992 *Farm Abandonment in Medieval and Post-Medieval Iceland: an interdisciplinary study.* Oxford: Oxbow Monograph 17.

Symonds, J. 1997 The Flora MacDonald Project. *Current Archaeology* 152, 304–307.

Symonds, J. 1998 Gearraidh Bhailteas. *Discovery and Excavation in Scotland 1998*, 104.

Symonds, J. 1999a Toiling in the vale of tears: everyday life and resistance in South Uist, Outer Hebrides, 1760–1860. *International Journal of Historical Archaeology* 3.2, 101–122.

Symonds, J. 1999b Songs remembered in exile? Integrating unsung archives of Highland life. In Gazinch-Schwartz, A. and Holtorf, C. (eds) *Folklore and Archaeology*. London: Routledge, 106–128.

Symonds, J. 1999c Surveying the remains of a Highland myth: investigations at the birthplace of Flora MacDonald, Airigh Mhuilinn, South Uist. In Harper, M. and Vance, M.E. (eds) *Myth, Migration and the Making of Memory: Scotia and Nova Scotia c.1700–1990*. Edinburgh: John Donald Publishers Limited, 73–88.

Symonds, J. 2000 The Dark Island revisited: an approach to the historical archaeology of Milton, South Uist. In Atkinson, J.A., Banks, I. and McGregor, G. (eds) *Townships to Farmsteads: Rural settlement studies in Scotland, England and Wales.* Oxford: British Archaeological Reports Brit. Ser. 293, 196–209.

Symonds, J. and Badcock, A. 2001 Airigh Mhuilinn. *Discovery and Excavation in Scotland 2000* (NS) 1, 96.

Symonds, J., Beaudry, M. and Brighton, S. 1998 Milton House. *Discovery and Excavation in Scotland 1998*, 104.

Taylor, M. 1978 *The Lewis Chessmen*. London: British Museum.

Taylor, M. 1999 The wood. In Parker Pearson, M. and Sharples, N.M. (eds) *Between Land and Sea: Excavations at Dun Vulan, South Uist*. Sheffield: Sheffield Academic Press, 188–192.

Teichert, M. 1975 Osteometrische Untersuchungen zur Berechnung der Wideristhohe bei Schafen. In Clason, A. (ed.) *Archaeozoological Studies*. Amsterdam: North Holland/ American Elsevier, 51–69.

Ter Braak, C.J.F. and Smilauer, P. 2002 *CANOCO Reference Manual and Canondraw for Windows User's Guide: Software for Canonical Community Ordination (version 4.5).* Ithaca, New York: Microcomputer Power.

Thom, V.M. 1986 *Birds in Scotland.* Staffordshire: Poyser.

Thompson, R. and Oldfield, F. 1986 *Environmental Magnetism*. London: Allen and Unwin.

Tutin, T.G., Heywood, V.H. *et al* 1964–80 *Flora Europaea.* Cambridge: Cambridge University Press

Ulery, A.L. and Graham, R.C. 1993 Forest fire effects on soil colour and texture. *Journal of the Soil Science Society of America* 57,135–140.

van der Plicht, J. 1993 The Groningen radiocarbon calibration program. *Radiocarbon* 35, 231–37.

van der Veen, M. 1992 *Crop Husbandry Regimes: An archaeobotanical study of farming in northern England 1000 BC – AD 500.* Sheffield: Sheffield Archaeological Monograph 3.

Vigne, J.D. 1992 The meat and offal (MOW) method and the relative proportion of ovicaprines in some ancient meat diets of the north-western Mediteranean. *Revista di Studi Ligure* 57, 21–47.

von den Driesch, A. 1976 *A Guide to the Measurement of Animal Bones from Archaeological Sites*. Cambridge, Mass: Harvard University (Peabody Museum Bulletin 1).

Walker, B., McGregor, C. and Stark, G 1996 *Thatch and Thatching Techniques: A guide to conserving Scottish thatching tradition.* Edinburgh: Historic Scotland.

Walker, J. 1764 *Report on the Hebrides*. Edinburgh: John Donald

Ward, G.K. and Wilson, S.R. 1978 Procedures for comparing and combining radiocarbon age determinations: a critique. *Archaeometery* 20, 19–31.

Ward, M. 1999 The animal bones: an evaluation of the faunal remains from Norse period Kilphedir. University of Sheffield: Unpublished MSc dissertation.

Waters, M.R. 1996 *Principles of Geoarchaeology. A North American perspective*. Tucson: University of Arizona Press.

Wattez, J. and Courty, M.-A. 1987 Morphology of ash of some plant materials. In Fedoroff, N., Bresson, M. and. Courty M.-A. (eds) *Micromorphologie des Sols – Soil Micromorphology*. Plaisir: Association Française pour l'Étude du Sol, 667–683.

Welander, R.D.E., Batey, C. and Cowie, T.G. 1987 A Viking burial from Kneep, Uig, Isle of Lewis. *Proceedings of the Society of Antiquaries of Scotland* 117, 149–174.

Wheeler, A. 1969 *The Fishes of the British Isles and North-West Europe.* London: Macmillan.

Wheeler, A. 1976 The fish bones from Buckquoy, Orkney. In Ritchie, A. Excavation of Pictish and Viking-age farmsteads at Buckquoy, Orkney. *Proceedings of the Society of Antiquaries of Scotland* 108 (1976–77), 211–214.

Wheeler, A. and Jones A.K.G. 1989 *Fishes.* Cambridge: The University Press.

Wilson, D.G. 1984 The carbonization of weed seeds and their representation in macrofossil assemblages. In van Zeist, W. and Casparie, W.A. (eds) *Plants and Ancient Man: Studies in Palaeoethnobotany*. Rotterdam: Balkema, 201–206.

Young, T.P. 2002 *Slags from Bornish, S Uist*. Cardiff: GeoArch (Report 2002/6).

Zvelebil, M. 1991 Cill Donnain. Unpublished SEARCH interim report, University of Sheffield.

Index

D

E

F

G

H